Graphics Programming
in C

M&T BOOKS

Save yourself the time and trouble of manual file entry ...

Order the
Graphics Programming in C
programs disk today!!

Source code for all the G drive and G tools libraries as described in the book are on the disk. The graphics packages can be copied directly and tried out in the demonstration programs. C programmers will find useful algorithms which can be modified to fit in with their own software development efforts. Advanced C programmers will find new, improved, faster, and more efficient graphics algorithms, and most of the background information needed for reference in branching off into new programming areas.

To order, return this postage-paid self-mailer with your payment of $20, plus sales tax if you are a California resident, to: M&T Books, 501 Galveston Drive, Redwood City, CA 94063. Or, call toll-free 800-533-4372 (In CA 800-356-2002). Ask for Item #020-6.

YES! Please send me the *Graphics Programming in C*
program disk for $20 _____

California residents add applicable sales tax _____% _____

TOTAL _____

_____ Check enclosed. Make payable to M&T Books.

Charge my ____ VISA ____ MasterCard ____ American Express

Card # _____ Exp. date _____

Name _____

Address _____

City _____ State _____ Zip _____

BUSINESS REPLY MAIL
FIRST CLASS PERMIT 871 REDWOOD CITY, CA

POSTAGE WILL BE PAID BY ADDRESSEE

M&T BOOKS

501 Galveston Drive
Redwood City, CA 94063

NO POSTAGE
NECESSARY
IF MAILED
IN THE
UNITED STATES

——— PLEASE FOLD ALONG LINE AND STAPLE OR TAPE CLOSED ———

Graphics Programming in C

A Comprehensive Resource for Every C Programmer

Covers CGA, EGA, and VGA graphic displays and includes a complete toolbox of graphic routines and sample programs.

Roger T. Stevens

M&T BOOKS

M&T Publishing, Inc.
Redwood City, California

M&T Books
A Division of M&T Publishing, Inc.
501 Galveston Drive
Redwood City, CA 94063

M&T Books
General Manager, Ellen Ablow
Editorial Project Manager, Michelle Hudun
Editor, David Rosenthal
Cover Art Director, Michael Hollister
Cover Designer, Kate Paddock
Illustrator, Lynn Sanford

Library of Congress Cataloging in Publication Data

Stevens, Roger T., 1927–
    Graphics Programming in C: a comprehensive resource for every C programmer: covers CGA, EGA, and VGA graphic displays and includes a complete toolbox of graphic routines and sample programs/Roger T. Stevens. -- 1st ed.
    p. cm.
    Includes index.
    1. C (Computer program language) 2. Computer graphics.
I. Title
QA76.73.C15S735 1988
006.6'765-dc19   88-23674
                                        CIP

ISBN 1-55851-018-4   (book) $24.95
ISBN 1-55851-019-2   (book/disk) $39.95
ISBN 1-55851-020-6   (disk) $20.00

92   91   90   89   5   4   3   2

Limits of Liability
and Disclaimer of Warranty

The Author and Publisher of this book have used their best efforts in preparing the book and the programs contained in it. These efforts include the development, research, and testing of the theories and programs to determine their effectiveness.

The Author and Publisher make no warranty of any kind, expressed or implied, with regard to these programs or the documentation contained in this book. The Author and Publisher shall not be liable in any event for incidental or consequential damages in connection with, or arising out of, the furnishing, performance, or use of these programs.

How to Order
the Accompanying Disk

Source code for all the GDrive and GTools libraries as described in the book are on the disk. The graphics packages can be copied directly and tried out in the demonstration programs. C programmers will find useful algorithms which can be modified to fit in with their own software development efforts. Advanced C programmers will find new, inproved, faster, and more efficient graphics algorithms, and most of the background information needed for reference in branching off into new programming areas.

The disk is $20, plus sales tax if you are a California resident. Order by sending a check, or credit card number and expiration date, to:

Graphics Programming in C Disk
M&T Books
501 Galveston Drive
Redwood City, CA 94063

Or, you may order by calling our toll-free number between 8 A.M. and 5:00 P.M. Pacific Standard Time: 800/533-4372 (800/356-2002 in California). Ask for **Item #020-6**.

For Barbara

Without whose unlimited patience this book wouldn't have been possible.

Acknowledgments

All of the software in this book was written in Turbo C version 1.0 and then checked with a copy of Turbo C version 1.5 furnished by Borland International, 4585 Scotts Valley Drive, Scotts Valley, CA 95066. The software was also checked with Microsoft C 5.0 furnished by Microsoft Corp., 16011 NE 36th Way, Redmund, WA 98073.

All programs using the VGA mode were run on a system which included the Vega VGA card furnished by Video Seven, Inc., 46335 Landing Parkway, Fremont, CA 94538 and a NEC Multisync Plus color monitor furnished by NEC Home Electronics (U.S.A.) Inc.

Contents

Chapter 6: Using the ROM BIOS
Video Services with C 109

1

Introduction

Early in the history of computing, it was recognized that some easier method than programming in assembly language was needed to make computer programming as simple and fast as possible. Ideally, almost anyone should be able to write a program that would permit the computer to do all sorts of sophisticated and wonderful things. Furthermore, the wonderful high-level language that would permit these people to do these things so easily should not reduce the flexibility of the user-computer interface, and it should be as fast or faster in execution than the computer language itself. From these ideal fantasies, a number of real life languages have grown—some of them in a thoroughly planned manner and others rather haphazardly. What usually isn't foreseen until the language has been around awhile and has developed a certain maturity is how effective of those compromises were that were made in its creation. Does the user really have flexibility, or has he been put into a straight jacket? Is the price of a simple user interface a considerable reduction in computing speed?

The C language has been around since 1972. Although C is not a new language, it is one of the most powerful computer languages in existence. It has withstood the ravages of time and is still the preferred tool of most professional programmers for personal computer use. C has turned out to be extremely fast and flexible. Although the price paid for these advantages is a lack of constraints on programmers, it is not excessively difficult to learn to use C effectively and quickly. Up until recently, newcomers to C programming have faced a rather discouraging prospect, however. Since C has few restrictions, some of its constructs can be rather unusual and cryptic. In fact, every year *Micro/Systems Journal* reports on the results of the Obfuscated C Code Contest, which gives awards for the most obscure C code. I defy even the most experienced programmer to make sense of the winning entries at first reading. Hence, the new user must usually learn by trial and error, and that usually means a lot of error. For the learner, programming was a torturous process, requiring that the programmer use his favorite editor to generate a program listing, then return to DOS to compile and link the program, then return to the editor to seek out and correct errors. When a program finally compiled and linked correctly, it could then be run to determine if it really did what was intended; if not, the entire process had to be repeated. All this changed in late 1986 when Borland came out with Turbo C, which uses the same type of integrated environment that made Turbo Pascal famous. You can now edit, compile, and link from a single environment. When errors are encountered, the program returns to the editor and directs the cursor to the error location where you can quickly and easily make corrections. In such an environment, it is easy to learn C and to become quickly a proficient C programmer. Fearing being surpassed, Microsoft soon followed with a similar all-in-one environment in Quick C. Learning C is now a simple and pleasant experience. The ranks of those who recognize the power and effectiveness of C for programming are increasing daily.

Graphics and C

Originally, C was developed to work with computers whose primary interface was through a teletype channel. This encouraged short and concise constructs. It did not, however, offer any incentive for including graphics capabilities. In fact, until the advent of the IBM Personal Computer, the wide variety of hardware environments running the C language made standardized graphics environment an impossibility. Now that there is a large base of compatible PCs, graphics standardization should be possible. In fact, C has thus far grown up in an informal fashion, so that an ANSI standard for C is only now being considered for adoption. Why doesn't it include a graphics standard? One reason is that it is tailored for a much wider variety of computer environments than is represented by the IBM PC. Another reason may well be that it is more difficult to agree on what should be included in a graphics capability than it is to settle on language fundamentals. Everyone wants something different in their graphics package; nobody quite agrees with how the other guy does it.

Right now, the best solution appears to be something similar to this book, which details the fundamentals of graphics processes for the IBM PC family and its clones. Using this material, the reader can be satisfied with the included graphics libraries of functions, or can modify them to meet his own specific requirements.

Which C Should I Use?

Originally, all of the graphics functions in this book were written specifically for Turbo C, version 1.0, which did not contain any graphics capabilities. Almost immediately, some commercial graphics packages for Turbo C appeared. Many of them quickly modified versions of more general C graphics packages. Some of these have significant drawbacks. One, for example, requires that you first load a driver which takes up 100K bytes of memory. This doesn't leave too much room for Turbo C to maneuver in, and Turbo C in the integrated environment option is somewhat of a memory hog. Another drawback is that these programs do not furnish source code, so there is no way that you can develop an understanding of what is going on. Often the prepackaged functions do almost, but not quite, what you would like them to do. With some understanding and a source code listing, a simple modification may make the function perfect for you. But if it's in a closed black box, you don't have this luxury.

Borland was fairly quick in remedying the deficiency caused by the lack of graphics capabilities in Turbo C. Turbo C version 1.5 includes the Borland Graphics Interface which provides 70 supplied graphics functions that are supposed to be standardized from one Borland language to another (the same are used in Turbo Pascal Version 4.0, for example). Although the functions in this book were developed before I had access to Turbo C Version 1.5, they all run perfectly on the new version. I have tried running some of the displays in my demonstration programs using the Borland graphics functions from Turbo C version 1.5. Some, but not all of the needed functions are available; when functions are available, the demos are fast and can be programmed without too much difficulty. However, I prefer some of my own techniques to Borland's. If you feel this way or want to include some of the functions Borland does not have, then you need to study this book.

All of the functions in this book will also run with Microsoft C 5.0. When I attempted to determine how compatible my original Turbo C functions were with Microsoft C, I discovered some interesting differences. First, Turbo C permits initializing arrays within a function, but Microsoft C does not. Second, Turbo C dynamically allocates the size of the stack, so that large arrays can temporarily be declared within a function without any problems. In Microsoft C, the stack size is determined at compile time; if there are any large arrays in functions, you must use the /F option of the compiler to declare your array size, and declare one large enough for your biggest array. Otherwise, the stack will be set to the default size of 2K and your program will bomb out with an error message reporting stack overflow. Finally, for input and output from a port, Turbo C uses the commands *inport, outport, inportb* and *outportb*. Microsoft uses the commands *inpw, outpw*, *inp*, and *outp*. Turbo C also understands the Microsoft form of these commands, but Microsoft C does not understand the Turbo C form. Therefore, although the Turbo C commands are easier to understand, it is best to use the Microsoft C form of these commands in your programming so that you achieve the most portability possible.

What about QuickC? It is supposed to be fully compatible with Microsoft C which in my graphics programs case appears to be true. They all run equally well on QuickC. QuickC also shares the Microsoft C limitation of fixed stack size, which must be given consideration if you have long arrays in your functions. However a limitation of QuickC is that it can only support one user library. So when using QuickC, make sure all of your library functions are in a single library. Personally, I prefer Turbo C, with its WordStar-like editor for programming. But Microsoft C is supposed to produce very fast and compact code. If you want to market a C program commercially, you might want to develop it with Turbo C and then use Microsoft C for the final compilation.

A Word About Hardware

All PC clones are alike, but some are more alike than others. If you do not have a true blue IBM PC, you may find occasional glitches and differences that trap you when you least expect it. In developing the functions described in this book, I used a collection of boards from different sources. They are listed below to show you what the base line was. If you encounter strange and apparently hardware-related difficulties, look for some critical differences between your hardware and mine. The hardware used is:

Motherboard: Bullet-286e from Wave Mate, Inc. Torrance, CA. This board is a drop-in replacement for the XT motherboard, but contains an 80286 and 1 Megabyte of 0 wait state memory. The memory between 640K and 1M is used for a hard disk cache.

Floppy Disk Controller: MCT-FDC-1.2 from JDR Microdevices,
Los Gatos, CA. This board supports either 360K or 1.2M
disk drives.

Floppy Disk Drives: 1 Fujitsu 1.2 Megabyte disk drive.
1 Mitsubishi 360 Kbyte floppy disk drive.

I/O Board: MCT-IO from JDR Microdevices.

Hard Disk Controller: MCT-RLL from JDR Microdevices.

Hard Disk Drive: LaPine LT300 30 Megabyte from Advanced Computer Products, Santa Ana, CA.

Keyboard: Surplus Honeywell keyboard from B. G. Micro, Dallas, TX.

Monochrome Display Card: Poni from Hercules Compatible from California Digital, Carson, CA.

Monochrome Monitor: Center from JDR Microdevices.

CGA Card: Zuckerboard Color Graphics Board from Logicsoft, Farmingdale, NY.

CGA Monitor: Acorn RGB Monitor from JDR Microdevices.

EGA Card: MCT-EGA from JDR Microdevices.

EGA Monitor: Casper EGA Monitor from JDR Microdevices.

VGA Card: Vega VGA from Video Seven, Fremont, CA.

VGA Monitor: NEC Multisync Plus

Printer: EPSON FX-86e.

Description of this Book

In attempting to develop a complete graphics environment for C, I found that there were a lot of pieces of information available, but that I had to go to dozens of sources to collect all of the required data. Many of the sources contained errors which apparently had never been caught. Others tended to use inefficient code, which is a real no-no when speed is essential. It is the purpose of this book to present all of the information that you need to do graphics programming in the C language The functions of the Color/Graphics Adapter (CGA), the Hercules Graphics Card, the Enhanced Graphics Adapter (EGA), and the Video Graphics Array (VGA) are all described in sufficient detail to permit you to program direct interfaces with them. The ROM BIOS video services are fully described, including those new services that have been added to service the EGA and the VGA.

Use of C to call the ROM BIOS video services for a series of basic graphics tools is described as well as a similar set of tools for use with the Hercules Graphics Card. Various methods of displaying a point on the screen are described, including use of the ROM BIOS video services, direct memory access to the CGA and Hercules Graphics Card, and writing of a pixel through the use of the EGA or VGA's graphics controller registers, both with C port calls and in-line assembly language. Improved, faster algorithms are described for drawing and filling lines, rectangles, rounded rectangles, polygons, ovals, circles, arcs, and Bezier and B-Spline curves.

Details are given on how to create and move graphics cursors. Techniques for coordinate transformation are discussed. The basic techniques for creating three-dimensional figures are presented. Use of dot matrix characters in the graphics mode is described, including how to overcome the color limitations of the ROM BIOS services for writing text to a graphics screen and how to write characters vertically instead of horizontally. The use of pop up windows and menus in the graphics modes is considered. Finally, the book describes how to put together a graphics library and how to print hard copies of graphics display screens. In conclusion, the use of fractals, both as an interesting mathematical phenomena and as a possible future technique for vast compression of graphics data is examined.

This book is intended for all levels of programmers interested in the C language. For the beginner, the graphics packages can be copied directly and tried out in the demonstration programs and then in some original software. The intermediate C programmer can find useful algorithms here which he can modify to fit in with his own software development efforts. Finally, the advanced C programmer will find here both new, improved, faster and more efficient graphics algorithms, and most of the background information that he needs for reference in branching off into new programming frontiers. Using the demonstration programs, programmers can get a good idea of the capabilities that the graphics functions provide and find some hints for expanding to additional interesting displays or developing new and useful functions.

2

Graphics
and the C Language

In the beginning, the C language was created to facilitate the writing of better and more efficient operating systems. At the time, there was little interest in computer graphics, since most computer input/output (I/O) was by means of punched cards, hard copy printouts, or teletype. Consequently, C did not include any graphics manipulation capabilities. As C proliferated, lack of graphics standardization and the desire to make C as universal and portable as possible between computers discouraged making graphics manipulation an inherent part of the C language.

The current situation is much different. There is an extensive base of IBM Personal Computers, PCs, XTs, ATs and many many clones. Most of them are capable of producing graphics displays, and several de facto graphics standards have arisen. These include the Color/Graphics Adapter (CGA) for medium resolution color displays, the Enhanced Graphic Adapter (EGA) for high resolution color displays, the Video Graphics Array (VGA), IBM's even higher resolution displays with capability for 16 or 256 colors out of 256K possible variations, and the Hercules Graphics Card (HGA) for high resolution monochrome displays. A version of C could be written with built-in manipulation of these graphics interfaces, but C standards are now long established and extend over many more computers than the IBM PC compatibles, so it is unlikely that such a modification will occur.

Using C with IBM PC Compatibles

Turbo C 1.0 and the early Microsoft Cs did not include any graphics capabilities. The new Turbo C version 1.5 has the Borland Graphic Interface with 70 graphics functions supplied. Microsoft C 5.0 also contains graphics functions, although they are not compatible with Turbo C. If you want to have graphics functions that are compatible with both of these versions of the C language, you need to know something about the inner working of the language and its functions. Fortunately C, whether Turbo C or Microsoft C, is rich in methods for direct communications with computer peripherals. At the highest level, both Turbo C and Microsoft C contain a DOS library and header, both of which, among other things, establish a means of entering data into any of the registers. These registers are the core of operation of the 8086 family of computer chips. The register interface is used by inserting the statement:

```
union REGS nnnnnn;
```

in the program. This sets up a structure of variables of the form:

```
nnnnnn.h.ah
nnnnnn.h.al
nnnnnn.h.bh
....
nnnnnn.x.ax    ,etc.
```

The *.h.ah*, *.h.al*, *.h.bh*, etc. refer to the high and low bytes of the a, b, etc. registers. Values that are entered into these variables will be transferred to the actual microprocessor registers when an interrupt command is run. The *.x.ax, etc.* refers to the full registers, so the value entered into the variable will be entered into the register as full two-byte variable. Normally, variables will be entered as hexadecimal values, which in C is done by the convention of preceding them by a *0x*. For example:

```
reg.h.bh = 0xF3;
```

or

```
reg.x.bx = 0xC42E;
```

Note that it is the programmer's responsibility to make sure that the appropriate value is entered. If a value larger than that which can be contained in a single byte is entered into an .h variable, for example, the results will be unexpected and no doubt unpleasant. A similar method of accessing the segment registers is also available through the structure:

```
struct SREGS nnnnn;
```

Once register contents have been established, the command:

```
int86(mmmm,&inreg,&outreg);
```

can be run. The *mmmm* may be a numerical (hex, decimal, or whatever) value, or the name of a variable containing a value. It is the number of the DOS interrupt which will be executed by the command. The *&inreg* is the address of *inreg* which must be defined by union *REG*, and *&outreg* is similarly the address of *outreg*. When the interrupt is executed, the data that has been loaded in the registers defined by the *inreg* union will be transferred to the actual microprocessor registers and used by the interrupt. When the interrupt is complete, the contents of the microprocessor registers will be transferred to the *outreg* variables. If it is desirable to separate the input from the output variables, these two parameters of *int86* should have different names; if only one set of register values is needed, they may both have the same name. A similar command which includes accessing the segment registers is:

```
int86x(mmmm,&inreg,&outreg,&segreg);
```

where *segreg* is defined to be of the structure *SREGS*.

DOS display commands are rather primitive, but by executing interrupt number 16 (hexadecimal 10), any one of the ROM BIOS video services can be executed. These are described in detail in Chapter 3. They provide almost all of the capabilities that are needed for creating graphics displays, although there are a few eccentricities that will be described later. Only a few of the ROM BIOS video services require access to the segment registers. For those, the *int86x* expression is required; for all others, *int86* is satisfactory.

At the next lower level, C contains the commands

```
inp(aaaa,bbbb);
inpw(aaaa,bbbb);
```

and

```
out(aaaa,bbbb);
outw(aaaa,bbbb);
```

which permit direct communication with any of the computer input or output ports. The *aaaa* refers to the port number and the *bbbb* is the value of a byte or a variable containing the value of a byte. In the case of the *inp* command, a byte is read from the designated port (in this case the *bbbb* must be the name of the variable to which the data from the port is to be read). In the case of the *outp* command, if *bbbb* is the value of a byte, it is output directly to the designated port; if it is a variable name, the contents of the variable are output to the designated port. The *inpw* and *outpw* commands transfer a word between the computer and the port rather than a byte. Turbo C prefers a different form of these commands as follows:

Microsoft C	Turbo C
inp	inportb
outp	outportb
inpw	inport
outpw	outport

However, Turbo C will recognize the Microsoft form of these commands while Microsoft C does not recognize the Turbo C form. Communication to the display screen requires both reading and writing to the memory that is reserved for the display screen and access to ports which control data flow from the hardware display adapter to the screen. Manipulating display data in this manner requires some fairly extensive knowledge of the internal working of the graphics adapter being used. Chapter 3 describes the manner in which the software interfaces with the CGA and the Hercules Graphics Card. Chapter 4 gives some details about the inner workings about the EGA and the VGA. The parallel printer port works in a different manner still. It is described briefly in Chapter 22.

At the very lowest level, communications to the display adapters may be in the form of assembly language instructions. Turbo C provides for the use of in-line assembly language code in a program. This requires that the Microsoft Assembler (version 3.0 or later) be included on the disk at the time the program is being compiled. The Turbo C compiler must be running in the right mode; this can be assured by including the statement *# pragma inline* at the beginning of the program. The assembly language portion of the program is then entered in the following manner:

```
asm MOV AX,BX
asm CMP AX,CX
etc.
```

Each assembly language statement is preceded by the reserved word *asm*. Note that standard assembly language statements are used and that they do not end in a semicolon, punctuation typical of most C language statements. (The semicolon is optional, however; no harm will be done if it is inserted.) If comments are inserted, they must be written in C style (that is, preceded by /* and succeeded by */). Attempting to use the Microsoft Assembler comment style, where anything following a semicolon on a line is considered to be a comment, will result in disaster since Turbo C will think that everything following the semicolon is a new C statement.

Microsoft C does not support in-line assembly language, but does permit creating separate assembly language modules and linking them to the C program. Fortunately, we will rarely require assembly language programs for our graphics routines.

What Method Should Be Used for Graphics

The immediate question that arises is "Which of the above methods should be used for generating a graphics display?" Regardless of which graphics adapter is being used, a graphics display is created by drawing figures on the display pixel by pixel. Any desired geometric figure can be displayed on the screen by plotting each point; only fairly simple mathematics is required to specify the equation of most geometric figures, which lets the computer determine where each point should be plotted. The problem is speed. Displaying anything that is fairly complex requires plotting a very large number of points, which can be a very slow process. The higher level technique of using the ROM BIOS services for graphic interface is certainly the best when speed is not a problem. It is compatible with all graphics adapters (except the Hercules Graphics Board) and all IBM clones and requires minimal knowledge of what is going on inside the graphic adapter cards. On the other hand, it is the slowest and sometimes has undesirable limitations on what may be done. In-line assembly language is the fastest technique but is the most obscure and is incompatible with Microsoft C. It requires a lot of knowledge of what goes on inside those cards to get it right. Once someone has written workable assembly language routines, however, anyone can use them or incorporate them in his programs.

Interchanging Libraries

In this book, the *gtools* and *gdraws* functions for the CGA, EGA, and VGA are set up to be the same, with minor changes throughout the *gdraws* functions incorporated by *#ifdef* statements. The *gtools* functions for these three cards are listed in Appendix D and the *gdraws* functions in Appendix E. The demonstration programs for the three three cards are listed in Appendix F. If you are going to compile the *gdraws* functions and include them in a library, you need to have a header function *gdraws.h* which has a define statement like:

```
#define CGA
```

where you use CGA, EGA, or VGA, depending upon the graphics adapter card that you have in your system. The functions are set up to use the highest resolution graphics capability of which your graphics adapter card is capable. However, since all IBM graphics cards are downward compatible, you can run the CGA graphics modes with the EGA or VGA card and the EGA modes with the VGA card, providing that you use the correct *gdraws* library for the card whose mode you are emulating (the CGA library for mode 4 or the EGA library for mode 16, for example). You can create this library by recompiling all of your *gdraws* functions with the correct *#define* statement in your header file for the mode that you want to use. You also need to be careful to remove the *getAdapt* calls in the demonstration programs and force the program to believe that you have a different adapter card. This will become clearer as you continue reading this book. Suppose that you want to switch back and forth between various graphics modes in the same program. You would have to include copies of the pertinent routines from each library and use the *getMode* function to determine which mode you were in before running any of the graphics functions. We could have built a single all-encompassing library, but the mode tests would have had to be made before running each function. Since this would be very time consuming, and since the usefulness of the capability is questionable, the libraries were kept separate.

Where Do We Go from Here

The decisions that are involved in developing functions and sub-routines that can be used with C to provide a full range of graphics capabilities all boil down to determining the best compromises for achieving maximum speed without undue complexity. For rarely used functions, using ROM BIOS services is the best solution. Where functions are used frequently,. elegant lower-level programming is needed. Techniques for drawing geometric figures and displaying text in the fastest possible manner are required. After the basic tools are given in the next few chapters, we will begin to look at the best way to plot pixels on the screen and to draw various geometric figures. Finally, we will talk about generating windows and menus. There are several commercial packages on the market which provide full sets of graphics tools for working with the C language, but they often do not quite fit a particular application. Since they do not supply source code or try to give you any understanding of the fundamentals, there is no way that you can modify them. It is essential that you understand the thoughts and decisions that go into creating a graphics package if you are to use it to its best advantage. That is what this book is all about.

3

The Color/Graphics Adapter and Hercules Graphics Card

Using the ROM BIOS video services, a lot of C graphics programming for the CGA, EGA, or VGA cards can be done with very little understanding of the inner workings of the cards themselves. Very often, however, speed or other constraints make it desirable to interface directly with the VGA, EGA, or CGA. Only the direct technique can be used for interfacing with the Hercules Graphics card since it is not supported by the ROM BIOS video services. Frequently used functions, such as the plotting of a point to the graphics screen, require the direct interfacing approach to achieve sufficient speed and flexibility. To perform direct interfaces and to intelligently make compromises between speed and complexity, some knowledge of the inner workings of each graphics card is essential. This chapter provides information about the CGA and the Hercules Graphics Card that is of interest to the C graphics programmer. Detailed circuitry discussions will be avoided. The general method of functioning of each card will be described , as will in more detail the interfaces that the programmer can affect.

Memory Assignment

The IBM PC family makes use of memory-mapped displays. That is to say, the information which is used to create the screen display is stored in a special section of computer memory, from where the display adapter reads it and converts it directly to the display. The advantage of this over a terminal, which contains its own separate memory, is substantial. Computer communication to a terminal is usually through a serial port; even at baud rates of 9600 per second, the time required to generate a new display is several seconds. The computer can rewrite a corresponding amount of its own memory almost instantaneously, so that no delay is incurred in writing the memory-mapped display. If you have had the experience of sitting at a terminal and waiting for the display to change or scroll, you will appreciate what a significant improvement memory-mapped display represents. The memory assigned to the display functions is the area from A0000H to BFFFFH. Figure 3-1 shows the memory assignments for the most popular display cards.

Figure 3-1: Display Memory Assignment

Mode	Card	Type	Pg	Charac-ters	Pixels	Colors	Start Address
0H,1H	CGA	Text	1	40x25	320x200	16	B8000H
0H,1H	CGA	Text	2	40x25	320x200	16	B8800H
0H,1H	CGA	Text	3	40x25	320x200	16	B9000H
0H,1H	CGA	Text	4	40x25	320x200	16	B9800H
0H,1H	CGA	Text	5	40x25	320x200	16	BA000H
0H,1H	CGA	Text	6	40x25	320x200	16	BA800H
0H,1H	CGA	Text	7	40x25	320x200	16	BB000H
0H,1H	CGA	Text	8	40x25	320x200	16	BB800H
0H,1H	EGA	Text	1	40x25	320x350	16/64	B8000H
0H,1H	EGA	Text	2	40x25	320x350	16/64	B8800H
0H,1H	EGA	Text	3	40x25	320x350	16/64	B9000H
0H,1H	EGA	Text	4	40x25	320x350	16/64	B9800H
0H,1H	EGA	Text	5	40x25	320x350	16/64	BA000H
0H,1H	EGA	Text	6	40x25	320x350	16/64	BA800H
0H,1H	EGA	Text	7	40x25	320x350	16/64	BB000H
0H,1H	EGA	Text	8	40x25	320x350	16/64	BB800H
0H,1H	VGA	Text	1	40x25	360x400	16/256K	B8000H
0H,1H	VGA	Text	2	40x25	360x400	16/256K	B8800H
0H,1H	VGA	Text	3	40x25	360x400	16/256K	B9000H
0H,1H	VGA	Text	4	40x25	360x400	16/256K	B9800H
0H,1H	VGA	Text	5	40x25	360x400	16/256K	BA000H
0H,1H	VGA	Text	6	40x25	360x400	16/256K	BA800H
0H,1H	VGA	Text	7	40x25	360x400	16/256K	BB000H
0H,1H	VGA	Text	8	40x25	360x400	16/256K	BB800H
2H,3H	CGA	Text	1	80x25	640x200	16	B8000H
2H,3H	CGA	Text	2	80x25	640x200	16	B9000H
2H,3H	CGA	Text	3	80x25	640x200	16	BA000H
2H,3H	CGA	Text	4	80x25	640x200	16	BB000H
2H,3H	EGA	Text	1	80x25	640x350	16/64	B8000H
2H,3H	EGA	Text	2	80x25	640x350	16/64	B9000H
2H,3H	EGA	Text	3	80x25	640x350	16/64	BA000H

Figure 3-1 (continued)

2H,3H	EGA	Text	4	80x25	640x350	16/64	BB000H
2H,3H	EGA	Text	5	80x25	640x350	16/64	BC000H
2H,3H	EGA	Text	6	80x25	640x350	16/64	BD000H
2H,3H	EGA	Text	7	80x25	640x350	16/64	BE000H
2H,3H	EGA	Text	8	80x25	640x350	16/64	BF000H
2H,3H	VGA	Text	1	80x25	720x400	16/256K	B8000H
2H,3H	VGA	Text	2	80x25	720x400	16/256K	B9000H
2H,3H	VGA	Text	3	80x25	720x400	16/256K	BA000H
2H,3H	VGA	Text	4	80x25	720x400	16/256K	BB000H
2H,3H	VGA	Text	5	80x25	720x400	16/256K	BC000H
2H,3H	VGA	Text	6	80x25	720x400	16/256K	BD000H
2H,3H	VGA	Text	7	80x25	720x400	16/256K	BE000H
2H,3H	VGA	Text	8	80x25	720x400	16/256K	BF000H
4H,5H	CGA	Graphics	1	40x25	320x200	4	B8000H
4H,5H	EGA	Graphics	1	40x25	320x200	4/64	B8000H
4H,5H	VGA	Graphics	1	40x25	320x200	4/256K	B8000H
6H	CGA	Graphics	1	80x25	640x200	2	B8000H
6H	EGA	Graphics	1	80x25	640x200	2/64	B8000H
6H	VGA	Graphics	1	80x25	640x200	2/256K	B8000H
7H	MA	Text	1	80x25	720x350	4	B0000H
7H	EGA	Text	2	80x25	720x350	4	B1000H
7H	EGA	Text	3	80x25	720x350	4	B2000H
7H	EGA	Text	4	80x25	720x350	4	B3000H
7H	EGA	Text	5	80x25	720x350	4	B4000H
7H	EGA	Text	6	80x25	720x350	4	B5000H
7H	EGA	Text	7	80x25	720x350	4	B6000H
7H	EGA	Text	8	80x25	720x350	4	B7000H
7H	VGA	Text	1	80x25	720x400	4	B0000H
7H	VGA	Text	2	80x25	720x400	4	B1000H
7H	VGA	Text	3	80x25	720x400	4	B2000H
7H	VGA	Text	4	80x25	720x400	4	B3000H
7H	VGA	Text	5	80x25	720x400	4	B4000H
7H	VGA	Text	6	80x25	720x400	4	B5000H
7H	VGA	Text	7	80x25	720x400	4	B6000H
7H	VGA	Text	8	80x25	720x400	4	B7000H
DH	EGA	Graphics	1	80x25	320x200	16/64	A0000H
DH	EGA	Graphics	2	80x25	320x200	16/64	A2000H
DH	EGA	Graphics	3	80x25	320x200	16/64	A4000H
DH	EGA	Graphics	4	80x25	320x200	16/64	A6000H
DH	EGA	Graphics	5	80x25	320x200	16/64	A8000H

33

Figure 3-1 (continued)

DH	EGA	Graphics	6	80x25	320x200	16/64	AA000H
DH	EGA	Graphics	7	80x25	320x200	16/64	AC000H
DH	EGA	Graphics	8	80x25	320x200	16/64	AE000H
DH	VGA	Graphics	1	80x25	320x200	16/256K	A0000H
DH	VGA	Graphics	2	80x25	320x200	16/256K	A2000H
DH	VGA	Graphics	3	80x25	320x200	16/256K	A4000H
DH	VGA	Graphics	4	80x25	320x200	16/256K	A6000H
DH	VGA	Graphics	5	80x25	320x200	16/256K	A8000H
DH	VGA	Graphics	6	80x25	320x200	16/256K	AA000H
DH	VGA	Graphics	7	80x25	320x200	16/256K	AC000H
DH	VGA	Graphics	8	80x25	320x200	16/256K	AE000H
EH	EGA	Graphics	1	80x25	640x200	16/64	A0000H
EH	EGA	Graphics	2	80x25	640x200	16/64	A4000H
EH	EGA	Graphics	3	80x25	640x200	16/64	A8000H
EH	EGA	Graphics	4	80x25	640x200	16/64	AC000H
EH	VGA	Graphics	1	80x25	640x200	16/256K	A0000H
EH	VGA	Graphics	2	80x25	640x200	16/256K	A4000H
EH	VGA	Graphics	3	80x25	640x200	16/256K	A8000H
EH	VGA	Graphics	4	80x25	640x200	16/256K	AC000H
FH	EGA	Graphics	1	80x25	640x350	4	A0000H
FH	EGA	Graphics	2	80x25	640x350	4	A8000H
FH	VGA	Graphics	1	80x25	640x200	4	A0000H
FH	VGA	Graphics	2	80x25	640x200	4	A8000H
10H	EGA	Graphics	1	80x25	640x350	16/64	A0000H
10H	EGA	Graphics	2	80x25	640x350	16/64	A8000H
10H	VGA	Graphics	1	80x25	640x350	16/256K	A0000H
10H	VGA	Graphics	2	80x25	640x350	16/256K	A8000H
11H	VGA	Graphics	1	80x30	640x480	2/256K	A0000H
12H	VGA	Graphics	1	80x30	640x480	16/256K	A0000H
13H	VGA	Graphics	1	40x25	320x200	256/256K	A0000H
--	Hercules	Text	1	80x25	720x348	4	B0000H
--	Hercules	Text	2	80x25	720x348	4	B8000H
--	Hercules	Graphics	1	80x25	720x348	4	B0000H
--	Hercules	Graphics	2	80x25	720x348	4	B8000H

In the text types of memory, each character location utilizes two bytes of memory. The first byte contains the ASCII code of the character to be displayed. The second byte contains a character attribute. For monochrome displays, this byte indicates whether the character is to be boldface, blinking, normal video, or reverse video. For color, the attribute byte includes the foreground and background colors. Figure 3-2 shows the contents of the attribute byte for monochrome and color text modes. The display adapter card reads the two bytes for each character, sets internal registers to produce the desired attributes, and uses a table to convert the ASCII code to the necessary dots on the raster to display the character. The beginning page address contains the character to be displayed at the upper left corner of the screen (column 0 and row 0), followed by its attribute. The remaining characters on that row are stored in sequence, then the characters for the next row, and so forth.

Figure 3-2: Text Attribute Byte for Monochrome and Color

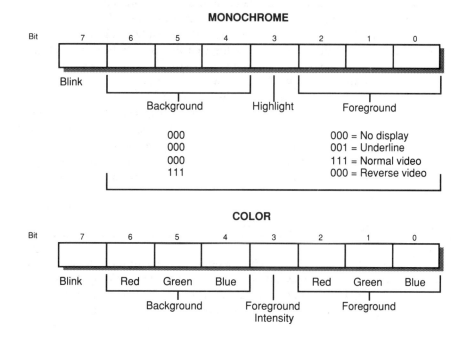

For color displays, the CGA utilizes two bits per pixel. These bits can represent any one of four different conditions that permit four different colors on the graphics screen.

Since there are eight bits in a byte, each memory byte can store color graphics data for four pixels. Monochrome graphics displays require only one bit per pixel, since the pixel is either on or off. Thus data for eight monochrome pixels can be stored in a memory byte. Since memory is read a byte at a time, the programmer who wishes to directly control a single pixel must read the memory byte containing the desired pixel, take the necessary logical actions to modify only the bits associated with this pixel, and then rewrite the modified byte to memory.

The EGA and VGA differ from the CGA and the Hercules Graphics Board in that they have four memory planes, all with the same set of addresses. Internal circuitry on the EGA or VGA determines, from the specified color of a pixel, which combination of the planes should have the corresponding bits set. The four bits (one from each plane) identify one of sixteen palettes (colors). Thus for the EGA or VGA, addressing a particular memory bit location retrieves (indirectly) four bits, one from each of four memory planes. Display data appears in sequential addresses from these adapters, with the beginning page address containing data for the eight pixels starting at the top left hand corner of the display. The graphics modes of the CGA and Hercules Card are different and do not simply follow in sequence. The Hercules board stores the first line of data beginning at the starting address, but the next line is stored at the starting address plus an offset of 2000H. The third line follows the first, and the process continues with all the odd lines consecutive, beginning at the starting address, and all the even lines consecutive, beginning at the starting address plus 2000H. The CGA uses a similar technique, except that the interlacing is fourfold. In other words, the first line is written at the starting address, the second line at the starting address plus 2000H, the third line at the starting address plus 4000H, and the fourth line at the starting address plus 6000H. The fifth line follows the first line and so forth.

The Hercules Graphics Card

The Hercules Graphics Card has become a de facto standard for high resolution monochrome text and graphics. It is a good place to start looking at graphics cards, since its requirement to be compatible with IBM-built cards makes its architecture similar; but due to the lack of support for this card in ROM BIOS, we must interact much more closely with its internal structure than in the case of other cards.

Figure 3-3 is a block diagram of the Hercules Graphics Card. In a typical computer monitor, an electron beam is swept across the cathode ray tube screen in a horizontal line, starting at the top left corner. When the sweep is complete, the beam is blanked and moved back to the left side of the screen. Meanwhile, a vertical sweep moves the beam position down the screen, so that each horizontal line is positioned below the previous one. When the bottom of the screen is reached, the beam is again blanked and moved back to the top left hand corner. A high-frequency clock in the video adapter card divides each horizontal line into a number of time increments, each of which positions the beam at some point along the horizontal sweep. Thus, if we say that a particular display mode has a resolution of 640 pixels by 350 lines, it means that each pulse of the high frequency clock identifies one of 640 pixel positions along the horizontal lines and that 350 horizontal lines make up the display on the screen. The control circuitry in the display adapter is responsible for generating the high-frequency clock pulses, supplying a horizontal synch pulse that identifies the time when the sweep of each horizontal line should start, and supplying a vertical synch pulse that determines the beginning of each vertical sweep. Thus, the presence of the horizontal and vertical sync pulses marks the positioning of the beam at the top left hand of the screen.

Figure 3-3: Block Diagram of Hercules Graphics Card

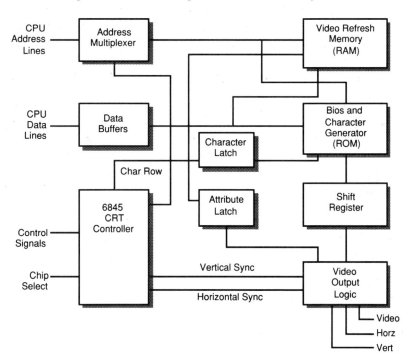

All of the rest of the circuitry in the display adapter is used to determine what the beam should do as it passes each pixel location. For monochrome displays, this basically boils down to a decision as to whether the beam should be turned on or off. For color displays, there are actually three electronic beams that travel synchronically, but activate red, green, and blue phosphers, so the display needs to use a combination of these three beams to activate at any particular point. If the display is analog, the intensity of the beam at each pixel location can be controlled rather than just turning it on or off. The basic technique used in the display adapters for graphics modes is to have random access memory on board the adapter board which has one or more bits assigned to each possible pixel position. The display adapter then checks the proper memory location for each pixel position just before the beam sweeps by this pixel position, and makes a decision as to what action the beam should take at that point. When a text mode is used, instead of looking to memory for each pixel position, the adapter looks for the memory location to define an entire ASCII character. Using the ASCII character code, it goes to an onboard character memory that contains the pixel characteristics for every pixel in the character. It selects the characteristic for the particular character line and pixel position being scanned, and allows that to determine the beam action for that pixel. In addition to controlling the display by sending characters or pixel information to the display memory, each adapter has a number of I/O ports that are used to pass control information to the adapter and status information from the adapter to the computer. These can be used to set registers on the display controller for particular display modes and sweep rates, and to activate features such as blinking or reverse video.

Figure 3-4: Internal Registers of 6845 CRT Controller

Register Number	Register Description	Hercules Text Value	Hercules Graphics Value
R0	Total Horizontal Cols	61H	35H
R1	Horizontal Display	50H	2DH
R2	Horiz Sync Position	52H	2EH
R3	Horiz Sync Width	0FH	07H
R4	Total Vertical Lines	19H	5BH
R5	Vertical Adjust	06H	02H
R6	Vertical Display	19H	57H
R7	Vert Sync Position	19H	57H
R8	Interlace Mode	02H	02H
R9	Max. Scan Line Address	0Dh	03H
R10	Cursor Start Register	0BH	00H
R11	Cursor End Register	0CH	00H
R12	Screen Start Address (MSB)	00H	00H
R13	Screen Start Address (LSB)	00H	00H
R14	Cursor Address (MSB)	00H	00H
R15	Cursor Address (LSB)	00H	00H
R16	Light Pen Register (MSB)	---	---
R17	Light Pen Register (LSB)	---	---

Like the CGA and the IBM monochrome adapter, the Hercules card is designed around a 6845 CRT controller integrated circuit. This integrated circuit has 18 programmable internal registers, which in the Hercules Card are accessed through two external ports: port 3B0H for setting the index register, and port 3B1H for transferring register data. Figure 3-4 lists the 6845 internal registers. The procedure is to first send the number of the desired register to the index port. This connects the selected register to the data port. Data is then written to or read from the data port. In addition, there are two other ports for communications with the Hercules Graphics Card. The contents of the registers accessed by ports is shown in Figure 3-5. Not very many of these ports and/or registers are useful to the programmer. The internal registers of the 6845 offer very flexible control of the CRT raster generation, but unfortunately, the flexibility exceeds the capability of a monitor to adapt to the inputs. The values given in Figure 3-3 must be output to the ports when initializing or switching between text and graphics modes. However, the programmer should not try to modify most of the values, since generation of the wrong horizontal and vertical signals could cause the monitor to self-destruct. The only registers that you can really afford to play around with are registers R10, R11, R14, and R15. The first two set up the cursor shape; they aren't used in the graphics mode. The last two set or read the cursor address; this information may be important, even in the graphics mode, where the cursor is not displayed, since the cursor location is the position where text characters are written.

Figure 3-5: Hercules Graphics Card I/O Ports

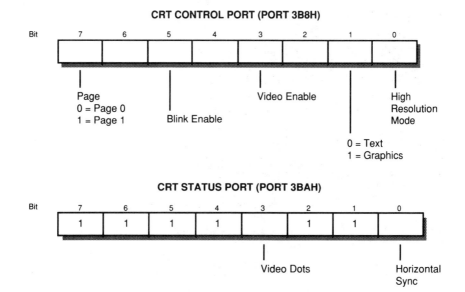

The CRT Control port allows the programmmer to turn the entire display on and off, to turn blinking characters on and off, and to choose between the text and graphics modes. Note, however, that it is not enough to switch the text/graphics bit; you must also reset all of the 6845 registers as shown in Figure 3-3.

The Hercules Graphics Card has 64K of display memory on board. In the graphics mode, two full display pages are available, addressed beginning at B0000H for page 0 and B8000H for page 1. Details of how this memory works were given above. One of the bits of the Control port (3B8H) determines which memory page is selected. The CRT Status port can be read by the user. Bit 0 monitors the horizontal sync signal and bit 3 monitors the stream of dots going out to the display. Neither of these signals is very useful.

The Hercules Board has its own self-contained clock; from this, when properly programmed, the 6845 CRT controller generates the horizontal and vertical sync signals that drive the monitor sweeps. The 6845 also generates a dot clock signal which provides outputs for every pixel position on the screen. For graphics modes, at the time when the horizontal and vertical sweeps cause the monitor CRT to be sweeping by each pixel position, the 6845 outputs the address of the appropriate location in video refresh memory. And, depending upon whether or not the memory contents indicate that a pixel should be painted on the screen, the video dot clock output is transmitted to the monitor video input. For text modes, at each line of a character position, the ASCII code of the the appropriate character is extracted from the video refresh memory by the 6845 together with an indication of the character line number used to address the character ROM. This ROM contains the dot pattern for that line of the selected character, which is sent through a shift register and output in serial fashion to activate the required video dots to provide a video output that forms the image of the character upon the screen. The Hercules board provides a single digital video output together with the horizontal and vertical video signals.

Color/Graphics Adapter

The CGA looks to software very similar to the Hercules Graphics Card; it is also built around the 6845 CRT Controller integrated circuit. Communicating with the 6845 takes place through two I/O ports, an Index port (3D0H) that determines which of the 6845 registers is connected to the data port, and the data port (3D1H) that transfers data between the computer and the selected register.

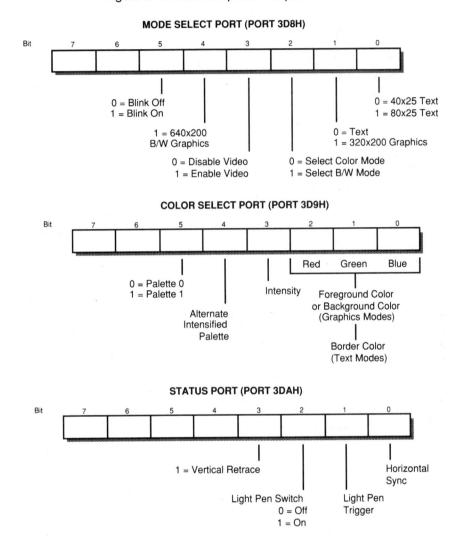

Figure 3-6: Color/Graphics Adapter I/O Ports

The description of the CGA 6845 registers is the same as for the Hercules Graphics Card. The values that go into these registers are controlled by the ROM BIOS and need not concern the programmer. In addition, the CGA has five other I/O ports. Two of these ports are for a light pen latch. The Clear Light Pen Latch port (3DBH) clears a flip-flop which is connected to the 6845's light pen input. This occurs whenever an output to the port occurs; the contents of the data transmitted are inconsequential. The flip-flop is cleared when the operator is

41

ready to enter a light pen position into the 6845. When the light pen detects a burst of light from the display as the electron beam of the CRT passes the light pen position, an output to the Set Light Pen Latch port (3DCH) occurs. This causes the current scan position data to be latched into the 6845 light pen registers. It can then be read from these registers into the computer whenever desired. Light pens have not found very much favor with users; they have typically been replaced with mice. Thus, this feature is not a very useful one.

Figure 3-7: Block Diagram of Color/Graphics Adapter

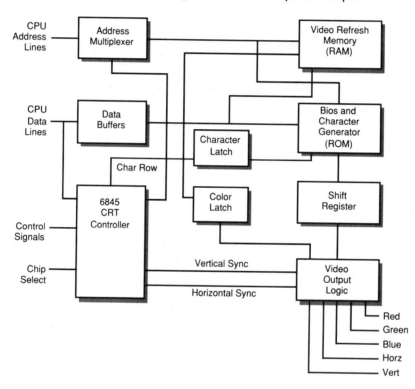

The remaining I/O ports and their functions are shown in Figure 3-6. Except in very special circumstances, there is no need for the programmer to directly concern himself with these registers. All of their functions can be exercised through the ROM BIOS Video Services, with less chance for a disastrous error and more capability for compatibility with clones and similar computers. When additional graphics speed is required, routines can be written to directly access display memory, but these do not normally require use of the CGA's I/O ports.

Figure 3-7 is a block diagram of the CGA, which is very similar to the Hercules Graphics Card. The arrangement of the data in memory is different and the number of bits required to designate a pixel in four colors instead of black and white are different, but this is all handled in the manner in which the 6845 CRT Controller is programmed. The most significant difference is in the output circuitry, which outputs separate Red, Green, and Blue video signals to drive an RGB color monitor, instead of the single video signal which is output by the Hercules card.

4

The Enhanced Graphics
Adapter and the
Video Graphics Array

The graphics modes and the adapters associated with them have already been shown in Figure 3-1. Note that there are several modes that are unique to the Video Graphics Array (VGA) including a high resolution mode with 256 shades of color. The VGA is also able to emulate all of the other adapters, by operating in their unique modes, sometimes with higher resolution, more pages of display memory, or additional colors. Therefore, software designed for any other IBM graphics adapter will work with the VGA. Likewise, the Enhanced Graphics Adapter (EGA) has some modes that only it (and the VGA) can support, but it also is designed to emulate the MA and CGA so that software designed for these adapters will work equally well on the EGA.

Hardware Considerations

Figure 4-1 is a block diagram of the EGA and VGA. Much of the circuitry for the two functions is identical; we will deal with the differences later. Both adapters essentially duplicate most of the registers of the other adapters, although instead of a 6845 CRT controller, they use several custom designed integrated circuits. These integrated circuits generate horizontal and vertical synch waveforms for the monitor and provide control of timing and memory access. However, unlike the earlier adapters, the VGA and EGA do not permit direct unrestricted access to their display memory. The memory addressing begins at memory address A0000H, and extends for as much as 64K. However, there are actually four memory planes that control the color shades. In the EGA, these planes select one of 16 colors from a possible 64; any or all of these 16 colors can be displayed on the screen at one time. A pixel is assigned one bit in each of the four memory planes, and these four bits are all considered to be at the same memory address. The memory data from all four planes is latched into internal registers by a memory read at the pixel address, and can then be modified and rewritten from the latches back to memory. Various graphics control registers on the board determine whether a memory read reads the contents of one of the memory planes, several simultaneously, or none at all. Meanwhile, the read causes existing data to be loaded to the board's internal registers. It may not be read from them, but may be modified and returned to memory. These inner workings are controlled by the settings of a number of registers that are accessed through I/O ports. These registers will be described below.

Figure 4-1: EGA/VGA Block Diagram

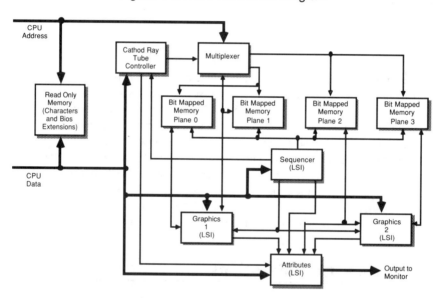

In addition to having a higher resolution mode than the EGA, the VGA differs in its capability for handling colors. The EGA uses the four attributes from the four memory planes to determine a digital color signal, which is sent to the monitor. Four binary attributes permit one of 16 colors to be sent out. The VGA, on the other hand, includes a digital-to-analog converter (DAC) to generate analog red, green, and blue signals that are sent to an analog monitor. Since each color can thus be infinitely varied in amplitude, a large number of shades are available. Most of the VGA modes use the four pixel bits from the four memory planes to select one of 16 colors, but instead of these being chosen from an available range of 64 colors, the possible range is now 256K. Figure 4-2 shows how this is accomplished.

Figure 4-2: VGA Color Select Block Diagram

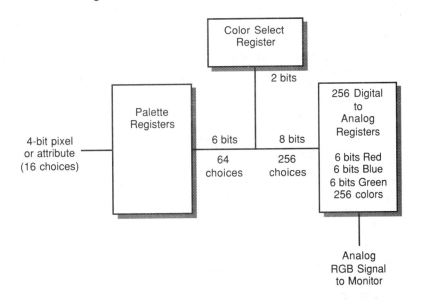

The four pixel or attribute bits from the four memory planes select one of 16 palette registers. Each palette register can be set with a six bit address, so that 16 from 64 addresses may be selected. These addresses are combined with two bits from the color select register, which is set with an I/O signal from the computer. Thus the combined signal permits selecting 16 color registers out of one of four groups of 64 DAC registers. Each DAC register contains three six-bit sets of data, one for red, one for blue, and one for green. These permit combining any one of 64 levels for each of the three colors, resulting in 256K shades of color. Figure 4-3 gives the default settings for the 256 DAC color registers. Each of these registers can have its default value changed using the ROM BIOS video services as described in Chapter 5. This, no doubt, means that there are port inputs or direct register manipulation techniques for changing these values, but they are not documented in the IBM technical manual.

Figure 4-3: Default Settings of VGA DAC Color Registers

Reg	R	G	B	Reg	R	G	B	Reg	R	G	B	Reg	R	G	B
00	00	00	00	20	00	00	3F	40	3F	3F	1F	60	2D	3F	2D
01	00	00	2A	21	10	00	3F	41	3F	27	1F	61	2D	3F	31
02	00	2A	00	22	1F	00	3F	42	3F	2F	1F	62	2D	3F	36
03	00	2A	2A	23	2F	00	3F	43	3F	37	1F	63	2D	3F	3A
04	2A	00	00	24	3F	00	3F	44	3F	3F	1F	64	2D	3F	3F
05	2A	00	2A	25	3F	00	2F	45	37	3F	1F	65	2D	3A	3F
06	2A	15	00	26	3F	00	1F	46	2F	3F	1F	66	2D	36	3F
07	2A	2A	2A	27	3F	00	10	47	27	3F	1F	67	2D	31	3F
08	15	15	15	28	3F	00	00	48	1F	3F	1F	68	00	00	1C
09	15	15	3F	29	3F	10	00	49	1F	3F	27	69	07	00	1C
0A	15	3F	15	2A	3F	1F	00	4A	1F	3F	2F	6A	0E	00	1C
0B	15	3F	3F	2B	3F	2F	00	4B	1F	3F	37	6B	15	00	1C
0C	3F	15	15	2C	3F	3F	00	4C	1F	3F	3F	6C	1C	00	1C
0D	3F	15	3F	2D	2F	3F	00	4D	1F	37	3F	6D	1C	00	15
0E	3F	3F	15	2E	1F	3F	00	4E	1F	2F	3F	6E	1C	00	0E
0F	3F	3F	3F	2F	10	3F	00	4F	1F	27	3F	6F	1C	00	07
10	00	00	00	30	00	3F	00	50	2D	2D	3F	70	1C	00	00
11	05	05	05	31	00	3F	10	51	31	2D	3F	71	1C	07	00
12	08	08	08	32	00	3F	1F	52	36	2D	3F	72	1C	0E	00
13	0B	0B	0B	33	00	3F	2F	53	3A	2D	3F	73	1C	15	00
14	0E	0E	0E	34	00	3F	3F	54	3F	2D	3F	74	1C	1C	00
15	11	11	11	35	00	2F	3F	55	3F	2D	3A	75	15	1C	00
16	14	14	14	36	00	1F	3F	56	3F	2D	36	76	0E	1C	00
17	18	18	18	37	00	10	3F	57	3F	2D	31	77	07	1C	00
18	1C	1C	1C	38	1F	1F	3F	58	3F	2D	2D	78	00	1C	00
19	20	20	20	39	27	1F	3F	59	3F	31	2D	79	00	1C	07
1A	24	24	24	3A	2F	1F	3F	5A	3F	36	2D	7A	00	1C	0E
1B	28	28	28	3B	37	1F	3F	5B	3F	3A	2D	7B	00	1C	15
1C	2D	2D	2D	3C	3F	1F	3F	5C	3F	3F	2D	7C	00	1C	1C
1D	32	32	32	3D	3F	1F	37	5D	3A	3F	2D	7D	00	15	1C
1E	38	38	38	3E	3F	1F	2F	5E	36	3F	2D	7E	00	0E	1C
1F	3F	3F	3F	3F	3F	1F	27	5F	31	3F	2D	7F	00	07	1C
80	0E	0E	1C	A0	1C	14	14	C0	00	10	00	E0	0B	0B	10
81	11	0E	1C	A1	1C	16	14	C1	00	10	04	E1	0C	0B	10
82	15	0E	1C	A2	1C	18	14	C2	00	10	08	E2	0D	0B	10
83	18	0E	1C	A3	1C	1A	14	C3	00	10	0C	E3	0F	0B	10
84	1C	0E	1C	A4	1C	1C	14	C4	00	10	10	E4	10	0B	10
85	1C	0E	18	A5	1A	1C	14	C5	00	0C	10	E5	10	0B	0F
86	1C	0E	15	A6	18	1C	14	C6	00	08	10	E6	10	0B	0D

Figure 4-3 (continued)

87	1C	0E	11	A7	16	1C	14	C7	00	04	10	E7	10	0B	0C
88	1C	0E	0E	A8	14	1C	14	C8	08	08	10	E8	10	0B	0B
89	1C	11	0E	A9	14	1C	16	C9	0A	08	10	E9	10	0C	0B
8A	1C	15	0E	AA	14	1C	18	CA	0C	08	10	EA	10	0D	0B
8B	1C	18	0E	AB	14	1C	1A	CB	0E	08	10	EB	10	0F	0B
8C	1C	1C	0E	AC	14	1C	1C	CC	10	08	10	EC	10	10	0B
8D	18	1C	0E	AD	14	1A	1C	CD	10	08	0E	ED	0F	10	0B
8E	15	1C	0E	AE	14	18	1C	CE	10	08	0C	EE	0D	10	0B
8F	11	1C	0E	AF	14	16	1C	CF	10	08	0A	EF	0C	10	0B
90	0E	1C	0E	B0	00	00	10	D0	10	08	08	F0	0B	10	0B
91	0E	1C	11	B1	04	00	10	D1	10	0A	08	F1	0B	10	0C
92	0E	1C	15	B2	08	00	10	D2	10	0C	08	F2	0B	10	0D
93	0E	1C	18	B3	0C	00	10	D3	10	0E	08	F3	0B	10	0F
94	0E	1C	1C	B4	10	00	10	D4	10	10	08	F4	0B	10	10
95	0E	18	1C	B5	10	00	0C	D5	0E	10	08	F5	0B	0F	10
96	0E	15	1C	B6	10	00	08	D6	0C	10	08	F6	0B	0D	10
97	0E	11	1C	B7	10	00	04	D7	0A	10	08	F7	0B	0C	10
98	14	14	1C	B8	10	00	00	D8	08	10	08	F8	00	00	00
99	16	14	1C	B9	10	04	00	D9	08	10	0A	F9	00	00	00
9A	18	14	1C	BA	10	08	00	DA	08	10	0C	FA	00	00	00
9B	1A	14	1C	BB	10	0C	00	DB	08	10	0E	FB	00	00	00
9C	1C	14	1C	BC	10	10	00	DC	08	10	10	FC	00	00	00
9D	1C	14	1A	BD	0C	10	00	DD	08	0E	10	FD	00	00	00
9E	1C	14	18	BE	08	10	00	DE	08	0C	10	FE	00	00	00
9F	1C	14	16	BF	04	10	00	DF	08	0A	10	FF	00	00	00

CRT Controller Registers

This is a good place to begin looking at the EGA and VGA, because these are the registers that emulate the 6845 CRT controller and make earlier software believe that nothing has changed. Like the 6845, there is an index register which determines which internal register will receive data and a number of data registers. The index register is addressed at port 3B4 if the adapter is running in monochrome modes and 3D4 if it is running the CGA, EGA, or VGA modes. The data register is addressed at 3B5 for monochrome and 3D5 for color. Figure 4-4 compares the CRT controller registers with the 6845 CRT controller registers. Many of the registers are the same for the EGA board as for boards using the 6845 CRT controller. However, there are enough differences to cause some possible troubles. As far as IBM is concerned, you shouldn't be fooling around with the contents of these registers anyway. In systems without an EGA card, the ROM BIOS video services provide you with the interfaces you need.

Figure 4-4: CRT Controller Registers

Register Number	6845 Register Description	EGA Register Description
R0	Total Horizontal Columns	Total Horizontal Columns
R1	Horizontal Display End	Horizontal Display End
R2	Horiz Sync Position	Start Horizontal Blank
R3	Horiz Sync Width	End Horizontal Blank
R4	Total Vertical Lines	Start Horizontal Retrace
R5	Vertical Adjust	End Horizontal Retrace
R6	Vertical Display	Vertical Total
R7	Vert Sync Position	Overflow
R8	Interlace Mode	Preset Row Scan
R9	Max. Scan Line Address	Max Scan line
R10	Cursor Start Register	Cursor Start Position
R11	Cursor End Register	Cursor End Position
R12	Screen Start Address (MSB)	Start Address (MSB)
R13	Screen Start Address (LSB)	Start Address (LSB)
R14	Cursor Address (MSB)	Cursor Location (MSB)
R15	Cursor Address (LSB)	Cursor Location (LSB)
R16	Light Pen Register (MSB)	Vertical Retrace Start (Write only) Light Pen High (Read only)
R17	Light Pen Register (LSB)	Vertical Retrace End (Write only) Light Pen Low (Read only)
R18	---	Vertical Display End
R19	---	Offset
R20	---	Underline Location
R21	---	Start Vertical Blank
R22	---	End Vertical Blank
R23	---	Mode Control
R24	---	Line Compare

The ROM BIOS itself does the proper initialization without any necessity for direct intervention with the registers. The EGA and the VGA have a ROM BIOS extension on board which automatically becomes a part of the BIOS and provides the proper initialization and interfaces with the EGA or VGA. Certainly there does not appear to be any reason why it would be profitable to try to directly access the EGA CRT controller registers rather than allow the BIOS to perform these tasks for you.

We have seen that the Hercules Graphics Card is not supported by IBM, and that the only way to switch it from its default text mode to the graphics mode is by reinitializing most of the CRT controller registers with new data. Then, when returning to the text mode, they must be reset to their default values. Thus if you run software designed for a Hercules card on a computer which has an EGA card, you might unintentionally send data to the EGA CRT controller registers. There is a very good chance that this will produce a totally unreadable display, and there is even a possibility that you will set sweep rates which will cause the CRT monitor to fail completely. Consequently, it is very important to make sure that the system does contain a Hercules card and not some other adapter card before sending out data to the controller registers. A function such as *getAdap()*, which is described in Chapter 6, will do this job and report back if the Hercules card is there. Only after this affirmation should the data be sent out.

General Registers

These are four registers that are used for general purpose activities in the EGA and VGA. Figure 4-5 shows the contents of these registers. There is probably never any reason for you to need to access these registers in the course of normal programming.

Figure 4-5: General Registers

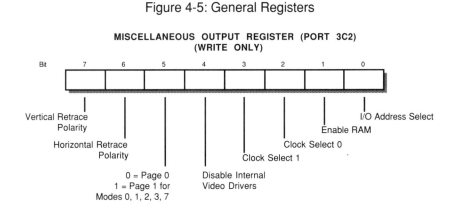

MISCELLANEOUS OUTPUT REGISTER (PORT 3C2)
(WRITE ONLY)

Figure 4-5 (continued)

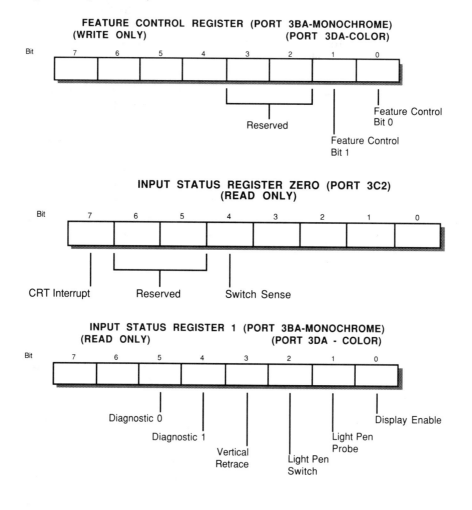

Sequencer Registers

There are five sequencer data registers that mainly control timing of the display signals. These are write-only registers that are accessed through two I/O ports. Port 3C4 accesses the sequencer index register, which must first be set with an index from 0 to 4. Data is then output to port 3C5. This data enters the register whose index was output in the previous step.

Figure 4-6 shows the contents of the sequencer registers. The reset register needs to be set before each change in the clocking mode register and the clocking mode register has to have key values changed when the display mode is changed. However, the ROM BIOS video service command to *set mode* handles this automatically. Since such changes are very infrequent, there is no time penalty for using the ROM BIOS video services, and there is therefore no reason why you should ever have to access these registers directly. Similarly, you should not need to access the Character Map Select register, since there are new ROM BIOS functions (described in Chapter 5) to cover the loading and setting of fonts that make it unnecessary for you to directly access this register to set character font addresses.

Figure 4-6: Sequencer Registers

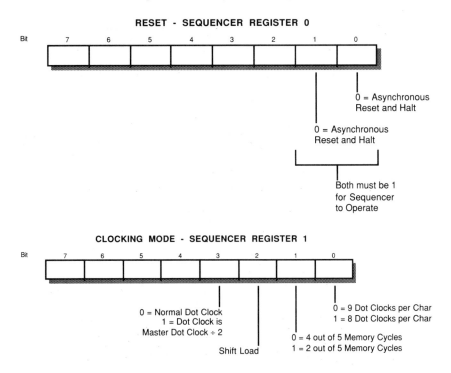

Figure 4-6 (continued)

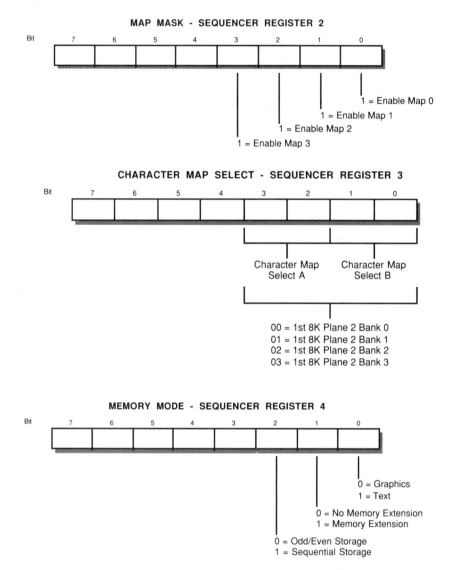

MAP MASK - SEQUENCER REGISTER 2

1 = Enable Map 0
1 = Enable Map 1
1 = Enable Map 2
1 = Enable Map 3

CHARACTER MAP SELECT - SEQUENCER REGISTER 3

Character Map Select A
Character Map Select B

00 = 1st 8K Plane 2 Bank 0
01 = 1st 8K Plane 2 Bank 1
02 = 1st 8K Plane 2 Bank 2
03 = 1st 8K Plane 2 Bank 3

MEMORY MODE - SEQUENCER REGISTER 4

0 = Graphics
1 = Text
0 = No Memory Extension
1 = Memory Extension
0 = Odd/Even Storage
1 = Sequential Storage

The memory mode register also gets changed depending upon the display mode, and this also is taken care of by the *set mode* ROM BIOS service. This leaves only the Map Mask register to consider. This register determines how many map planes you can simultaneously write to with a single memory write. Changing the value input to this register is one of the methods for writing selected colors to the screen. Another method of color control is to change the value of the Set/Reset Register that is part of the Graphics Register Set. If you are using the Graphics Registers to control color, you should set this register to write to all planes simultaneously. If you want to be sure, you can send an 0FH to this register to make sure that all four planes are enabled, but the ROM BIOS has already initialized this register to 0FH when *set mode* selected mode 10H, so this register output does not really need to be repeated.

Attribute Registers

Figure 4-7 shows the contents of the attribute registers. The attribute registers primarily are concerned with the palette color selection. All of the registers are addressed through I/O port 3C0H. When the first output is made to this port, it contains the index for the following output. This then activates a toggle within the EGA/VGA so that the next output to the port goes to the register whose index was sent in the first output. Accepting this data causes the toggle to work again, so the next command sets the index again. This index register also uses bit 5 as the Palette Address Source. It must be set to zero when you want to load data to any of the palette registers, and then returned to one when you wish to return to the display mode.

The use of 16 individual palette registers marks a completely different way of handling colors from that of the CGA. You will recall that the CGA had two color palettes of four colors each. With either, you could set the background color to any of the eight unintensified colors. The remaining colors for the first palette were green, red, and brown; for the second palette they were cyan, magenta, and white.

You can specify 16 colors with the EGA. By defaults, they are the eight unintensified colors (black, blue, green, cyan, red, magenta, brown, and light gray) and eight intensified ones (dark gray, light blue, light green, light cyan, light red, light magenta, yellow and white).

Each of the 16 palette registers corresponds to one of the 16 color numbers, and you can program any one of them for any combination of the three primary colors and the three intensified primary colors. This can all be handled by some additions to the ROM BIOS video services, which will be described later. Basically, the ROM BIOS video services can handle all of the necessary programming of the Attribute Registers so that you will not have to access them directly.

Figure 4-7: Attribute Registers

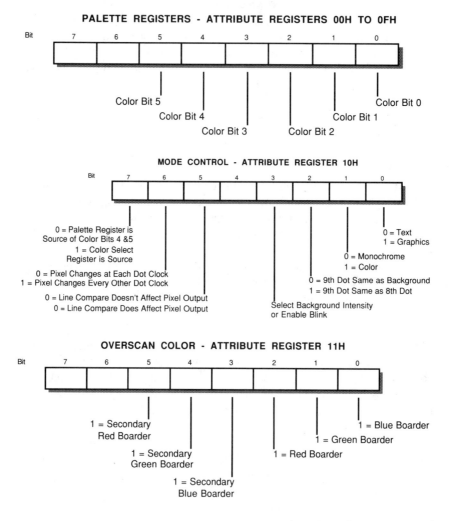

(continued on next page)

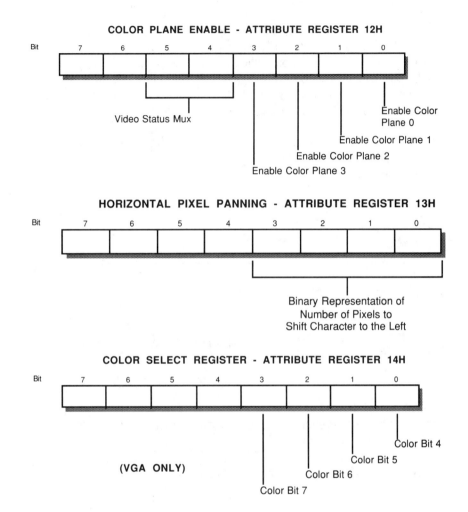

As previously described, the VGA has a Color Select Register which is Attribute register 14H. This register supplies additional bits to the color selection data so that it and the output of the Palette Register supply an eight-bit address to the DAC color registers.

Graphics Controller Registers

These are the registers that you as a programmer are most interested in, since they provide the quickest access possible to the display memory. They are shown in Figure 4-8. For the EGA, there are two position registers: Graphics 1 Position

Register at port address 3CCH, and Graphics 2 Position Register at port address 3CAH. These registers control the response of the graphics chips to the processor data bus; for proper operation of the EGA, Graphics 1 Position Register must always be programmed to 00 and Graphics 2 Position Register must always be programmed to 01. Fortunately, the ROM BIOS takes care of this for you, so you can forget about these registers. These registers do not exist in the VGA.

The remaining registers consist of an index register at port address 3CEH and nine data registers at port 3CF, one of which is selected by writing its index to the index register before data is transmitted.

Figure 4-8: Graphics Data Registers

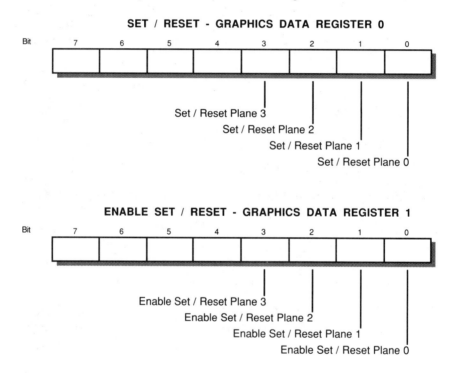

(Figure 4-8 continued)

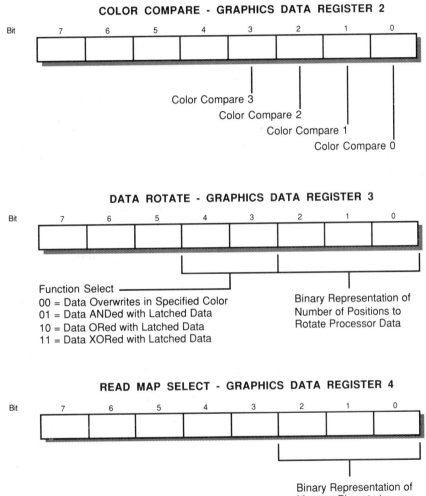

COLOR COMPARE - GRAPHICS DATA REGISTER 2

Bit 7 6 5 4 3 2 1 0

Color Compare 3
Color Compare 2
Color Compare 1
Color Compare 0

DATA ROTATE - GRAPHICS DATA REGISTER 3

Bit 7 6 5 4 3 2 1 0

Function Select
00 = Data Overwrites in Specified Color
01 = Data ANDed with Latched Data
10 = Data ORed with Latched Data
11 = Data XORed with Latched Data

Binary Representation of
Number of Positions to
Rotate Processor Data

READ MAP SELECT - GRAPHICS DATA REGISTER 4

Bit 7 6 5 4 3 2 1 0

Binary Representation of
Memory Plane to be
Read by Processor

59

Figure 4-8 (continued)

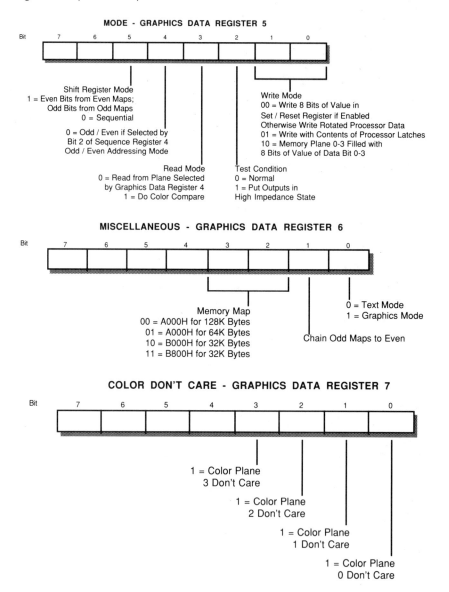

MODE - GRAPHICS DATA REGISTER 5

Shift Register Mode
1 = Even Bits from Even Maps;
Odd Bits from Odd Maps
0 = Sequential

0 = Odd / Even if Selected by
Bit 2 of Sequence Register 4
Odd / Even Addressing Mode

Read Mode
0 = Read from Plane Selected
by Graphics Data Register 4
1 = Do Color Compare

Write Mode
00 = Write 8 Bits of Value in
Set / Reset Register if Enabled
Otherwise Write Rotated Processor Data
01 = Write with Contents of Processor Latches
10 = Memory Plane 0-3 Filled with
8 Bits of Value of Data Bit 0-3

Test Condition
0 = Normal
1 = Put Outputs in
High Impedance State

MISCELLANEOUS - GRAPHICS DATA REGISTER 6

Memory Map
00 = A000H for 128K Bytes
01 = A000H for 64K Bytes
10 = B000H for 32K Bytes
11 = B800H for 32K Bytes

Chain Odd Maps to Even

0 = Text Mode
1 = Graphics Mode

COLOR DON'T CARE - GRAPHICS DATA REGISTER 7

1 = Color Plane
3 Don't Care

1 = Color Plane
2 Don't Care

1 = Color Plane
1 Don't Care

1 = Color Plane
0 Don't Care

Figure 4-8 (continued)

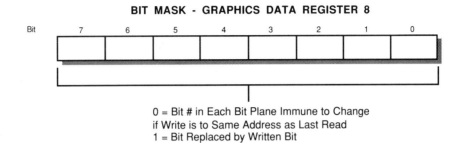

BIT MASK - GRAPHICS DATA REGISTER 8

0 = Bit # in Each Bit Plane Immune to Change
if Write is to Same Address as Last Read
1 = Bit Replaced by Written Bit

It is not self-evident from Figure 4-8 just how the graphics data registers should be used. One method of writing pixels involves writing the color for the selected pixel into the Set/Reset Register (Graphics Data Register 0). This permits the selected planes to be written to; however, the Set/Reset Enable Register (Graphics Data Register 1) must be set for these planes to be enabled. This normally means that an 0FH should be sent to Register 1, since if it is not enabled, data from the processor will be written. The function select in the Data Rotate Register (Graphics Data Register 3) is next set for the desired method of writing data (overwrite, AND, OR, or XOR). Next, the Bit Mask Register (Graphics Data Register 8) must be set with a mask which has a bit set only in the pixel position that is to be written. If you want to write several adjacent pixels with the same color, you may have more than a single bit in this mask.) After these registers are set, you need to do a read at the address where you want the pixel written, so that those pixels that you don't want to change will be made immune to change by the zeroes in the Mask Register. Then you do a write to this same address, which causes the bits to be changed in the planes enabled in Set/Reset Register 0.

In this mode of operation, what you write out to the memory address is unimportant; normally one sends 0FFH, just to be safe. Note that this all depends upon the Mode Register (Graphics Data Register 5) having the write mode set to 0; however, the register is normally initialized to zero, so that you shouldn't have to change it. Finally, after you are through writing pixels, you need to reset registers 0, 1, and 3 to zero and register 8 to 0FFH.

Another technique is similar to the above, and seems to be a little faster. It makes use of the sequencer registers to set the color instead of the graphics set/reset registers. The code for writing a pixel using this method is shown in Figure 4-9.

Figure 4-9: Code to Write a Pixel to the EGA

```
void plot(int x, int y, int color)
{
    #define seq_out(index,val)      {outp(0x3C4,index);\
                                      outp(0x3C5,val);}
    #define graph_out(index,val)    {outp(0x3CE,index);\
                                      outp(0x3CF,val);}

    unsigned int offset;
    int dummy, mask;
    char far * mem_address;

    offset = (long)y * 80L + ((long)x / 8L);
    mem_address = (char far *) 0xA0000000L + offset;
    mask = 0x80 >> (x % 8);
    graph_out(8,mask);
    seq_out(2,0x0F);
    dummy = *mem_address;
    *mem_address = 0;
    seq_out(2,color);
    *mem_address = 0xFF;
    seq_out(2,0x0F);
    graph_out(3,0);
    graph_out(8,0xFF);
}
```

You might also want to read a pixel from the screen by directly accessing the EGA registers. Figure 4-10 lists the code to perform this task. First, the correct memory address and correct location for the mask need to be established in the same way that they were for writing a pixel.

Figure 4-10: Code to Read a Pixel from the EGA

```
int readPixel (int x, int y)
{
    #define DISPLAY_OUT(index,val)  {outp(0x3CE,index);\
                                      outp(0x3CF,val);}
    int i,j,color=0;
    unsigned char mask, exist_color;
    char far *base;
    base = (char far *) (0xA0000000L + ((long)y * 80L +
```

```
    ((long)x/8L)));
mask = 0x80 >> (x % 8);
for (i=0; i<4; i++)
{
    DISPLAY_OUT(4,i);
    DISPLAY_OUT(5,0);
    exist_color = *base & mask;
    if (exist_color != 0)
        color |= 0x01<<i;
}
return color;
}
```

We are now going to assemble the color attribute of the selected pixel in the four least significant bits of *color*. This is done by first zeroing color and then setting the Graphics Data Register 4 to permit reading only one color plane (with a different plane being read in each of four passes. Graphics Data Register 5 is then set to the read mode and the display address is read and masked. If the result is zero (the color being checked is present at the desired pixel), then the existing value of *color* is ORed with 01 and the result is shifted left by one bit (except for the last pass). The result in *color* at the end of the pass is each of the four least significant bits set if the color it represents was set on the corresponding color plane for the pixel being examined.

5

ROM BIOS Video Services

The ROM BIOS video services provide a means of displaying text and graphics to the IBM PC display screen, which is essentially independent of the type of display used. By using only these services, the programmer is virtually guaranteed that his software will work with any IBM compatible machine and with any of the various compatible color or monochrome displays (with the exception of the graphics mode of the Hercules Graphics Card). The penalty that is paid for this flexibility is a lack of speed and certain restrictions as to what can be done with the services. The basic approach, then, is to use the ROM BIOS services for operations performed a small number of times, and to think seriously about faster techniques for operations that are highly repetitive. For example, you are not likely to set the video mode more than once at the beginning of the program, so there is no reason to use anything besides the ROM BIOS service number 0 to perform this operation. The fact that it takes a few more microseconds than optimum to perform its function is unimportant. On the other hand, writing a pixel to the screen is likely to be done thousands of times for a single display. In this case, the extra microseconds begin to add up to significant delays, and it is time to think about using techniques that are faster than the ROM BIOS services.

All of the ROM BIOS video services are called by generating interrupt 16 (10H). The service to be selected is determined by placing the service number in register AH before the interrupt is generated. Often the service requires entry of various parameters in the other microprocessor registers before the interrupt is generated. Sometimes data is produced by the service and stored in the other registers for your use after the interrupt has terminated. There are 16 ROM BIOS video services that may be used with any computer and display combination. Seven other ROM BIOS video services (divided into a number of subservices) can be used only in conjunction with an EGA or VGA adapter board and their associated displays. The ROM BIOS of the computer is supplemented by a ROM BIOS on the EGA or VGA board, which permits operation of these additional services.

The remainder of this chapter provides tables that define each of the video services. These tables should supply all of the information that you need to make uses of these services, either through interfaces with Turbo or Microsoft C or directly in assembly language.

Set Video Mode (ROM BIOS Video Service 00H)

The Set Video Mode service will set the system to any video mode that is compatible with whatever video board the system is using, except for the Hercules Graphics Card which is not supported by the ROM BIOS video services. Usually it is necessary to change the values in several of the video board registers to change the mode. Enough information has been given in chapters 3 and 4 so that you can determine just what has to be done to set the various modes directly, but it is much simpler to use this ROM BIOS service. The video modes supported by this service are shown in Figure 5-1. The service is described in Figure 5-2.

Figure 5-1: Video Modes Supported by ROM BIOS Video Service 0

Mode	Type	Colors	Pgs	Pixels	Alpha	Char	Adapter
00H	Text	16	8	320x200	40x25	8x8	CGA
00H	Text	16/64	8	320x350	40x25	8x14	EGA
00H	Text	16/256K	8	320x400	40x25	9x16	VGA
01H	Text	16	8	320x200	40x25	8x8	CGA
01H	Text	16/64	8	320x350	40x25	8x14	EGA
01H	Text	16/256K	8	360x400	40x25	9x16	VGA
02H	Text	16	8	640x200	80x25	8x8	CGA
02H	Text	16/64	8	640x350	80x25	8x14	EGA
02H	Text	16/256K	8	720x400	80x25	9x16	VGA
03H	Text	16	8	640x200	80x25	8x8	CGA
03H	Text	16/64	8	640x350	80x25	8x14	EGA
03H	Text	16/256K	8	720x400	80x25	9x16	VGA
04H	Graphic	4/256K	1	320x200	40x25	8x8	CGA/EGS/VGA
05H	Graphic	4/256K	1	320x200	40x25	8x8	CGA/EGS/VGA
06H	Graphic	1/256K	1	640x200	80x25	8x14	CGA/EGA/VGA

(continued on next page)

07H	Text	4	8	720x350	80x25	9x14	MA
07H	Text	4	8	720x400	80x25	9x16	VGA
0DH	Graphic	16/256K	8	320x200	40x25	8x8	CGA/EGA/VGA
0EH	Graphic	16/256K	8	640x200	80x25	8x8	CGA/EGA/VGA
0FH	Graphic	4	2	640x400	80x25	8x14	CGA/EGA/VGA
10H	Graphic	16x256K	2	640x350	80x25	8x14	EGA/VGA
11H	Graphic	2x256K	1	640x480	80x30	8x16	VGA
12H	Graphic	16x256K	1	640x480	80x30	8x16	VGA
13H	Graphic	256/256K	1	320x200	40x25	8x8	VGA

Figure 5-2: ROM BIOS Video Service 00H

Service 0 (00H): Set Video Mode

INPUT TO BIOS	OUTPUT FROM BIOS
AH = 00H	No data returned.
AL = Video Mode	

Description: This service sets the video mode to that specified in the AL register. At the same time, the screen memory buffer is cleared, so resetting to the same mode can be used to clear the screen. This method of clearing the screen, however, may be objectionably slow on some clones. The Hercules modes are not supported by IBM and therefore cannot be set by this service.

Set Cursor Size (ROM BIOS Video Service 01H)

This service sets the number of character lines which the cursor occupies. Each cursor line is filled for the width of the character (8 or 9 pixels depending upon the mode and adapter card). The cursor can take from one line up to a full character height (8 lines for low resolution modes, 14 lines for high resolution modes, and 16 lines for some VGA modes). For all modes except the VGA, you may select any line as the starting line and any line as the ending line. If you choose an ending line that is smaller than the starting line, the cursor will wrap around so that you have a two part cursor, with the first part at the bottom of the character position and the second part at the top. With the VGA, if the starting line is greater than the ending line, the cursor will not appear. The cursor does not appear on the display in the CGA and EGA graphics modes, making this service useless for them. For VGA graphics modes, the cursor can appear on graphics modes if the Cursor Emulation subservice of ROM BIOS video service 12H is set. This service is described in Figure 5-3.

Figure 5-3: ROM BIOS Video Service 01H

Service 1 (01H): Set Cursor Size

INPUT TO BIOS	OUTPUT FROM BIOS
AH = 01H CH = Starting cursor scan line CL = Ending cursor scan line	No data returned.

Description: The cursor appears in the text modes only; graphics modes have no cursor. The cursor is a blinking line or lines of the foreground color. Characters generated by the Color Graphics Adapter have eight scan lines; those generated by the Monochrome Adapter or Enhanced Graphics Adapter have fourteen scan lines. In either case, the scan lines are numbered consecutively from top to bottom, beginning with line 0. The cursor size and position are as specified by the contents of CH and CL. The first cursor line is specified by CH; the last is specified by CL. If CL is less than CH, the cursor wraps around so that it appears in two parts. If bit 5 of CH is set by entering 32 (20H), the cursor is turned off.

Set Cursor Position
(ROM BIOS Video Service 02H)

This service sets the cursor to a specified row and column position. For purposes of specifying cursor position, the screen is divided into a number of character positions. Depending upon the current mode of operation, the entire display width will be divided into 40 or 80 character positions. The height of the screen is always divided into 25 character lines, except for modes 11H and 12H, which have 30 lines. The cursor position will still be stored, even if in a graphics mode, where the cursor is not displayed. The ROM BIOS video services for writing a text character to the screen use this stored cursor position data to determine where the character will be written, both for text and graphics displays. This service is described in Figure 5-4.

Figure 5-4: ROM BIOS Video Service 02H

Service 2 (02H): Set Cursor Position

INPUT TO BIOS	OUTPUT FROM BIOS
AH = 02H BH = Page Number (0 for CGA graphics modes) DH = Row DL = Column	No data returned.

Description: This service sets the position of the cursor in terms of row and column coordinates. Cursor position can be set and read in both text and graphic modes, even though the cursor does not appear in the graphic modes. The first cursor position is at the top left corner of the screen, and has coordinates (0,0). The maximum row position is 24; the maximum column position is 39 for 40-column displays and 79 for 80-column displays. If numbers higher than these are used, the cursor will be off screen and will not be displayed. The minimum page number is 0; the maximum is 7 for 40-column displays and 3 for 80-column displays. The page number must be 0 for graphics modes. The cursor position is kept track of separately for each page.

Read Cursor Position

This service permits you to read out the cursor position and also the current cursor starting and ending lines. The latter information is not apt to be too useful, but the former may be important if you have been writing a string of characters and are not sure where you left off. Of course, in text modes, you can see the cursor position on the screen, but you cannot do this in graphics modes, so you must depend upon this service. Another use for this service is to provide an index for branching to several menu commands, one of which has been selected by placing the cursor on a line of text. This service is described in Figure 5-5.

Figure 5-5: ROM BIOS Video Service 03H

Service 3 (03H): Read Cursor Position

INPUT TO BIOS	OUTPUT FROM BIOS
AH = 03H	DH = Row number
BH = Page Number	DL = Column number
	CH = Cursor starting scan line
	CL = Cursor ending scan line

Description: This service reads the cursor position, returning the row in DH and the column in DL. For text modes, it reports the cursor size and shape by returning the starting scan line in CH and the ending scan line in CL.

Read Light Pen Position
(ROM BIOS Video Service 04H)

Light pens are virtually obsolete, so this service is essentially worthless. It is not supported by the VGA. It is described in Figure 5-6.

Figure 5-6: ROM BIOS Video Service 04H

Service 4 (04H): Read Light Pen Position

INPUT TO BIOS	OUTPUT FROM BIOS
AH = 04H	AH = 0: Not triggered
	= 1: Triggered
	DH = Character row number
	DL = Character column number
	CH or CX = Pixel raster line number
	BX = Pixel column number

Description: This service reports light pen status, when a light pen is installed. If the light pen has not been triggered, a 0 is returned in AH. If the light pen has been triggered, a 1 is returned in AH and the triggered position is returned in two forms. The position in terms of character coordinates is returned as a row in DH and a column in DL. The position in terms of pixel column number is returned in BX. The pixel raster line coordinate is returned in CH for old graphics modes and in CX for new EGA modes.

Set Active Display Page
(ROM BIOS Video Service 05H)

Most video modes have more than one page of memory available. By switching from one to another you can call up a completely different display, work with it for awhile, and then recall your original display. This is the video service to use to accomplish this task. It is described in Figure 5-7.

Figure 5-7: ROM BIOS Video Service 05H

Service 5 (05H): Set Active Display Page

INPUT TO BIOS	OUTPUT FROM BIOS
AH = 05H AL = Active Page	No data returned.

Description: This service sets the active display page. The maximum number of display pages for each mode is given in Figure 5-1, Video Modes Supported by ROM BIOS video service 0. If this service is not called, the display is taken by default from page 0.

Scroll Window Up
(ROM BIOS Video Service 06H)

This useful service creates a window of any desired size and scrolls the contents up as many lines as desired, filling in with blank lines at the bottom. When the number of lines is specified as zero, the entire window is filled with blank lines of the color specified by the attribute byte. The use of the attribute byte is strange, however. For CGA modes, the attribute byte uses two bits to specify the color of one of four columns, alternately. Thus the desired color must be repeated four times to avoid vertical stripes. For the EGA modes, the specified foreground color is used for the blanks, not the background color as one might expect. This service is described in Figure 5-8.

Figure 5-8: ROM BIOS Video Service 06H

Service 6 (06H): Scroll Window Up

INPUT TO BIOS	OUTPUT FROM BIOS
AH = 06H	No data returned.
AL = Number. of character lines to scroll	
BH = Display attribute for blank lines	
CH = Row number for upper left corner	
CL = Column number for upper left corner	
DH = Row number for lower right corner	
DL = Column number for lower right corner	

Description: This service defines a window on the display screen and permits scrolling up of its contents. The contents of CH and CL defines the upper left corner of the window; DH and DL defines the lower right corner. The contents of the window are scrolled up the number of lines specified in AL. The lines that are scrolled off the top disappear and are lost. A corresponding number of blank lines having the attribute specified in BH are inserted at the bottom of the window. If AL is set to 0 or to a greater number of lines than the window contains (DH-CH), then the entire window is filled with blank lines having the attributes specified in BH. Note that when this service is used in EGA modes, the foreground color attribute is the color that is filled in on the blank lines, rather than the background color as one might expect. For CGA modes, the color must be repeated four times in the attribute byte to avoid vertical stripes.

Scroll Window Down
(ROM BIOS Video Service 07H)

This is essentially the same as the above service except that it scrolls down (filling in with blank lines at the top) instead of up. This service is described in Figure 5-9.

Figure 5-9: ROM BIOS Video Service 07H

Service 7 (07H): Scroll Window Down

INPUT TO BIOS	OUTPUT FROM BIOS
AH = 07H	No data returned.
AL = Number of lines to scroll	
BH = Display attribute for blank lines	
CH = Row number for upper left corner	
CL = Column number for upper left corner	
DH = Row number for lower right corner	
DL = Column number for lower right corner	

Description: This service defines a window on the display screen and permits scrolling down of its contents. The contents of CH and CL define the upper left corner of the window; DH and DL define the lower right corner. The contents of the window are scrolled down the number of lines specified in AL. The lines that are scrolled off the bottom disappear and are lost. A corresponding number of blank lines having the attribute specified in BH are inserted at the top of the window. If AL is set to 0 or to a greater number of lines than the window contains (DH-CH), then the entire window is filled with blank lines having attributes specified in BH. Note that when this service is used in EGA modes, the foreground color attribute is the color that is filled in on the blank lines, rather than the background color as one might expect. For CGA modes, the color must be repeated four times in the attribute byte to avoid vertical stripes.

Read Character and Attribute (ROM BIOS Video Service 08H)

This is an interesting service since it works in graphics as well as text modes. In the text modes, the ASCII value of any character that has been written to the screen and adjacently its attribute byte is stored in display memory. This service finds the proper place in memory and returns these two bytes. Anything may be written on the screen in the graphics mode, including text characters, lines, points, or even text overdrawn with something else. In this case, the service compares the contents of the character position with all of the character matrices used to write characters in the graphics mode, and reports back the ASCII value if it finds a character that matches. If there is no match, it returns a 00H. No attribute byte is returned in the graphics modes. This service is described in Figure 5-10.

Figure 5-10: ROM BIOS Video Service 08H

Service 8 (08H): Read Character and Attribute

INPUT TO BIOS	OUTPUT FROM BIOS

AH = 08H
BH = Active page (not
    required in CGA
    graphics modes)
	AH = attribute of text character
	
	AL = ASCII character at
	    cursor location

Description: This service reads the character from the screen at the current cursor location. In the text modes, the character read will always match some ASCII character that has been written to the screen (if only a space (20H)) and that ASCII character designation will appear in AL. For text, the attribute byte will appear in AH, with bit meanings as shown below. In the graphics modes, the character read from the screen is compared with the character generation table used to write alphanumerics to the screen. If a match is found, the ASCII designation of the matched character is reported in AL; if there is no match, AL returns a 0. In graphics mode, the contents returned in AH are meaningless.

TEXT MODES

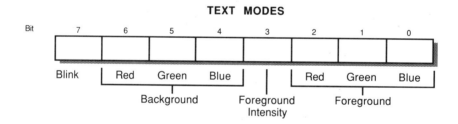

Write Character and Attribute (ROM BIOS Video Service 09H)

This service writes a character to the screen. In the text mode, both foreground and background colors can be specified. In the graphics mode, only the foreground color can be specified; the currently specified background color is used for the background. Note that the current background color may not be the color which is shown on the unwritten part of your display, so character backgrounds may be something different from what you were expecting. This service is described in Figure 5-11.

Figure 5-11: ROM BIOS Video Service 9

Service 9 (09H): Write Character and Attribute

INPUT TO BIOS	OUTPUT FROM BIOS
AH = 09H AL = ASCII character to be written to screen BL = Attribute of character to be written BH = Active display page (not used in graphics modes) CX = Number. of times to write character and attribute to screen	No data returned.

Description: This service writes the character in AL to the screen at the current cursor position with attributes specified in BL. The attributes for text modes and for graphics modes are shown below. In graphics modes, bit 7 causes the character color to be XORed with the background color. (This guarantees that the character will be visible unless the foreground is zero (black). When bit 7 is not set, the foreground color of the characters replaces the background color. CX must be set to 1 if a single character is to be written. Setting CX to some number is a useful way to fill in blanks or repeat characters. Failing to enter a value in CX creates a disaster.

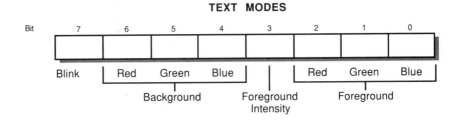

TEXT MODES

(continued on next page)

GRAPHICS MODES

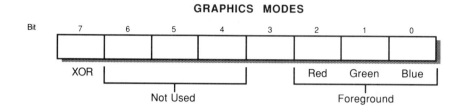

Write Character (ROM BIOS Video Service 0AH)

This relatively useless service is the same as service 09H for graphics modes and is the same as service 09H for text modes except that it does not specify a character attribute. In text modes, the character is written with the current foreground and background colors. This service is described in Figure 5-12.

Figure 5-12: ROM BIOS Video Service 0AH

Service 10 (0AH): Write Character

INPUT TO BIOS	OUTPUT FROM BIOS

AH = 0AH
 AL = ASCII character to be written to screen
 BL = Color attribute of character to be
     written to screen when in graphic modes
 BH = Active display page (not used in
     graphic modes)
 CX = Number of times character and attribute
     are to be written to screen.
	No data returned.

Description: This service is the same as service 9, except that in text modes it does not change the current screen color attributes. In graphics modes the color attributes behave as shown below. In graphics modes, bit 7 causes the character color to be XORed with the background color. (This guarantees that the character will be visible unless the foreground is zero (black). When bit 7 is not set, the foreground color of the characters replaces the background color. CX must be set to 1 if a single character is to be written. Setting CX to some number is a useful way to fill in blanks or repeated characters. Failing to enter a value in CX creates a disaster.

(continued on next page)

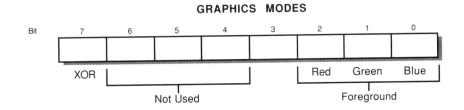

GRAPHICS MODES

Set Color Palette (ROM BIOS Video Service 0BH)

This service selects one of two medium-resolution palettes for the Color/Graphics Adapter. It is described in Figure 5-13. It should not be used when the Enhanced Graphics Adapter or Video Graphics Array is present, since although it will properly set the background color, at the same time it will remap some of the other colors in a way that you don't want. Instead, use ROM BIOS video service 10H, Subservice 0 to set the colors for the EGA.

Figure 5-13: ROM BIOS Video Service 0BH

Service 11 (0BH): Set Color Palette

INPUT TO BIOS	OUTPUT FROM BIOS

AH = 0BH
 BH = 0; Set border or background color
    = 1; Set Palette
 BL = Background Color when in Graphics Mode
     and BH = 0
    = Border Color when in Text Mode and BH = 0
    = 0; Set Palette to 0 when BH = 1 and in Mode 4
    = 1; Set Palette to 1 when BH = 1 and in Mode 4
 DH = Row
 DL = Column
	No data returned.

Description: This service sets the palette or background/border color. When in color mode 4 and BH = 1, the palette is set as shown below. When BH = 0 and in the graphics modes, the background and border colors are set to the color given in BL. When BH = 0 and in the text modes, the border color is set to the color given in BL. This service only works properly on CGA modes 4 and 5. When used with the EGA or VGA modes to set background color, the background color is set properly, but some of the foreground colors are mapped to different colors.

Palette 0	Palette 1
0 = current background color 1 = green (2) 2 = red (4) 3 = brown (6)	0 = current background color 1 = cyan (3) 2 = magenta (50 3 = white (7)

Write Pixel Dot (ROM BIOS Video Service 0CH)

This service writes a pixel to the screen at a specified location with color and writing method (replace, AND, OR or XOR) as specified. It is described in Figure 5-14.

Figure 5-14: ROM BIOS Video Service 0CH

Service 12 (0CH): Write Pixel Dot

INPUT TO BIOS	OUTPUT FROM BIOS
AH = 0CH AL = Pixel color and write method (0-FH & 80H-8FH) BH = Display Page DX = Pixel row number CX = Pixel column number	No data returned.

Description: The pixel color is shown below. If bit 7 of AL is set, the specified pixel color is XORed with the current color of the pixel; if bit 7 is 0, the specified color replaces the existing color.

(continued on next page)

AL (Decimal)	AL (Hex)	Color
0 or 128	0 or 80	Black
1 or 129	1 or 81	Blue
2 or 130	2 or 82	Green
3 or 131	3 or 83	Cyan
4 or 132	4 or 84	Red
5 or 133	5 or 85	Magenta
6 or 134	6 or 86	Brown
7 or 135	7 or 87	Light Gray
8 or 136	8 or 88	Dark Gray
9 or 137	9 or 89	Light Blue
10 or 138	A or 8A	Light Green
11 or 139	B or 8B	Light Cyan
12 or 140	C or 8C	Light Red
13 or 141	D or 8D	Light Magenta
14 or 142	E or 8E	Yellow
15 or 143	F or 8F	Bright White

Read Pixel Dot (ROM BIOS Video Service 0DH)

This service reads a pixel and its color from the screen. It is described in Figure 5-15.

Figure 5-15: ROM BIOS Video Service 0DH

Service 13 (0DH): Read Pixel Dot

INPUT TO BIOS	OUTPUT FROM BIOS
AH = 0DH BH = Display Page DX = Pixel raster line number CX = Pixel column number	AL = Pixel color.

Description: This service reads the color of the pixel at row DX and column CX into AL. The color codes are the same as for service 12 above except that bit 7 is never set.

Write Character in TTY Mode (ROM BIOS Video Service 0EH)

This service writes a character to the screen in the TTY mode, where the bell, backspace, line feed, and carriage return characters are intercepted and executed rather than being displayed. This service is described in Figure 5-16.

Figure 5-16: ROM BIOS Video Service 0EH

Service 14 (0EH): Write Character in TTY Mode

INPUT TO BIOS	OUTPUT FROM BIOS
AH = 0EH	No data returned.
AL = ASCII character to be written to screen	
BH = Active display page (not used in graphic modes)	
BL = Foreground color of character (applies only in graphics modes)	

Description: This service writes the character in AL to the screen at the current cursor position using current screen attributes. The cursor advances one position, and wrapping to a new line or line scrolling takes place as needed. In the graphics modes, the character is displayed in the foreground color specified in BL. The ASCII characters 07H, 08H, 0AH, and 0DH are not displayed by this service. Instead, they cause the following actions to be taken:

> 07H = beep from the computer speaker
> 08H = backspace the cursor one character position
> 0AH = line feed (move cursor to the next line)
> 0DH = carriage return (move the cursor to the beginning of the line.

Get Current Video Mode (ROM BIOS Video Service 0FH)

This service returns the current video mode and the number of characters per line. It is described in Figure 5-17.

Figure 5-17: ROM BIOS Video Service 0FH

Service 15 (0FH): Get Current Video Mode

INPUT TO BIOS	OUTPUT FROM BIOS
AH = 0FH	AL = Current display mode
	AH = Number of characters per line
	BH = Active display page number

Description: This service returns the current video display mode, the number of characters per line, and the number of the active display page.

Set EGA/VGA Palette Registers (ROM BIOS Video Service 10H)

This service consists of fourteen subservices. All of these subservices are concerned with setting of the color and palette registers for the EGA and VGA. The first four subservices work either with the EGA or VGA. They are concerned with setting the 16 palette registers. They should not be used with VGA mode 13H, since in this mode the palette registers are required to remain in their default state to serve as indexes to the DAC color registers. For this mode, colors should be changed by directly changing the DAC color registers. The remaining ten subservices work with the VGA only. Figures 5-18 to 5-31 describe the subservices of service 10H.

Figure 5-18: ROM BIOS Video Service 10H Subservice 00H

Service 16 (10H)   Set Individual EGA Palette Registers
Subservice 00H   (for systems using EGA/VGA only)

INPUT TO BIOS	OUTPUT FROM BIOS
AH = 10H	No data returned.
AL = 0	
BH = Color	
BL = Palette number	

Description: This service and subservice sets the color for a particular palette register. Each palette register determines the color which will be produced by a particular color number. Palette 0 is the background color (0), palette 1 is color attribute 1, etc.

Figure 5-19: ROM BIOS Video Service 10H Subservice 01H

Service 16 (10H)   Set EGA/VGA Overscan
Subservice 01H: (for systems using EGA/VGA only)

INPUT TO BIOS	OUTPUT FROM BIOS
AH = 10H	No data returned.
AL = 1	
BH = Overscan color	

Description: This service and subservice sets the color of the overscan border.

Figure 5-20: ROM BIOS Video Service 10H Subservice 02H

Service 16 (10H)   Set Palette Registers
Subservice 02H   (for systems using EGA/VGA only)

INPUT TO BIOS	OUTPUT FROM BIOS
AH = 10H	No data returned.
AL = 2	
ES:DX = Pointer to 17 byte table of palette and overscan values	

Description: This service and subservice transfers 17 bytes pointed to by ES:DX to the 16 palette registers and the overscan register. This permits remapping of all displayable colors with a single command.

Figure 5-21: ROM BIOS Video Service 10H Subservice 03H

Service 16 (10H)   Toggle EGA Blinking
Subservice 03H   (for systems using EGA/VGA only)

INPUT TO BIOS	OUTPUT FROM BIOS
AH = 10H	No data returned.
AL = 3	
BL = 0 : Toggle Intensity	
= 1 : Toggle Blinking	

Description: The intensity bit is initially set for low intensity and the blinking bit is set for no blinking. When this service is called with BL equal to zero, the intensity bit is switched to the opposite state (high intensity if currently low or low intensity if currently high). When this service is called with BL equal to one, the blinking bit is switched to the opposite state (blinking if currently not blinking or not blinking if currently blinking).

Figure 5-22: ROM BIOS Video Service 10H Subservice 07H

Service 16 (10H)   Read Individual VGA Palette
Subservice 07H   Register (for systems using VGA only)

INPUT TO BIOS	OUTPUT FROM BIOS
AH = 10H	BH = Palette register value
AL = 07H	
BL = Palette register number	

Description: This service and subservice reads the color for a particular palette register.

Figure 5-23: ROM BIOS Video Service 10H
Subservice 08H

Service 16 (10H) Read Overscan Register
Subservice 08H (for systems using VGA only)

INPUT TO BIOS	OUTPUT FROM BIOS
AH = 10H	BH = Overscan register value
AL = 08H	

Description: This service and subservice reads the color of the overscan border.

Figure 5-24: ROM BIOS Video Service 10H
Subservice 09H

Service 16 (10H) Read All Palette Registers
Subservice 09H (for systems using VGA only)

INPUT TO BIOS	OUTPUT FROM BIOS
AH = 10H	Data returned to table
AL = 09H	pointed to by ES:DX
ES:DX = Pointer to 17 byte table of palette and overscan values	

Description: This service and subservice transfers 17 bytes of data giving the values of the 16 palette registers and overscan register to the memory location pointed to by ES:DX.

Figure 5-25: ROM BIOS Video Service 10H Subservice 10H

Service 16 (10H)   Set Individual Color Register
Subservice 13H   (for systems using VGA only)

INPUT TO BIOS	OUTPUT FROM BIOS
AH = 10H	No data returned.
AL = 10H	
BX = Color register number	
CH = Green value	
CL = Blue value	
DH = Red Value	

Description: This subservice sets an individual DAC color register (numbered 00H to FFH) to a six bit value for *red*, *blue*, and *green*.

Figure 5-26: ROM BIOS Video Service 10H Subservice 12H

Service 16 (10H)   Set Block of Color Registers
Subservice 12H   (for systems using VGA only)

INPUT TO BIOS	OUTPUT FROM BIOS
AH = 10H	No data returned.
AL = 12H	
BX = Number of first color register	
CX = Number of registers to be set	
ES:DX = Pointer to table of color values	

Description: This service and subservice sets a designated number of color registers with colors values from the table pointed to by ES:DX. The values in the table should be in the order *red, green, blue, red, green, blue*, etc.

Figure 5-27: ROM BIOS Video Service 10H Subservice 13H

Service 16 (10H) Select Color Page
Subservice 13H (for systems using VGA only)

INPUT TO BIOS	OUTPUT FROM BIOS
AH = 10H	No data returned.
AL = 13H	
BL = 0 :Select paging mode	
= 1 :Select page	
BH = 0 :Selects 4 pages of 64 color registers (if BL = 0)	
= 1 :Selects 16 pages of 16 color registers (if BL = 0)	
= Number of color page (if BL = 1)	

Description: This service and subservice selects the color page or the color page mode.

Figure 5-28: ROM BIOS Video Service 10H Subservice 15H

Service 16 (10H) Read Individual Color Register
Subservice 15H (for systems using VGA only)

INPUT TO BIOS	OUTPUT FROM BIOS
AH = 10H	CH = Green value
AL = 15H	CL = Blue value
BX = Number of color register	DH = Red value

Description: This service and subservice reads the color values from a selected color register.

Figure 5-29: ROM BIOS Video Service 10H Subservice 17H

Service 16 (10H)   Read Block of Color Registers
Subservice 17H   (for systems using VGA only)

INPUT TO BIOS	OUTPUT FROM BIOS
AH = 10H	Data returned to table
AL = 17H	pointed to by ES:DX
BX = Number of first color register	
ES:DX = Pointer to table to receive color values	

Description: This subservice reads a block of color registers and returns the values to the table pointed to by ES:DX in the order *red*, *green*, *blue*, *red*, *green*, *blue*, etc.

Figure 5-30: ROM BIOS Video Service 10H Subservice 1AH

Service 16 (10H)   Read Current Color Page Number
Subservice 1AH   (for systems using VGA only)

INPUT TO BIOS	OUTPUT FROM BIOS
AH = 10H	BH = Current Page
AL = 1AH	BL = Paging Mode

Description: This service and subservice reads the current color page and color paging mode.

Figure 5-31: ROM BIOS Video Service 10H Subservice 1BH

Service 16 (10H)   Sum Color Values to Gray Scale
Subservice 1BH   (for systems using VGA only)

INPUT TO BIOS	OUTPUT FROM BIOS
AH = 10H	No data returned.
AL = 1BH	
BX = First color register to be summed	
CX = Number of registers to sum	

Description: This service and subservice reads the R, G, and B values in the color registers, performs a weighted summation (30% red + 59% green + 11% blue) and writes the result into the R, G, and B components of the color registers. The original contents of the color registers is over-written.

Character Generator Routines (ROM BIOS Video Service 11H)

This service consists of 15 subservices, which are concerned with loading and specifying fonts. All of these subservices are used by either the EGA or VGA. These subservices are described in figures 5-32 to 5-46.

Figure 5-32: ROM BIOS Video Service 11H Subservice 0

Service 17 (11H)   Load User Font
Subservice 00H   (for systems using EGA/VGA only)

INPUT TO BIOS	OUTPUT FROM BIOS
AH = 11H AL = 00H : Load user text font with total video environment reset BL = Block to load BH = Number of bytes per character CX = Count to store DX = Character offset into table ES:BP = Pointer to user table	No data returned.

Description: This service loads a user character font into the loadable character generator. An offset may be specified for the beginning of the load.

Figure 5-33: ROM BIOS Video Service 11H Subservice 01H

Service 17 (11H)   Load ROM Monochrome Character Set
Subservice 01H   (for systems using EGA/VGA only)

INPUT TO BIOS	OUTPUT FROM BIOS

AH = 11H
AL = 01H : Load ROM monochrome
          character set with total video
          environment reset
BL = Block to load
	No data returned.

Description: This service loads the ROM monochrome character set with 8x14 character cell.

Figure 5-34: ROM BIOS Video Service 11H Subservice 02H

Service 17 (11H)   Load ROM 8x8 Double Dot
Subservice 02H   (for systems using EGA/VGA only)

INPUT TO BIOS	OUTPUT FROM BIOS
AH = 11H	No data returned.
AL = 02H	
BL = Block to load	

Description: This service loads the 8x8 double dot character set into the specified block.

Figure 5-35: ROM BIOS Video Service 11H Subservice 03H

Service 17 (11H)   Set Block Specifier
Subservice 03H   (for systems using EGA/VGA only)

INPUT TO BIOS	OUTPUT FROM BIOS
AH = 11H	No data returned.
AL = 03H	
BL = Character generator block specifier	

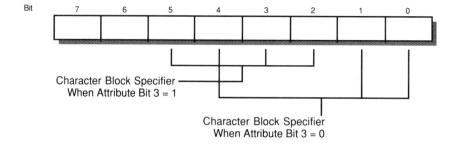

Description: This service allows you to determine which two of four-character sets are to be selected by the settings of the attribute bit. IBM recommends that a function call with:
     AX = 1000H
     BX = 0712H

be run just before this service is called, to properly set palette colors. If both block values are the same attribute, bit 3 determines foreground intensity.

Figure 5-36: ROM BIOS Video Service 11H Subservice 04H

Service 17 (11H)   Load ROM 8x16 Character Set
Subservice 04H   (for systems using EGA/VGA only)

INPUT TO BIOS	OUTPUT FROM BIOS
AH = 11H	No data returned.
AL = 04H	
BL = Target Block	

Description: This service loads the 8x16 character set into the specified block.

Figure 5-37: ROM BIOS Video Service 11H Subservice 10H

Service 17 (11H)   Load User Font
Subservice 10H   (for systems using EGA/VGA only)

INPUT TO BIOS	OUTPUT FROM BIOS
AH = 11H	No data returned.
AL = 10H	
BH = Number of bytes per character	
BL = Block to load	
DX = Character offset into table	
ES:BP = Pointer to user table	

Description: This subservice is similar to subservice 00H except that a MODE SET call must be issued immediately before this subservice is called, page zero must be active, and the character height will be recalculated.

Figure 5-38: ROM BIOS Video Service 11H Subservice 11H

Service 17 (11H)   Load ROM Monochrome Character Set
Subservice 11H   (for systems using EGA/VGA only)

INPUT TO BIOS	OUTPUT FROM BIOS
AH = 11H AL = 11H BL = Block to load	No data returned.

Description: This service loads the ROM monochrome character set (using the 8x14 cell) into the specified block.

Figure 5-39: ROM BIOS Video Service 11H Subservice 12H

Service 17 (11H)   Load ROM 8x8 Double Dot
Subservice 12H   (for systems using EGA/VGA only)

INPUT TO BIOS	OUTPUT FROM BIOS
AH = 11H AL = 12H BL = Block to load	No data returned.

Description: This service loads the 8x8 double-dot character set into the selected block.

Figure 5-40: ROM BIOS Video Service 11H
Subservice 13H

Service 17 (11H)   Load ROM 8x16 Character Set
Subservice 14H   (for systems using EGA/VGA only)

INPUT TO BIOS	OUTPUT FROM BIOS
AH = 11H	No data returned.
AL = 14H	
BL = Target Block	

Description: This service loads the 8x16 character set into the specified block.

Figure 5-41: ROM BIOS Video Service 11H
Subservice 20H

Service 17 (11H)   Set High Order Character Pointer
Subservice 20H   (for systems using EGA/VGA only)

INPUT TO BIOS	OUTPUT FROM BIOS
AH = 11H	No data returned.
AL = 20H	
ES:BP = Pointer to user table for graphics characters having ASCII codes 128 to 255	

Description: This subservice stores a pointer to the table of graphics characters represented by ASCII codes 128 to 255.

Figure 5-42: ROM BIOS Video Service 11H Subservice 21H

Service 17 (11H)   Set Character Pointer
Subservice 21H   (for systems using EGA/VGA only)

INPUT TO BIOS	OUTPUT FROM BIOS
AH = 11H	No data returned.
AL = 21H	
BL = 1: 14 rows on screen	
2: 25 rows on screen	
3: 43 rows on screen	
CX = Bytes per character	
ES:BP = Pointer to user table for all	
graphics characters.	

Description: This subservice stores a pointer to the table of all graphics characters.

Figure 5-43: ROM BIOS Video Service 11H Subservice 22H

Service 17 (11H)   Load Graphics ROM 8x14 Character
Subservice 22H   Set (for systems using EGA/VGA only)

INPUT TO BIOS	OUTPUT FROM BIOS
AH = 11H	No data returned.
AL = 22H	
BL = 1: 14 rows on screen	
BL = 2: 25 rows on screen	
BL = 3: 43 rows on screen	

Description: This service loads the 8x14 character set for the graphics mode.

Figure 5-44: ROM BIOS Video Service 11H Subservice 23H

Service 17 (11H)　　　Load Graphics ROM 8x8 Character
Subservice 23H　　　　Set (for systems using EGA/VGA only)

INPUT TO BIOS	OUTPUT FROM BIOS
AH = 11H	No data returned.
AL = 23H	
BL = 1: 14 rows on screen	
BL = 2: 25 rows on screen	
BL = 3: 43 rows on screen	

Description: This service loads the 8x8 character set for the graphics mode.

Figure 5-45: ROM BIOS Video Service 11H Subservice 24H

Service 17 (11H)　　　Load Graphics ROM 8x16 Character
Subservice 24H　　　　Set (for systems using EGA/VGA only)

INPUT TO BIOS	OUTPUT FROM BIOS
AH = 11H	No data returned.
AL = 24H	
BL = 1: 14 rows on screen	
BL = 2: 25 rows on screen	
BL = 3: 43 rows on screen	

Description: This service loads the 8x16 character set for the graphics mode.

Figure 5-46: ROM BIOS Video Service 11H Subservice 30H

Service 17 (11H)   Return Character Generator Data
Subservice 30H   (for systems using EGA/VGA only)

INPUT TO BIOS	OUTPUT FROM BIOS
AH = 11H	CX = Bytes per character
AL = 30H	DL = One less than the
BH = 0 INT 1FH pointer	number of character
BH = 1 INT 43H pointer	rows on the screen
BH = 2 ROM 8x14 pointer	ES:BP = Requested Pointer
BH = 3 ROM 8x8 pointer	
BH = 4 ROM 8x8 upper 128 pointer	
BH = 5 ROM alpha supplement	
9x14 pointer	
BH = 8 ROM 8x16pointer	
BH = 9 ROM alpha supplement	
9x16 pointer	

Description: This service returns the requested pointer information.

Alternate Select (ROM BIOS Video Service 12H)

This service consists of nine subservices concerned with handling video information and printing functions. The first two subservices are used by both the EGA and VGA. The remaining subservices are used by the VGA only. The subservices are shown in Figures 5-47 to 5-56.

Figure 5-47: ROM BIOS Video Service 12H Subservice 10H

Service 18 (12H)   Get EGA/VGA Information
Subservice 10H   (for systems using EGA/VGA only)

INPUT TO BIOS	OUTPUT FROM BIOS

AH = 12H
BL = 10H
	BH = 0 : Color Mode in
	    effect
	   = 1 : Monochrome Mode
	    in effect
	BL = Memory value
	   = 00H : 64K
	   = 01H : 128K
	   = 10H : 192K
	   = 11H : 256K
	CH = Feature bits
	CL = Switch setting

Description: This service returns information on the status of the EGA or VGA display.

Figure 5-48: EGA Configuration Switch Settings

Configuration Switch Settings						
SW1	SW2	SW3	SW4	Enhanced Adapter	Monochrome Adapter	Color Graphics Adapter
On	Off	Off	On	Primary Color Display 40x25	Secondary	--
Off	Off	Off	On	Primary Color Display 80x25	Secondary	--
On	On	On	Off	Primary En- hanced Display Emulation Mode	Secondary	--
Off	On	On	Off	Primary En- hanced Display Hi Res Mode	Secondary	--

(continued on next page)

On	Off	On	Off	Primary Monochrome	--	Secondary 40x25
Off	Off	On	Off	Primary Monochrome	--	Secondary 80x25
On	On	On	On	Secondary Color Display 40x25	Primary	--
Off	On	On	On	Secondary Color Display 80x25	Primary	--
On	Off	On	On	Secondary Enhanced Display Emulation Mode	Primary	--
Off	Off	On	On	Secondary Enhanced Display Hi Res Mode	Primary	--
On	On	Off	On	Secondary Monochrome	--	Primary 40x25
Off	On	Off	On	Secondary Monochrome	--	Primary 80x25

The VGA does not have physical switches; instead, adapter information is stored in memory and read with this ROM video service.

Figure 5-49: ROM BIOS Video Service 12H Subservice 20H

Service 18 (12H)   Select Alternate Print Screen Routine
Subservice 20H   (for systems using EGA/VGA only)

INPUT TO BIOS	OUTPUT FROM BIOS
AH = 12H BL = 20H	

Description: This service changes the interrupt address so that the *PrtSc* key initiates an alternate print screen routine that is compatible with the capabilities of the EGA and VGA boards, including 43 line display.

Figure 5-50: ROM BIOS Video Service 12H Subservice 30H

Service 18 (12H):   Select Scan Lines for Alpha
Subservice 30H   Numeric Modes
                       (for systems using VGA only)

INPUT TO BIOS	OUTPUT FROM BIOS
AH = 12H	
BL = 30H	
AL = 0: 200 scan lines	
= 1: 350 scan lines	
= 2: 400 scan lines	

Description: This subservice selects the number of scan lines and the default character set for an alphanumeric mode. It takes effect at the next MODE SET call.

Figure 5-51: ROM BIOS Video Service 12H Subservice 31H

Service 18 (12H)   Default Palette Loading During Mode Set
Subservice 31H   (for systems using VGA only)

INPUT TO BIOS	OUTPUT FROM BIOS
AH = 12H	
BL = 31H	
AL = 0 Enable palette loading	
= 1 Disable palette loading	

Description: This service determines whether or not the default palette will be loaded during a Mode Set. If AL = 0, the default will be loaded; if AL = 1, the palette will be unchanged.

99

Figure 5-52: ROM BIOS Video Service 12H Subservice 32H

Service 18 (12H)   Video Enable/Disable
Subservice 32H   (for systems using VGA only)

INPUT TO BIOS	OUTPUT FROM BIOS
AH = 12H	
BL = 32H	
AL = 0 Enable video	
= 1 Disable video	

Description : This subservice enables or disables the video input port and buffer address decode.

Figure 5-53: ROM BIOS Video Service 12H Subservice 33H

Service18 (12H)   Sum to Gray Scale
Subservice 33H   (for systems using VGA only)

INPUT TO BIOS	OUTPUT FROM BIOS
AH = 12H	
BL = 33H	
AL = 0 Enable summing	
= 1 Disable summing	

Description: This subservice determines whether the summing to gray scale feature is enabled or disabled.

Figure 5-54: ROM BIOS Video Service 12H Subservice 34H

Service 18 (12H)   Cursor Emulation
Subservice 34H   (for systems using VGA only)

INPUT TO BIOS	OUTPUT FROM BIOS
AH = 12H BL = 34H AL = 0 Enable emulation = 1 Disable emulation	

Description: This subservice determines whether or not cursor data will be mapped in accordance with the current character height definition.

Figure 5-55: ROM BIOS Video Service 12H Subservice 35H

Service 18 (12H)   Display Switch
Subservice 35H   (for systems using VGA only)

INPUT TO BIOS	OUTPUT FROM BIOS

AH = 12H
BL = 35H
AL = 0. Initial switch off adapter
    = 1: Initial switch on
        planar display
    = 2: Switch iff active
        display
    = 3: Switch on active
        display
ES:DX = Pointer to 128 byte buffer
	AL = 12H: Valid call

Description: This subservice selects or deselects a video device; calls to *0* or *1* to initialize must preceed calls to *2* and *3*.

101

Figure 5-56: ROM BIOS Video Service 12H Subservice 36H

Service 18 (12H)   Video Screen On/Off
Subservice 36H   (for systems using VGA only)

INPUT TO BIOS	OUTPUT FROM BIOS
AH = 12H	No data returned.
BL = 36H	
AL = 0: Enable video output	
= 1: Disable video output	

Description: This subservice enables or disables the video output to the monitor display. When disabled all outputs are at the black level.

Write Character String (ROM BIOS Video Service 13H)

This service consists of four subservices. Two subservices permit writing a string of characters to the screen, beginning at a specified location and with a specified attribute for all of the characters to be written, and with cursor moved or not moved. The remaining two subservices write both the characters using attributes that are embedded in the string following each character, with cursor moved or not moved. These subservices are described in Figures 5-57 to 5-60.

Figure 5-57: ROM BIOS Video Service 13H
Subservice 00H

Service 19 (13H)   Write Character String
Subservice 00   (for systems using VGA only)

INPUT TO BIOS	OUTPUT FROM BIOS
AH = 13H	No data returned.
AL = 00H	
BH = Page Number	
BL = Attribute	
CX = Number of characters in string	
DH = Row	
DL = Column	
ES:BP = Pointer to beginning of string	

Description: This service writes the character string beginning with ES:BP and starting at the screen location given in DH and DL with the attribute given in BL. At the end of the service, the cursor is at its original position.

Figure 5-58: ROM BIOS Video Service 13H
Subservice 01H

Service 19 (13H)   Write Character String
Subservice 01H   (for systems using EGA/VGA

INPUT TO BIOS	OUTPUT FROM BIOS
AH = 13H	No data returned.
AL = 01H	
BH = Page Number	
BL = Attribute	
CX = Number of characters in string	
DH = Row	
DL = Column	
ES:BP = Pointer to begin- ning of string	

(continued on next page)

Description: This service writes the character string which begins at ES:BP starting at the screen location given in DH and DL with the attribute given in BL. At the end of the service, the cursor is positioned at the end of the string.

Figure 5-59: ROM BIOS Video Service 13H Subservice 02H

Service 19 (13H)   Write Character String
Subservice 02H   (for systems using EGA/VGA only)

INPUT TO BIOS	OUTPUT FROM BIOS
AH = 13H	No data returned.
AL = 02H	
BH = Page Number	
CX = Number of characters and attributes in string	
DH = Row	
DL = Column	
ES:BP = Pointer to beginning of string	

Description: This service writes the character string which begins at ES:BP starting at the screen location given in DH and DL. The string consists of alternate characters and attributes. Each character is written to the screen with the attribute following it in the string. At the end of the service, the cursor is positioned at the beginning of the string.

Figure 5-60: ROM BIOS Video Service 13H
Subservice 03H

Service 19 (13H)   Write Character String
Subservice 03H   (for systems using EGA/VGA only)

INPUT TO BIOS	OUTPUT FROM BIOS
AH = 13H	No data returned.
AL = 02H	
BH = Page Number	
CX = Number of characters and attributes in string	
DH = Row	
DL = Column	
ES:BP = Pointer to beginning of string	

Description: This service writes the character string beginning with ES:BP, and starting at the screen location given in DH and DL. The string consists of alternate characters and attributes. Each character is written to the screen with the attribute following it in the string. At the end of the service, the cursor is positioned at the end of the string.

Read/Write Display Combination Code
(ROM BIOS Video Service 1AH

This service reads or writes the Display Combination Code in low memory. This service is automatically performed by the system and requires no programmer intervention. The service is described in Figure 5-61.

Figure 5-61: ROM BIOS Video Service 1AH

Service 26 (1AH)   Read/Write Display Combination
                          Code (for systems using EGA/VGA only)

INPUT TO BIOS	OUTPUT FROM BIOS
AH = 1AH	AL = 1AH for valid call
AL = 00H :Read DCC	BH = Alternate display
= 01H :Write DCC	code when reading
BH = Alternate Display	DCC
code when writing DCC	BL = Active Display code
BL = Active Display code	when reading DCC
when writing DCC	

Description: This service is a system function not ordinarily used by the programmer.

Return Functionality/State Information (ROM BIOS Video Service 1BH

This service reads the functionality/state table from the VGA into a designated buffer. It can determine if a VGA card is present in the system. This service is described in Figure 5-62.

Figure 5-62: ROM BIOS Video Service 1BH

Service 27 (1BH)   Return Functionality/State Data
                          (for systems using EGA/VGA only)

INPUT TO BIOS	OUTPUT FROM BIOS
AH = 1BH	AL = 1BH for valid call
ES:BP = Pointer to target	Data in table pointed to
buffer	by ES:BP

Description: This service reads the functionality/state table to a designated buffer.

Save/Restore Video State
(ROM BIOS Video Service 1CH)

This service saves or restores video data to a designated buffer. The service is described in Figure 5-63.

Figure 5-63: ROM BIOS Video Service 1CH

Service 28 (1CH)   Save/Restore Video State
                      (for systems using EGA/VGA only)

INPUT TO BIOS	OUTPUT FROM BIOS
AH = 1CH	AL = 1CH for valid call.
AL = 00H: Return size of save/restore buffer	BX = Save/restore buffer size block count for AL = 0
= 01H: Save video state	
= 02H: Restore video state	
CX = 01H: Video hardware state	
= 02H: Video data areas	
= 04H: Video DAC state and color registers	
ES:BP = Pointer to save/ restore buffer	

Description: This service saves and restores the video state.

107

6

Using the ROM BIOS
Video Services with C

For functions that are needed occasionally to produce graphics effects, speed is not a problem, and the ROM BIOS services are ideal. To conveniently use these services with C, we need a set of functions that can be called from C and their descriptions. These functions are described in the following paragraphs.

Determining the Video Mode

Many of the ROM BIOS video services described below are independent of the type of video adapter and of the video operation mode. There are some routines that will need to know just which video mode is being used. For example, to run any graphic routines you must be in a graphics mode; attempting to run them in text modes is useless. It is also important to know the number of pixel columns and pixel raster lines on the screen when drawing lines or other geometric figures. Either or both of these can be smaller for lower resolution display modes than for high resolution modes. If you design a program to fill the screen with a high resolution display, the upper parts of it will be beyond the limits of a low resolution display and only part of your graphics will appear. On the other hand, if your program is designed to display a full screen on a low resolution display, it may only fill the upper left quadrant of a high resolution display. Thus, it is important to know which mode you are operating in and also to be able to set the system to a different mode. We will discuss the former problem first.

All of the IBM-supported display modes were shown in Figure 5-1. The two modes used by the Hercules Graphics Card appear in Figure 6-1. It is important to note that the EGA and the VGA emulate a number of the modes that are used by the CGA and the Monochrome Adapter. The VGA emulates all of the EGA modes. Both of these advanced adapters can supply improved resolution in some of their emulation modes. Where programming is concerned, however, the improvements are totally transparent.

Figure 6-1: Hercules Graphics Adapter Video Modes.

Mode	Type	Colors	Pages	Alpha Format	Reso- lution	Char Cell	Mem Size	Buffer Start
--	Text	b/w	2	80x25	720x348	9x14	64K	B0000
--	Graphic	b/w	2	80x25	720x348	9x14	64K	B0000
None of the ROM BIOS video services will work with the Hercules Graphics Adapter.								

Programs that are designed to run with the CGA or the MA will run in identical fashion using the EGA or the VGA. Note that if a standard RGB color monitor is connected to the EGA or VGA, all of the CGA graphics modes will be run in exactly the same manner and with the same resolution as if a CGA card was installed. (It is hard to imagine, though, why you would want to use an EGA or VGA card with a standard monitor.) When the system is booted up, it must start with some default video mode. This mode differs depending upon which video adapter card is being used. Figure 6-5 shows the default modes for various adapter cards.

Figure 6-2: Default Modes of Video Adapters

VGA	EGA	CGA	MDA	Compaq	Hercules
3	3	3	7	2	7

Figure 6-3 is the C function for reading the current video mode of the system. The video mode is returned by the function. The parameter passed by the function (*ncols) returns the number of character columns in the display.

Figure 6-3: Function to Return Display Mode

getMode() = Returns Current Video Mode

```
int getMode(int *ncols)
{
        reg.h.ah = 0x0F;
        int86 (0x10,&reg,&reg);
        *ncols = reg.h.ah;
        return reg.h.al;
}
```

Identifying the Video Adapter

There is no single location where information is stored that can identify which video adapter or adapters are present in a particular system. Hence a function that returns the identity of the video adapter must do some detective work by examining several sources and drawing conclusions from a combination of results. The very first thing to do is to check for the presence of the Video Graphics Array. ROM BIOS video service 1BH reads a lot of information about the VGA into a designated buffer. For our purposes here, we are only interested in the fact that if the VGA is present, this service returns a 1BH in register AL. If the VGA is absent, the service does nothing, and AL is empty.

Many PC operations are controlled by data in memory locations 0400H to 05FFH. The area from 0400H to 04FFH is called the BIOS data area by IBM; the area from 0500H to 05FFH is referred to as the user read/write memory. This data is loaded by the BIOS during start-up, either from information in the BIOS itself or by reading switches and data lines that tell something about the hardware set up. The first place to look is at memory location 0487H. This byte contains information about an EGA board if one is present. Figure 6-4 shows the meaning of the bits in this data location. In examining this memory location, we want to determine if an EGA board is present. Most of the information given in the byte is not important to us. It is sufficient to know that if there is an EGA board present, this byte will be non-zero, whereas if there is no EGA board, the byte will be zero. Thus, if we examine this byte and find it non-zero, we do not need to proceed further; we can report that the video adapter is an EGA.

Figure 6-4: EGA Data (Memory Location 0487H)

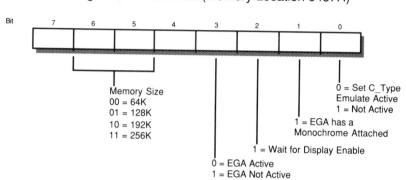

The two equipment bytes are located at 0410H and 0411H. These bytes give the status of various options available on the PC system. Figure 6-5 shows the equipment list information.

Figure 6-5: Equipment List (Memory Locations 0410H and 0411H)

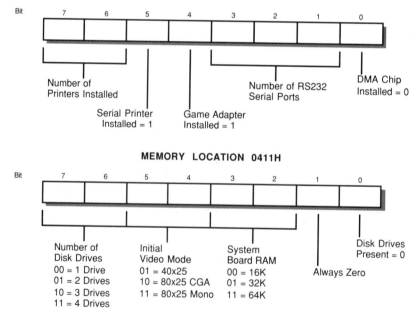

The initial video mode bits 4 and 5 at 0411HAll are the most useful in determining the type of video adapter present although they don't help much. A value of 11 indicates an MDA or a Hercules adapter; a 00 could be an EGA, a CGA or a Compaq. Combining this information with the initial mode operation in Figure 6-2, however, enables us to identify most common adapters but cannot enable us to distinguish between the Hercules and monochrome adapters. We can nonetheless distinguish the Hercules adapter, since it keeps the vertical retrace status bit (bit 7 of the Hercules status port) at one during normal scanning of the raster and only resets it to zero during vertical retrace. The MA board always keeps this bit low. Hence if we examine this bit enough times to be sure that the vertical retrace period has been completed and at any time see a value of one, then the Hercules Graphics Adapter is present.

Figure 6-6 is the listing of a function to determine which graphics adapter is present. This function returns a *C* for the Color Graphics Adapter, an *E* for the Enhanced Graphics Adapter, an *M* for the Monochrome Display Adapter, a *Q* for the Compaq Graphics Adapter, a *V* for the Video Graphics Array, and an *O* for other adapters not identified by the function.

Figure 6-6: Function to Return Adapter Type Information

```
         getAdapter()  =  Returns  Adapter  Type
```

```
char getAdapter()
{
    union REGS reg;
    struct SREGS inreg;
    int EGA, adapter, mode, herc, i, n;
    char type, buffer[64];
    char far *address;
    segread(&inreg);
    inreg.es = inreg.ds;
    reg.x.di = buffer;
    reg.x.ax = 0x1B00;
    int86x(0x10,&reg,&reg,*inreg);
    if (reg.h.al == 0x1B);
        type = 'V';
    else
    {
        int86(0x11,&reg,&reg);
        adapter = (reg.h.al & 0x30) >> 4;
        mode = getMode(&n);
```

```
    address = (char far *)0x00000487;
    EGA = *address;
    type = 'O';
    if (EGA)
        type = 'E';
    else
    {
        if(adapter == 3)
        {
            for (i=0; i<=0x1000; i++)
            {
                if (inp  (0x3BA) & 0x80)
                {
                    type = 'H';
                    break;
                }
            }
            if (type == 'O')
                type = 'M';
        }
        else
        {
            if ((adapter == 2) || (adapter == 0))
            {
                if (mode == 2)
                    type = 'Q';
                else
                    type = 'C';
            }
        }
    }
    return (type);
}
```

This function for determining which adapter is present depends upon examining the default video mode to which the system is set when it is initialized. Therefore, the function must be run before the setMode function is used to change the video mode. If you plan to make use of adapter information at any time during your program, run this function first and save the result. If you use setMode first, the chances are high that the getAdapter function will always report that the adapter is *O*.

Setting the Video Mode

If you want to use anything other than the default mode, you must set the system to the new video mode. Since all default modes are text modes, the mode must be set before using graphics. Figure 6-7 lists a function for setting the video mode, which does not work with the Hercules Graphics Adapter. Functions for use with this card will be described in Chapter 7.

Figure 6-7: Function to Set Video Mode

```
            setMode() = Sets Video Mode
```

```
void setMode(int mode)
{
        reg.h.ah = 0;
        reg.h.al = mode;
        int86 (0x10,&reg,&reg);
}
```

Positioning the Cursor

While the cursor does not appear on the graphics display, the cursor position is recorded, and it is at the current cursor position that textual data is written to the display. Consequently, the capability to specify a cursor position is important. The function that will position the cursor is given in Figure 6-8. Normally this is called before a function that writes textual data to the screen.

Figure 6-8: Function to Set Cursor Position

```
  gotoxy() = Moves Cursor to Specified x,y Position
             and Page
```

```
void gotoxy(int column, int row, int page)
{
    reg.h.ah = 2;
    reg.h.bh = page;
    reg.h.dh = row;
    reg.h.dl = column;
```

```
    int86 (0x10,&reg,&reg);
}
```

Reading the Cursor Position

It is sometimes important to know where the cursor is and to take action depending upon that position. In text modes, you can usually see the cursor; in graphics modes it does not appear on the display, so a routine to read the cursor position is essential. Such a function is given in Figure 6-9.

Figure 6-9: Function to Return the Current Cursor Position

```
        getxy() = Gets the Current Cursor Position
```

```
void getxy(int *column, int *row, int page)
{
    reg.h.ah = 3;
    reg.h.bh = page;
    int86 (0x10,&reg,&reg);
    *row = reg.h.dl;
    *column = reg.h.dh;
}
```

Setting the Active Page

All of the text modes and some of the graphics modes are capable of storing more than one page of display data. It is then possible to switch rapidly from one page to another. This is not only useful in transitioning from one set of data to another, but also it can provide a limited animation capability by rapidly switching back and forth between two slightly different picture screens. Figure 6-10 gives the function to switch from one active page to another.

Figure 6-10: Function to Set Active Page

```
        setPage() = Sets the Active Display Page
```

```
void setPage(int page)
{
    reg.h.ah = 5;
```

```
    reg.h.al = page;
    int86 (0x10,&reg,&reg);
}
```

Determining the Active Page

It is sometimes necessary to determine exactly what page is currently being displayed. When the need arises, this function does the job.

Figure 6-11: Function to Return the Active Page Number

```
           getPage() = Returns Active Page Number
```

```
int getPage(void)
{
    reg.h.ah =0x0F;
    int86(0x10,&reg,&reg);
    return (reg.h.bh);
}
```

Clearing the Screen

There are a number of ways to clear the screen of all data to prepare for a fresh beginning. The technique used here is fast and efficient. It makes use of the window capabilities built into the ROM BIOS. The function creates a window that is the size of the full screen and then scrolls the window up zero lines.

Setting the number of lines to zero causes the window scrolling function to fill the entire window with blank lines. Some care is required in specifying the color parameter that is passed to this function. Figure 6-12 shows the standard character attribute byte as it is defined for text and graphic modes.

Figure 6-12: Display Character Attribute Byte

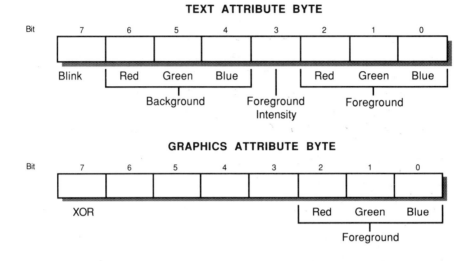

In the text modes, passing a parameter having this format results in the screen being blanked to the specified background color. The foreground color is also preserved. Now, any text display function (such as *printf*) will display characters having the foreground color on a background of the background color. For the VGA and EGA in the graphics modes, the screen will be blanked to the foreground color given by this attribute. The CGA graphic modes are different. Each two bits of the attribute set the color for one of four columns on the display. This pattern repeats across the screen. Therefore, if you want to clear the screen to a solid color background rather than vertical stripes, you must repeat the color four times in the attribute byte. This function does this for color graphics modes.

Figure 6-13: Function to Clear Screen

cls() = Clears the Screen

```
void cls(char colors)
{
    char ch;
    int columns,mode;
    mode = getMode(&columns);
    if (columns == 80);
    {
```

```
    if ((mode == 0x11) || (mode == 0x12))
        reg.x.dx = 0x1D4F;
    else
        reg.x.dx = 0x184F;
    reg.h.bh = colors;
}
else
{
    reg.x.dx = 0x1828;
    switch (colors)
    {
        case 1:     reg.h.bh = 0x55;
                    break;
        case 2:     reg.h.bh = 0xAA;
                    break;
        case 3:     reg.h.bh = 0xFF;
                    break;
        default:    reg.h.bh = 0;
    }
}
reg.x.ax = 0x0600;
reg.x.cx = 0;
int86(0x10,&reg,&reg);
gotoxy(0,0,getPage());
}
```

Creating an Empty Window

The ROM BIOS video services include the capability to create windows. A window can be the full size of the screen or any specified part of it. Once a window is established, you can write data into it and use it just like a full display screen. Using the function shown in Figure 6-14 will make a window pop up on your screen for uses such as menu selection. There is no simple function, however, for making the window disappear and for restoring the original display. To restore the original display, you have to save the screen contents somewhere in memory and read them back to the screen after you are finished with the window.

Figure 6-14: Function to Create an Empty Window

```
          setWindow() = Creates an Empty Window

void setWindow(int x1,int y1,int x2,int y2,int color)
{
    reg.h.ah = 6;
    reg.h.al = 0;
    reg.h.bh = color;
    reg.h.cl = x1;
    reg.h.ch = y1;
    reg.h.dl = x2;
    reg.h.dh = y2;
    int86 (0x10,&reg,&reg);
}
```

Scrolling the Window

Two companion functions, shown in figures 6-15 and 6-16, allow you to scroll up or down one line in the window that you have created. Figure 6-15 gives the function to scroll the window up one line.

Figure 6-15: Function to Scroll Window Up One Line

```
 scrollWindowUp() = Scrolls Window One Line Upward

void scrollWindowUp (int x1, int y1, int x2, int y2,
                     int color)
{
    reg.h.ah = 6;
    reg.h.al = 1;
    reg.h.bh = color;
    reg.h.cl = x1;
    reg.h.ch = y1;
    reg.h.dl = x2;
    reg.h.dh = y2;
    int86 (0x10,&reg,&reg);
}
```

Figure 6-16: Function to Scroll Window Down One Line

```
    scrollWindowDn = Scrolls Window One Line Down
```

```
void scrollWindowDn (int x1, int y1, int x2, int y2,
                     int color)
{
    reg.h.ah = 7;
    reg.h.al = 1;
    reg.h.bh = color;
    reg.h.cl = x1;
    reg.h.ch = y1;
    reg.h.dl = x2;
    reg.h.dh = y2;
    int86 (0x10,&reg,&reg);
}
```

Reading a Character from the Screen

When reading a character from the screen, if the character matches the pattern of any character that may be written to the screen from the character set, then the ASCII value of the character is returned. If there is no match, 00 is returned. This function works for all graphics modes. In text modes, there is always a match since you can only write to the screen from the character set. Furthermore, it is also possible in text modes to use the ROM BIOS function to obtain the character attribute. Attribute identification can then be a viable possibility; in the graphics mode it is meaningless.

Figure 6-17: Function to Read a Character from the Screen

```
    readChar = Reads a Character from the Screen
```

```
int readChar(int page, char *attr)
{
reg.h.ah = 8;
reg.h.bh = page;
int86 (0x10,&reg,&reg);
return (reg.h.al);
*attr = reg.h.ah;
}
```

Writing a Character to the Screen

The function listed in Figure 6-18 is the principal tool used in writing text to the screen. Parameters passed by this function are the character to be written, the attribute of the character, and the page to which the character will be written. The characteristics of the attribute byte are given in Figure 6-11. Note that only the foreground color of the character may be specified; the character will be written with the current background color and at the current cursor location. The function, however, will not advance the cursor. This is the programmer's responsibility before writing another character.

Figure 6-18: Function to Write a Character to the Screen

```
writChar = Writes a Character to the Screen
          with Specified Attribute
```

```
void writChar(char ch, int color, int page)
{
    reg.h.ah = 9;
    reg.h.al = ch;
    reg.h.bl = color;
    reg.h.bh = page;
    reg.x.cx = 1;
    int86 (0x10,&reg,&reg);
}
```

Writing a String to the Screen

When writing a string of text to the screen, the address of the first character of the string is passed to the function. The function writes the first character at the current cursor location with the specified attribute and on the specified display page. The function then advances the cursor, writes the next character, and so on until 00 is encountered, marking the end of the string. If the cursor advances beyond the end of a line, it is repositioned at the beginning of the next line.

Figure 6-19: Function to Write a String to the Screen

```
      writString = Writes a String to the Screen
                 with Specified Attribute
```

```
void writString(char *str, int color, int page)
{
    int col, row, width, i = 0;
    getMode (&width);
    getxy(&col,&row,page);
    while (str[i])
    {
        if (col > width - 1)
        {
            col = 0;
            row++;
        }
        writChar(str[i++], color, page);
        gotoxy(++col, row, page);
    }
}
```

Setting the CGA Palette

When the system is in the CGA color mode 4, either of two palettes, each having four colors, may be used to display data. These palette colors are shown in Figure 6-20. The function listed in Figure 6-21 sets the palette to one of these two selections.

Figure 6-20: CGA Palette Colors

Color Number	Palette 0 Color	Palette 1 Color
0	Current background color	Current background color
1	Green (2)	Cyan (3)
2	Red (4)	Magenta (5)
3	Brown (6)	White (7)

Figure 6-21: Function to Set CGA Palette

```
┌─────────────────────────────────────────────────────────┐
│      setCGAPalette = Sets Palette for CGA Modes           │
└─────────────────────────────────────────────────────────┘

void setCGAPalette(int paletteNo)
{
    reg.h.ah = 0x0B;
    reg.h.bl = paletteNo;
    reg.h.bh = 1;
    int86 (0x10,&reg,&reg);
}
```

Setting the EGA/VGA Palette

Figure 6-22 is a function to set the EGA/VGA Palette. In the 16 color modes, the EGA displays 16 colors that are by default those colors given in Figure 16-4. However, any of 64 colors may be assigned to each of the 16 color numbers by this command. The color is a number from 0 to 63 passed to *color* and the number from one to 16 passed to *palette* determines the assignment of that color.

Figure 6-22: Function to Set EGA Palette

```
┌─────────────────────────────────────────────────────────┐
│      setEGAPalette = Sets Palette for EGA Modes           │
└─────────────────────────────────────────────────────────┘

void setEGApalette(int palette, int color)
{
    reg.h.ah = 0x10;
    reg.h.al = 0x00;
    reg.h.bl = palette;
    reg.h.bh = color;
    int86 (0x10,&reg,&reg);
}
```

Setting the Background Color

The same ROM BIOS video service that sets the palette can be used with different parameters to set the background color when in the CGA modes. Unfortunately, this service does not perform properly in the EGA color mode; it sometimes deceivingly appears to work for EGA. It correctly sets the background color, but it also changes the mapping of some of the foreground colors. You may think that you've set the background correctly until you try to display a foreground color and see that it is different from what you expected. The function listed in Figure 6-23 first checks to determine the current mode. If a CGA mode is encountered, it uses the CGA Set Palette service to set the background color. If an EGA mode is encountered, the function uses ROM BIOS video service 10H to set the background color. This new BIOS service is only available if the EGA card is installed.

Figure 6-23: Function to Set Background Color

```
    setBackground = Sets Background Color

void setBackground(int color)
{
    int mode,n;
    mode = getMode(&n);
    if (mode >= 10)
    {
        reg.h.ah = 0x10;
        reg.h.al = 0;
        reg.h.bl = 0;
        reg.h.bh = color;
        int86 (0x10,&reg,&reg);
    }
    else
    {
        reg.h.ah = 0x0B;
        reg.h.bl = color;
        reg.h.bh = 0;
        int86 (0x10,&reg,&reg);
    }
}
```

Setting the Color Paging Mode

This function permits selecting a color paging mode for the VGA only. The first mode has four pages, each consisting of 64 color registers, and the second mode has 16 pages, each consisting of 16 color registers. This function works for all EGA and VGA modes except mode 13H. Note that after a setMode function call, the DAC color registers are initialized so that the first 64 register colors correspond to the EGA colors, and all resets are set to zero. The function is listed in Figure 6-24.

Figure 6-24: Function to Set Color Paging Mode

```
    setColorPageMode = Sets Color Paging Mode

void setColorPageMode(int mode)
{
    reg.x.ax = 0x1013;
    reg.h.bl = 0;
    reg.h.bh = mode;
    int86(0x10,&reg,&reg);
}
```

Setting the Color Page

This function sets the color page for the selected set of DAC color registers. The maximum value of the color page is either 3 or 15, depending upon the color paging mode set by the previous function. Note the initial color register setting data given for the previous function and note also that this function does not work for mode 013H.

Figure 6-25: Function to Set Color Page

```
    setColorPage = Sets Page of Color Registers

void setColorPage(int page_no)
{
    reg.x.ax = 0x1013;
    reg.h.bl = 1;
    reg.h.bh = page_no;
    int86(0x10,&reg,&reg);
}
```

Reading an Individual Color Register

This function reads an individual specified DAC color register and returns the red, green, and blue values.

Figure 6-26: Function Read Individual Color Register

```
readColorReg = Reads Individual Color Register Setting
```

```
void readColorReg(int color_reg,int *red, int *green,
    int *blue)
{
    reg.x.ax = 0x1015;
    reg.x.bx = color_reg;
    int86(0x10,&reg,&reg);
    *green = reg.h.ch;
    *blue =reg.h.cl;
    *red = reg.h.dh;
    int86(0x10,&reg,&reg);
}
```

Writing an Individual Color Register Value

This function writes six-bit red, green, and blue color values into a specified DAC color register.

Figure 6-27: Function to Write Individual Color Register Data

```
writeColorReg = Writes Color Data to Individual Color
                Register
```

```
    void writeColorReg(int color_reg,int red, int green,
        int blue)
    {
        reg.x.ax = 0x1010;
        reg.x.bx = color_reg;
        reg.h.ch = green;
        reg.h.cl = blue;
        reg.h.dh = red;
        int86(0x10,&reg,&reg);
    }
```

Writing a Pixel to the Screen

Almost all graphics operations require writing figures to the screen one pixel at a time. This ROM BIOS video service performs that function and will work with any of the IBM supported video adapter cards and graphics modes. It is very slow, however.

The necessity to activate an interrupt, to save all registers, to perform the operations, to restore registers again, and to return to the original program uses a lot of overhead, regardless of the efficiency of the code that actually writes the pixel to the screen. Consequently, this method of writing a pixel is seldom used. Nevertheless, the function is shown for reference in Figure 6-28. More direct and faster techniques for writing a pixel to the screen will be described in Chapter 8.

Figure 6-28: Plot Function using ROM BIOS Video Services

```
plot() = Plots a point at (x,y) with color
         using ROM BIOS Video Services
```

```c
void plot(int x, int y, int color) n
{
    reg.h.ah = 0x0C;
    reg.h.al = color;       /* pixel color value */
    reg.h.bh = 0;
    reg.x.cx = x;
    reg.x.dx = y;
    int86 (0x010, &reg,&reg);
}
```

Reading a Pixel from the Screen

There are many situations where it is necessary to determine the color of a pixel at a particular screen location. The function listed in Figure 6-29 goes to a specified pixel raster row and pixel column location and returns the attribute of the pixel found there. The attribute byte returned is that for graphic modes in which the three least significant bits specify the pixel color.

Figure 6-29: Function to Read Pixel from the Screen

readPixel = Read a Pixel from the Screen

```
int readPixel(int x, int y)
{
    reg.h.ah = 0x0D;
    reg.x.cx = x;
    reg.x.dx = y;
    int86 (0x10,&reg,&reg);
    return (reg.h.al);
}
```

7

Graphics Functions for the Hercules Graphics Card

The Hercules Graphics Card is not supported by the ROM BIOS video services. A similar set of functions to those developed in Chapter 6 is needed for the Hercules Graphics Card, but we have to develop these functions through direct accessing of the the registers and display memory on the Hercules card. To make the graphics functions in this book as compatible as possible with different adapter cards, this chapter will develop a set of functions for the Hercules card that have the same names as those that were developed for the other graphics adapters using the ROM BIOS video services. These functions will be placed in one library, and the ROM BIOS video service derived functions will be placed in another. Then, for most programs, referencing the proper library in the project file will permit the program to run either on a Hercules Graphics Adapter or the EGA/CGA. These functions, however, offer somewhat less capability than the ROM BIOS video functions of Chapter 6 since some of the ROM BIOS services cannot easily be duplicated for the Hercules card, and the Hercules card itself only supports a monochrome monitor, so no color functions are available.

Identifying the Video Adapter

The function described in Chapter 6 that works for any adapter card, including the Hercules, is repeated here in Figure 7-1. Therefore, this chapter will be essentially self-contained with complete Hercules functions.

Figure 7-1: Function to Identify Video Adapter

```
                   getAdapter() = Returns Adapter Type
```

```
char getAdapter()
{
    union REGS reg;
    struct SREGS inreg;
    int EGA, adapter, mode, herc, i, n;
    char type, buffer[64];
    char far *address;
    segread(&inreg);
    inreg.es = inreg.ds;
    reg.x.di = buffer;
    reg.x.ax = 0x1B00;
    int86x(0x10,&reg,&reg,*inreg);
    if (reg.h.al == 0x1B);
        type = 'V';
    else
    {
        int86(0x11,&reg,&reg);
        adapter = (reg.h.al & 0x30) >> 4;
        mode = getMode(&n);
        address = (char far *)0x00000487;
        EGA = *address;
        type = 'O';
        if (EGA)
type = 'E';
        else
        {
if(adapter == 3)
{
    for (i=0; i<=0x1000; i++)
    {
        if (inp  (0x3BA) & 0x80)
        {
    type = 'H';
    break;
        }
    }
    if (type == 'O')
        type = 'M';
```

```
        }
    else
    {
        if ((adapter == 2) || (adapter == 0))
        {
            if (mode == 2)
    type = 'Q';
            else
    type = 'C';
        }
    }
            }
        }
        return (type);
    }
```

Determining the Video Mode

The Hercules Graphics Adapter has two modes of operation: text and graphics. These are shown in Figure 7-2. They do not correspond to any of the IBM designated modes, so the ROM BIOS video service routine for getting the mode does not recognize them or assign them a number. When the ROM BIOS video services select a video mode, they enter the mode number into memory address 449H. For the internal Hercules *setMode* and *getMode* functions, we have used *0* for the text mode and *1* for the graphics mode. Figure 7-3 lists a function for getting the mode when a Hercules card is present. It will return the mode number as it exists in memory address 449H.

Figure 7-2: Hercules Graphics Adapter Video Modes

Mode	Type	Colors	Pages	Alpha Format	Reso-lution	Char Cell	Mem Size	Buffer Start
01H	Text	b/w	2	80x25	720x348	9x14	64K	B0000
02H	Graphic	b/w	2	80x25	720x348	9x14	64K	B0000s
None of the ROM BIOS video services will work with the Hercules Graphics Adapter.								

Figure 7-3: Function for Getting Mode of the Hercules Card

```
        getMode() = Returns Current  Video Mode

int getMode (int *ncols)
{
    char mode;
    char far *address;

    address = (char far *)0x00000449;
    mode = *address;
    *ncols = 80;
    return mode;
}
```

Setting the Video Mode

This function switches the mode of the Hercules board between the text and graphics modes. In addition to sending the proper data to the 6845 CRT Controller to switch modes, it inserts a mode number (00H for text or 01H for graphics in memory location 449H). Figure 7-4 lists the function.

Figure 7-4: Function to Set Video Mode

```
        setMode() = Sets Video Mode

void setMode(int mode)
{
    char i,graph_reg_data[12] = {0x35,0x2D,0x2E,
        0x07,0x5B,0x02,0x57,0x57,0x02,0x03,0x00,
        0x00},text_reg_data[12] = {0x61,0x50,0x52,
        0x0F,0x19,0x06,0x19,0x19,0x02,0x0D,0x0B,
        0x0C};
    char far * address

    if (mode == 0x00);
    {
        outp (0x3BF,0);
        outp (0x3B8,0);
        for (i=0; i<12; i++)
        {
```

```
        outp (0x3B4,i);
        outp (0x3B5,text_data[i]);
    }
    for (i=0;  i<=0x7FFF;  i+=2)
    {
        address = (char far *)0xB0000000L + i;
        *address = 0x00;
        *address = 0x07;
    }
    outp (0x3B8,0x28);
}
else
{
    outp (0x3BF,3);
    outp (0x3B8,2);
    for (i=0;  i<12;  i++)
    {
        outp (0x3B4,i);
        outp (0x3B5,graph_reg_data[i]);
    }
    for (i=0;  i<=0x7FFF;  i++)
    {
        address = (char far *)0xB0000000L + i;
        *address = 0x00;
        address = (char far *)0xB8000000L + 2*i;
        *address = 0x00;
    }
    outp (0x3B8,0x0A);
}
address = (char far *)0x00000449L;
*address = mode;
}
```

Positioning the Cursor

While the cursor does not appear on the graphics display, the cursor position is recorded. Textual data is written to the display at the current cursor position, which is the reason why the capability to specify a cursor position is important. The function that will position the cursor is given in Figure 7-5. To make this function compatible with the same function using the ROM BIOS services, the parameter *page* is passed to the function. However, the function ignores this parameter and sets the cursor position for the currently active page. Normally, this function is called just before a function that writes textual data to the screen.

Figure 7-5: Function to Set Cursor Position

```
gotoxy() = Moves Cursor to Specified x,y Position
                     and Page

void gotoxy(int column, int row, int page)
{
    reg.x.ax = 80*row + column
    outp (0x3B4,14);
    outp (0x3B5,reg.h.ah);
    outp (0x3B4,15);
    outp (0x3B5,reg.h.al);
}
```

Reading the Cursor Position

It is sometimes important to know where the cursor is in order to take appropriate action. In text modes, you can usually see the cursor. In graphics modes, it does not appear on the display, so a routine to read the cursor position is essential. Such a function is given in Figure 7-6. Although the parameter *page* is passed to the function, the function ignores the parameter and gets the cursor position of the currently displayed page.

Figure 7-6: Function to Get Cursor Position

```
getxy() = Gets the Current Cursor Position

void getxy(int *column, int *row, int page)
{
    outp (0x3B4,14);
    inp (0x3B5,reg.h.ah);
    outp (0x3B4,15);
    inp (0x3B5,reg.h.al);
    *row = reg.x.ax/80;
    column = reg.x.ax % 80;
}
```

Setting the Active Page

The Hercules Graphics Card has two pages of video data that are either in the text or graphics mode. In the graphics mode, one page begins at address B00000H and the other at B8000H. Figure 7-7 lists the function to switch from one active page to another.

Figure 7-7: Function to Set Active Page

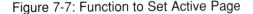

```
        setPage() = Sets the Active Display Page

  void setPage(int page)
  {
      if (page == 1)
          outp (0x3B8, 0x8A);
      else
          outp (0x3B*,0x0A);
  }
```

Determining the Active Page

The function given in Figure 7-8 returns the active page number.

Figure 7-8: Function to Determine Active Page

```
        getPage() = Returns Active Page Number

  int getPage(void)
  {
      char ch;

      inp(0x3B8,ch);
      if (ch == 0x8A);
          return 1;
      else
          return 0;
  }
```

It is sometimes necessary to determine exactly what page is active. When that is necessary, this function does the job.

Clearing the Screen

Clearing the screen with the Hercules Graphics Card simply requires setting all of the memory on the active page to zero. It is best to turn off the screen while doing this and then turn it back on. Figure 7-9 lists the function for clearing the Hercules screen. This funcjtion permits clearing to black or white.

Figure 7-9: Function for Clearing the Hercules Screen

```
                    cls() = Clears the Screen
```

```c
void cls(char colors)
{
    char ch;
    char far *address;
    unsigned char ch;
    unsigned int i;
    if (color == 1)
        colors = 0xFF;
    outp(0x3B8,2);
    ch = inp(0x3B8);
    if (ch == 0x8A)
    {
        for (i=0; i<0x7FFF; i++)
        {
            address = (char far *) 0xB8000000L + i;
            *address = colors;
            outp(0x3B8,0x8A);
        }
    }
    else
    {
        for (i=0; i<0x7FFF; i++)
        {
            address = (char far *) 0xB0000000L + i;
            *address = 0;
        }
        outp(0X3B8,0x0A);
    }
}
```

Creating an Empty Window

The ROM BIOS video services include the capability to create windows. A window can be the full size of the screen or any specified part of it. Once a window is established, you can write data into it and use it exactly like a full display screen. It would be easy enough to devise a similar function for the Hercules Graphics Card that could create a window in the sense that a particular specified area of the screen can be blanked. However, it is impossible for this procedure to be easily tied to the text and pixel writing routines. Input data is limited to the bounds of the window and wraps around to the next line when the right window boundary is reached. This requires interactions between several routines that we would rather avoid. Therefore, this function will not be duplicated in the Hercules set of functions. If you are trying to write programs that will work equally well in either IBM or Hercules modes, you need to avoid the series of window functions.

Scrolling the Window

Assuming that a method existed that limited character writing to within a Hercules window in a manner similar to that used by the IBM ROM BIOS window functions for IBM supported video adapters, it would not be too difficult to scroll the data within a window. A series of memory moves should accomplish this with a minimum of effort. But since the decision was made not to implement the basic window function, there is no need to include the scrolling functions. They should be avoided if you plan for your program to be compatible with both IBM and Hercules video modes.

Reading a Character from the Screen

This is another function that needs to be avoided if you plan on using the Hercules Card. The ROM BIOS video services provide a pattern-matching routine that determines whether one of the standard character set patterns appears on the graphics displays at a designated character position. Since we have to generate our own routines for writing characters to the Hercules card in the graphics mode, we intend to avoid the constraint that characters appear only in the standardized character positions. This would make the character matching task much too complex to be worth pursuing.

Writing a Character to the Screen

Writing characters to the Hercules Graphics screen is not simply a matter of transferring information from a set of characters built into ROM to a shift register. Consequently, we are deferring discussion of this topic until Chapter 16, which discusses techniques for writing graphics characters in much greater detail. Note that this statement does not apply to the Hercules card in its text mode when it appears to the computer exactly as if it were an IBM Monochrome Adapter.

Color Functions

Chapter 6 described a number of functions for setting up and modifying the color capabilities of the various color adapter cards. None of these functions apply to the Hercules card, which is strictly a monochrome adapter.

Writing a Pixel to the Screen

Chapter 8 provides detailed descriptions of techniques for writing a pixel to the screen, including a method specifically for the Hercules Graphics Card. Refer to that chapter for details of this function.

Reading a Pixel from the Screen

The method used to read a pixel from the screen is similar to that which is used to write a pixel. Figure 7-10 lists a function to perform this task. The method of addressing the correct point in display memory is described in detail in connection with the point plotting function in Chapter 8.

Figure 7-10: Function for Reading a Pixel from the Screen using the Hercules Graphics Card

```
readPixel() = Reads a pixel from the screen at
              point (x,y) for Hercules Graphics
              Card
```

```
int readPixel(int x, int y)
{
```

```
unsigned int offset;
int page,pixel;
char mask;
char far *address;

 page = getPage();
 offset = 0x2000 * (y%4) + 0x8000 * page +
     90 * (y/4) + x/8;
 mask = 0x80 >> (x%8);
 address = (char far *) 0xB0000000L + offset;
 pixel = *address & mask;
 if (pixel != 0) pixel = 1;
 return(pixel);
}
```

8

Displaying a Point
on the Screen

Chapter 6 introduced a ROM BIOS video service based technique for plotting a point on the display screen. This function is convenient, but slow. Point plotting is the most important of all graphics functions. It is central to the drawing of lines, rectangles, oval, and other figures. This whole chapter is devoted to it.

There are two ways to send data to the display screen in the graphics display mode. The first involves writing a text character to the screen at positions defined by the cursor row and column. (Writing text characters will be described in more detail later). The shape of EACH text character is stored in a font table. All other information to be displayed on the screen (circles, rectangles, lines or other shapes) must be written to the screen a pixel at a time. A point on the screen may be located at any position where a display pixel can occur. The number of pixel locations on the display varies with the display mode. For the high resolution EGA display, there are 640 pixel columns and 350 pixel rows, for a total of 224,000 discrete locations. One can see that many pixels must be written to the screen to draw even a small line. Fortunately, it is seldom necessary to fill in every one of the 224,000 pixels individually to create a graphics display. The pixel plotting routine will be called many times for any one display. Therefore, it is important to write each pixel as fast as possible to minimize the wait to complete a screen drawing. In designing graphics plotting routines, however, the programmer must often make compromises between speed and the flexibility obtained by using higher level techniques. The rest of this chapter will describe several point plotting routines, beginning with the most flexible (and slowest) using the ROM BIOS services, and proceeding to those that make use of direct insertion into memory or via control ports by means of output instructions or direct assembly language. The latter have to be tailored for the particular graphics adapter card that is used, but they offer the fastest speed.

Plotting a Point with the ROM BIOS Video Services

Figure 8-1 is a listing of the function to plot a single point (pixel) using the ROM BIOS video services. (You can compare this function with more improved functions that will be described later in the chapter.) This is a good place to start in considering point plotting functions, since this routine is compatible with any IBM video adapter that supports a graphics mode. However, this function cannot be used with the Hercules Graphics Card. It is also exceedingly slow, since it makes use of interrupts, which not only take time, but also involve saving all registers on the stack and restoring them after the function has been completed. The interrupt also has to begin by reading the proper address from a table and jumping to the correct interrupt servicing routine.

Figure 8-1: Plot Function using ROM BIOS Video Services

```
          plot() = Plots a point at (x,y) with color
                   using ROM BIOS Video Services

void plot(int x, int y, int color) n
{
    reg.h.ah = 0x0C;
    reg.h.al = color;       /* pixel color value */
    reg.h.bh = 0;
    reg.x.cx = x;
    reg.x.dx = y;
    int86 (ROM, &inreg,&outreg);
}
```

Plotting a Point with the Color Graphics Adapter

In our search for a more rapid means of plotting points, let's start with systems that use the IBM Color Graphics Adapter or its equivalent, including the EGA or VGA Adapter when it is emulating the CGA (set to mode 4, for example). In mode 4, the CGA has one page of graphics data located at address B8000H. Each pixel, beginning at the top left hand corner of the screen, is represented by two bits. These bits form a binary number that represents the pixel color from 0 to 3 as defined by the selected palette. For page 0, all of the even numbered raster lines have their data stored consecutively beginning at address B8000H. All of the odd numbered lines have their data stored consecutively beginning at address BA000H. There are 320 pixel columns, so at two bits per pixel and eight bits per byte, there are 80 bytes for each display line. Fortunately, with the CGA, it is possible to directly address the display memory and load it with data. The above information provides all of the clues to find the proper address for each pixel that we want to write to the CGA display memory. Figure 8-2 gives the resulting function. The offset from the starting address is a sum that begins with 2000H if the line is odd, or with zero if the line is even. We then add 80H bytes for each odd (or even) line and finally add one byte for each four pixel columns.

Figure 8-2: Plot Function for CGA Using Direct Memory Access

```
        plot() = Plots a point at (x,y) with color
for  CGA  mode  4,  sending  data  directly  to  dis-
play memory
```

```
void plot(int x, int y, int color)
{
    int offset, mask, page,temp;
    char far *address;

    offset = 0x2000 * (y%2) + 80 * (y/2)) + x/4;
    mask  =   0xC0 >> ((x%4)*2);
    address = 0xB8000000L + offset;
    temp = *address;
    *address = temp & ~mask;
    mask = (color & 0x03) << (6-(x%4) * 2);
    temp = *address;
    *address = temp | mask;
}
```

The mask selects the two bits that are to be modified. It is found by multiplying the result of the column number mod 4 by two and then using this result to determine how many places to the right to shift hex C0 (binary 11000000). We next AND the contents of the base address plus the offset (which includes the offsets for the x and y values plus that for the page number) with the inverse of the mask ANDed with the negative of the mask. The result puts zeroes in the two bits of interest and leaves the rest of the bits unchanged. Then a new mask is calculated which places the color number in the same selected two bits. This is ORed with the data obtained from the memory address, and the result is written back into that address in memory. This results in a pixel being displayed on the screen at the selected location and in the specified color. While in mode 4, draw some points with the *plot* function that uses the ROM BIOS video services, and then with this routine that directly addresses video memory. Note how much faster the latter is.

Plotting a Point
with the Hercules Graphics Adapter

The Hercules Graphics Adapter is similar to the CGA in that it is possible to directly address the display memory. Like the CGA, the memory is interleaved, but instead of the odd/even scheme used by the CGA, Hercules uses a factor-of-four interleaving scheme, with rows 0, 4, 8, etc. starting at memory location B0000H (for page 0) and running consecutively; rows 1,5,9, etc. starting at B2000H; rows 2,5,10, etc. starting at B4000H; and rows 3, 7, 11, etc. starting at B6000H. Hercules also has two video graphics pages. The resolution is 720 pixel columns by 348 pixel raster rows. Only a single bit is used to represent each pixel. Since the display is monochrome, if the pixel is one the bit is displayed; if it is zero, the bit is blank. Thus, 90 bytes are required per raster line.

Memory locations for the first few lines using the various graphics adapters are:

Line	CGA Beginning Address	Hercules Beginning Address	EGA/VGA Beginning Address
0	B8000	B0000	A0000
1	BA000	B2000	A0050
2	B8050	B4000	A00A0
3	BA050	B6000	A00F0
4	B80A0	B005A	A0140
5	BA050	B205A	A0190
6	B80F0	B405A	A0230
7	BAoF0	B605A	A0230
8	B8140	B00B4	A0280

Figure 8-3 is a listing of a function for plotting a point on the Hercules Graphics Adapter system. The method of determining the offset and mask is similar to that used with the CGA, except that the mask is now a single bit. The selected bit location does not have to be reset; it is simply turned on if the parameter *color* is 1 or off if *color* is zero. For the Hercules card there is no option; ROM BIOS video services will not write pixels to the card, so that the function of Figure 8-3 must be used.

Figure 8-3: Plot Function for Hercules Graphics Adapter

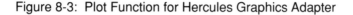

```
    plot() = Plots a point at (x,y) in black or white
for Hercules Graphics Adapter, sending data directly to
display memory
```

```
void plot(int x, int y, int color)
{
    unsigned int offset;
    int page,temp;
    char mask;
    char far *address;

    page = getPage();
    offset = 0x2000 * (y % 4) + 0x8000 * page +
        (90 * (y/4)) + x/8;
    mask =  0x80 >> (x%8);
    address = 0xB0000000L + offset;
    temp = *address;
    if (color == 1)
        *address = temp | mask;
    else
        *address = temp &~mask;
}
```

Plotting a Point
with the Enhanced Graphics Adapter

IBM Personal Computer systems seem to be moving in the direction of having the Enhanced Graphics Adapter or the Video Graphics Array as the minimum display capability. Hence we will take a little more time to examine how to implement the point plotting function for this piece of equipment. Unlike the adapters previously discussed, the EGA and VGA hardware and software are designed to discourage direct memory access. The memory portion of the adapter is located at address A0000H. It consists of four memory planes: three for the primary colors of red, blue, and green, and one for intensity. The addresses of these planes overlap, so that all four planes have a starting address of A0000H. Hardware and software control which planes are written to when a particular location is addressed. Control is through a set of registers. (See Chapter 4 for detailed description). Figure 8-4 lists a function for plotting a colored point to the screen using the EGA control registers.

Figure 8-4: Plot Function for Enhanced Graphic Adapter Using C Port Output Functions

```
        plot() = Plots a point at (x,y) in color
    for Enhanced Graphics Adapter, using Turbo C port
    output functions
```

```c
void plot(int x, int y, int color)
{
    #define seq_out(index,val)   {outp(0x3C4, index);\
                                   outp(0x3C5, val);}
    #define graph_out(index, val) {outp(0x3CE,index);\
                                   outp(0x3CF, val);}

    extern int OPERATOR;
    unsigned int offset;
    int dummy, mask;
    char far *mem_address;

    offset = (long)y * 80L + ((long)x / 8L);
    mem_address = (char far *) 0xA0000000L + offset;
    mask = 0x80 >> (x % 8);
    graph_out(8,mask);
    graph_out(3,OPERATOR);
    seq_out(2,0x0F;
    dummy = *mem_address;
    *mem_address = 0;
    seq_out(2,color);
    *mem_address = 0xFF;
    seq_out(2,0x0F);
    graph_out(3,0);
    graph_out(8,0xFF);
}
```

First, it is important to note how C handles far addresses. It makes use of a long integer that combines the segment and offset addresses side by side. Thus, when EGA address is defined as 0xA0000000, it refers to an actual memory address of A00000H. Determining the memory address of a particular pixel is really simpler than with the other types of adapters, since the EGA and VGA do not use interleaving; all lines of data are placed consecutively in memory. Each pixel takes up only a single bit (at a particular address; actually there are four bits defining a pixel, one at this same address in each of the four memory planes) so there are 80 bytes to a line for a pixel column resolution of 640. The variable *offset* computes the offset in a similar manner to that used for the CGA and Hercules point plotting functions, and then adds in the base memory address to yield the precise byte in EGA/VGA memory where the selected pixel is to be written. The variable *mask* selects the appropriate bit of that byte as in the previous functions. Although it is possible to directly address each of the four memory planes, if the control registers are set properly, it is much safer and equally as fast to indirectly modify memory through the control registers, since direct addressing would require more register setting than the indirect method. This process begins by doing a dummy read of the data at *color_address*. This memory location cannot actually be read; anything read into the variable *dummy* at this step is meaningless. When the computer attempts to read this memory, however, the contents of the address from all four memory planes are stored in data registers in the EGA/VGA board. Next, the color is written to the sequencer map mask register to permit enabling only those memory planes corresponding to the color to which the pixel is to be set. Next, *OPERATOR* is loaded into register 3, the data rotate register. Although we are not using the rotate function, bits 3 and 4 of this register determine how the color of the pixel to be written will interact with the existing pixel on the screen. If bits 4 and 3 are 00B, the existing data will be replaced by the specified color. If they are 01B, the specified color will be ANDed with the existing data. If they are 10B, the color will be ORed with the existing data. Finally, if they are 11B, the color will be XORed with the existing data. Taking into account the position of these bits in the byte, the hex numbers to be written for these conditions are 00H, 08H, 10H, and 18H, respectively. The mask information is then loaded into the bit mask register, register 8. Next, 0xFF is written to the selected memory address, causing the desired pixel to be set to the designated color. Finally, the three registers that were sent data in the above operation are reinitialized, and further access is shut off until they are reopened. The resulting plot function is self-contained. Some additional speed increase may be gained by modifying it for special cases. We seldom wish to plot a single point. If we plan to draw a line, for example, it will probably be all in one color and the data will be treated in the same way (replace, AND, etc.). Consequently, we don't need to reset the registers between successive writes. The three registers need only be reinitialized at the end of the line-drawing function.

Of course, some flexibility is lost by having several tailored point-plotting functions or by incorporating a specialized routine in a number of different drawing functions. It all depends upon which is most important, flexibility or speed.

Improving the EGA Plot Function with Assembly Language

Figure 8-5 shows the plot routine of Figure 8-4 rewritten in assembly language to still further improve the speed of operation. Using assembly language, a single port instruction can be used to output two bytes to adjacent port addresses in a single operation. This permits sending each index to the index register and then the accompanying data to the indexed register with one instruction. This function depends upon the setting of register values directly and upon the use of in-line assembly code. Both of these capabilities are only available in Turbo C. If you are using Microsoft C, you will have to manipulate variables on and off the stack, and will have to write the assembly language program as a completely separate module which will be linked to the rest of the program when *link* is run. Even with Turbo C, there are some cautions to the taken into consideration, before adopting this routine. First, Turbo C permits in-line assembly language if each line is headed by the word *asm*. Note that unlike ordinary C instructions, these lines do not have to end with a semicolon. However, any comments must be delineated in C language fashion with the /*.....*/ beginning and ending and not preceded by a semicolon as are ordinary assembly language comments. Second, a program having in-line assembly language instructions cannot be compiled in the integrated environment. It must be compiled using the *tcc* command-line Turbo C compiler. Also, in order to assemble the assembly language instructions, the Microsoft Macro Assembler version 3.0 or later must be present on the same disk as your Turbo C compiler. Third, Turbo C permits direct setting of the contents of the microprocessor registers using the variables _AH, _BX, _ES, etc.; but, since other C processes may use these registers, great care must be taken in how they are initialized. For example, it is tempting to want to avoid the interim variables used in Figure 8-5 and, instead, set up the lines of code:

```
_DI = (long)y + 80L + ((long)x / 8L);
_CH = 0x80 >> (x % 8);
```

It is quite possible, however, that the mathematical operations performed in computing the value to insert in CH will make use of DI and thereby destroy the value that was set into it. It is best to set all the registers at once and then go immediately to assembly language. But even this has some pitfalls. For example, setting the ES segment register is performed by first loading the value into

150

AL and then transferring it to ES. If you are looking for the most highly optimized code, and you like to live dangerously, you can possibly find an order for
setting the registers that will not be destructive. You must choose a proposed
order, compile the program, and then look at the resulting *.exe* file with DEBUG.
You can search for part of your assembly language code and then look just before
it to see how the registers are set up. If there is any use of a register after your
value has been entered into it, you will have to try again with a different order.
Finally, suppose you have the bright idea (as I did) of keeping the assembly
language portion of your program separate from the remainder of the program,
compiling it, and making the object module a part of your project file so that the
rest of your code can be handled in the integrated environment. This would not
work for me using Turbo C 1.0. If I compiled both my main program and my
module with *tcc* and set up a project file for the main program in C and the module in object form, and then went to *tc* for the integrated environment, everything
would run just fine. But as soon as I made a change in the main program (even
just adding or deleting a blank line) and recompiled from within the integrated
environment, the program would fail to run and would either display garbage or
go off to never-never land or both. However, if I placed the module in object
form in a library and made that library part of my project file, everything would
work fine. Chapter 20 will describe in detail how to set up libraries for the
graphics functions. Don't be discouraged by all of these difficulties. With a little
experimentation you can set up a library that includes the *plot* function in its assembly language form and achieve gratifying results.

Figure 8-5: EGA Plot Function Using Assembly Language

```
        plot() = Plots a point at (x,y) in color
   for Enhanced Graphics Adapter, using assembly
   language at critical points
```

```c
void plot(int x, int y, int color)
{

    unsigned int offset;
    int dummy, mask;
    char far * mem_address;

    offset = (long)y * 80L + ((long)x / 8L);
    mask = 0x80 >> (x % 8);
    _ES = 0xA000;
    _BX = offset;
    _CX = color;
```

```
    _AX = mask;

    asm MOV     AH,AL
    asm MOV     AL,08
    asm MOV     DX,03CEH
    asm OUT     DX,AX
    asm MOV     AX,0FF02H
    asm MOV     DL,0C4H
    asm OUT     DX,AX
    asm OR      ES:[BX],CH
    asm MOV     BYTE PTR ES:[BX],00
    asm MOV     AH,CL
    asm OUT     DX,AX
    asm MOV     BYTE PTR ES:[BX],0FFH
    asm MOV     AH,0FFH
    asm OUT     DX,AX
    asm MOV     DL,0CEH
    asm MOV     AX,0003
    asm OUT     DX,AX
    asm MOV     AX,0FF08H
    asm OUT     DX,AX
}
```

9

Coordinate Systems and Clipping Boundaries

Those functions that are involved with reading or writing pixels on the screen, such as the *plot* functions which were developed in the previous chapter, make use of the screen coordinate system. This differs depending upon the display adapter used and the display mode. For the EGA high resolution mode, for example, the 0,0 point is at the top left hand of the screen; the x pixels increase to the right from 0 to 639 (a total of 640); and the y pixels increase downward from 0 to 349 (a total of 350). For CGA color mode 4, the x coordinate should be between 0 and 199 and the y coordinate between 0 and 319. For the Hercules Graphics Card, the x coordinate should be between 0 and 719 and the y coordinate between 0 and 347. We have assumed that the functions will not be given numbers outside these limits. What happens to our display if the function is supplied with coordinates that are outside the limits? Sometimes the computer will assume that some of the points to be plotted are off the display and will do nothing. At other times, because of the limitations on the size of integers, there may be a foldover, and the part of the figure to be drawn which is beyond the edge of the display may appear at the other edge of the display or somewhere else on the screen. Therefore, we need to give some attention to placing some limitations on the coordinate values, unless we are very sure that programmers will never exceed the display limits.

Another problem that we have not yet considered is that the programmer may want to define the screen in terms of some arbitrary set of coordinates. Instead of 0 to 639 for an x coordinate, he may want the limits to be -100 to + 100 kilometers. In fact, even if we don't want to scale up the coordinates to match distances or some other real quantities, the screen coordinates are not very easy to work with. First, since they differ for different adapters and display modes, all of the screen coordinates in a program have to be changed when the program is run in a different mode or with a different adapter. Second, the coordinates do not define a square pixel; that is, if you draw a rectangle with each side 50 units long, it will not be a square. Instead, the vertical sides will be longer than the horizontal sides. Similarly, if you specify a circle (an oval with an aspect ratio of one), it will not appear as a circle, but rather as an oval. In order to make something look like a circle on the screen, you need to specify an aspect ratio of 0.73. Finally, the orientation of the screen coordinates, with y increasing in a downward direction, is different from almost every other coordinate system.

The mathematics and techniques used in coordinate definition and and scaling and those required for setting clipping boundaries involve similar considerations. Both topics will be considered in this chapter.

System Coordinates

BASIC solves the coordinate problem by setting up "WORLD COORDINATES", a coordinate system easy to work with but totally unrelated to everything else. Being able to start from scratch with this C library of graphics functions, we are going to define a set of "System Coordinates" which are easy to use but are related to screen coordinates in a manner that makes the mathematics as simple as possible. Our first requirement is that the point (0,0) be at the center of the screen. Second, we will set up the coordinate system to minimize conversions of the x coordinate when the high resolution EGA or VGA cards are used. To do this we set the x coordinate limits to be -319 and +320, with x increasing to the right. Since this is the same range as the EGA and VGA high resolution x coordinates, converting from "System Coordinates" to screen coordinates in the x dimension simply involves an addition of 319.

The non-squareness of the screen coordinate system involves two factors—the display screen dimensions and the resolution in each direction. The display is defined to have a 3:4 ratio (vertical height is three units; horizontal length is 4 units). Since we have 640 pixel positions in the x dimension, for squareness, we would expect to have 480 (3/4 times 640) pixel positions in the y dimension. We will define our "System Coordinates" to be square, so that the y coordinates have a range from -239 to +240. The y dimension will be defined in the conventional manner, where y increases in the upward direction and decreases in the downward direction. The VGA has exactly 480 pixel positions in the y direction, so only a simple addition is involved in the conversion. The situation for the other adapters gets a little more complicated. The y dimension for the EGA high resolution modes only has 350 pixel positions. Now we have to think a bit about the conversion mathematics. At all costs, we want to avoid floating point arithmetic and even integer division, since these are time consuming processes. However, we can quickly do division by powers of two by a shifting process. Looking at the ratio 350/480, which is what we need to use in changing the scale of system y coordinates to screen y coordinates, we see that it is very close to 93/128. In fact, the position error across the screen is never more than one pixel. We then rescale the y coordinates by multiplying in integer form by 93 and then shifting right seven places to accomplish the 128 division. Then, because of the perverse reverse direction in which screen y coordinates are defined, we must subtract the result from 175 to get our system y coordinates going in the right direction.

The other modes that need to be considered are CGA modes having screen coordinates of 640 x 200 and of 320 x 200 and the Hercules Graphics Card having screen coordinates of 720 x 348. Again, simple integer techniques can be used which will result of errors in position of at most one pixel. Figure 9-1 shows the mathematical operations for each of the adapter modes. You can substitute the proper expressions in the plot routine of Figure 9-2, or in whatever *plot* function you are using, and then work in system coordinates independent of which adapter you have in your system or which mode you have selected.

Figure 9-1: Mathematics for Changing from System Coordinates to Screen Coordinates

Screen Coordinates	x conversion	y conversion
640 x 480	x = x + 319	y = 240 - y
640 x 350	x = x + 319	y = 175-((93*y)>>7)
640 x 200	x = x + 319	y = 100-((53*y)>>7)
320 x 200	x = x>>1 + 159	y = 100-((53*y)>>7)
720 x 348	x = x + (x>>4) + 359	y = 174-((93*y)>>7)

Figure 9-2 is a new version of the *plot* function given in the previous chapter, with the correct mathematics included so that it converts from system coordinates to screen coordinates in the EGA high resolution mode at the most primitive level. You can substitute the conversion factors given in Figure 9-1 to make this plot function work with any desired adapter. While this slows the point plotting function, the decrease in speed is not appreciable, and doing this at this lowest level is the simplest and most effective way of accomplishing the purpose.

Figure 9-2: Plot Function with Coordinate Conversion

```
plots() = converts from system coordinates to EGA
          high resolution screen coordinates and
          plots a point on the screen in the desig-
          nated color.
```

```c
#include "gdraws.h"

void plots(int x, int y, int color)
{
    #define seq_out(index,val)      {outp(0x3C4,index);\
                                     outp(0x3C5,val);}
    #define graph_out(index,val)    {outp(0x3CE,index);\
                                     outp(0x3CF,val);}
    unsigned int offset;
    int dummy, mask;
    char far * mem_address;

    x = x + 319;
    y = 175 - ((93*y) >> 7);
    offset = (long)y * 80L + ((long)x / 8L);
    mem_address = (char far *) 0xA0000000L + offset;
    mask = 0x80 >> (x % 8);
    graph_out(8,mask);
    seq_out(2,0x0F);
    dummy = *mem_address;
    *mem_address = 0;
    seq_out(2,color);
    *mem_address = 0xFF;
    seq_out(2,0x0F);
    graph_out(3,0);
    graph_out(8,0xFF);
}
```

Coordinate Scaling

If you want to scale to some other set of coordinates than the System Coordinates
we have chosen, the task may be equally simple in finding the right ratio to
permit use of shifting for division and in determining the right offsets to add or
subtract. However, if you want to include a flexible coordinate scaling capability

that can be changed as desired, you may have to go to floating point arithmetic, divisions, and perhaps to inserting the scaling routine at some higher order places than at the point-plotting level. A trade-off must be made between performing the scaling action at a primitive level, where a lot of overhead is used in performing the mathematical operations for every point that is to be plotted, or going to a higher level where only a few calculations are needed for a large number of points. On a more general basis, but using the same procedures that we did before, lets assume that we will define minimum and maximum coordinates that can be expressed with integers—that is, the limiting coordinate values must be between -32768 and +32767. Furthermore, no fractional positions can be specified. This is not too great a restriction, and it will speed things by allowing us to use integer arithmetic rather than floating point. Suppose we define the limits of our screen as being xMIN, yMIN, xMAX, and yMAX. Now the actual pixel position of a point on the screen for EGA high resolution mode is:

```
px = (x - xMIN) * 640 / (xMax - xMin)     (Eq. 9-4)

py = (y - yMIN) * 350 / (yMAX - yMIN)     (Eq. 9-5)
```

You probably want to use long integers within the calculation so that you don't overflow when the multiplication takes place. (You don't want to do the division first, because the result will be rounded off to an integer, resulting in your point being plotted to only one of two positions, the beginning or end of the display.)

You can do this scaling at the point plotting level, but there are no complications in implementing it at the line, rectangle or oval drawing level. For lines, you need only to compute the pixel coordinates of the beginning and end of the line. For the *drawOval* routine, you need to convert the x and y coordinates of the oval's center and the radius using the expression:

```
pb = b * 350 / (yMAX - yMIN)          (Eq. 9-6)
```

You may want to build such mathematics into your figure drawing functions and also add a function for setting the values of the maximum and minimum coordinates. Or perhaps you prefer to keep all of the drawing functions in display coordinates and perform the conversions in your regular software.

Another consideration is whether you are trying to create software that is compatible with all possible monitor/adapter card configurations. If you set up all of your drawing functions to perform the coordinate conversions, but use a pair of variables, xRES and yRES, instead of the numbers 640 and 350 that are in the equations above, you can write a function that not only sets the minimum and maximum values for the display coordinates, but also checks the type of adapter present and the mode that has been set and inserts the proper numbers into xRES and yRES (640 and 480 for VGA high resolution, 640 and 350 for EGA high resolution, 320 and 200 for CGA mode 4, or 720 and 348 for the Hercules Graphics Card).

Uses of Clipping

Clipping is used to assure that points are not displayed outside of a designated area. This area may be whole screen, in which case the clipping boundaries are used to assure that data at addresses outside the boundaries do not appear at strange places on the screen. As a minimum, we want to establish a clipping rectangle, and whatever points fall outside this rectangle will not be displayed. For the EGA high resolution mode, this clipping rectangle would have its top left hand corner at coordinates (0,0) and its bottom right hand corner at coordinates (639,349). There are other uses of clipping, however. Suppose we want to define a rectangular window on the screen and display only that part of a drawing that falls within this window. The remainder of the screen may contain other things that we do not wish to disturb. Then we can define a smaller clipping rectangle, say (20,20) and (500,250). Whatever techniques we develop to perform the clipping action should be equally applicable to any smaller window that we define. In fact, if you are really concerned with windows, you should provide the capability for defining a number of them and be able to specify that any particular figure that you are about to draw goes to the particular window that you specify.

Clipping at the Most Primitive Level

The simplest, but not the fastest way to perform clipping is at the level where each individual point is being plotted. Consider the following fragment of C language software:

```
if ((x >= XSTART) && (x <= XEND) && (y >= YSTART)
        && (y <= YEND)
        plot(x, y, color);
```

These statements assure that the point to be plotted will always be within the bounds of the rectangle defined by (XSTART,YSTART) and (XEND,YEND). It is assumed that no point is ever plotted without having this condition satisfied and that you have some means of defining XSTART, YSTART, XEND, and

YEND, which are the clipping rectangle and all of which are global variables. You can build this condition right into your most basic point plotting routine and never have to worry about clipping again. The cost is in speed. Every time that you plot a point, four conditional tests have to be met. So assuming that the point is within the bounds to be plotted, all of these tests have used up time and the plotting function becomes much slower.

Sophisticated Clipping

What happens if we decide to clip at a more sophisticated level instead of on a point by point basis? Suppose we decide to clip by defining new beginning and end points for each line that extends beyond the clipping rectangle so that these points are within or at the edge of the clipping rectangle. We then have to do this not only for straight lines, but also for circles, ovals, and any other figures that involve direct plotting instead of *drawLine* function. The mathematics for this is apt to become rather complicated. Nevertheless, when it boils down to a few program statements, if the line length is long enough so that a large number of points are involved, the increase in time required to compute new line beginning and end points is going to be offset by the fact that these calculations only need to be done once for each line; whereas the testing of the plotted point has to be done once for each point in the line. On the other hand, if you are plotting some complex curve by stringing together a lot of small line segments which contain only a few pixels each, the so-called sophisticated technique may very well turn out to be much slower than the primitive one. You need to carefully consider what your applications will be before you make a decision as to which way to go.

Clipping Lines

As an example such trade-off, we'll consider in detail how to go about clipping a line. The generalized equation of a line is:

```
y = mx +b                    (Eq. 9-1)
```

where m is the slope of the line and b is an offset. We'll consider a line that has the beginning point (x1, y1) and the ending point (x2, y2). We shall assume that

```
x1 < x2
```

by definition. Now suppose we are looking for a new point on the line (x3, y3). Substituting in equation 9-1 and solving the resulting system of equations, we find that:

$$y3 = (x3 - x1)(y2 - y1)/(x2 - x1) + y1 \qquad (Eq. \ 9\text{-}2)$$

and

$$x3 = (y3 - y1)(x2 - x1)/(y2 - y1) + x1 \qquad (Eq. \ 9\text{-}3)$$

Our procedure to obtain new line end points is as follows:

1. If x1 and y1 are within the clipping rectangle, leave the point alone.

2. If x1<XMIN, solve equation 12.2 for y3 with x3=XMIN.

3. If a new set of points was found in step 2, it are used to replace (x1, y1). Now, if y1<YMIN, solve equation 12.3 for x3 with y3=YMIN. If y1>YMAX, solve equation 12.3 for x3 with y3=YMAX. Use these new points, if the were computed, to replace (x1, y1).

4. If x2 and y2 are within the clipping rectangle, leave the point alone. Otherwise follow steps 2 and 3 for (x2, y2).

Figure 9-3 lists a function to obtain these new beginning and ending points for a line.

Figure 9-3: Function to Clip Lines

```
clipLine() = Computes new beginning and ending
             points for a line (if needed) so that
             it will be within the bounds of the
             clipping rectangle.
```

```
void clipLine(int *x1, int *y1, int *x2, int *y2)
{
    int temp;

    if (*x1 > XMAX)
    {
        *x1 = 0;
        *x2 = 0;
```

```
    *y1 = 0;
    *y2 = 0;
}
if (*x1<XMIN)
{
    *y1 = *y1 + (XMIN - *x1)*(*y2 - *y1)/
        (*x2 - *x1);
    *x1 = XMIN;
}
if (*y1<YMIN)
{
    *x1 = (YMIN - *y1)*(*x2 - *x1)/(*y2 - *y1) +
        *x1;
    *y1 = YMIN;
}
if (*y1>YMAX)
{
    *x1 = (YMAX - *y1)*(*x2 - *x1)/(*y2 - *y1) +
        *x1;
    *y1 = YMAX;
}
if (*x1 > XMAX)
{
    *x1 = 0;
    *x2 = 0;
    *y1 = 0;
    *y2 = 0;
}
if (*x2>XMAX)
{
    *y2 = *y2 + (XMAX - *x2)*(*y2 - *y1)/
        (*x2 - *x1);
    *x1 = XMAX;
}
if (*y1<YMIN)
{
    *x1 = (YMIN - *y1)*(*x2 - *x1)/(*y2 - *y1) +
        *x1;
    *y1 = YMIN;
}
if (*y1>YMAX)
{
```

```
        *x1 = (YMAX - *y1)*(*x2 - *x1)/(*y2 - *y1) +
            *x1;
        *y1 = YMAX;
    }
```

10

Drawing Lines
and Rectangles

Most of the figures that you will draw on the display screen will be composed of simple geometric shapes such as line segments, rectangles, ovals, or circles. Because each of these curves contain a large number of points to be plotted, the algorithms used to determine the location of each point must be such that computer processing time is minimized, so that the curve can be drawn in a reasonable amount of time. The most commonly used technique for determining the location of points to be drawn to form well behaved curves is Bresenham's algorithm. With proper ingenuity in selecting a decision function, this algorithm can be very fast and efficient.

Bresenham's Algorithm

Figure 10-1 shows the situation where we have just plotted a point P which is either on the curve that we are trying to plot or as close to it as we can get, given the discrete nature of the pixels on a monitor screen. Points Q1 through Q8 are the possible choices for the next point. Bresenham's algorithm starts by using information on the direction in which x and y are changing to reduce the number of choices to three. For example, if over the portion of the curve that we are considering, both x and y are increasing, points Q1, Q4, Q6, Q7, and Q8 are ruled out because the result in the decrease of one or both coordinates. The only remaining candidates are Q2, Q3, and Q5. Next, the slope of the curve is considered. If the slope is between 0 and 1, Q2 is ruled out; if between 1 and ∞, Q5 is ruled out. The choice is thus narrowed down to two points.

Figure 10-1: Possibilities for Next Point to be Plotted

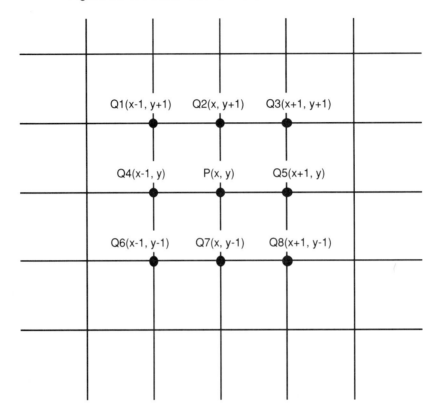

Figure 10-2 shows how the process for narrowing down to two points can be tabulated. A decision variable is then defined, which has a value of zero when the curve is exactly half way between the two points, and which is minus if the curve is closer to one point and positive if it is closer to the other. The whole key to the proper use of Bresenham's algorithm is to select a decision variable that can be computed for each point to be plotted with the very minimum of computer actions. Based upon the sign of the decision variable, one of the two points is selected and plotted and the procedure begins all over again for the next point.

Figure 10-2: Narrowing Down to Two Possible Points

x	y	Slope	Points
Increasing	increasing	1 to ∞	Q2, Q3
Increasing	increasing	0 to 1	Q3, Q5
Increasing	decreasing	0 to -1	Q5, Q8
Increasing	decreasing	-1 to ∞	Q7, Q8
decreasing	increasing	0 to -1	Q1, Q4
decreasing	increasing	-1 to ∞l	Q1, Q2
decreasing	decreasing	0 to 1	Q4, Q6
decreasing	decreasing	1 to ∞	Q6, Q7

Drawing a Line

Figure 10-3 is a function for drawing a line using Bresenham's algorithm. I've seen four or five line drawing programs using Bresenham's algorithm (and several much slower ones that don't). This is the fastest that I've found. It is interesting to note that for a straight line, the information as to whether the x or y coordinate is increasing faster is sufficient to determine a decision variable (x or y) that only depends upon one coordinate. Instead of modifying this variable by incrementing or decrementing it by the fractional change in the x or y coordinate per pixel change, the decision variable is modified by the entire change in each coordinate over the entire line length. This preserves the same change per pixel ratio, but eliminates a lot of floating point multiplications and divisions.

Figure 10-3: Function for Drawing a Line

```
drawline()  = Draws a line from x1,y1 to x2,y2 in
              selected color
```

```
void drawLine(int x1,int y1,int x2,int y2,int color)
{
    #define sign(x) ((x) > 0 ? 1: ((x) == 0 ? 0: (-1)))

    int dx,dy,dxabs,dyabs,i,px,py,sdx,sdy,x,y;

    dx = x2 - x1;
    dy = y2 - y1;
    sdx = sign(dx);
    sdy = sign(dy);
```

165

```
dxabs = abs(dx);
dyabs = abs(dy);
x = 0;
y = 0;
px = x1;
py = y1;
if (dxabs >= dyabs)
{
    for (i=0; i<=dxabs; i++)
    {
        y += dyabs;
        if (y>=dxabs)
        {
            y -= dxabs;
            py += sdy;
        }
        plots(px,py,color);
        px += sdx;
    }
}
else
{
    for (i=0; i<=dyabs; i++)
    {
        x += dxabs;
        if (x>=dyabs)
        {
            x -= dyabs;
            px += sdx;
        }
        plots(px,py,color);
        py += sdy;
    }
}
}
```

Finally, note one example of the subtlety that must be used in programming for maximum speed. Once the macro is defined for the sign of a variable, the temptation is to use it within the *for* loops to determine the sign of dx or dy. However, what the C compiler does is substitute the actual code for the macro whenever it is encountered. The signs of dx and dy are unchanged throughout the *for* loops, so we don't want to use several computer operations to redetermine them with each loop iteration. Therefore, one computation of each sign is made outside the loop and each is assigned to a variable that is used within the loop. Figure 10-4 shows a typical result of using the function listed in Figure 10-3 to draw a line.

Figure 10-4: Sample Line Plot

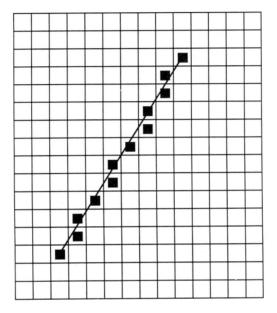

Drawing Wide Lines

The function listed above draws lines that are only a single pixel wide. Drawing wider lines presents somewhat of a problem. Of course, you could draw several lines with the end points of each line a pixel offset from the original line. It would be nice to have a more elegant (and faster) technique, however. Fortunately, there is a way to do this. Looking at the sample line in Figure 10-4, it is evident that this line (in which the difference between the beginning and ending y coordinates is larger than the distance between the beginning and ending x coordinates) can be widened by placing new pixels on either side (x-1 and x+1) of each pixel that was originally drawn. Similarly, if the difference in x coordinates is greater than the difference in y coordinates, the pixels to widen the line are placed above and below each one that was originally drawn. Why make such a point of this? Consider what would happen if we arbitrarily decided to widen a line by putting pixels on both sides of the original ones. All vertical lines would be widened just fine, but all horizontal lines would still be only one pixel wide. Similarly, if we decided to widen by putting pixels above and below, all horizon-

tal lines would be widened but vertical would not. The criteria given above determines which method to use in each given case and works correctly for all
cases. Fortunately, the algorithm that is being used in the line function neatly
separates these two situations, so that a *for* loop in each case can select the proper
coordinates for plotting the extra pixels needed for a wider line. Figure 10-5 is
the line drawing function rewritten to provide for wide lines and for lines of different styles (solid, dotted, dashed, etc. Note that the specified beginning and
ending coordinates of the line correspond to the center of the line.

Line Style

We don't always want solid straight lines. Sometimes we need dotted or dashed
or center lines. The generally accepted method of drawing such lines is through
the use of a pattern. For the function we are using, the pattern is 32 bits long
and is contained in an unsigned long integer. The technique used is to set up a
mask that begins having only the most significant bit set. Each time a pixel is
generated for plot in the *drawLine* function, the mask is shifted one bit to the
right. When the mask becomes zero, it is reset again to a one in the most
significant bit. Each time that we are ready to plot a point to the screen, the
mask is ANDed with the pattern. If the pattern contains a one in that bit position, the result is non-zero; if the pattern contains a zero, the result is zero. We
then actually plot the point on the screen if the result is non-zero, indicating a
one at that bit position in the pattern. The result is that points are plotted along
the line for all ones in the pattern and spaces are left for zeroes. The pattern may
be selected to be almost any kind of dashed or dotted line that is desired. Eight
typical lines are included in the header file *gdraws.h* which is used in connection
with the drawing package and is described in Chapter 20. One caution: if you are
generating a curve by using very small line segments, the line segments may not
be long enough to reproduce the entire pattern. Since the pattern begins again
each time *drawLine* is called, don't be surprised if you get a solid line or only
part of a pattern.

Figure 10-5: Drawing Lines with Different Widths and Styles

```
drawLine() = Draws a line from x1,y1 to x2,y2 in
             selected color with adjustable line
             width and selectable line styles
```

```
void drawLine(int x1,int y1,int x2,int y2,int color)
{
    #define sign(x) ((x) > 0 ? 1: ((x) == 0 ? 0: (-1)))
```

```
extern unsigned long int PATTERN;
extern int LINEWIDTH;
int dx,dy,dxabs,dyabs,i,j,px,py,sdx,sdy,x,y;
unsigned long int, mask=0x80000000;

dx = x2 - x1;
dy = y2 - y1;
sdx = sign(dx);
sdy = sign(dy);
dxabs = abs(dx);
dyabs = abs(dy);
x = 0;
y = 0;
px = x1;
py = y1;
if (dxabs >= dyabs)
{
    for (i=0; i<=dxabs; i++)
    {
        mask = mask ? mask : 0x80000000;
        y += dyabs;
        if (y>dxabs)
        {
            y -= dxabs;
            py += sdy;
        }
        if (PATTERN & mask)
        {
            for (j=-LINEWIDTH/2; j<=LINEWIDTH/2;
                j++)
                plots(px,py+j,color);
        }
        px += sdx;
        mask >>= 1;
    }
}
else
{
    for (i=0; i<=dyabs; i++)
    {
        mask = mask ? mask : 0x80000000;
        x += dxabs;
        if (x>dyabs)
        {
            x -= dyabs;
```

```
                px += sdx;
        }
        if (PATTERN & mask)
        {
            for (j=-LINEWIDTH/2; j<=LINEWIDTH/2;
                j++)
                plots(px+j,py,color);
        }
        py += sdy;
        mask >>= 1;
    }
  }
}
```

Figure 10-5 is a new version of the *drawLine* function which provides for setting the line width and style. Line width is set into a global variable called *LINEWIDTH*. The style is set into a global variable called *PATTERN*. Remember, this *drawLine* function is likely to be slower than the one given in Figure 10-3 for solid lines, so if the utmost in speed is essential, you might want to forego the extra features or to keep both functions in your library for use under different circumstances. Figure 10-6 is a simple function that you can add to your graphics library to select line style.

Figure 10-6: Function to Select Line Style

```
setLineStyle() = Selects the style of line to be drawn
```

```
void setLineStyle(int style)
{
    extern unsigned long PATTERN;

    unsigned long int style_type[8] = { 0xFFFFFFFF,
        0xC0C0C0C0,0xFF00FF00,0xFFF0FFF0,0xF000F000,
        0xFFFF0000,0xFFFFF0F0,0xFFF0F0F0};

    PATTERN = style_type(style);
}
```

Drawing a Rectangle

The simplest way to draw a rectangle is by just drawing the four lines of which it is composed. Figure 10-7 lists a function to perform this job. Note that the function makes sure that the corner points are not written twice. This might be a problem if the XOR operator were chosen for the plotting of points, since XOR-ing twice gets back to the original background color, leaving gaps. The straight line function that was developed above processes horizontal and vertical lines almost as fast as diagonal ones. Thus the function in Figure 10-7 doesn't exact too great a penalty in speed of operation. In fact, a function was developed that plotted all of the points for the rectangle directly, but for some reason it wasn't as fast as the function in Figure 10-7.

Figure 10-7: Drawing a Rectangle with Straight Lines

```
drawRect() = Draws a Rectangle with no overlap at
             corners
```

```
  void drawRect(int x1,int y1,int x2,int y2,int color)
{
    extern unsigned long int PATTERN;
    unsigned long int mask=0x80000000;
    PATTERN = style[LINESTYLE];
    drawLine(x1-LINEWIDTH/2,y1,
            x2+LINEWIDTH/2,y1,color);
    drawLine(x1-LINEWIDTH/2,y2,
            x2+LINEWIDTH/2,y2,color);
    drawLine(x1,y1+LINEWIDTH/2,
            x1,y2-LINEWIDTH/2,color);
    drawLine(x2,y1+LINEWIDTH/2,
            x2,y2-LINEWIDTH/2,color);
}
```

Filling a Rectangle

Often we want to fill a rectangle on the screen with a solid color. As usual, the simplest way is also the slowest; that is, to just draw a set of lines from the left boundary to the right boundary of the rectangle. The top line is at the upper boundary. The end point locations are then moved down one pixel and another line is drawn. This process continues until the last line is drawn at the bottom boundary. Figure 10-8 lists a function to perform the rectangle fill.

Figure 10-8: Filling a Rectangle with Straight Lines

```
fillRect() = Fills a Rectangle with a Specified Color
```

```
void fillRect(int x1, unsigned int y1, int x2,
```

```
unsigned int y2, int color)
{
    int i,j;

    for (i=y1; i<=y2; y++)
    {
        drawLine(x1,i,x2,i,color);
    }
}
```

A faster method of filling a rectangle can be devised using the ROM BIOS video service for Scrolling a Window. When the number of lines to be scrolled is set to zero, this service fills an entire specified window with a designated color. Unfortunately, there are a couple of problems. First, the window size is specified in character position coordinates, while we wish to specify the rectangle dimensions in pixel coordinates. Each display line in the EGA high resolution display mode, for example, has 640 pixels, but can only identify 80 characters, so we have to divide the pixel column location by 8 to obtain the equivalent character column. Similarly, there are 350 pixel raster lines, but only 25 rows of characters, so the pixel raster line must be divided by 14 to obtain the equivalent character row. Unfortunately, these divisions seldom come out even. We have to make sure that we don't, therefore, draw a character column or row that is outside the original specified rectangle dimensions. Once we do this, there is still likely to be part of a row or column that does not get filled in at all four edges of the rectangle. To fill these, we start by drawing lines around the edges of the rectangle until we reach an exact character boundary. This is right for the top and right edges, but we need one more line on the bottom and right, so these are drawn also. Then the character boundaries of the window are calculated. The ones on the right and bottom must be decreased by one or we will draw to big a window. The window scrolling service is then called to fill the rest of the rectangle. This results in a lot faster fill than when filling by drawing a line at a time. If you watch it work on a demonstration program, you will see the line by line fill around the edges, which is representative of the speed of the fill when drawing all lines. But once the borders are complete, the rest of the fill takes place almost instantaneously. Figure 10-9 lists a function to fill a rectangle using this technique. The window scrolling technique will work with any of the IBM graphics adapters, but the function as written assumes 14 line characters, which is only true of the high resolution modes of the EGA and VGA. All of the 14s should be changed to 8s in order for the function to work with the CGA. Also the coordinate conversion needs to be modified for use with any othe the other adapters, as described in Chapter 9. Since the Hercules Card does not support window scrolling, this technique will not work for it. Note that the technique only works properly if the border fill-in is done with single pixel width lines. Therefore, the *LINEWIDTH* parameter is changed to one for the duration of this function and then restored to its original value. If you are going to use this technique, you should note that the *drawLine* function that is used must be in terms of screen pixel coordinates for the function to work properly. Thus, you will need a special version of the *drawLine* function, which simply replaces the two calls to the *plots* function with calls to the *plot* function instead. However, for the EGA and VGA, there is a faster way to do fills, which is described below.

Figure 10-9: Filling a Rectangle Using Window Scrolling

```
fillRect() = Fills a Rectangle with a Specified Color
```

```
void fillRect(int x1, unsigned int y1, int x2,
    unsigned int y2, int color)
{
    int line_temp;
    line_temp = LINEWIDTH;
    LINEWIDTH = 1;
    x1 += 319;
    x2 += 319;
    y1 = 175 - ((93*y1) >> 7);
    y2 = 175 - ((93*y2) >> 7);
    while ((x1 % 8 != 0) && (x1<=x2))
    {
        drawLine(x1,y1,x1,y2,color);
        x1++;
    }
    while ((x2 % 8 != 0) && (x2>=x1))
    {
        drawLine(x2,y1,x2,y2,color);
        x2--;
    }
    drawLine(x2,y1,x2,y2,color);
    while ((y1 % 14 != 0) && (y1<=y2))
    {
        drawLine(x1,y1,x2,y1,color);
        y1++;
    }
    drawLine(x1,y2,x2,y2,color);
    while ((y2 % 14 != 0) && (y2>=y1))
    {
        drawLine(x1,y2,x2,y2,color);
        y2--;
    }
    drawLine(x1,y2,x2,y2,color);
```

```
    x1=x1/8;
    x2=(x2/8)-1;
    y1=y1/14;
    y2=(y2/14)-1;
    if ((x2>=x1) && (y2>=y1))
        window(x1,y1,x2,y2,color);
    LINEWIDTH = line_temp;
}
```

The faster method depends upon using the plot technique more efficiently than we do when we plot a single pixel to the screen in a plot operation. Our normal *plot* function plots a single point to the screen, even though it must operate on a whole byte of memory. The function does a dummy read to store the byte in the EGA/VGA registers, modifies the desired pixel with a mask, and then causes the modified data to be written back to display memory. In filling a rectangle, most of the time we want to do the same thing to all of the pixels in a byte. Consequently we can use a mask that modifies all eight pixels in the byte in one operation and then rewrite the byte to display memory. The result is more than eight times faster than writing individual pixels as done by the method of drawing straight lines. In addition, several of the EGA registers addressed through I/O ports do not need to be changed except at the beginning and end of the process, further increasing the speed of operation. This works well except at the left and right edges of the rectangle, where if the specified locations are not at the division between two bytes, a special mask must be devised to only write the desired pixels. This mask depends upon the rectangle x coordinate specified. Figure 10-10 lists a function that performs the special byte-at-a-time operation for the main portion of the rectangle and generates and uses the masks that are necessary to complete the fill at the left and right edges. This function has its coordinate conversion from system coordinates to screen coordinates set up for VGA mode 12H. That section of the function would have to be modified to work with the EGA high resolution mode.

Figure 10-10: Filling a Rectangle using Direct Outputs

```
fillRect() = Fills a Rectangle with a Specified Color
```

```
void fillRect(int x1, int y1, int x2, int y2,
    int color)
{
    int i,first,last,begin,end,start_mask,end_mask,
        mask,dummy;
    long int y1L, y2L, j;
    #define seq_out(index,val)       {outp(0x3C4,index);\
                                      outp(0x3C5,val);}
```

```
#define graph_out(index,val)   {outp(0x3CE,index);\
                                 outp(0x3CF,val);}
unsigned int offset;
char far * mem_address;

x1 += 319;
x2 += 319;
y1L = (240 - y1)*80L;
y2L = (240 - y2)*80L;
begin = x1/8;
end = x2/8;
first = x1 - begin*8;
last = x2 - end*8 + 1;
start_mask = 0xFF >> first;
end_mask = 0xFF << (8-last);
for (j=y1L; j<=y2L; j+=80)
{
    offset = j + begin;
    mem_address = (char far *) 0xA0000000L +
        offset;
    graph_out(8,start_mask);
    seq_out(2,0x0F);
    dummy = *mem_address;
    *mem_address = 0;
    seq_out(2,color);
    *mem_address = start_mask;
    for (i=begin+1; i<end; i++)
    {
        offset = j + i;
        mem_address = (char far *) 0xA0000000L +
            offset;
        graph_out(8,0xFF);
        seq_out(2,0x0F);
        dummy = *mem_address;
        *mem_address = 0;
        seq_out(2,color);
        *mem_address = 0xFF;
    }
    offset = j + end;
    mem_address = (char far *) 0xA0000000L +
        offset;
    graph_out(8,end_mask);
    seq_out(2,0x0F);
    dummy = *mem_address;
    *mem_address = 0;
    seq_out(2,color);
```

```
        *mem_address = end_mask;
        seq_out(2,0x0F);
        graph_out(3,0);
        graph_out(8,0xFF);
    }
}
```

11

Drawing Ovals, Circles, and Arcs

Drawing ovals, circles, and arcs is a much more complicated process than drawing straight lines. With a variation of Bresenham's algorithm, however, we can develop functions that will perform these actions quickly and efficiently. These techniques will work well with any well-behaved curve, particularly those that are conic sections, such as parabolas and hyperbolas. These latter curves, however, do not appear in graphics often enough to require special functions dedicated especially to them. If they are needed in a particular application, it is usually sufficient to represent the curve by a succession of small straight line segments.

Pixel Dimensions

The equation of a circle is:

$$x^2 + y^2 = r^2 \qquad\qquad \text{(Eq. 11-1)}$$

where r is the radius of the circle. This depends upon a unit of measurement having the same length in the x and y dimensions. If that is not the case, the circle will be distorted in one dimension and will thus appear as an oval. Unfortunately, except for the high resolution mode of the VGA (which is set up to have square pixels), the characteristics of the PC displays are such that unit pixel dimensions are different along the x and y axes. Consider the EGA display in its high resolution graphics mode (mode 10H). There are 640 pixels along the x axis and 350 along the y axis. The display is not square; the ratio of the entire length along the x axis to that along the y axis is 4:3. Thus the relative length of a pixel along the x axis is 4/640, or .00625, whereas the relative length of a pixel along the y axis is 3/350, or .00857. If we select the y pixel length as our reference, we then have to multiply all of the x values by 1.3712 to obtain the same length in both axes.

The equation for an oval (or ellipse) is:

$$x^2/a^2 + y^2/b^2 = 1 \qquad\qquad (Eq. 11-2)$$

The aspect ratio, which is passed as a parameter in the *drawOval* function, is:

$$aspect\ ratio = b/a \qquad\qquad (Eq. 11-3)$$

In normal space where x and y are of the same scale, the equation of the oval becomes that of a circle when the aspect ratio is one. With non-square pixels, the circle drawn using the aspect ratio of one is distorted into an ellipse, so that some fudge factor aspect ratio needs to be used to change the ellipse back to a circle. This is overly complex and is one of the reasons that we chose in chapter 9 to set up a set of "System Coordinates" that has square pixels. To refresh your memory, the system coordinates have point (0,0) at the center of the screen. The x coordinate limits are -319 at the left side of the screen and +320 at the right side of the screen. The y coordinate limits are -239 at the bottom of the screen and +240 at the top of the screen. The resulting ratio is 480/640 which is the same as the 3/4 ratio of vertical to horizontal screen length, which makes the pixels square. As a result, ovals drawn with an aspect ratio of one will be circles. If they do not appear as circles on your screen, you need to correct the vertical to horizontal length ratio by changing the vertical size with the monitor vertical size control. The most accurate way to do this is not with a circle displayed, but with the display of rotated rectangles, where you can adjust the vertical size until the angles of the rotated rectangle corners are exactly ninety degrees. This is described in further detail in Chapter 21.

Drawing an Oval

Figure 11-1 lists the algorithm for drawing an oval using Bresenham's circle algorithm. The basic technique is the same as that described for using this algorithm to draw straight lines in the previous chapter. Only a quarter of the oval is actually computed; because of symmetry, this can be reflected and plotted four times to make the complete oval. For the quarter circle that is calculated, x is always increasing and y is decreasing. This fact makes it possible to narrow down the possible choices for the next point to three. The quarter circle is broken into two parts: 1) the slope of the circle is more than 1, and 2) the slope is less than one. This eliminates one of the three points. Finally, a decision variable is used to compare the slope of the line between the previously plotted point and each of the two choices to the slope of the circle at that point, and select the point which gives the closest match. Different decision variables are used for each of the two eighths of the circle.

Figure 11-1: Function for Drawing an Oval

```
drawOval() = Draws an oval centered at x,y with
             radius b, aspect ratio 'aspect' and
             in selected color
```

```c
void drawOval(int x, int y, int b, int color,
     float aspect)
{
    int col, i, row;
    float aspect_square;
    long a_square, b_square, two_a_square,
        two_b_square, four_a_square,  four_b_square,d;

    aspect_square = aspect*aspect;
    b -= LINEWIDTH/2;
    for (i=1; i<=LINEWIDTH; i++)
    {
        b_square = b*b;
        a_square = b_square/aspect_square;
        row = b;
        col = 0;
        two_a_square = a_square << 1;
        four_a_square = a_square << 2;
        four_b_square = b_square << 2;
        two_b_square = b_square << 1;
        d = two_a_square * ((row  -1)*(row )) +
            a_square + two_b_square*(1-a_square);
        while (a_square*(row ) > b_square * (col))
        {
            plots(col+x,row+y,color);
            plots(col+x,y-row, color);
            plots(x-col,row+y,color);
            plots(x-col,y-row,color);
            if (d>= 0)
            {
                row--;
```

```
            d -= four_a_square*(row);
        }
        d += two_b_square*(3 + (col << 1));
        col++;
    }
    d = two_b_square * (col + 1)*col +
        two_a_square*(row * (row  -2) +1) +
        (1-two_a_square)*b_square;
    while ((row) + 1)
    {
        plots(col+x,row+y,color);
        plot(col+x,y-row, color);
        plots(x-col,row+y,color);
        plots(x-col,y-row,color);
        if (d<= 0)
        {
            col++;
            d += four_b_square*col;
        }
        row--;
        d += two_a_square * (3 - (row <<1));
    }
    b++;
    }
}
```

There are several decision variables that can be used with Bresenham's circle algorithm. The one used here appears to give the smoothest and best looking ovals and circles of any that I have tried. Figure 11-2 shows several circles that were drawn using this function.

Filling an Oval

We often would like to have an oval or circle that is filled in with a solid color. Using exactly the same oval drawing function that is listed above in Figure 11-1, we can replace the plot drawing routines with the line drawing function. Note that each pair of point plotting calls has the same x coordinate, but different y coordinates. By drawing a line from one y coordinate to the other along the x coordinate, we not only plot the two end points, but also fill in the distance between them.

Figure 11-2: Circles

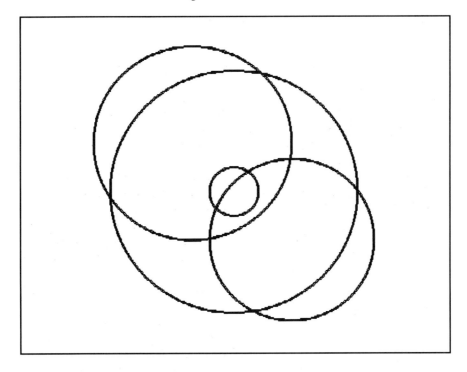

The result is a totally filled in oval. Figure 11-3 lists a function that accomplishes this task. It is sped up by including the point plotting within the function itself. It also includes coordinate conversion suitable for the VGA high resolution mode. These conversions are different for other adapter cards. A sample of filled-in ovals is shown in Figure 11-4 (see color section). The eyes in the smiling face are circles filled in with the background color; the mouth is made with several line segments.

Figure 11-3: Function to Fill an Oval

```
fillOval() = Draws an oval centered at x,y with
             radius b, aspect ratio 'aspect' and
             fills it with selected color.
```

```
void fillOval(int x, int y, int b, int color,
     float aspect)
{
    union REGS reg;
```

```
#define seq_out(index,val)      {outp(0x3C4,index);\
                                 outp(0x3C5,val);}
#define graph_out(index,val)    {outp(0x3CE,index);\
                                 outp(0x3CF,val);}

unsigned int offset;
char far * mem_address;
int col, col1, row, row1, dummy, i, mask;
float aspect_square;
long a_square, b_square, two_a_square,
    two_b_square, four_a_square, four_b_square,d;
char far *base;

aspect_square = aspect*aspect;
a_square = b*b/aspect_square;
b_square = b*b;
row = b;
col = 0;
x += 319;
y = 240 -y;
two_a_square = a_square << 1;
four_a_square = a_square << 2;
four_b_square = b_square << 2;
two_b_square = b_square << 1;
d = two_a_square * ((row  -1)*(row )) + a_square +
    two_b_square*(1-a_square);
while (a_square*(row ) > b_square * (col))
{
    for (i=y-row; i<=y+row; i++)
    {
        offset = (long)i * 80L + ((long)
            (x + col) / 8L);
        mem_address = (char far *) 0xA0000000L
            + offset;
        mask = 0x80 >> ((x + col) % 8);
        graph_out(8,mask);
        seq_out(2,0x0F);
        dummy = *mem_address;
        *mem_address = 0;
        seq_out(2,color);
        *mem_address = 0xFF;
        offset = (long)i * 80L + ((long)
```

```
                      (x - col) / 8L);
          mem_address = (char far *) 0xA0000000L
              + offset;
          mask = 0x80 >> ((x - col) % 8);
          graph_out(8,mask);
          seq_out(2,0x0F);
          dummy = *mem_address;
          *mem_address = 0;
          seq_out(2,color);
          *mem_address = 0xFF;
          seq_out(2,0x0F);
          graph_out(3,0);
          graph_out(8,0xFF);
      }
      if (d>= 0)
      {
          row--;
          d -= four_a_square*(row);
      }
      d += two_b_square*(3 + (col << 1));
      col++;
  }
  d = two_b_square * (col + 1)*col +
      two_a_square*(row*(row  -2) +1) +
      (1-two_a_square)*b_square;
  while ((row) + 1)
  {
      for (i=y-row; i<=y+row; i++)
      {
          offset = (long)i * 80L + ((long)
              (x + col) / 8L);
          mem_address = (char far *) 0xA0000000L
              + offset;
          mask = 0x80 >> ((x + col) % 8);
          graph_out(8,mask);
          seq_out(2,0x0F);
          dummy = *mem_address;
          *mem_address = 0;
          seq_out(2,color);
          *mem_address = 0xFF;
          offset = (long)i * 80L + ((long)
              (x - col) / 8L);
```

183

```
        mem_address = (char far *) 0xA0000000L
            + offset;
        mask = 0x80 >> ((x - col) % 8);
        graph_out(8,mask);
        seq_out(2,0x0F);
        dummy = *mem_address;
        *mem_address = 0;
        seq_out(2,color);
        *mem_address = 0xFF;
        seq_out(2,0x0F);
        graph_out(3,0);
        graph_out(8,0xFF);
    }
    if (d<= 0)
    {
        col++;
        d += four_b_square*col;
    }
    row--;
    d += two_a_square * (3 - (row <<1));
    }
}
```

Drawing an Arc

It is generally accepted that using Bresenham's algorithm to compute a part of a circle and then reflecting to plot several parts at once is the best and fastest method of drawing full circles. When it comes to drawing arcs, however, several authors resort to other, less efficient circle algorithms because they feel that attempts to use Bresenham's algorithm become much too complicated. Nevertheless, it turns out that this fast and efficient technique can be used for all sizes of arcs with considerable success. Figure 11-5 lists a function for drawing arcs with a technique similar to that used for drawing circles above.

Figure 11-5: Function to Draw an Arc

```
drawArc() = Draws an arc centered at xc,yc with
            radius b, aspect ratio aspect,
            starting angle start_angle in tenths
            of a degree and ending angle end_angle
            in tenths of a degree.
```

```c
void drawArc (int xc, int yc, int b, int start_angle,
    int end_angle, int color, float aspect)
{
    const float pi = 3.14159625;
    int col, i, j, row,start_sector,end_sector,
        x_start_test,x_end_test;
    int arcTest[9] = {0,0,0,0,0,0,0,0,0};
    float aspect_square;
    long a_square, b_square, two_a_square,
    two_b_square, four_a_square, four_b_square,d;

    aspect_square = aspect*aspect;
    b -= LINEWIDTH/2;
    for (j=1; j<=LINEWIDTH; j++)
    {
        b_square = b*b;
        a_square = b_square/aspect_square;
        row = b;
        col = 0;
        two_a_square = a_square << 1;
        four_a_square = a_square << 2;
        four_b_square = b_square << 2;
        two_b_square = b_square << 1;
        d = two_a_square * ((row  -1)*(row )) +
            a_square + two_b_square*(1-a_square);
        start_sector = start_angle/450;
        end_sector = end_angle/450;
        x_start_test = xc + sqrt(a_square) *
            cos(start_angle * pi/1800);
        x_end_test = xc + sqrt(a_square) *
            cos(end_angle*pi/1800);
        if (start_sector == end_sector)
            arcTest[start_sector] = 4;
        else
```

```
{
    arcTest[start_sector] = 1;
    arcTest[end_sector] = 3;
    for (i=start_sector+1; i!=end_sector; i++)
    {
    arcTest[i] = 2;
    if (i==8)
        i=-1;
    }
}
while (a_square*(row ) > b_square * (col))
{
    plotArc1 (xc+col, yc-row, 6, color,
        arcTest, x_start_test, x_end_test);
    plotArc2 (xc+col, yc+row, 1, color,
        arcTest, x_start_test, x_end_test);
    plotArc1 (xc-col, yc-row, 5, color,
        arcTest, x_start_test, x_end_test);
    plotArc2 (xc-col, yc+row, 2, color,
        arcTest, x_start_test, x_end_test);
    if (d>= 0)
    {
        row--;
        d -= four_a_square*(row);
    }
    d += two_b_square*(3 + (col << 1));
    col++;
}
d = two_b_square * (col + 1)*col +
    two_a_square*(row * (row  -2) +1) +
    (1-two_a_square)*b_square;
while ((row) + 1)
{
    plotArc1 (xc+col, yc-row, 7, color,
        arcTest, x_start_test, x_end_test);
    plotArc2 (xc+col, yc+row, 0, color,
        arcTest, x_start_test, x_end_test);
    plotArc1 (xc-col, yc-row, 4, color,
        arcTest, x_start_test, x_end_test);
    plotArc2 (xc-col, yc+row, 3, color,
        arcTest, x_start_test, x_end_test);
    if (d<= 0)
```

```
        {
            col++;
            d += four_b_square*col;
        }
        row--;
        d += two_a_square * (3 - (row <<1));
    }
    b++;
    }
}
void plotArc1 (int x, int y, int sector, int color,
     int arcTest[], int x_start_test, int x_end_test)
{
    if (arcTest[sector] == 0)
        return;
    if (arcTest[sector] == 2)
        plots(x,y,color);
    if ((arcTest[sector] == 1) && (x>=x_start_test))
        plots(x,y,color);
    if ((arcTest[sector] == 3) && (x<=x_end_test))
        plots(x,y,color);
    if ((arcTest[sector] == 4) && (x>=x_start_test)
        && (x<=x_end_test))
        plots(x,y,color);
}


void plotArc2 (int x, int y, int sector, int color,
    int arcTest[], int x_start_test, int x_end_test)
{
    if (arcTest[sector] == 0)
        return;
    if (arcTest[sector] == 2)
        plots(x,y,color);
    if ((arcTest[sector] == 1) && (x<=x_start_test))
        plots(x,y,color);
    if ((arcTest[sector] == 3) && (x>=x_end_test))
        plots(x,y,color);
    if ((arcTest[sector] == 4) && (x>=x_end_test)
        && (x<=x_start_test))
        plots(x,y,color);
```

Those computations which involve floating point math occur only once for each arc drawn. The same point-plotting scheme is used with a simple testing technique to determine when and when not to plot a point. Figure 11-6 shows how the oval algorithm plots the parts of a circle.

Figure 11-6: Method of Plotting Arcs

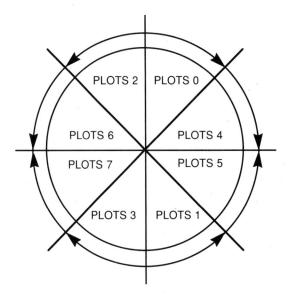

If you look at Figure 11-2, the oval drawing function, you will note that the *plots* function is called eight times. Each of these eight locations plots one-eighth of the circle. I have arbitrarily designated these *plots* calls as *plots* numbers 0 to 7 in the order they occur in the function. The figure identifies each *plots* call, shows the portion of the circle on a display which is drawn by that particular call, and shows the direction in which that arc is plotted. The technique that has been chosen is to select the x and y coordinates of the oval center, a starting and ending angle, a radius, and a color. For each of the eight 45 degree sectors of the circle or oval, a variable is used to keep track of its status in plotting the arc. These statuses are shown in Figure 11-7.

Figure 11-7: Segment Status for Arc Drawing

Status	Meaning
0	No part of the arc appears in this segment
1	The arc starts but does not end in this segment
2	The arc extends through this entire segment
3	The arc ends but does not start in this segmen
4	The arc starts and ends in this segment

It can be seen that they represent all possible conditions for each sector. A fairly simple if statement for each condition can determine whether a point should be plotted. In addition, all of the different possibilities for directions of plotting can be encompassed in only two subroutines. The resulting function plots arcs to one-tenth degree accuracy (within the limits of the pixel resolution) at high speeds. Figure 11-8 shows several arcs drawn using this function.

Figure 11-8: Arcs

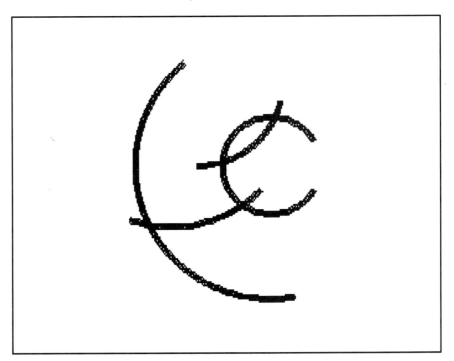

Filling an Arc

Finding a fast way to fill the segment comprising an arc and lines from each end
of the arc to the oval center appears to be very difficult. The only way that I have
found to fill an arc is to draw a line from the center to each point on the arc as it
is plotted. Even this does not suffice if a line is drawn which is only a single
pixel wide. Certain pixels throughout the segment will be missed and thus a few
pixel size holes will be left in interesting patterns. To overcome this, the function that has been developed uses a line that is three pixels wide. This does a
perfect fill job, but leaves the terminations of the segments at the center three
pixels wide instead of one. Normally, this amount of accuracy will be adequate.
If you really want the most precise algorithm, you might try drawing a one pixel
wide line halfway out and then changing it to three pixels wide for the remainder
of the line. Figure 11-9 is the function that has been developed to fill arc segments. Figure 11-10 shows some filled-in arcs drawn using this function.

Figure 11-9: Function to Fill an Arc

```
fillArc() = Draws an arc centered at xc,yc with
            radius b, aspect ratio aspect,
            starting angle start_angle in tenths
            of a degree and ending angle end_angle
            in tenths of a degree, and fills it
            with a specified color.
```

```
void fillArc (int xc, int yc, int b, int start_angle,
     int end_angle, int color, double aspect)
{
    const float pi = 3.14159625;
    int col, i, row,start_sector,end_sector,
        x_start_test,x_end_test;
    int arcTest[9] = {0,0,0,0,0,0,0,0,0};
    double aspect_square;
    long a_square, b_square, two_a_square,
    two_b_square, four_a_square, four_b_square,d;
    aspect_square = aspect*aspect;
    b_square = b*b;
    a_square = b_square/aspect_square;
    row = b;
    col = 0;
    two_a_square = a_square << 1;
    four_a_square = a_square << 2;
```

```
four_b_square = b_square << 2;
two_b_square = b_square << 1;
d = two_a_square * ((row  -1)*(row )) + a_square +
    two_b_square*(1-a_square);
start_sector = start_angle/450;
end_sector = end_angle/450;
x_start_test = xc + sqrt(a_square) *
    cos(start_angle*pi/1800);
x_end_test = xc + sqrt(a_square) *
    cos(end_angle*pi/1800);
if (start_sector == end_sector)
    arcTest[start_sector] = 4;
else
{
    arcTest[start_sector] = 1;
    arcTest[end_sector] = 3;
    for (i=start_sector+1; i!=end_sector; i++)
    {
        arcTest[i] = 2;
        if (i==8)
            i=-1;
    }
}
lineWidth = 3;
while (a_square*(row ) > b_square * (col))
{
    fillArc1 (xc,yc,xc+col, yc+row, 6, color,
        arcTest, x_start_test, x_end_test);
    fillArc2 (xc,yc,xc+col, yc-row, 1, color,
        arcTest, x_start_test, x_end_test);
    fillArc1 (xc,yc,xc-col, yc+row, 5, color,
            arcTest, x_start_test, x_end_test);
    fillArc2 (xc,yc,xc-col, yc-row, 2, color,
            arcTest, x_start_test, x_end_test);
    if (d>= 0)
    {
        row--;
        d -= four_a_square*(row);
    }
    d += two_b_square*(3 + (col << 1));
    col++;
}
```

```
      d = two_b_square * (col + 1)*col +
          two_a_square*(row * (row  -2) +1) +
          (1-two_a_square)*b_square;
      while ((row) + 1)
      {
          fillArc1 (xc,yc,xc+col, yc+row, 7, color,
              arcTest, x_start_test, x_end_test);
          fillArc2 (xc,yc,xc+col, yc-row, 0, color,
              arcTest, x_start_test, x_end_test);
          fillArc1 (xc,yc,xc-col, yc+row, 4, color,
              arcTest, x_start_test, x_end_test);
          fillArc2 (xc,yc,xc-col, yc-row, 3, color,
              arcTest, x_start_test, x_end_test);
          if (d<= 0)
          {
              col++;
              d += four_b_square*col;
          }
          row--;
          d += two_a_square * (3 - (row <<1));
      }
}


void fillArc1 (int xc, int yc,int x, int y,
    int sector, int color, int arcTest[],
    int x_start_test, int x_end_test)
{
    if (arcTest[sector] == 0)
        return;
    if (arcTest[sector] == 2)
        drawLine(xc,yc,x,y,color);
    if ((arcTest[sector] == 1) && (x>=x_start_test))
        drawLine(xc,yc,x,y,color);
    if ((arcTest[sector] == 3) && (x<=x_end_test))
        drawLine(xc,yc,x,y,color);
    if ((arcTest[sector] == 4) && (x>=x_start_test) &&
        (x<=x_end_test))
        drawLine(xc,yc,x,y,color);
}

void fillArc2 (int xc, int yc,int x, int y,
```

```
       int sector, int color, int arcTest[],
       int x_start_test, int x_end_test)
{
    if (arcTest[sector] == 0)
        return;
    if (arcTest[sector] == 2)
        drawLine(xc,yc,x,y,color);
    if ((arcTest[sector] == 1) && (x<=x_start_test))
        drawLine(xc,yc,x,y,color);
    if ((arcTest[sector] == 3) && (x>=x_end_test))
        drawLine(xc,yc,x,y,color);
    if ((arcTest[sector] == 4) && (x>=x_end_test) &&
        (x<=x_start_test))
        drawLine(xc,yc,x,y,color);
}
```

Figure 11-10: Filled-in Arcs

Although there doesn't seem to be any simpler algorithm for filling an arc, the program shown in Figure 11-9 can be modified in some ways to make it run faster if you are using the Enhanced Graphics Adapter or Video Graphics Array. Essentially, what has been done is to incorporate stripped down versions of the line drawing and point plotting functions into the *fillarc* function. The number of outputs to the EGA/VGA registers is reduced to the minimum, and as a result, the function runs faster than that of Figure 11-9. The improved version of the function is listed in Figure 11-11.

Figure 11-11: Improved VGA Function to Fill an Arc

```
void fillArc (int xc, int yc, int b, int start_angle,
    int end_angle, int color, float aspect)

{
    int col, i, row,start_sector,end_sector,
        x_start_test,x_end_test;
    int arcTest[9];
    float aspect_square;
    long a_square, b_square, two_a_square,
        two_b_square, four_a_square, four_b_square,d;

    for (i=0; i<8; i++)
        arcTest[i] = 0;
    aspect_square = aspect*aspect;
    a_square = b*b/aspect_square;
    b_square = b*b;
    row = b;
    col = 0;
    xc += 319;
    yc = 240 - yc;
    two_a_square = a_square << 1;
    four_a_square = a_square << 2;
    four_b_square = b_square << 2;
    two_b_square = b_square << 1;
    d = two_a_square * ((row  -1)*(row )) + a_square +
        two_b_square*(1-a_square);
    start_sector = start_angle/450;
    end_sector = end_angle/450;
    x_start_test = xc+sqrt(a_square)*
        cos(start_angle*.0017453);
    x_end_test = xc+sqrt(a_square)*
        cos(end_angle*.0017453);
    if (start_sector == end_sector)
```

```
        arcTest[start_sector] = 4;
else
{
    arcTest[start_sector] = 1;
    arcTest[end_sector] = 3;
    for (i=start_sector+1; i!=end_sector; i++)
    {
        arcTest[i] = 2;
        if (i==8)
            i=0;
    }
}
while (a_square*(row ) > b_square * (col))
{
    fillArc1 (xc,yc,xc+col, yc+row, 6, arcTest,
        x_start_test, x_end_test,color);
    fillArc1 (xc,yc,xc+col, yc-row, 1, arcTest,
        x_start_test, x_end_test,color);
    fillArc1 (xc,yc,xc-col, yc+row, 5, arcTest,
        x_start_test, x_end_test,color);
    fillArc1 (xc,yc,xc-col, yc-row, 2, arcTest,
        x_start_test, x_end_test,color);
    if (d>= 0)
    {
        row--;
        d -= four_a_square*(row);
    }
    d += two_b_square*(3 + (col << 1));
    col++;
}

d = two_b_square * (col + 1)*col +
    two_a_square*(row * (row  -2) +1) +
    (1-two_a_square)*b_square;
while ((row) + 1)
{
    fillArc1 (xc,yc,xc+col, yc+row, 7, arcTest,
        x_start_test, x_end_test,color);
    fillArc1 (xc,yc,xc+col, yc-row, 0, arcTest,
        x_start_test, x_end_test,color);
    fillArc1 (xc,yc,xc-col, yc+row, 4, arcTest,
        x_start_test, x_end_test,color);
```

```
        fillArc1 (xc,yc,xc-col, yc-row, 3, arcTest,
            x_start_test, x_end_test,color);
        if (d<= 0)
        {
            col++;
            d += four_b_square*col;
        }
            row--;
            d += two_a_square * (3 - (row <<1));
    }
}

void fillArc1 (int xc, int yc,int x, int y, int sector,
    int arcTest[], int x_start_test, int x_end_test,
    int color)
{

    union REGS reg;
    #define seq_out(index,val)      {outp(0x3C4,index);\
                                     outp(0x3C5,val);}
    #define graph_out(index,val)    {outp(0x3CE,index);\
                                     outp(0x3CF,val);}

    unsigned int offset;
    int dummy, mask,dx,dy,i,tx=0,ty=0,sdx,sdy,
        dxabs,dyabs;
    char far * mem_address;

    switch (sector)
    {
        case 4:
        case 5:
        case 6:
        case 7:
            if (arcTest[sector] == 2)
                break;
            if ((arcTest[sector] == 1) &&
                (x>=x_start_test))
                break;
            if ((arcTest[sector] == 3) &&
                (x<=x_end_test))
                break;
```

```
        if ((arcTest[sector] == 4) &&
            (x>=x_start_test) && (x<=x_end_test))
            break;
        return;
    case 0:
    case 1:
    case 2:
    case 3:
        if (arcTest[sector] == 2)
            break;
        if ((arcTest[sector] == 1) &&
            (x<=x_start_test))
            break;
        if ((arcTest[sector] == 3) &&
            (x>=x_end_test))
            break;
        if ((arcTest[sector] == 4) &&
            (x>=x_end_test) && (x<=x_start_test))
            break;
        return;
}
if ((sector <= 1) || (sector >= 6))
    sdx = 1;
else
    sdx = -1;
if (sector > 3)
    sdy = 1;
else
    sdy = -1;
dxabs = (x-xc)*sdx;
dyabs = (y-yc)*sdy;
if (dxabs >= dyabs)
{
    for (i=0; i<= dxabs; i++)
    {
        ty+= dyabs;
        if (ty>dxabs)
        {
            ty -= dxabs;
            yc +=sdy;
        }
        offset = (long)yc * 80L + ((long)xc / 8L);
```

```
        mem_address = (char far *) 0xA0000000L
            + offset;
        mask = 0x80 >> (xc % 8);
        graph_out(8,mask);
        seq_out(2,0x0F);
        dummy = *mem_address;
        *mem_address = 0;
        seq_out(2,color);
        *mem_address = 0xFF;
        offset = (long)(yc + 1) * 80L +
            ((long)xc / 8L);
        mem_address = (char far *) 0xA0000000L
            + offset;
        graph_out(8,mask);
        seq_out(2,0x0F);
        dummy = *mem_address;
        *mem_address = 0;
        seq_out(2,color);
        *mem_address = 0xFF;
        seq_out(2,0x0F);
        graph_out(3,0);
        graph_out(8,0xFF);
        xc+= sdx;
    }
}
else
{
for (i=0; i<= dyabs; i++)
{
    tx+= dxabs;
        if (tx>dyabs)
        {
            tx -= dyabs;
            xc +=sdx;
        }
        offset = (long)yc * 80L + ((long)xc / 8L);
        mem_address = (char far *) 0xA0000000L
            + offset;
        mask = 0x80 >> (xc % 8);
        graph_out(8,mask);
        seq_out(2,0x0F);
        dummy = *mem_address;
```

```
*mem_address = 0;
seq_out(2,color);
*mem_address = 0xFF;
offset = (long)yc * 80L +
    ((long)(xc + 1) / 8L);
mem_address = (char far *) 0xA0000000L
    + offset;
mask = 0x80 >> ((xc + 1) % 8);
graph_out(8,mask);
seq_out(2,0x0F);
dummy = *mem_address;
*mem_address = 0;
seq_out(2,color);
*mem_address = 0xFF;
seq_out(2,0x0F);
graph_out(3,0);
graph_out(8,0xFF);
yc+= sdy;
            }
        }
    }
```

12

Drawing Rounded Rectangles and Polygons

In this chapter, we'll look at even more complex geometric figures. Drawing and filling them involves complicated computer code, and as a result, they are more time consuming than some of the figures that we previously encountered. They can, however, provide some unique and unusual displays, and are often well worth the time required to create them.

Drawing a Rounded Rectangle

The rounded rectangle provides a pleasing frame for displaying text or graphics figures. The function to create it is listed in Figure 12-1, and is set up with inputs of two pairs of coordinates (x1,y1 and x2,y2) which mark the top left and bottom right corners of a rectangle. These are the corner locations if the rectangle were not rounded. Other inputs are the radius for rounding and the color. The function makes use of a simplified line drawing algorithm and the oval drawing function which was described in Chapter 11. However, the user is not permitted to specify the aspect ratio for the rounding of the corners; it is assumed that circular rounding should be used. The line drawing algorithm simply plots two horizontal lines by plotting all points at the same y dimension from the x beginning (which is in from the specified starting point by the x radius) to the end of the x line (which is also toward the center from the specified end point by the x radius). Extra one-pixel-wide lines are plotted on both sides of the specified y starting and ending values until the line width which is in the global variable LINEWIDTH is achieved. Note that the line width must be specified as an odd number of pixels; if it is not, the actual width will be the next larger odd number. The vertical sides of the rectangle are plotted in a similar way, starting beyond the y starting point by the y radius and ending before the y ending point by the same amount.

Figure 12-1: Function to Draw a Rounded Rectangle

```
drawRoundRect() = Draws a rectangle with rounded
                  corners, with upper right and lower
                  left corners of the unrounded rectangle
                  specified, the radius of the rounded
                  corners specified, and the color speci-
                  fied.
```

```c
void drawRoundRect(int x1, int y1, int x2, int y2,
    int b, int color)
{
    int a, xr, yr, col,i,j,row,xend,yend,flag;
    long a_square, b_square, two_a_square,
        two_b_square, four_a_square, four_b_square,d;

    yr = b;
    xr = b;
    xend = x2-xr;
    yend = y2+yr;
    for (j=-LINEWIDTH/2; j<=LINEWIDTH/2; j++)
    {
        for (i=x1+xr; i<=xend; i++)
        {
            plots(i,y1+j,color);
            plots(i,y2-j,color);
        }
    }
    for (j=-LINEWIDTH/2; j<=LINEWIDTH/2; j++)
    {
        for (i=y1-yr; i<=yend; i++)
        {
            plots(x1+j,i,color);
            plots(x2+j,i,color);
        }
    }
    b -= LINEWIDTH/2;
    a = b;
    for (i=0; i<LINEWIDTH; i++)
```

```
{
    b_square = b*b;
    a_square = a*a;
    row = b;
    col = 0;
    two_a_square = a_square << 1;
    four_a_square = a_square << 2;
    four_b_square = b_square << 2;
    two_b_square = b_square << 1;
    d = two_a_square * ((row  -1)*(row )) +
        a_square + two_b_square*(1-a_square);
    while (a_square*(row ) > b_square * (col))
    {
        plots(col+xend,yend-row,color);
        plots(col+xend,y1-yr+row, color);
        plots(x1+xr-col,yend-row,color);
        plots(x1+xr-col,y1-yr+row,color);
        if (d>= 0)
        {
            row--;
            d -= four_a_square*(row);
        }
            d += two_b_square*(3 + (col << 1));
            col++;
    }
    d = two_b_square * (col + 1)*col + two_a_square
        * (row * (row  -2) +1 ) + (1-two_a_square)
        * b_square;
    while (row)
    {
        plots(col+xend,yend-row,color);
        plots(col+xend,y1-yr+row, color);
        plots(x1+xr-col,yend-row,color);
        plots(x1+xr-col,y1-yr+row,color);
        if (d<= 0)
        {
            col++;
            d += four_b_square*col;
        }
        row--;
        d += two_a_square * (3 - (row <<1));
    }
```

```
        b++;
        a++;
    }
}
```

You will remember that the version of Bresenham's circle algorithm that was used to generate ovals and circles produced a quarter of a circle, which was then plotted four times with the correct mirroring to draw a whole circle. We use the same technique here, except that instead of specifying the same center for each quadrant, each quadrant is offset by the proper amount so that its beginning and ending points join the line segments that have previously been plotted.

Filling a Rounded Rectangle

Figure 12-2 lists the function for filling a rounded rectangle. The function takes the same input parameters that are used for the *drawRoundRect* function, namely the x and y coordinates of the top left and bottom right corners of the unrounded rectangle, the radius (in the y direction) for rounding, and the color to be used for the fill. The procedure that is used here is to first fill two regular rectangles with the *fillRect* function. One of these has the same top and bottom dimensions as the desired rounded rectangle but its right and left edges are set in from the desired edges of the rounded rectangle by the rounding radius. The other has its right and left edges the same as the desired rounded rectangle but is set in from the top and bottom by the rounding radius. These overlap each other, but can still be drawn much faster than by any other technique, because the technique used for filling regular rectangles is very fast. The result is a sort of cross, with the four rounded corners remaining to be filled in.

Figure 12-2: Function to Fill a Rounded Rectangle

```
fillRoundRect() = Fills a rectangle with rounded
                  corners, with upper right and lower
                  left corners of the unrounded rectangle
                  specified, the radius of the rounded
                  corners specified, and the color speci-
                  fied.
```

```
void fillRoundRect(int x1, int y1, int x2, int y2,
    int b, int color)
{
    int a, xr, yr, col,i,j,row,xend,yend,flag;
```

```
long a_square, b_square, two_a_square,
two_b_square, four_a_square, four_b_square,d;

yr = b;
xr = b-2
xend = x2-xr;
yend = y2+yr;
b -= LINEWIDTH/2;
a = b;
b_square = b*b;
a_square = a*a;
fillRect(x1,y1-yr,x2,y2+yr,color);
fillRect(x1+xr,y1,x2-xr,y2,color);
row = b;
col = 0;
two_a_square = a_square << 1;
four_a_square = a_square << 2;
four_b_square = b_square << 2;
two_b_square = b_square << 1;
d = two_a_square * ((row  -1)*(row )) +
    a_square + two_b_square*(1-a_square);
while (a_square*(row ) > b_square * (col))
{
    drawLine(xend,yend-row,col+xend,yend-row,
        color);
    drawLine(xend,y1-yr+row,col+xend,y1-yr+row,
        color);
    drawLine(x1+xr,yend-row,x1+xr-col,yend-row,
        color);
    drawLine(x1+xr,y1-yr+row,x1+xr-col,y1-yr +
        row,color);
    if (d>= 0)
    {
        row--;
        d -= four_a_square*(row);
    }
    d += two_b_square*(3 + (col << 1));
    col++;
}
d = two_b_square * (col + 1)*col + two_a_square
    * (row * (row  -2) +1) + (1-two_a_square) *
    b_square;
```

```
while (row)
{
    drawLine(xend,yend-row,col+xend,yend-row,
        color);
    drawLine(xend,y1-yr+row,col+xend,y1-yr+row,
        color);
    drawLine(x1+xr,yend-row,x1+xr-col,yend-row,
        color);
    drawLine(x1+xr,y1-yr+row,x1+xr-col,y1-yr +
        row,color);
    if (d<= 0)
    {
        col++;
        d += four_b_square*col;
    }
    row--;
    d += two_a_square * (3 - (row <<1));
}
b++;
a++;
}
```

The same *drawOval* type of programming used in drawing a rounded rectangle is used to do this, except that instead of plotting points to create the rounded lines, lines are drawn from the center x coordinate out to the intersection of the circle arc for each y pixel line. The four quarters of the circle are again computed with a single set of calculations and then all four rounded corners are filled simultaneously using the same computed values but with different offsets and signs to place them at the proper locations. You will note that in calculating the x radius (xr), some fudging has been done to obtain the best matching of the rounded areas to the rest of the rectangle.

Variable Argument Lists

Suppose we want to draw a polygon, but don't want to limit ourselves to a specific number of sides. One time that we call the polygon function, we may want to draw a triangle by specifying three vertices; the next time we may wish to have an octagon, which has eight vertices. Fortunately, C has a means by which a variable number of arguments may be passed to a function. This set of functions is in the C reference book as the va_... functions. The implementation is that of ANSI X3J11 draft C, which is a little bit different from the techniques used in some older compilers. The prototype function description is:

```
void function_name(int xxxx, int yyyy, ...)
```

where, of course, the function type need not be void, but can be anything you require. The first two int's (*xxxx* and *yyyy*) represent the names of fixed variables that are always passed by the function call. There can be any number of these and they may be of any type. The three dots (...) indicate that a variable number of additional parameters may be passed by the function. When you are making a specific function call, you may replace the dots by any number of parameters that you wish to pass. Now let's look at what happens inside the function. To begin with, somewhere you must have the include statement:

```
#include <stdarg.h>
```

in order to permit the compiler to access the library which contains the appropriate functions. Next in your argument declarations you must include the statement:

```
va_list zzzz;
```

where *zzzz* is the name of a parameter into which you want to load each of the parameters passed to the function in turn. Next, before you attempt to use any of the parameters in the variable length list, you need the statement:

```
va_start(zzzz,yyyy);
```

where *zzzz* is the same parameter name that you assigned to receive the variable length information, and *yyyy* is the name of the last fixed parameter in the function before the beginning of the variable length list of parameters. You have now started the process. From now on, every time that you call the function va_arg, it will obtain the next parameter in the variable argument list. For example, the statement:

```
k = va_arg(zzzz,int);
```

will obtain the next variable from the list, in integer form, and place it in *k*. The two parameters that are passed to va_arg are the parameter name (*zzzz*) that you assigned to receive data, and the type of argument (int, char, etc.) that you expect to be in the list. Note that you never really do anything useful with *zzzz* since the data actually returns to whatever variable you put before the equals sign (*k* in this case). Nevertheless, you must use some name in place of *zzzz* throughout to make the function work. You should also observe that you have unlimited flexibility to mix data types in the variable length argument list, but it is your responsibility as a programmer to build the code into your function that will sort out these types in a desired order and then to make sure that each time you call the function, the parameters in the list have the proper types for their relative positions.

Unfortunately, this set of functions does not give you any indication as to when the variable length parameter list comes to an end. This would certainly be a nice feature, but at this point it is also the programmer's responsibility to include as the last member of the list something that the function can take as a signal to stop reading values from the list. If you don't do this, your function is apt to keep on reading values off the stack forever. Finally, before you leave your function, you must include the statement:

```
va_end(zzzz);
```

where *zzzz* is the same name you assigned in va_start. If you don't include this statement, your program can later do weird and unpredictable things that are hard to track down.

There are various *v* versions to the *printf, scanf*, etc. functions which are designed to be used with this set of variable length argument list functions to permit passing on variable length lists to them after you have performed whatever manipulations you desire on the data. They are not pertinent to our graphics purposes, and therefore will not be considered in detail here.

The variable argument list functions have some limitations on the number of parameters that may be passed using Turbo C. These will be described in the following section.

Drawing a Polygon with Variable Length Argument List

Figure 12-3 lists the function to draw a polygon using the variable length argument list functions for the EGA adapter. This is a good example of how to use these functions. The *drawPoly* function passes one fixed argument: *color*, which is the color of the lines that are drawn to make up the polygon. Next follow a variable length series of integers, of which each pair are the x and y display coordinates of a vertex of the polygon. Finally, the last number in the argument list must be more negative than -320 to indicate to the function that the end of the coordinate list has been reached. The *drawPoly* function begins by setting up the va_list and then runs a *while* loop that reads points from the variable length list to the members of an two arrays, *xpoint* and *ypoint*, which store up to 150 pairs of points. When the first value more negative than -320 is encountered, this loop is terminated. The function then checks to ascertain if at least three pairs of coordinates were transferred. If not, a valid polygon has not been defined, so the function returns without doing anything.

Figure 12-3: Function to Draw a Polygon Using Variable Argument List

```
drawPoly() = Draws a Polygon in Specified Color
             using xy coordinate sets given.  Last
             entry must be negative.
```

```
void drawPoly(int color,...)
{
    #include <stdarg.h>
    va_list coord;
    int xpoint[150],ypoint[150],i=0,j;
    va_start(coord,color);
    while (((xpoint[i]=va_arg(coord,int)) >= -320)
        && ((ypoint[i]=va_arg(coord,int)) >= -320)
        && i<=150))
        i++;
    if (i<3) return;
    for (j=0; j<i-1; j++)
        drawLine(xpoint[j],ypoint[j],xpoint[j+1],
            ypoint[j+1],color);
    drawLine(xpoint[0],ypoint[0],xpoint[i-1],
        ypoint[i-1],color);
    va_end(coord);
}
```

The program then begins a *for* loop that first draws a line from the first pair of coordinates to the second, then another line from the second pair to the third, and so forth until a line is drawn from the next-to-last pair of coordinates to the last pair. The *for* loop is then complete. Next, the function draws the final line from the last pair of coordinates back to the first pair. There is no restriction on the coordinate positions by this function. They can be selected so that the lines are drawn to bound some enclosed surface, or they can be chosen so that they cross each other within the bounded surface. Strictly speaking, only in the first case does the function define a polygon. The function is deliberately left with the extra flexibility, and all sorts of interesting figures can be drawn with it.

Some Limitations

The above function should now meet all of our polygon drawing requirements. But does it really? Suppose you want to draw a figure containing a whole lot of line segments—hundreds of them. First, the above function may not be the best way to do it, since including several hundred arguments in a function call can be unwieldy and inconvenient. But more important, if you are using Turbo C in the integrated environment, there apparently seems to be a definite limitation on the number of arguments that can be passed by the va_... family of functions. Somewhere between 100 and 200 arguments, everything seems to go sour. Usually, what seems to happen is that the stack overflows during compilation. First, Turbo C reports 30,000 or so warnings and a similar number of errors. Then Turbo C halts the computer (sometimes with a message saying "Fatal stack overflow error—System halted" and sometimes with no message at all). Everything stops; the computer cannot even be reset with Control-Alternate-Delete.

You need to turn off the computer power completely and start over again. Hopefully you saved the program you were working on before all this happened; if not, it's gone and you have to type it back in again. Because of these limitations, we have another version of the function for drawing polygons, which is described below. Inasmuch as both of these serve useful purposes, we have given the second a different name, so that both functions may be kept in the library for use as desired.

Drawing a Polygon Using a Coordinate Array

Figure 12-4 is a function for drawing a polygon using an array of coordinate points. To keep the function as similar to the *drawPoly* function as possible, a single array of points is used, with the first point being an x coordinate, the second a y coordinate, the third an x coordinate, and so forth. At the cost of modifying the coding somewhat from the previous function, you can use a structure of arrays or a multidimensioned array to store the points, possibly in a more understandable form. Usually in typing coordinates, however, one types an x coordinate, followed by a comma, followed by a y coordinate. This corresponds well with a single-dimensioned array; the only problem occurs if you drop out one coordinate. The function passes the address of the *point* array and thus doesn't need to worry about the va_... functions, nor about overflowing the stack.

In this function, the *point* array is first scanned to determine its end which, like the preceeding function, is a number more negative than -320. You could use a more elegant technique in which you process points until an end marker is encountered.

Figure 12-4: Function to Draw a Polygon Using Array

```
draw2Poly() = Draws a Polygon in Specified Color
              using xy coordinate sets from an array.
```

```
void draw2Poly(int color, int point[300])
{
    int i,j;

    for (i=0; i<=300; i++)
        if (point[i] < 0)
            break;
    if (i<=5) return;
    for (j=0; j<i-2; j+=2)
        drawLine(point[j],point[j+1],point[j+2],
            point[j+3],color);
    drawLine(point[0],point[1],point[i-2],point[i-1],
    color);
}
```

Comments on Filling Polygons

While it is very easy to look at a polygon and know what is inside and what should be filled and what is outside and should not be filled, this is a much more difficult task for the computer. The simplest approach might be to sort all of the boundary points in order of their y coordinates and then, beginning at the first x coordinate on each line, draw a solid line until the next x coordinate is encountered. Figure 12-5 shows what happens when this approach is used on a relatively simple figure. One whole section of the figure is missed. Topology tells us that there is an answer to this—that if we draw lines across any bounded surface, we are inside whenever we have made an odd number of boundary crossings and outside whenever we have made an even number of crossings. You can verify this for yourself with Figure 12-6. There are a few additional problems, however. In any case, the first consideration is to sort the coordinates. This is addressed below.

Figure 12-5: Failure of Simple Approach to Filling

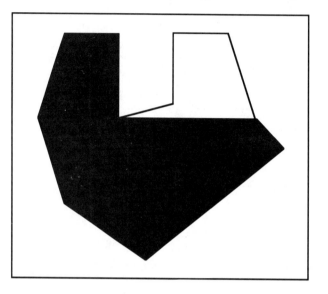

Figure 12-6: Determining Inside or Out by Counting Boundary Crossings

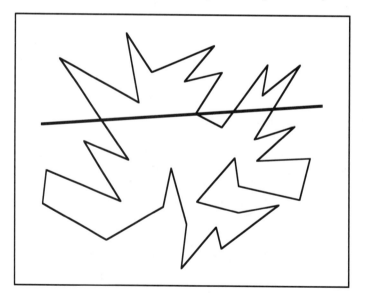

Sorting Coordinate Pairs

There are a number of sorting techniques—some of them very simple, but very lengthy if very many items are to be sorted, and others are more sophisticated and much shorter. The one that has been chosen for use here is the Shell Sort, named after its creator, Donald Shell. It is very simple to program, and is about as fast as you can get for the number of items to be sorted here. The Shell Sort function is listed in Figure 12-7.

Figure 12-7: Shell Sort Function

```
sort() = Performs a Shell sort, first on
         y[1][nnnn] and then on y[0][nnnn]
         within the y[1]'s.
```

```
void sort(int index, int y[2][4000][2])
{
    int d=4,i,j,k,temp;

    while (d<=index)
        d*=2;
    d-=1;
    while (d>1)
    {
        d/=2;
        for (j=0; j<=(index-d); j++)
        {
            for (i=j; i>=0; i-=d)
            {
                if ((y[i+d][1] < y[i][1]) ||
                    ((y[i+d][1] == y[i][1]) &&
                    (y[i+d][0] <= y[i][0])))
                {
                    temp = y[i][1];
                    y[i][1] = y[i+d][1];
                    y[i+d][1] = temp;
                    temp = y[i][0];
                    y[i][0] = y[i+d][0];
                    y[i+d][0] = temp;
                }
            }
        }
    }
```

```
      }
}
```

We are sorting an array of coordinates of two dimensions, such that y[0][nnnn] is the nnnnth x coordinate and y[1][nnnn] is the nnnnth y coordinate. We want to sort *index* of these coordinate pairs first in the order of their y coordinates, and then within a particular y value in the order of their x coordinates. Figure 12-8 shows how the Shell Sort technique works with some sample coordinates. It begins by partitioning the entire array to be sorted into very small partitions, essentially of two numbers each. The distance between numbers in a partition is maximum. Each pair is compared and swapped if necessary so that the smaller is in the leftmost of the two positions previously occupied by the two coordinates, and the larger is in the rightmost position. Since we are sorting first on the y coordinate and then on the x, we first test the y coordinate to see if a swap is necessary. Only if the two y's are equal do we make the further check on the two x's to determine whether to swap. Next, the partition size is doubled, so that each has four members. They are now positioned closer together. The tests and swaps are made for all members of the partition (shown connected by lines) and swaps occur so that the partition's positions in the array are filled with partition members in ascending order from left to right. This process continues until the partition size encompasses the entire array. Now all swaps necessary to get everything in final sorted order are made. Note, however, that by the last sort everything is nearly in correct position and only swaps of adjacent positions are necessary. The increase in speed using the Shell Sort comes about because, although it is inefficient in the number of tests that it must make, it is very effective in minimizing the number of swaps. Since a swap takes a lot more computer time than a test, the computer time is minimized.

Figure 12-8: Shell Sort Technique

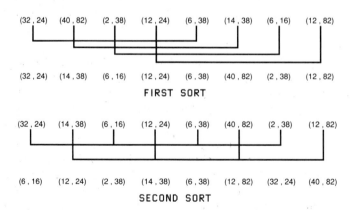

Figure 12-8 (continued)

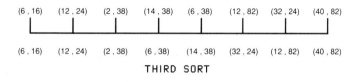

THIRD SORT

Filling a Polygon

Now that we know how to sort a list of coordinates, we are ready to attempt a function to fill a polygon. The final function is listed in Figure 12-9. This function makes use of the variable length argument list, and at the beginning will look familiar to you from the corresponding *drawPoly* function. However, at the point where we previously drew lines to connect up the vertices of the polygon, we now have some code that looks very much like the inner workings of the *drawLine* function (the version that does not include handling of line widths or styles) except that in addition to plotting each point on a line that is computed, the coordinates of the point are stored (whenever there is a change in the value of the *y* coordinate) in an array called (appropriately enough) *coordinates*. Another difference from *drawPoly* is that instead of drawing each line segment separately, the entire polygon is drawn as a single line. We continue looping through the point plotting part of the function, but when we reach one set of end points, we simply change the destination parameters and keep right on plotting points.

Figure 12-9: Function to Fill a Polygon Using Variable Argument List

```
fillPoly() = Fills a Polygon with Specified Color.
             Polygon vertices are xy coordinate sets
             given.  Last entry must be more
             negative than 320.
```

```
void fillPoly(int color,...)
{
    #include <stdarg.h>
    #define sign(x)  ((x)>0 ? 1: ((x) == 0 ? 0: (-1)))

    int dx, dy, dxabs, dyabs, i, index=0, j, k, px,
        py, sdx, sdy, x, y, xpoint[150], ypoint[150],
        toggle, old_sdy,sy0;
    long int check;
```

```c
int *x_coord, *y_coord;

va_list coord;

x_coord = (int *) malloc(4000 * sizeof(int));
y_coord = (int *) malloc(4000 * sizeof(int));
va_start(coord,color);
for (i=0; i<150; i++)
{
    xpoint[i] = va_arg(coord,int) + 319;
    ypoint[i] = 240 - va_arg(coord,int);
    if ((xpoint[i] < 0) || (ypoint[i] > 480))
        break;
}
va_end(coord);
xpoint[i] = xpoint[0];
ypoint[i] = ypoint[0];
if (i<3) return;
px = xpoint[0];
py = ypoint[0];
if (ypoint[1] == ypoint[0])
{
    x_coord[index] = px;
    y_coord[index++] = py;
}
for (j=0; j<i; j++)
{
    dx = xpoint[j+1] - xpoint[j];
    dy = ypoint[j+1] - ypoint[j];
    sdx = sign(dx);
    sdy = sign(dy);
    if (j==0)
    {
        old_sdy = sdy;
        sy0 = sdy;
    }
    dxabs = abs(dx);
    dyabs = abs(dy);
    x = 0;
    y = 0;
    if (dxabs >= dyabs)
    {
```

```
        for (k=0; k<dxabs; k++)
        {
            y += dyabs;
            if (y>=dxabs)
            {
                y -= dxabs;
                py += sdy;
                if (old_sdy != sdy)
                {
                    old_sdy = sdy;
                    index--;
                }
                x_coord[index] = px+sdx;
                y_coord[index++] = py;
            }
            px += sdx;
            pattern_plot(px,py,color);
        }
    }
    else
    {
        for (k=0; k<dyabs; k++)
        {
            x += dxabs;
            if (x>=dyabs)
            {
                x -= dyabs;
                px += sdx;
            }
            py += sdy;
            if (old_sdy != sdy)
            {
                old_sdy = sdy;
                if (sdy != 0)
                    index--;
            }
            pattern_plot(px,py,color);
            x_coord[index] = px;
            y_coord[index++] = py;
        }
    }
}
```

```
index--;
if (sy0 + sdy== 0)
    index--;
sort(index,x_coord,y_coord);
toggle = 0;
for (i=0; i<index; i++)
{
    if ((y_coord[i] == y_coord[i+1]) &&
        (toggle == 0))
    {
        for (j=x_coord[i]; j<=x_coord[i+1];
            j++)
            pattern_plot(j,y_coord[i],color);
        toggle = 1;
    }
    else
        toggle = 0;
}
free(x_coord);
free(y_coord);
}
```

From our previous discussion, it appeared that all we had to do after we had a set of ordered coordinates was count the number of times we crossed one of the lines, fill when that number was odd, and not fill when it was even. That works most of the time. The problems occur when we come to a place where the direction of the *y* coordinate changes. If there is a peak or valley where only a single value of the *y* occurs, the inside-outside algorithm becomes confused because the beginning and end of the filled area are actually the same point. For a peak, the function then will not shut off the fill and a line will be drawn from the apex all the way across the screen. (If other parts of the polygon occur on this row, but separated from this apex, the fills and not fills will all be backwards after the apex is encountered. Similarly, at the valley, the fill will be shut off, but not restarted, so that from then on areas to be filled will be blank and areas that should be blank will be filled. We attempt to cope with all of these situations by the way we collect coordinate sets for the *coordinates* array. We assume that critical line segment junction points only occur when the sign of the y coordinate changes. This means that we might have a problem with a single set of coordinates at a point. To avoid this, we reduce the array index by one when a sign change is encountered. This essentially writes the present set of coordinate values over the previous set, which represented the apex of the line segment junction. Effectively, this rounds off the point to something at least two pixels wide, and thus assures that there is no singularity. The only time that this fails to work is when a line segment doubles back on the previous one. You would be well advised not to let this happen. There are also problems when a horizontal line is drawn, in that we do not want to record a coordinate set for the *y* change of direction for this line when fill should continue beyond the line. In addition, some special precautions need to be taken to assure that the junction of the beginning and end of the polygon is treated properly. The net result of all this is a well-behaved set of coordinates, but not one which necessarily defines the very last pixel of the boundary line, particularly at the apexes. This is why we draw the outline of the polygon while we are collecting coordinates. This assures that the outline of the polygon is exactly as specified.

Now that we have a well behaved set of coordinates, we use the sort routine to sort them and then fill or not fill operations for each row based upon whether we have an odd or zero number of line crossings.

Note that we use the function *pattern_plot* to plot each point throughout the 'fillPoly' function. This function when driven by a color value between 0 and 15 (hex 0 to F) behaves just like the *plot* function. Through the use of other values for *color*, it can be made to do shading in two colors. Shading is discussed in detail in Chapter 19. The full description of the *pattern_plot* function will be found in that chapter.

Coping with a Large Array

In developing the function described above, we encounter another problem. Within the function, we need a large array: one capable of handling all of the co-ordinates for the beginning and ending of each line that we are going to draw across the polygon. With Turbo C, this is no problem. We can simply define the array within the function; Turbo C will make this array a part of the stack, and will dispense it when the function is terminated. Since Turbo C dynamically allocates stack space as required, everything will work just fine. Unfortunately, Microsoft C by default assigns a size of 2K bytes to the stack. Our array of 4000 integers for *x_coord* and 4000 more for *y_coord* will cause the compiler to fail with a "stack overflow" message. We can either assign a much larger stack size when we compile any program using this function, or else we need to use some other way of handling the large array. We can do this by defining the addresses of the start of each array with the statement:

```
int *x_coord, *y_coord;
```

We then include at the beginning of the program the statements:

```
x_coord = (int *) malloc(4000 * sizeof(int));
y_coord = (int *) malloc(4000 * sizeof(int));
```

The C function *malloc* is a standard function that assigns a memory space. It takes one parameter; the size of the memory space assigned. So the two statements above assign space for 4000 integers for each array, with the beginnings at the start of *x_coord* and *y_coord*. At the end of this function, we need to use a *free* function to release the memory for each of these arrays; otherwise it becomes lost to program use forever.

Filling a Polygon Using a Coordinate Array

The same problems that occur with the *drawPoly* function when two many sets of coordinates are used can also occur with the *fillPoly* function. Therefore another form of the function has been prepared which uses a coordinate array. It is similar to the previous function in the same way that *draw2Poly* is similar to *drawPoly*. This function is listed in Figure 12-10.

Figure 12-10: Function to Fill a Polygon Using an Array of Coordinates

```
fillPoly() = Fills a Polygon with Specified Color.
             Polygon vertices are xy coordinate sets
             given.  Last entry must be more
             negative than -320.
```

```
void fill2Poly(int color,int point[600])
{
    #define sign(x)  ((x)>0 ? 1: ((x) == 0 ? 0: (-1)))

    int dx, dy, dxabs, dyabs, i, index=0, j, k, px, py,
    sdx, sdy, x, y, toggle, old_sdy, sy0;
    int dx, dy, dxabs, dyabs, i, index=0, j, k, px, py,
    sdx, sdy, x, y, toggle, old_sdy, sy0;
    int *x_coord, *y_coord;
    x_coord = (int *) malloc(4000 * sizeof(int));
    y_coord = (int *) malloc(4000 * sizeof(int));
    for (i=0; i<=600; i++)
    if (point[i] < -320)
        break;
```

```
point[i] = point[0];
point[i+1] = point[1];
if (i<=5) return;
px = point[0];
py = point[1];
if (point[1] == point[3])
{
    x_coord[index] = px;
    y_coord[index++] = py;
}
for (j=0; j<i-2; j+=2)
{
    dx = point[j+2] - point[j];
    dy = point[j+3] - point[j+1];
    sdx = sign(dx);
    sdy = sign(dy);
    if (j==0)
    {
        old_sdy = sdy;
        sy0 = sdy;
    }
    dxabs = abs(dx);
    dyabs = abs(dy);
    x = 0;
    y = 0;
    if (dxabs >= dyabs)
    {
        for (k=0; k<dxabs; k++)
        {
            y += dyabs;
            if (y>=dxabs)
            {
                y -= dxabs;
                py += sdy;
                if (old_sdy != sdy)
                {
                    old_sdy = sdy;
                    index--;
                }
                x_coord[index] = px+sdx;
                y_coord[index++] = py;
            }
```

```
                    px += sdx;
                    plots(px,py,color);
                }
            }
            else
            {
                for (k=0; k<dyabs; k++)
                {
                    x += dxabs;
                    if (x>=dyabs)
                    {
                        x -= dyabs;
                        px += sdx;
                    }
                    py += sdy;
                    if (old_sdy != sdy)
                    {
                        old_sdy = sdy;
                        if (sdy != 0)
                            index--;
                    }
                    plots(px,py,color);
                    x_coord[index] = px;
                    y_coord[index] = py;
                    index++;
                }
            }
        }
        index--;
        if (sy0 + sdy == 0)
            index--;
        sort(index,x_coord,y_coord);
        toggle = 0;
        for (i=0; i<index; i++)
        {
            if ((y_coord[i] == y_coord[i+1]) &&
                (toggle == 0))
            {
                for (j=x_coord[i]; j<=x_coord[i+1];
                    j++)
                    plots(j,y_coord[i],color);
```

13

Drawing Bezier
and B-Spline Curves

If you want to draw a pleasing curved line, you can always create it from a large number of small line segments connected together. Each line segment can be drawn with the *drawLine* function. But specifying each tiny segment is a drag, and it's sometimes difficult to get the line to look like a free flowing curve instead of patched together segments. Two techniques are available for creating such curves after specifying only a few points. The Bezier curve connects two end points and has its curving portion determined by a number of control points. While all of the control points influence every portion of the Bezier curve, the B-spline curve is influenced only by the four points nearest to the present location on the curve. The blending function for the B-spline curve also sharpens up the influence of the nearest control point more than does the Bezier curve. The result is that the Bezier curve provides a very free-flowing curve between two points, while the B-spline curve provides a smoothed curve that follows closer to the irregular line drawn between the control points.

The Bezier Curve

The Bezier curve was first developed by the French mathematician Pierre Bezier (pronounced "bay-zee-AY") in the early 1970s for use in the automated design of automobiles by Renault. The equations for the curve can be expressed in two different ways: as a closed-form summation and in matrix form. The summation form is:

$$P(u) = \sum_{i=0}^{n} p_i B_{i,n}(u) \qquad (Eq.\ 13\text{-}1)$$

This says that the location of any particular point is the sum of the product of each control point and the blending function. The blending function is:

$$B_{i,n}(u) = C(n,i) \ u; \ (1 - u)^{n-1} \qquad \text{(Eq. 13-2)}$$

where C is the binomial coefficient:

$$C(n,i) = n!/(i!(n-i)!) \qquad \text{(Eq. 13-3)}$$

For a Bezier curve having four control points, the matrix form of this expression is:

$$P(u) = [t^3 \quad t^2 \quad t \quad 1] \ B \begin{bmatrix} p_1 \\ p_2 \\ p_3 \\ p_4 \end{bmatrix} \qquad \text{(Eq. 13-4)}$$

where

$$B = \begin{bmatrix} -1 & 3 & -3 & 1 \\ 3 & -6 & 3 & 0 \\ -3 & 3 & 0 & 0 \\ 1 & 0 & 0 & 0 \end{bmatrix} \qquad \text{(Eq. 13-5)}$$

The mathematics of equations 13-1 through 13-3 can be elegantly and compactly expressed in C. Figure 13-1 lists the function to draw Bezier curves with any reasonable number of control points. By having the end point of one Bezier curve common with the beginning control point of a second Bezier curve, you can combine two curves into a single one. By connecting all of the control points together with straight lines, one generates what is called the "convex hull" for a particular Bezier curve.

Figure 13-1: Function to Draw a Bezier Curve

```
                drawBezier() = draws a Bezier curve
```

```
void drawBezier(int segments, int color,...)
{
    #include <stdarg.h>

    float blend(int i, int n, float u);

    va_list coord;
    int xpoint[20],ypoint[20],i=0,j,oldx,oldy,
        px,py,last;
    float b,u,x,y;

    va_start(coord,color);
    while (((xpoint[i]=va_arg(coord,int)) >= -320)
        && ((ypoint[i]=va_arg(coord,int)) >= -320)
        && (i<=20))
        i++;
    va_end(coord);
    last = (i-1);
    for (i=0; i<=segments; i++)
    {
        u = (float)i/segments;
        x = 0;
        y = 0;
        for (j=0; j<=last; j++)
        {
            b = blend (j,last,u);
            x += xpoint[j]*b;
            y += ypoint[j]*b;
        }
        px = x;
        py = y;
        if (i>0)
            drawLine(oldx,oldy,x,y,color);
            oldx = x;
            oldy = y;
    }
}
```

```
float blend(int i, int n, float u)
{
    int c,j,k=1,g=1;
    float f;

    for (c=n; c>i; c--)
    k *= c;
    for (c=n-i; c>1; c--)
        g *= c;
    f = (float)k/g;
    for (j=1; j<=i; j++)
        f *= u;
    for (j=1; j<=n-i; j++)
        f *= (1-u);
    return (f);
}
```

Usually, if the convex hull is a closed polygon, the entire Bezier curve lies within it. Figure 13-2 and Figure 13-3 show the convex hulls and resulting Bezier curves for a single curve and two joined curves, respectively.

Figure 13-2: Bezier Curve

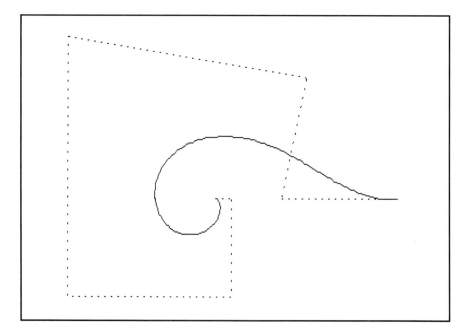

Figure 13-3: Two Bezier Curves

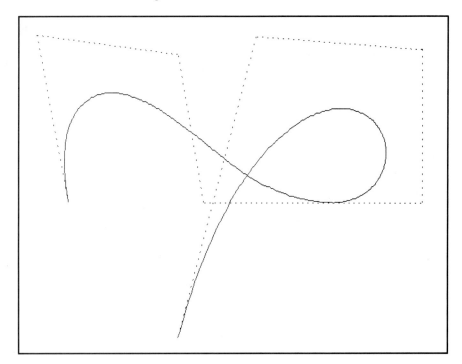

The B-Spline Curve

There is a whole family of B-spline curves, depending upon how many control points are allowed to influence the curve at any given time. The equation in matrix form for the B-Spline curve in which four control points exert influence at any one time is:

$$P(u) = [t^3 \quad t^2 \quad t \quad 1] \, B \begin{bmatrix} p_{i-1} \\ p_i \\ p_{i+1} \\ p_{i+2} \end{bmatrix} \qquad (Eq. \ 13\text{-}6)$$

where

$$B = \begin{bmatrix} -1 & 3 & -3 & 1 \\ 3 & -6 & 3 & 0 \\ -3 & 0 & 3 & 0 \\ 1 & 4 & 1 & 0 \end{bmatrix} \qquad (Eq.\ 13\text{-}7)$$

Figure 13-4 lists a function to draw this type of B-Spline curve. The result of computing a B-Spline curve is shown in Figure 13-5 together with a graph of the connected control points (see color section).

Figure 13-4: Function to Draw a B-Spline Curve

drawBspline() = draws a B-Spline curve

```
{
    #include <stdarg.h>
    va_list coord;
    int xpoint[20],ypoint[20],i=1,j,x,y,oldx,oldy,
        last;
    float u,nc1,nc2,nc3,nc4;

    va_start(coord,color);
    while (((xpoint[i]=va_arg(coord,int)) >= -320)
        && ((ypoint[i]=va_arg(coord,int)) >= -320)
        && (i<=20))
        i++;
    va_end(coord);
    xpoint[0]=xpoint[1];
    ypoint[0]=ypoint[1];
    oldx=xpoint[0];
    oldy=ypoint[0];
    for (j=i; j<=i+1; j++)
    {
        xpoint[j]=xpoint[j-1];
        ypoint[j]=ypoint[j-1];
    }
    last = j;
    for(i=1; i<=last-3; i++)
    {
        for (u=0; u<=1; u+=1.0/segments)
```

```
{
    nc1=-(u*u*u/6)+u*u/2-u/2+1.0/6;
    nc2=u*u*u/2-u*u+2.0/3;
    nc3=(-u*u*u+u*u+u)/2+1.0/6;
    nc4=u*u*u/6;
    x = (nc1*xpoint[i-1]+nc2*xpoint[i]+
        nc3*xpoint[i+1] +nc4*xpoint[i+2]);
    y = (nc1*ypoint[i-1]+nc2*ypoint[i]+
        nc3*ypoint[i+1]+nc4*ypoint[i+2]);
    drawLine(oldx,oldy,x,y,color);
    oldx=x;
    oldy=y;
  }
 }
}
```

14

Translation and Rotation

One of the areas where the computer really excels is in the simple but manually tedious mathematics needed to translate graphics figures from one part of the screen to another, or to rotate entire figures around a predetermined axis. Nevertheless, we are embarking on an area which offers dangers and requires careful thought and investigation. Although the mathematics is simple, it can become highly repetitive in some situations, and, especially where floating point arithmetic is used without a math coprocessor, the additional time can objectionably slow down graphics routines. Furthermore, we are in that gray area where it is hard to decide whether the functions required should be a part of our graphics tools collection or should be tailored for particular application programs. We shall discuss the problems involved and offer up some tools in the remainder of this chapter.

Translation

Translation simply means moving a graphics figure to a different part of the screen, without altering its shape or orientation. It is simply accomplished; all that is needed is to add or subtract a fixed amount from the x coordinate and a different fixed amount from the y coordinate of each point to be plotted. This is a last resort, however. Translating the end points of a line, for example, is all the extra computation you need to do, and the plotting of all points on the line can be done as fast as if the line were not translated. In general, if translation is all you want to do, you can do it at the input to any of the figures for which functions have been developed, and the reduction in speed will be negligible.

If you want to keep the same orientation that a figure originally had, but change the position and size of the figure, the problem becomes a little more complex. You probably need to perform a multiplication and division for scaling in addition to the translation function. If this can be done at the higher level of circles, rectangles, etc., the additional overhead is negligible, even if you have to use floating point arithmetic. If you have to do it at the *drawLine* level, especially where many lines are being drawn in a fill operation, the overhead may be objectionable. In such cases, it is important to perform your operations in integer arithmetic and to avoid division at all costs. The way to do this is to select a fractional ratio for your scaling that has a denominator with a power of two. Then, the multiplication by the numerator can be performed normally and the division can be accomplished by shifting the product the appropriate number of places to the right—a very fast operation. You need to be careful in choosing the numerator not to exceed the bounds of signed integer arithmetic. Integers can be within the range of -32768 to +32767. If you note that our "System Coordinates" will never exceed ±320 in magnitude, you can see that we can have multipliers of up to 102 without difficulty.

Rotation

Figure 14-1 shows the mathematics involved in rotating a point from one set of axes to another in two dimensions, when the center of the coordinate system remains at the same position. If we want to apply this to our graphics activities, we need to decide whether we will let the center of the coordinate system be at point (0,0) of our system coordinates, or whether we should select some other point about which to rotate. We then have to decide what level to do our rotations at for each figure or shape that we are interested in. Several examples are given in the sections that follow; the resulting rotate functions are included in the *gdraws* library, and examples of their use are shown in the demonstration program. These do not exhaust the possibilities; rather, they are examples to show you some of the decisions that were made so that you can develop your own rotation functions.

Figure 14-1: Establishing Rotation Formulas

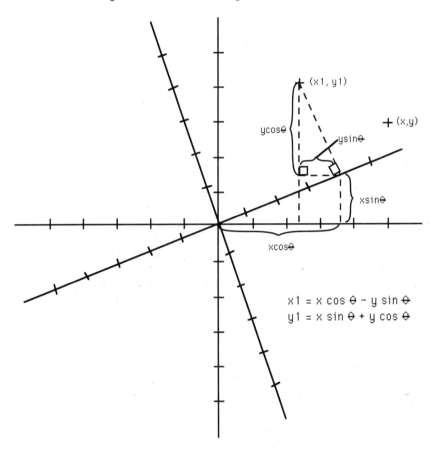

$$x1 = x \cos \theta - y \sin \theta$$
$$y1 = x \sin \theta + y \cos \theta$$

Rotating a Rectangle

Figure 14-2 lists a function to rotate a rectangle. It was decided to create a pair of global variables, XCENTER and YCENTER, which are set for the system coordinates of the point about which we wish to rotate the rectangle. This can be the center of the rectangle or any other arbitrary point. The rectangle consists of four lines, connecting four vertices. We first compute the positions of each of these vertices after the rotation takes place, and then draw lines between the new vertices. Note that for this calculation, we assume a coordinate system of XCENTER and YCENTER for the rotation, and then move the center of the coordinate system back to (0,0) of the system coordinates after the rotation has taken place.

233

Figure 14-3 shows the results of rotating a rectangle through 180 degrees in 15 degree steps (see color section).

Figure 14-2: Function to Rotate a Rectangle

```
rotateRect() = draws a rectangle rotated from its
               normal position by an angle 'ANGLE'
               in degrees around (XCENTER, YCENTER)
```

```c
void rotateRect(int x1, int y1, int x2, int y2,
    int color)
{
    int nx1,nx2,nx3,nx4,ny1,ny2,ny3,ny4;
    float angle;

    angle = .01745329*(360 - ANGLE);
    nx1 = (x1 - XCENTER)*cos(angle) -
        (y1 - YCENTER)*sin(angle) + XCENTER;
    ny1 = (x1 - XCENTER)*sin(angle) +
        (y1 - YCENTER)*cos(angle) + YCENTER;
    nx3 = (x2 - XCENTER)*cos(angle) -
        (y2 - YCENTER)*sin(angle) + XCENTER;
    ny3 = (x2 - XCENTER)*sin(angle) +
        (y2 - YCENTER)*cos(angle) + YCENTER;
    nx2 = (x2 - XCENTER)*cos(angle) -
        (y1 - YCENTER)*sin(angle) + XCENTER;
    ny2 = (x2 - XCENTER)*sin(angle) +
        (y1 - YCENTER)*cos(angle) + YCENTER;
    nx4 = (x1 - XCENTER)*cos(angle) -
        (y2 - YCENTER)*sin(angle) + XCENTER;
    ny4 = (x1 - XCENTER)*sin(angle) +
        (y2 - YCENTER)*cos(angle) + YCENTER;

    drawLine(nx1-LINEWIDTH/2,ny1,nx2+LINEWIDTH/2,
        ny2,color);
    drawLine(nx2-LINEWIDTH/2,ny2,nx3+LINEWIDTH/2,
        ny3,color);
    drawLine(nx3,ny3+LINEWIDTH/2,nx4,ny4-
        LINEWIDTH/2,color);
    drawLine(nx4,ny4+LINEWIDTH/2,nx1,ny1-
        LINEWIDTH/2,color);
}
```

Rotating a Polygon

Figure 14-4 is a listing of a function to rotate polygons. The function is very similar to the *drawPoly* function and uses the va_arg functions to pass a variable parameter list as did the *drawPoly* function. We use the same technique as in the *rotateRect* function to rotate the beginning and end points of each line segment before drawing it with the *drawLine* function. As in the *rotateRect* function, the rotation takes place around an arbitrarily selected point (XCENTER,YCENTER). Figure 14-5 shows the display generated by rotating a triangle through 360 degrees in 15 degree increments (see color section).

Figure 14-4: Function to Rotate a Polygon

```
rotatePoly() = draws a polygon rotated from its
               normal position by an angle 'ANGLE'
               in degrees around (XCENTER, YCENTER)
```

```
extern int ANGLE,XCENTER,YCENTER;

void rotatePoly(int color,...)
{
    #include <stdarg.h>
    va_list coord;
    int point[600],i=0,j,x1,y1,x2,y2;
    float angle,param;

    va_start(coord,color);
    angle = .01745329*(360 - ANGLE);
    while (((point[i]=va_arg(coord,int)) >= -320)
        && (i<=600))
        i++;
    va_end(coord);
    point[i++] = point[0];
    point[i] = point[1];
    if (i<=5) return;
    for (j=0; j<i-2; j+=2)
    {
        x1 = (point[j] - XCENTER)*cos(angle) -
            (point[j+1] - YCENTER)*sin(angle) +
            XCENTER;
        y1 = (point[j] - XCENTER)*sin(angle) +
            (point[j+1] - YCENTER)*cos(angle) +
```

```
            YCENTER;
    x2 = (point[j+2] - XCENTER)*cos(angle) -
         (point[j+3] - YCENTER)*sin(angle) +
            XCENTER;
    y2 = (point[j+2] - XCENTER)*sin(angle) +
         (point[j+3] - YCENTER)*cos(angle) +
            YCENTER;
    drawLine(x1,y1,x2,y2,color);
  }
}
```

Rotating an Oval

From looking at the two functions described above, you might get the impression that a similar technique could be used with an oval to draw a rotated one by simply rotating the x and y center coordinates and the radius in some manner. Two things prevent this. First, the aspect ratio for any oval is defined in terms of the x and y axes. Any rotation implies a complex technique for determining the translation from one radius to the other. Second, the oval drawing functions use mirroring to plot four quadrants of the circle or oval at the same time, using a single set of calculations. The symmetry gets a lot more complicated in reference to the x and y axes after rotation occurs, making the mirroring technique difficult or impossible. If you wanted to tackle a fast technique for drawing rotated ovals, you might solve the equation for a rotated oval in terms of the original coordinate system and compute some new decision variables for Bresenham's algorithm that apply to this new equation.

The approach that was used here is simpler. First, it was assumed that the oval would only be rotated around its center and not around any arbitrary center point. Second, rotation takes place at the point-plotting level, where the coordinates of each point are rotated before plotting. Although the sine and cosine functions need only be solved once for the entire oval, there are still floating point multiplications required for each point to be plotted, which slows the routine considerably. It is probably worthwhile to multiply the sine and cosine functions by 1024 and then store them as long integers. Then all of the rotation multiplications could be performed in integer arithmetic followed by a shift right of 10 bit positions to obtain the proper answer in integer form. Figure 14-6 lists the resulting function to rotate ovals. An example of an oval rotated through 180 degrees in 15 degree increments is shown in Figure 14-7 (see color section).

Figure 14-6: Function to Rotate an Oval

```
rotateOval() = draws an oval centered at (xc,yc),
               with radius 'b' and aspect ratio
               around its center by 'ANGLE' degrees
```

```
void rotateOval(int x, int y, int b, int color,
    float aspect)
{
    int col, i, row,px,py;
    float aspect_square;
    long a_square, b_square, two_a_square,
        two_b_square, four_a_square, four_b_square,d;
    float angle,ca,sa;

    angle = .01745329*(360 - ANGLE);
    sa=sin(angle);
    ca=cos(angle);

    aspect_square = aspect*aspect;
    b -= LINEWIDTH/2;
    for (i=1; i<=LINEWIDTH; i++)
    {
        b_square = b*b;
        a_square = b_square/aspect_square;
        row = b;
        col = 0;
        two_a_square = a_square << 1;
        four_a_square = a_square << 2;
        four_b_square = b_square << 2;
        two_b_square = b_square << 1;
        d = two_a_square * ((row  -1)*(row )) +
            a_square + two_b_square*(1-a_square);
        while (a_square*(row ) > b_square * (col))
        {
            px = x + col*ca - (row)*sa;
            py = y + col*sa + row*ca;
            plots(px,py,color);
            px = x + col*ca + row*sa;
            py = y + col*sa - row*ca;
            plots(px,py,color);
            px = x - col*ca - row*sa;
```

```
            py = y - col*sa + row*ca;
            plots(px,py,color);
            px = x - col*ca + row*sa;
            py = y - col*sa - row*ca;
            plots(px,py,color);
            if (d>= 0)
            {
                row--;
                d -= four_a_square*(row);
            }
            d += two_b_square*(3 + (col << 1));
            col++;
        }

        d = two_b_square * (col + 1)*col +
            two_a_square*(row * (row  -2) +1) +
            (1-two_a_square)*b_square;
        while ((row) + 1)
        {
            px = x+ col*ca - (row)*sa;
            py = y + col*sa + row*ca;
            plots(px,py,color);
            px = x + col*ca + row*sa;
            py = y + col*sa - row*ca;
            plots(px,py,color);
            px = x - col*ca - row*sa;
            py = y - col*sa + row*ca;
            plots(px,py,color);
            px = x - col*ca + row*sa;
            py = y - col*sa - row*ca;
            plots(px,py,color);
            if (d<= 0)
            {
                col++;
                d += four_b_square*col;
            }
            row--;
            d += two_a_square * (3 - (row <<1));
        }
        b++;
    }
}
```

15

Generating Graphics Cursors

In the EGA and CGA graphics modes, the cursor does not appear on the graphic display. In VGA graphics modes, a ROM BIOS video service exists which can write a graphics cursor; if it is not activated, then the cursor does not appear on these graphics displays. However, for all of these displays the cursor position is stored and can be changed just as if it actually were displayed. When writing text characters to any of these graphics displays, the position of the non-existent cursor is used to mark the beginning of the text. There are many cases where we want to identify a position on the graphics screen, and in fact, we may wish to do so with greater precision than is available with the normal cursor identifying location. For text characters, it is perfectly satisfactory to identify a character location, but in a graphics display, it may often be desirable to identify a precise point on the screen down to the actual pixel row and column. To do this, it is necessary to identify our own cursor with a routine that does not make use of the ROM BIOS video services. Let's consider what we would like such a routine to contain.

First, we need a pair of global variables that contain the cursor x and y pixel positions. As the cursor moves around the screen, these variables will be changed to indicate the cursor position. Then, when the program exits from the cursor moving routine, the position data can be used to take any kind of action that depends upon selecting a particular screen position.

The second requirement is that the cursor have higher resolution than the text cursor. We would like to have a point or crosshair or some similar indicator for cursor so that an exact pixel location can be identified. We would like to be able to move the cursor pixel by pixel for high accuracy, but since this kind of accuracy really slows the movement of the cursor across the screen, we want to have a faster and coarser movement as an alternative. Finally, we would like to have at least a couple different shapes for the cursor.

Figure 15-1 lists a cursor function that will provide all of these capabilities. This function provides two cursor shapes, an arrow and a cross. The cursor function passes a parameter which selects the cursor type. If the type is *0*, the arrow is selected; if it is *1*, the cross is selected. The cursor is displayed as a pattern of pixels on a 16 by 16 matrix. Each of the two matrices for the two cursor shapes consists of 16 unsigned integers, each containing 16 bits. Each integer of the matrix represents the bit pattern for a cursor row; the 16 integers of the matrix make up the 16 rows of the cursor.

Figure 15-1: Function to Generate and Move Cursor

```
move_cursor() = draws a cursor on the screen and
                moves it based upon user keyboard
                inputs
```

```c
void move_cursor(int type,int color)
{
    int i,j,k,xoff=0,yoff=0,ch,fast = 1, temp;
    unsigned int mask, cursor_pattern[2][16] =
        {0x8000,0xC000,0xE000,0xF000,0xF800,0xFC00,
        0xFE00,0xFF00,0xF800,0xD800,0x8C00,0x0C00,
        0x0600,0x0600,0x00,0x00,0x0100,0x0100,0x0100,
        0x0100,0x0100,0x7FFC,0x0100,0x0100,0x0100,
        0x0100,0x0100,0x0100};
    char far *base;

    if (type == 1)
    {
        xoff = -8;
        yoff = -6;
    }
    temp = OPERATOR;
    OPERATOR = 0x18;
    do
    {
        for (i=0; i<16; i++)
            {
                for (j=0; j<16; j++)
                    {
```

```
            mask = 0x8000 >> j;
            if ((mask & cursor_pattern
                [type][i]) != 0)
            plot(CURSOR_X+j+xoff+319,
                175 - ((CURSOR_Y*93 >> 7) +i
                + yoff, color);
        }
    }
ch = getch();
if (ch == 0)
    ch = getch() + 256;
for (i=0; i<16; i++)
{
    for (j=0; j<16; j++)
    {
        mask = 0x8000 >> j;
        if ((mask & cursor_pattern
            [type][i]) != 0)
        plot(CURSOR_X+j+xoff+319,
            175 - ((CURSOR_Y*93 >> 7) +i
            + yoff, color);
    }
}
switch(ch)
{
    case 27:
        fast = (++fast) % 2;
        break;
    case 333:
        if ((CURSOR_X < 303) &&
            (fast == 0))
            CURSOR_X++;
        if ((CURSOR_Xf < 294) &&
            (fast == 1))
            CURSOR_X += 10;
            break;
    case 331:
        if ((CURSOR_X > -318) &&
            (fast == 0))
            CURSOR_X--;
        if ((CURSOR_X > -309) &&
            (fast == 1))
```

```
                         CURSOR_X -= 10;
                         break;
                case 336:
                     if ((CURSOR_Y > -223 &&
                         (fast == 0))
                         CURSOR_Y--;
                     if ((CURSOR_Y > -214 &&
                         (fast == 1))
                         CURSOR_Y -= 10;
                         break;
                case 328:
                     if ((CURSOR_Y < 239) &&
                         (fast == 0))
                         CURSOR_Y++;
                     if ((CURSOR_Y < 230) &&
                         (fast == 1))
                         CURSOR_Y _+= 10;
                         break;
                }
            }
            while (ch != 0x0D);
        }
        OPERATOR = temp;
    }
}
```

Figures 15-2 and 15-3 show the cursor shapes provided by the two matrices. It is a simple matter to add as many more cursor shapes as you can think up—the only restriction being that they fit into the 16 by 16 matrix. The function must also take into consideration the fact that the cursor centering point of the cursor may be different for different shaped cursors. This is corrected for by two variables, *xoff* and *yoff*. For the arrow cursor, these offsets are both zero, and the reference point of the cursor is the top left corner of the matrix. For the crosshair cursor, the offsets are -8 in x and -6 in y, resulting in the center of the crosshairs being the reference point. The current reference point for the cursor is recorded in the global variables CURSOR_X and CURSOR_Y. After setting the offsets, the function enters a *do* loop in which it writes cursors and accepts keystroke inputs until a carriage return is entered. When the carriage return is encountered (the user hits the *Enter* key), the loop terminates and the function is complete. We would like to have the cursor movement relatively independent of the type of graphics adapter and monitor being used by the system. On the other hand, when we generate the cursor, we want to take advantage of every pixel of resolution on the screen display. Therefore the cursor position is stored in system coordinates, but the actual drawing of the cursor pattern is done in a matrix of screen pixel coordinates.

The resulting function is almost independent of which graphics adapter is being used. However, for resolution displays lower than the EGA or VGA high resolution modes for which these cursors were specifically designed, the cursor matrix may be too large or the cursor shape may be displeasing, in which case you will need to do some modification. Such modifications should be easy, once you take a close look at the code and understand how the function is implemented.

One of the main problems with a cursor function is restoring the original display when the cursor moves to a new position. Particularly for the EGA and VGA, there is no really fast way to send the 16x16 array representing the display area being replaced by the cursor to storage somewhere and then to recover it and send it back to the screen when the cursor moves to its next position. The practical limit here is that if we hold down one of the cursor arrow keys, we want the cursor to move across the screen as fast as keystrokes are being transmitted to the computer. What we don't want is for the cursor to keep moving for several seconds after the key is released before it catches up with the entered keystrokes and reaches the correct position. Techniques that read each pixel into an array and then write each pixel from that array back to the display when the cursor is moved are just not fast enough to meet this requirement. There is a technique that quite effectively solves this problem. We simply write the cursor to the screen using the XOR operator. Then, when the cursor is moved, we write the cursor first to the same position that it currently occupies. Two XORs in succession restore the data to its original condition, just as if the cursor were erased. Then we write the cursor to its new position and are ready for the next position command.

The disadvantage of this is that we don't have complete control of the cursor color with the XOR technique. For example, if we write a white cursor (color 0FH) to a blue (color 01H) screen, the result of the XOR will be color 0EH, which is yellow. You can also note that if the cursor passes across some different colors, it will contain a multicolored image that changes with the underlying color. This is not a serious drawback, however. The cursor is always highly visible, and we are mainly interested in it for positioning, not for its intrinsic beauty.

Figure 15-2: Arrow Cursor Pattern

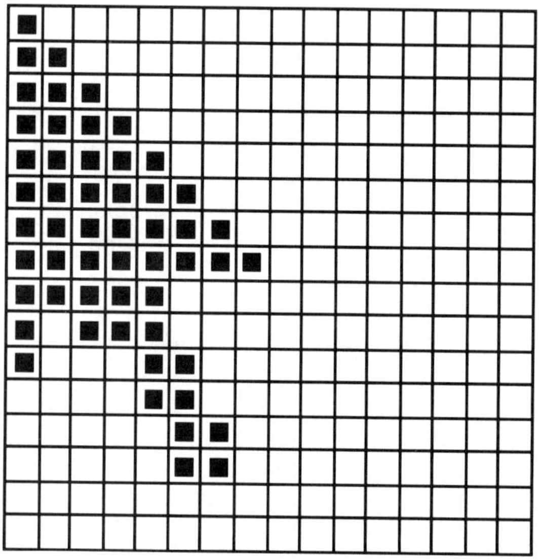

Figure 15-3: Crosshair Cursor Pattern

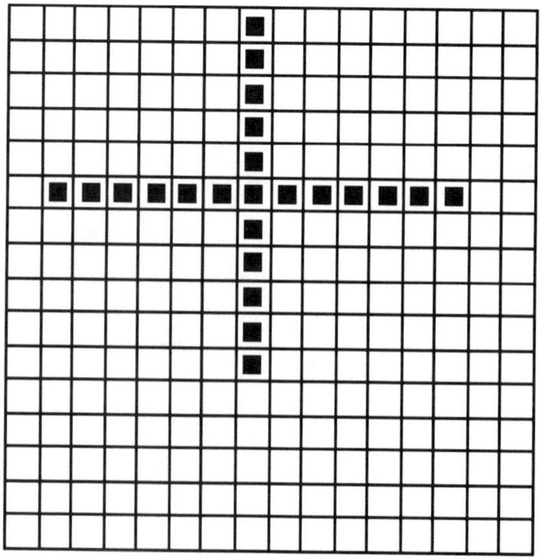

We write the cursor by starting at the upper left corner and scanning through each pixel positon in the 16x16 matrix. For each of the 16 lines which comprise the cursor, we have a rotating mask that extracts first the most significant bit of the character shape integer for that line, then the bit for the next pixel position, and so forth. If the character shape bit in that position is a *one*, we write a pixel to the screen at that pixel column. This occurs for each of the 16 character shape integers that correspond to the 16 lines of the cursor character.

The function now begins looking for character inputs from the keyboard using the *getch* function. Many of the special keys of the IBM PC keyboard are codes with two character inputs, the first being *00H* and the second some number that is the same as one of the ASCII character codes. To avoid ambiguities, if a zero is read from the keyboard, we read another input immediately and add 256 to it to obtain a unique number. Using this technique, the right arrow becomes 333, the left arrow is 331, the down arrow is 336 and the up arrow is 328. In addition to the carriage return, the function recognizes only these four arrow keys and the *escape* key. The *escape* key toggles between the default mode, in which each time an arrow key is hit, the cursor moves ten pixel units in the direction of the arrow, and a mode in which each time the arrow is hit, the cursor moves only one pixel in the arrow direction. Thus, hitting *ESC* changes from fast to slow cursor movement and then back again. Cases are set up in the function to check and make sure that moving the specified amount will not cause the cursor to exceed the bounds of the display; if the bounds are not exceeded, the CURSOR_X and CURSOR_Y variables are updated to show the new position and the cursor is moved accordingly. If the new value would pass the edge of the display, the arrow key is ignored and the cursor remains at its current position.

Note that the cursor writing action works in the following way. At the beginning of the *do* loop, the cursor is written to the screen. Next a character is read from the keyboard, and the cursor is written to the screen again. This erases the cursor from its present position. The keys are checked to see what action should occur. Then the cursor positon variables are updated and the loop is gone through again, beginning with the writing of a new cursor to the screen, if the key that was struck was not the *Ent* key. It is important to observe what happens if you hit a key other than one of those specifically recognized by the *move_cursor* function. When the *getch* routine transfers the keyboard input to the function, the cursor is erased; since the key is unrecognized, the cursor coordinates are unchanged, and another pass through the loop rewrites the cursor to the same position that it was originally in. This function establishes limits on cursor motion that are expressed in system coordinates, so it works equally well with any graphics adapter card and monitor.

16

Using Text in
Graphics Displays

The simplest way to write text to the screen is by means of ROM BIOS video service number 9. This service writes characters to the screen with any specified foreground color and with the current background color. As in many cases, using the ROM BIOS video service has some drawbacks. The sections that follow will discuss these and offer some alternative solutions.

Writing a Character to the Screen

The function listed in Figure 16-1 is the principal tool used to write text to the screen. Parameters passed by this function are the character to be written, the attribute of the character, and the page to which the character will be written. The function writes the character at the current cursor location. The function does not advance the cursor. This is the programmer's responsibility before writing another character. The characteristics of the attribute byte are given in Figure 5-10. Note that only the foreground color of the character may be specified; the character will be written with the current background color, and also at the current cursor location.

Figure 16-1: Function to Write a Character to the Screen
Using ROM BIOS Video Services

```
       writChar = Writes a Character to the Screen
                  with Specified Attribute
```

```
void writChar(char ch, int color, int page)
{
```

```
        reg.h.ah = 9;
        reg.h.al = ch;
        reg.h.bl = color;
        reg.h.bh = page;
        reg.x.cx = 1;
        int86 (0x10,&reg,&reg);
}
```

There are several limitations in the use of the function just described. The first, and perhaps most important of these, is that the background color of the character cannot be specified, but must be the background color that has been defined for the whole display. Suppose that we want to have a menu in which the items are all in the same foreground color, but the background color of the selected menu item is to be of a contrasting color. This is simply done using ROM BIOS video service number 9 in the text mode, but the same thing is impossible in the graphics mode.

Another case in which this lack of control is annoying is when a screen or window has been filled with some specified color. This may now appear as if it were a background color, but as each character is written to the screen, it will have the default background color, which is probably different from the color that was used to fill in the window. For graphics purposes, another drawback of the above function is that it is limited to the character positions. The screen, for text purposes, is defined as 25 lines of 80 characters (in the high resolution modes). A character must be exactly in one of these positions.

If you are using text to specify dimensions or labels for geometric shapes, the position that you want the text to be in may be a fraction of the character position. The EGA high resolution graphics screen has a resolution of 640x350 pixels and the VGA high resolution graphics has a resolution of 640x480 pixels; it would be nice if any one of these pixel locations could be specified as the corner of a character box. Finally, when doing graphics, it is often desirable to write characters vertically on the screen. There is no ROM BIOS method for doing this.

Generic Character Plotting Routine

Figure 16-2 is a generic routine for plotting horizontal and vertical characters in normal and large sizes. Basically, this function lays out an 8x14 array on the screen and then selects the image of the designated character from a character table. Each character in the table is represented by 14 eight-bit bytes. The function plots a pixel on the screen in the foreground color for each *one* in the character matrix, and a pixel in the background color for each bit that is *zero*.

The ROM BIOS and/or graphics adapter board may have a character table already built-in, but it is not always easy to identify the location in such a way that the software is portable from one machine to another. Therefore, these routines make use of a character table that is included in an array of 1302 characters. The character table is part of the global variables that are stored in the *chars.h* header file, which can be found in Appendix C. Appendix C also includes an 8x8 pixel character table for CGA graphics modes.

Each byte represents eight pixels which are one line of a character, with a one indicating that the pixel should be plotted in the foreground color and a zero indicating that it should be in the background color. There are 14 bytes for the 14 lines of each character in the EGA/VGA modes and eight bytes for the eight lines of each character in the CGA modes. Thus, the table contains data for 93 characters. This includes alphanumerics and punctuation characters, but not the special IBM line-drawing characters which were deemed unnecessary for the graphics application. If you are interested in adding additional special characters, you need to plot which pixels to turn on and convert them to hexidecimal numbers, then simply expand the character table to add them. (Note that the position in the table where they are added will determine the ASCII code that calls the character. You can go for lower ASCII code characters by placing them at the beginning of the table, but you will need to modify the software somewhat.)

Figure 16-2: Generic Character Writing Function

```
plot_char = generic Character Writing Function.
            Writes a character at a specified pixel
            position with specified foreground and
            background colors
```

```c
void plot_char(int x, int y, int char_offset,
    int color, int type)
{
    #define seq_out(index,val)    {outp(0x3C4,index);\
                                   outp(0x3C5,val);}
    #define graph_out(index,val)  {outp(0x3CE,index);\
                                   outp(0x3CF,val);}

    unsigned int offset;
    char far * mem_address;
```

```
unsigned char char_test;
int i, j, k, m, start, end,height,width,
    foreground,background,point_color,dummy,mask;

foreground = color & 0x0F;
background = (color & 0xF0) >> 4;
switch(type)
{
    case 0:
    case 1:
        start = 0;
        end = 1;
        break;
    case 2:
        start = 0;
        end = 4;
        break;
    case 3:
        start = 1;
        end = 4;
}
for (i=0; i<14; i++)
{
    for (j=0; j<8; j++)
    {
        for (m=start; m<end; m++)
        {
            for (k=start; k<end; k++)
            {
                switch(type)
                {
                    case 0:
                        height = y+i;
                        width = x+j;
                        break;
                    case 1:
                        height = y-j;
                        width = x+i;
                        break;
                    case 2:
                    case 3:
                        height = y+4*i+k;
```

```
                width = x+4*j+m;
        }
        char_test = 0x80 >> j;
        if ((char_table[char_offset+i] &
            char_test) != 0)
            point_color = foreground;
        else
            point_color = background;
        offset = (long)(height) * 80L
            + ((long)(width) / 8L);
        mem_address = (char far *)
            0xA0000000L + offset;
        mask = 0x80 >> ((width) % 8);
        graph_out(8,mask);
        seq_out(2,0x0F);
        dummy = *mem_address;
        *mem_address = 0;
        seq_out(2,point_color);
        *mem_address = 0xFF;
            }
        }
        }
    }
    seq_out(2,0x0F);
    graph_out(3,0);
    graph_out(8,0xFF);
}
```

The color parameter is treated in the similar manner to the way the attribute byte is used in the text mode. Like both the text and graphics modes, the least significant four bits (bits 0, 1, 2, and 3) designate the foreground color. Note that unlike the text mode, any of the intensified colors can be used as a background color. Consequently the four most significant bits (bits 4, 5, 6, and 7) are needed to designate the background color. Figure 16-3 shows the decimal numbers corresponding to various color combinations. The character functions themselves are relatively simple. First, the color parameter is separated into foreground and background color variables. The first character in the table is a space (ASCII code 32 decimal). Thus the offset in the table is calculated by subtracting 32 from the ASCII character code and multiplying by 14, since 14 characters are required for each character.

Figure 16-3: Numbers Representing Color Combinations

Back-ground	Dark Gray	Light blue	Light Green	Light Cyan	Light Red	Light Magenta	Yel-low	Bright White
Bright White	143	159	175	191	207	223	239	255
Yellow	142	158	174	190	206	222	238	254
Light Magenta	141	157	173	189	205	221	237	253
Light Red	140	156	172	188	204	220	236	252
Light Cyan	139	155	171	187	203	219	235	251
Light Green	138	154	170	186	202	218	234	250
Light Blue	137	153	169	185	201	217	233	249
Dark Gray	136	152	168	184	200	216	232	248
Light Gray	135	151	167	183	199	215	231	247
Brown	134	150	166	182	198	214	230	246
Magenta	133	149	165	181	197	213	229	245
Red	132	148	164	180	196	212	228	244
Cyan	131	147	163	179	195	211	227	243
Green	130	146	162	178	194	210	226	242
Blue	129	145	161	177	193	209	225	241
Black	128	144	160	176	192	208	224	240

Back ground	Black	Blue	Green	Cyan	Red	Magenta	Brown	Light Gray
Bright White	15	31	47	63	79	95	111	127
Yellow	14	30	46	62	78	94	110	126
Light Magenta	13	29	45	61	77	93	109	125
Light Red	12	28	44	60	76	92	108	124
Light Cyan	11	27	43	59	75	91	107	123

(continued on next page)

Back ground	Black	Blue	Green	Cyan	Red	Magenta	Brown	Light Gray
Light Green	10	26	42	58	74	90	106	122
Light Blue	9	25	41	57	73	89	105	121
DarkGray	8	24	40	56	72	88	104	120
Light Gray	7	23	39	55	71	87	103	119
Brown	6	22	38	54	70	86	102	118
Magenta	5	21	37	53	69	85	101	117
Red	4	20	36	52	68	84	100	116
Cyan	3	19	35	51	67	83	99	115
Green	2	18	34	50	66	83	98	114
Blue	1	17	33	49	65	82	97	113
Black	0	16	32	48	64	81	96	112

All of the characters in the table are in their ASCII order, so that the offset always matches up to the proper character (see Appendix A for ASCII characters and their codes). Next, two *for* loops are used to scan the 8x14 pixel character box. At each pixel position, a mask is created which has a single bit at the appropriate position in the character from the character table. This mask is ANDed with the character for the appropriate line being drawn. If the result is non-zero, the pixel is plotted in the foreground color; if it is zero, the pixel is plotted in the background color. The vertical character drawing function is the same except for the scanning. Instead of starting at the top right, scanning across eight pixels, stepping down a line and repeating the operation 14 times, it starts at the bottom right, scans up eight pixels, steps over a column, repeating 14 times. The two functions listed in figures 16-4 and 16-5 will write characters to the VGA high resolution (640 x 480) screen with specified foreground and background colors. A slight modification in the coordinate conversion makes the function work with the EGA high resolution mode. Figure 16-4 writes characters horizontally from left to right. Figure 16-5 writes characters vertically from bottom to top. Both functions make use of the same table of character shapes.

Figure 16-4: Function to Write a Character to the Screen
Horizontally From Character Table

```
write_horz_char = Writes a Character to the Screen
                  horizontally at a specified pixel
                  position with specified foreground
                  and background colors
```

```
void write_horz_char(int x, int y, int ch, int color)
{

    int char_offset;

    x += 319;
    y = 240 - y;
    char_offset = (ch - 32) * 14;
    plot_char(x,y,char_offset,color,0);
    }
```

In the EGA high resolution mode, pixels are not square, but are longer in the vertical direction than in the horizontal direction, so the appearance of the characters is somewhat different when they are written vertically than when they are written horizontally. In all cases, however, the characters are highly legible. Each character is written in an 8x14 pixel box. The user specifies x and y coordinates. The horizontal character is written with the top left corner of the box at the specified pixel position. The vertical character is written with the top left corner of the character box at the pixel position, which results in the remainder of the character box extending up and to the right of the specified position coordinates. The functions are designed to take their position input in terms of system coordinates, but do the actual writing of characters in screen pixels so that there are no overlaps or missed points due to rounding off errors.

Figure 16-5: Function to Write a Character to the Screen
Vertically From Character Table

```
write_vert_char = Writes a Character to the Screen
                  vertically at a specified pixel
                  position with specified foreground
                  and background colors
```

```
void write_vert_char(int x, int y, int ch, int color)
{
```

```
int char_offset;

x += 319;
y = 240 - y;
char_offset = (ch - 32) * 14;
plot_char(x,y,char_offset,color,1);
}
```

Writing a String to the Screen

The function listed in Figure 16-6 uses the ROM BIOS video service based character writing routine to write a string of characters out to the screen. Positioning is done based upon the stored cursor position, even though the cursor cannot be seen in the graphics modes. The address of the first character of the string is passed to the function. The function writes the first character at the current cursor location with the specified attribute and on the specified display page. The function then advances the cursor and writes the next character and so on until 00 is encountered, which marks the end of the string. If the cursor advances beyond the end of a line, it is repositioned at the beginning of the next line.

Figure 16-6: Function to Write a String of Characters to the Screen
Based on a ROM BIOS Video Service

```
  writString = Writes a String to the Screen
             with Specified Attribute
```

```
void writString(char *str, int color, int page)
{
    int col, row, width, i = 0;
    getMode (&width);
    getxy(&col,&row,page);
    while (str[i])
    {
        writChar(str[i++], color, page);
        if (col > width - 1)
        {
            col = 0;
            row++;
        }
        gotoxy(++col, row, page);
    }
```

}

Writing a Character String
with the Custom Characters

Figure 16-7 lists a function for writing a string of characters to the screen horizontally using the custom character set described above. The function is similar in action to the one just described, but requires somewhat different details. The function depends upon a pixel coordinate location. It must advance the x coordinate eight pixels after each character is written. When the x coordinate is increased to the point where it is too near the right boundary of the screen (pixel number 639), the x coordinate is reset to zero and the y coordinate is increased by 14. Note that this function will only work with the EGA/VGA high resolution modes unless the 631 is replaced with some value appropriate to the mode being used.

Figure 16-7: Function to Write a String of Characters to the Screen Horizontally Using the Custom Characters

```
write_horz_str = Writes a String of characters
                 to the Screen horizontally begin-
                 ning at a specified pixel pos-
                 ition (x,y) and having specified
                 foreground and background colors
```

```c
void write_horz_str(int x, int y, char *string,
    int color)
{
    int char_offset,p=0;

    x += 319;
    y = 240 - y;
    while (string[p])
    {
        char_offset = (string[p] - 32) * 14;
        plot_char(x,y,char_offset,color,0);
        x += 8;
        if (x>632)
        {
            x=0;
```

```
            y += 14;
        }
        p++;
    }
}
```

Figure 16-8 is the equivalent function for writing a string to the screen vertically. It is similar to the previous function except that y is increased by eight for each character written, and when the pixel vertical location approaches too near the top of the screen, the column (x) value is increased by 14 and the raster line (y) value is reset to the bottom of the screen. This function will work well except in the EGA high resolution modes, since other modes do not have adequate resolution for the vertically oriented characters to be pleasing and legible.

Figure 16-8: Function to Write a String of Characters to the Screen Vertically Using the Custom Characters

```
write_vert_str = Writes a String of characters
                 to the Screen vertically, begin-
                 ning at a specified pixel pos-
                 ition (x,y) and having specified
                 foreground and background colors
```

```c
void write_vert_str(int x, int y, char *string,
    int color)
{
    int char_offset,p=0;

    x += 319;
    y = 240 - y;
    while (string[p])
    {
        char_offset = (string[p] - 32) * 14;
        plot_char(x,y,char_offset,color,1);
        y -= 8;
        if (y<8)
        {
            y=472;
            x += 14;
        }
        p++;
    }
```

```
}
```

Large and *Video* Characters

Using the same character table, a number of character writing variations are possible. Two functions are included here to give you some examples of what can be done. Figure 16-9 lists a function for writing big characters to the screen. The function is basically the same as that used for writing horizontal characters except that a 32x56 pixel matrix is used.

Figure 16-9: Function to Write a Big Character to the Screen
Horizontally Using the Custom Characters

```
write_big_char = Writes a big character to the
                 screen horizontally, beginning
                 at a specified pixel position
                 (x,y) and having specified fore-
                 ground and background colors
```

```
void write_big_char(int x, int y, int ch, int color)
{
    int char_offset;

    x += 319;
    y = 240 - y;
    char_offset = (ch - 32) * 14;
    plot_char(x,y,char_offset,color,2);
}
```

Each bit that was written as a single pixel for the horizontal character writing routine is written here as a cluster of 16 pixels (arranged 4x4) to make characters four times as big as normal. A companion for writing big strings is listed in Figure 16-10.

Figure 16-10: Function to Write a String of Big Characters

```
write_big_str = Writes a sting of big characters
                to the screen horizontally, begin-
                ning at a specified pixel position
                (x,y) and having specified fore-
                ground and background colors
```

```c
void write_big_str(int x, int y, char *string,
    int color)
{
    int p=0,char_offset;

    x += 319;
    y = 240 - y;
    while (string[p])
    {
        char_offset = (string[p] - 32) * 14;
        plot_char(x,y,char_offset,color,2);
        x += 32;
        if (x>607)
        {
            x=0;
            y += 56;
        }
        p++;
    }
}
```

The function *write_vid_char* is exactly the same as the function *write_big_char* except that a 3x3 cluster is used, so that there is a pixel width of background color space around each character. This gives an effect as if the characters were in a display of lights as on a motion picture marque. This function is listed in Figure 16-11 and a companion function for writing video strings is listed in Figure 16-12.

Figure 16-11: Function to Write a "Video" Character
to the Screen Horizontally

```
write_vid_char = Writes a "video" character to the
                 screen horizontally, beginning
                 at a specified pixel position
                 (x,y) and having specified fore-
                 ground and background colors
```

```
void write_vid_char(int x, int y, int ch, int color)
{
    int char_offset;

    x += 319;
    y = 240- y;
    char_offset = (ch - 32) * 14;
    plot_char(x,y,char_offset,color,3);
}
```

These are only two examples of various ways in which you can perform character generation using the C language. If you are not satisfied with the quality of the characters written by *write_big_char* you could create your own table of character shapes that would fill the 64x64 matrix without the need for increasing the cluster size. This could produce very pleasing characters in a variety of shapes. The penalty is that you need a storage array 16 times as big as the one you used for the existing character table.

Figure 16-12: Function to Write a String of "Video" Characters

```
write_vid_str = Writes a string of "video" char-
                acters to the screen horizontally,
                beginning at a specified pixel
                position (x,y) and having speci-
                fied foreground and background
                colors
```

```
void write_vid_str(int x, int y, char *string,
    int color)
{
    int p=0,char_offset;

    x += 319;
```

```
y = 240 - y;
while (string[p])
{
    char_offset = (string[p] - 32) * 14;
    plot_char(x,y,char_offset,color,3);
    x += 32;
    if (x>607)
    {
        x=0;
        y += 56;
    }
    p++;
}
}
```

17

Pop-up Windows and Menus

The capability to create windows which can be popped up at critical times in a program and be used to select a menu item or operate upon a display is one of the extremely useful features that makes software programs friendly to the user. The ROM BIOS video service functions for creating a window of a designated color and for scrolling text within it have already been described. As pointed out, however, the functions only create a window; they don't make any provision for recovering the display that was behind it when you are through with the window.

When you are writing a program which uses only text display modes, this is not too great a hardship. All of the text information for an entire screen can be captured quickly and placed in a buffer of only 2000 bytes. There are also times, regardless of what display mode you are in, when after you have made a selection from the window in the menu, you don't want the old display anymore—you are ready to go on to something new. In such situations, you don't really need to recover the previous display. But there are some cases where you want to make a choice and then return to the original display. If you are in the graphics mode, this becomes very difficult, especially for the EGA and VGA. Both these adapters have four memory planes, all basically at the same set of addresses. You can't access them directly. There is a ROM BIOS video service that has been described which will read a pixel color through the intervention of the EGA/VGA registers, but it is not particularly fast. If you were going to use it to retrieve and store a complete display, you would need to get 224,000 pixels in the EGA high resolution mode and even more for the VGA, and then either spend some time compressing them or else store 224,000 bytes somewhere. Then when you wanted to restore the display, you would have to use the *Write Pixel* video service to write all of these back to the screen. This process is much too lengthy. In fact, when researching how to draw graphics cursors, a function was written which did just this for the 16x16 matrix containing data under the cursor position. It was so slow that repeatedly using an arrow key to move the cursor inserted keystrokes far faster than the cursor could follow them, so that after the key was released, the cursor continued to move across the screen for some time. If this small portion of the display could not be saved efficiently, think what would happen if you wanted to store an entire display.

Saving Display Data

If you are using both memory pages in the EGA high resolution mode, or all of the available pages in on of the other EGA modes, or if you are using the VGA high resolution mode, (which has only one page), there isn't much you can do to efficiently save display data. If you are using the CGA or Hercules Graphics Card, the display memory is directly accessible and you may be able to do some direct block memory moves to save all or a portion of display memory. However, if you do have an EGA memory page available, you can use EGA direct memory transfer processes to save part or all of your display on the unused memory page and retrieve it afterward. Figure 17-1 lists a function to perform the storage and retrieval functions.

Figure 17-1: Function to Save and Restore Display Data

```
save_restore() = Transfers a rectangle from the
                 display designated by top left
                 corner (x1,y1) and bottom
                 right coner (x2,y2) to the
                 other display page (A00000 to
                 A8000 if 'type' is 0 or A8000
                 to A0000 if 'type' is 1
```

```c
void save_restore (int x1, int y1, int x2, int y2,
    int type)
{
    #define DISPLAY_OUT(index,val)   {outp(0x3CE,index);\
                                      outp(0x3CF,val);}
    unsigned char exist_color;
    char far *base1;
    char far *base2;
    int x,y;

    DISPLAY_OUT(5,0x01);
```

```
for (y=(y1-1)*14; y<=(y2+2)*14; y++)
{
    for (x=(x1-1)*8; x<=(x2+1)*8; x+=8)
    {
        base1 = (char far *) (0xA0000000L + ((long)y
            * 80L + ((long)x/8L)));
        base2 = (char far *) (0xA8000000L + ((long)y
            * 80L + ((long)x/8L)));
        if (type == 0)
        {
            exist_color = *base1;
            *base2 = 0x00;
        }
        else
        {
            exist_color = *base2;
            *base1 = 0x00;
        }
    }
}
DISPLAY_OUT(5,0);
}
```

It is assumed that the coordinates passed to the function are those from the window that is to be opened for use by the menu. In order to be sure that a sufficient area of the screen is saved, memory movement is controlled by two *for* loops that begin one character position before the window starting x and y positions and end one character position after the x and y ending positions. Position data for opening a window is given in terms of character column and row positions, where there are 80 columns of characters and 25 lines of characters on a display screen. The save/restore function needs to operate on a pixel by pixel basis. The EGA high resolution mode has 640 pixel column positions and 350 pixel row positions. This corresponds to 8 pixel column positions per character and 14 pixel row positions per character. Thus the x and y coordinates in character coordinates passed to the function are internally converted by multiplying the row by 14 and the column by 8 to obtain the corresponding pixel position data. The variables *base1* and *base2* are the memory addresses of the desired data in memory on page 0 and page 1, respectively. Page 0 starts at A0000H and page 1 starts at page A8000H. Unlike the case with the plotting functions that were described earlier, only one register has to be initialized before data transfer takes place. Graphics controller register 5 has to be set to 1, which puts the EGA into write mode 1. This causes data that is in the internal EGA processor latches to be transferred to memory when a memory write occurs. First, a dummy read is made at the address in display memory where each byte of data (a group of eight pixels) is stored. This dummy read causes the data for these eight pixels from each of the four memory planes to be latched into internal processor registers. Then a write instruction to the corresponding address on the other memory page causes the data from the internal registers to be written to the four memory planes associated with the write address. We learned in plotting points that this dummy write instruction worked well if we ANDed the data currently at that address with an 0FFH to write back the same data. This is not the case with write mode 1. The only way that it seems to work properly is if an 00H is written to the memory address. IBM, in their instruction material on the EGA, is not very clear about this. They seem to imply that the read is just a dummy instruction to cause the transfer of internal data, but this does not appear to be the case. At any rate, it should work for you if you write 00H.

The function is set up so that the if the parameter *type* is zero, data is transferred from page 0 to page 1, and if *type* is one, data is transferred from page 1 to page 0. Normally, the screen will be showing page 1. The first time that *save_restore* is used, *type* will be set to zero and the designated data from the area where the window is about to be displayed will be saved on page 1, where it is invisible. The window will then be written and then, when all menu operations are complete, the *save_restore* function will be run again with *type* set to one, which will transfer the invisible original data back to the proper position on the screen.

The Menu Function

Figure 17-2 shows the menu function. This is not meant to be a generalized all-purpose menu function, but rather an example of what can be done with such software. In particular, the text that is displayed in the window, the window size, and the colors are all internal to the program. If you were attempting to design a totally generalized menu function, you would probably want to have all of these parameters passed to the menu function, or make them global variables. You would also need to generalize the limitations on how far the cursor arrows move things up and down.

Figure 17-2: Function to Permit Selection of a Menu Item

```
menu()  = Displays a window and menu, returns the
          number of the menu item selected and
          restores the original display
```

```
int menu(int x1, int y1, int x2, int y2)
{
    int i,j,select=2,temp,ch;
    char string[5][30]={
        {"Select choice with arrows -- "},
        {"'Enter' to quit...            "},
        {"Six pointed star              "},
        {"Five pointed star             "},
        {"Rotated rectangles            "}};

    save_restore(x1,y1,x2,y2,0);
    temp = LINEWIDTH;
    LINEWIDTH = 3;
    setWindow(x1,y1,x2,y2,4);

    for (i=x1*8; i<=x2*8+8; i++)
    {
        for (j=0; j<LINEWIDTH; j++)
        {
            plot(i,y1*14 + j,14);
            plot(i,y2*14 + 14 - j,14);
        }
    }
    for (i=y1*14; i<=y2*14+14; i++)
    {
        for (j=0; j<LINEWIDTH; j++)
        {
            plot(x1*8+j,i,14);
            plot(x2*8 + 8 -j,i,14);
        }
    }
    write_horz_str(x1*8-309,(128*(175 - y1*14)/93)-20,
        string[0],79);
    write_horz_str(x1*8-309,(128*(175 - y1*14)/93)-40,
        string[1],79);
    write_horz_str(x1*8-309,(128*(175 - y1*14)/93)-60,
```

```
            string[2],47);
    write_horz_str(x1*8-309,(128*(175 - y1*14)/93)-80,
            string[3],79);
    write_horz_str(x1*8-309,(128*(175 - y1*14)/93)-100,
            string[4],79);
    while ((ch = getch()) != 13)
    {
        if (ch == 0x00)
            ch = getch() +256;
        switch(ch)
        {
            case 336:
                if (select < 4)
                {
                    write_horz_str(x1*8-309,
                        (128*(175 - y1*14)/93)
                        -(select+1)*20,
                        string[select],79);
                    write_horz_str(x1*8-309,
                        (128*(175 - y1*14)/93)
                        -(select+1)*20,
                        string[++select],47);
                }
                break;
            case 328:
                if (select > 2)
                {
                    write_horz_str(x1*8-309,
                        (128*(175 - y1*14)/93)
                        -(select+1)*20,
                        string[select],79);
                    write_horz_str(x1*8-309,
                        (128*(175 - y1*14)/93)
                        -(select+1)*20,
                        string[--select],47);
                }
        }
    }
    save_restore(x1,y1,x2,y2,1);
    LINEWIDTH = temp;
    return(select-1);
}
```

The menu program begins be calling the *save_restore* function to save the portion of display screen memory where the menu window is to be positioned. Next, the current value of the LINEWIDTH parameter is saved so that it can be restored later and LINEWIDTH is set to 3 to permit drawing a three-pixel wide line around the border of the menu window. Function *setWindow* is then called to create the empty window with a color of red. The coordinates for drawing the window are character position coordinates. We next want to draw a border around the window, but we can't use the *drawRect* function since its system coordinates are not compatible with exact matching of the boundaries of the window. Therefore, we make the proper conversions from character positions defined for the window to screen coordinates and draw the border pixel by pixel using the plot function. The *write_horz_str* function is then used to write the lines of the menu to the window. The first two lines are of general instructions and are written in white on red. The next line is the first selection and is written in white on green. The remaining two lines are the other two selections and are written in white on red.

Next a *while* loop is executed which gets characters from the keyboard until the *Enter* key is hit, at which time the function terminates. For each keyboard entry, the input character is checked to see if it is zero. A number of keyboard characters return a two byte sequence, the first byte being zero. If the keyboard entry is one of the two byte keys, when the zero is received, the second byte is read and increased by 256 so that there will be no conflict with a key that has a one-byte sequence when a key that has a two-byte sequence has its second byte the same as the single byte of a key having a one byte character output. The *switch* instruction is now used to test whether the character is an up or down arrow. If the character is an up arrow and the currently selected menu item is not the first, the currently selected item is rewritten in white on red and the item above is rewritten in white on green to indicate that it is now the currently selected one. The parameter *select* is also decremented to indicate the line number of the selected item. Similarly, if a down arrow was typed and if the currently selected item was not the last one, the currently selected item is rewritten in white on red and the next item down is rewritten in white on green to indicate that it is now the currently selected item. The *select* parameter in this case is incremented. This loop continues until the *Enter* key is hit. If any other keys than *up arrow*, *down arrow*, or *Enter* are hit, they are ignored. When the loop is terminated, the *save_restore* function is run to replace the menu window with the old display data. The LINEWIDTH parameter is restored to its original value. The *select* parameter is pointing to the line that was currently selected. Since the first two lines (lines 0 and 1) were general instructions, the first item selection has a number 2, the next 3, and so forth. We want to be conventional and have the selections numbered 1, 2, 3, ... so we subtract one from select, before returning it to the calling program.

269

Menu Demonstration Program

Figure 17-3 lists a program for demonstrating the *menu* function. It requires that you have established the *gtool* and *gdraws* libraries as described in Chapter 20. The program begins by drawing a large rectangle with two diagonal lines from corner to corner. Next, *menu* is called. This function saves the display portion where the window is to be opened and then creates a window with a contrasting color border and instructions to select one of three displays.

These displays, which are described in more detail in Chapter 21, are an outlined, six-pointed star, a filled circle containing a partially-filled five pointed star, and a series of rotated rectangles. The user selects one of these using the up and down arrow keys and then hits the *Enter* key. The window is then replaced with the original display material and the selected display is superimposed upon the existing one. This program demonstrates how a menu window is created, how a *menu* function is used to make a selection for further action, and how the original display is restored after the use of the menu is over. It is also a simple matter to modify this program to loop back so that the menu can continually reselect one of the three options to be superimposed upon the background display. This would be useful if you had a map display on which you wanted to superimpose one of several different overlays. In this mode, you would need to use the *save_restore* function to save all of the original display, or at least the portion of it where each overlay was going to appear, and restore it after you were finished with each overlay.

Figure 17-3: Menu Demonstration Program

```
    gmenu = Program to demonstrate the use of the
            'menu' function
```

```
/*


                            INCLUDES


                                                              */

#include <stdio.h>
#include <math.h>
#include <dos.h>
```

```
/*
    ┌─────────────────────────────────────────────────────────┐
    │                                                         │
    │                 USER WRITTEN INCLUDES                   │
    │                                                         │
    └─────────────────────────────────────────────────────────┘
                                                                   */


    #include "gtools.h"
    #include "gdraws.h"



/*
    ┌─────────────────────────────────────────────────────────┐
    │                                                         │
    │        GLOBAL VARIABLES USED BY GRAPHICS FUNCTIONS      │
    │                                                         │
    └─────────────────────────────────────────────────────────┘
                                                                   */




    int color = 2;
    int background_color = 0;
    int LINEWIDTH=1, OPERATOR=0, ANGLE, XCENTER, YCENTER;
    unsigned long int PATTERN=0xFFFFFFFF;
    char string[5][30]={{"Select choice with arrows -- "},
                    {"'Enter' to quit...          "},
                    {"Six pointed star            "},
                    {"Five pointed star           "},
                    {"Rotated rectangles          "}};



/*
    ┌─────────────────────────────────────────────────────────┐
    │                                                         │
    │                  FUNCTION DEFINITIONS                   │
    │                                                         │
    └─────────────────────────────────────────────────────────┘
                                                                   */

    int menu(int x1, int y1, int x2, int y2);
    void save_restore (int x1, int y1, int x2, int y2, int type);
    void wait(char title[]);
```

271

```
/*
┌─────────────────────────────────────────────────────┐
│                                                       │
│                  MAIN PROGRAM                         │
│                                                       │
└─────────────────────────────────────────────────────┘
                                                    */

main()
{
    int i, j, k, x, y, oldx, oldy, midpoint,select;
    double xd,yd,ampl,aspect;
    char ch;

    cls (1);
    ch = getAdapter();
    if ((ch != 'V') && (ch != 'E'))
        printf("Cannot Run Demo -- EGA or VGA Not "
            "Installed!");
    else
    {
        setMode(16);
        LINEWIDTH = 3;
        cls(1);
        drawRect(-309,210,310,-200,11);
        drawLine(-309,210,310,-200,11);
        drawLine(-309,-200,310,210,11);
        select = menu(2,2,37,8);
        switch (select)
        {
            case 1:

                LINEWIDTH = 2;
                drawPoly(11,-259, 90,-59, 90,-159,
                    -90,-999);
                drawPoly(11,-259,-20,-159,160,
                    -59,-20,-999);
                break;

            case 2:

                fillOval(161,34,107,9,1.0);
                fillPoly(14,60,66,262,66,104,-55,
                    161,140,218,-55,-999);
```

```
                break;
        case 3:

                LINEWIDTH = 1;
                color=3;
                XCENTER = -70;
                YCENTER = 35;
                for (ANGLE=0; ANGLE<180; ANGLE+=15)
                {
                        rotateRect(-220,100,80,-35,color);
                        color++;
                }
        }
        wait("");
    }
    setMode(3);
}

void wait(char title[])
{
    int tab,width;
    getMode(&width);
    tab = (width - strlen(title))/2;
    gotoxy(tab,0,0);
    writString(title,WHITE,0);
    tab = (width - 33)/2;
    gotoxy(tab,24,0);
    writString("Press any key to continue demo...",15,0);
    getch();
    cls(0);
}
```

18

Three-Dimensional Drawing

There are all kinds of ways to create the illusion of a three-dimensional figure on a two-dimensional display screen. Since the exact choices you will make are determined by the end use of your display and the type of figures that you want to draw, there aren't any absolute techniques for doing exactly what you want. We will discuss two methods of projection, one of which leans toward the drafting approach toward drawing, while the other leans more toward the artistic. The problems of how to project, how to rotate the image, how to remove hidden lines, and how to do shading will be discussed in this and the next chapter. Some demonstration programs will be given including some functions that you can add to your *gdraws* library.

Direct Projection

Suppose you have a three-dimensional space, with its three-dimensional coordinate system (x,y,z) centered at (0,0,0). We place this three-dimensional space so that its origin coincides with the origin of a plane, which is our display screen. Each of the axes of the three-dimensional coordinate system makes an angle with the display plane, where α is the angle between the display plane and x axis, β is the angle between the display plane and the y axis, and Γ is the angle between the display plane and the z axis. You may specify these angles to have any orientation between the space to the display plane that you desire. The most common orientation is that used for isometric drawing, where α and Γ are thirty degrees and β is ninety degrees. Another orientation that is used in some geometry books is for α and β to be zero and Γ to be 135 degrees.

Assuming you have settled upon the orientation that you want, each point within the (x,y,z) space can be projected upon the (vx,vy) display plane in a fairly simple fashion. Basically, there is only one line that can be drawn perpendicular to the display plane that intersects any particular point in the (x,y,z) space. When you draw this line, the point (vx,vy) where it intersects the display screen is where the projected point lies on the display screen. Once you have projected all of the points that you are interested in, in this manner, you have a two-dimensional representation of the three-dimensional space. Of course, you can't go around drawing perpendiculars from your screen to the space containing the original surfaces, but the equations for locating the projected points, assuming that you know the location of the original points, are rather simple. They are:

$$vx = x \cos \alpha + y \cos \beta + z \cos \Gamma \qquad \text{(Eq. 18-1)}$$

$$vy = x \sin \alpha + y \sin \beta + z \sin \Gamma \qquad \text{(Eq. 18-2)}$$

The only problem with doing this kind of projection is that is is less than obvious how to handle hidden surfaces or shading. In many cases, however, we don't really want to blank out the hidden surfaces. If we are looking at something that can be considered semi-transparent and where we want to see all of the surfaces at once, a technique that does not remove hidden surfaces is called for. You can then enhance the three-dimensional quality of the image by drawing the background lines before the foreground ones so that the foreground overwrites the background, and by using different colors for foreground and background lines.

Quadric Surfaces

An ideal subject for the above type of three-dimensional representation is the three-dimensional geometric surfaces found in solid geometry textbooks. One particular example of these is quadric surfaces. Quadrics are the three-dimensional shapes produced by rotating the traditional conic section curves in the third dimension. These shapes are the elliptic paraboloid, the hyperbolic paraboloid, the elliptic cone, the hyperboloid of one sheet, the hyperboloid of two sheets, and the ellipsoid. The equation for the elliptic paraboloid is:

$$x^2/a^2 + y^2/b^2 = z \qquad \text{(Eq. 18-3)}$$

The equation for the hyperbolic paraboloid is:

$$x^2/a^2 - y^2/b^2 = z \qquad \text{(Eq. 18-4)}$$

The equation for the elliptic cone is:

$$x^2/a^2 + y^2/b^2 - z^2/c^2 = 0 \qquad (Eq. \ 18-5)$$

The equation for the hyperboloid of one sheet is:

$$x^2/a^2 + y^2/b^2 - z^2/c^2 = 1 \qquad (Eq. \ 18-6)$$

The equation for the hyperboloid of two sheets is:

$$x^2/a^2 - y^2/b^2 - z^2/c^2 = 1 \qquad (Eq. \ 18-7)$$

The equation for the ellipsoid is:

$$x^2/a^2 + y^2/b^2 + z^2/c^2 = 1 \qquad (Eq. \ 18-8)$$

Figure 18-1 is a demonstration program to draw quadric surfaces with whatever axis orientations you may choose, using the high resolution mode of the EGA. Note carefully how this program makes use of the basic graphics tools that we developed in earlier chapters. The program has been set up with the proper offsets and scale factors to give a satisfactory appearance on the screen if you enter angles of 15, -15 and 90 degrees for α, β, and Γ, respectively. If you change the angles by a large amount, you may need to change offset and scaling for the figures to fit properly on the screen. Figure 18-2 shows the display of quadric surfaces (see color section).

Figure 18-1: Program to Generate Quadric Surfaces

```
#include <dos.h>
#include <stdio.h>
#include <math.h>

#include "gtools.h"
#include "gdraws.h"

float rad_per_degree=0.0174533, x_angle, y_angle,
    z_angle, step, x3, y3, z3;
int x,y,horz_scale,vert_scale,color,type,x_offset,
    y_offset;

float radians_to_degrees(float degrees);
void projection (float x_angle, float y_angle,
```

```
        float z_angle, float x3, float y3, float z3,
        int color);
void wait(char title[]);

main ()
{
    setMode(16);
    cls(0);
    gotoxy(10,10,0);
    printf("Enter x axis angle in degrees: ");
    scanf("%f",&x_angle);
    gotoxy(10,11,0);
    printf("Enter y axis angle in degrees: ");
    scanf("%f",&y_angle);
    gotoxy(10,12,0);
    printf("Enter z axis angle in degrees: ");
    scanf("%f",&z_angle);
    x_angle = radians_to_degrees(x_angle);
    y_angle = radians_to_degrees(y_angle);
    z_angle = radians_to_degrees(z_angle);
    cls(1);
    for (type=1; type<=6; type++)
    {
        switch (type)
        {
            case 1:
                x_offset = 130;
                y_offset = 160;
                horz_scale = 9;
                vert_scale = 2.2;
                for (y3=-6; y3<=6; y3+=.4)
                {
                    color = 3;
                    step = .05;
                    for (x3=-6; x3<=6; x3+=step)
                    {
                        z3 = x3*x3 + y3*y3;
                        projection(x_angle,
                            y_angle,z_angle,
                            x3,y3,z3,color);
                        if (x3>=0)
                        {
```

```
                step = .2;
                color = 12;
            }
        }
    }
    gotoxy(5,12,0);
    writString("Elliptic Paraboloid",11,0);
    break;
case 2:
    x_offset = 340;
    y_offset = 88;
    horz_scale = 12;
    vert_scale = 2;
    for (y3=-5; y3<=5; y3+=.4)
    {
        step = .1;
        color = 13;
        for (x3=-5; x3<=5; x3+=step)
        {
            z3 = y3*y3 - x3*x3;
            projection(x_angle,y_angle,
            z_angle,
            x3,y3,z3,color);
            if (x3>=0)
            {
                step = .4;
                color = 14;
            }
        }
    }
    gotoxy(30,12,0);
    writString("Hyperbolic Paraboloid ",11,0);
    break;
case 3:
    x_offset = 540;
    y_offset = 88;
    horz_scale = 7;
    vert_scale = 3;
    for (y3=-6; y3<=6; y3+=.75)
    {
        step = .2;
        color = 2;
```

```
                for (x3=-6; x3<=6; x3+=step)
                {
                    z3 = sqrt(y3*y3 + x3*x3)*2;
                    projection(x_angle,y_angle,
                        z_angle,
                        x3,y3,z3,color);
                    projection(x_angle,y_angle,
                        z_angle,
                        x3,y3,-z3,color);
                    if (x3>=0)
                    {
                        step = .5;
                        color = 14;
                    }
                }
            }
        gotoxy(60,12,0);
        writString("Elliptic Cone ",11,0);
        break;
    case 4:
        y_offset = 255;
        x_offset = 120;
        horz_scale = 7;
        vert_scale = 5;
        for (y3=-4; y3<=4; y3+=.5)
        {
            for (x3=-4; x3<=4; x3+=.2)
            {
                if (x3<0)
                    color = 13;
                else
                    color = 15;
                if (x3*x3+y3*y3>2)
                {
                    z3 = sqrt(y3*y3 +
                        x3*x3-2)*2;
                    projection(x_angle,
                        y_angle,z_angle,
                        x3,y3,z3,color);
                    projection(x_angle,
                        y_angle,z_angle,
                        x3,y3,-z3,color);
```

```
                    }
                }
            }
        gotoxy(0,23,0);
        writString(" Hyperboloid of one sheet",
            11,0);
        break;
    case 5:
        y_offset = 265;
        x_offset = 320;
        horz_scale = 2;
        vert_scale = 2;
        for (y3=-20; y3<=20; y3+=2)
        {
            for (x3=-20; x3<=20; x3+=.3)
            {
                if (x3<0)
                    color = 9;
                else
                    color = 13;
                if (y3*y3>=x3*x3+1)
                {
                    z3 = sqrt(y3*y3
                        - x3*x3 - 1);
                    projection(x_angle,
                        y_angle,z_angle,
                        x3,y3,z3,color);
                    projection(x_angle,
                        y_angle,z_angle,
                        x3,y3,-z3,color);
                }
            }
        }
        gotoxy(30,23,0);
        writString("Hyperboloid of two "
            sheets ",11,0);
        break;
    case 6:
        y_offset = 265;
        x_offset = 530;
        horz_scale = 60;
        vert_scale = 50;
```

```
                    for (y3=-.99; y3<=1; y3+=.15)
                    {
                        step = .015;
                        color = 11;
                        for (x3=-1; x3<=1; x3+=.03)
                        {
                            if (x3*x3+y3*y3<1)
                            {
                                z3 = sqrt(1-x3*x3 -
                                    y3*y3);
                                projection(x_angle,
                                    y_angle,
                                    z_angle,x3,y3,z3,
                                    color);
                                projection(x_angle,
                                    y_angle,
                                    z_angle,x3,y3,-z3,
                                    color);
                            }
                            if (x3>0)
                            {
                                step = .03;
                                color = 15;
                            }
                        }
                    }
                    gotoxy(63,23,0);
                    writString("Ellipsoid",11,0);
            }
        }
    wait("Quadric Surfaces");
}

float radians_to_degrees(float degrees)
{
    float angle;

    while (degrees >= 360)
        degrees -= 360;
    while (degrees < 0)
        degrees += 360;
    angle = rad_per_degree*degrees;
```

```
        return angle;
}

void projection (float x_angle, float y_angle,
    float z_angle, float x3, float y3, float z3,
    int color)
{
    float temp_x, temp_y;
    int x,y;

    temp_x = x3*cos(x_angle) + y3*cos(y_angle) +
        z3*cos(z_angle);
    temp_y = x3*sin(x_angle) + y3*sin(y_angle) +
        z3*sin(z_angle);
    x = x_offset + (temp_x*horz_scale);
    y = y_offset - (temp_y*vert_scale);
    plot (x,y,color);
}

void wait(char title[])
{
    int tab,width=80;
    tab = (width - strlen(title))/2;
    gotoxy(tab,0,0);
    writString(title,15,0);
    tab = (width - 33)/2;
    gotoxy(tab,24,0);
    writString("Press any key to continue demo...", 15,0);
    getch();
    cls(1);
}
```

The External Observer

Suppose we have a three-dimensional space in which the x and y coordinates are the same as our system coordinates. The x coordinate is zero at the center of the screen and increases positively as it goes toward the right or decreases negatively as it goes toward the left. The y coordinate is zero at the center of the screen and increases positively as it moves upward or decreases negatively as it moves downward. We take the point of view of an observer looking at the screen. The z coordinate is zero at the observer's position and decreases negatively as it moves ahead toward the screen or increases positively as it moves away from the screen and the observer. Thus we have a right-handed coordinates system with axes x, y, and z. The only effect that z will have on the two-dimensional display is on the apparent size of an object when it is projected upon the screen.

If the object is behind the screen, it's projected image on the screen will be smaller than the size of the real object; if the object is in front of the screen, its image on the screen will be larger than the real object. Figure 18-3 shows the geometry of the situation.

Figure 18-3: Geometry for Projecting z on a Screen

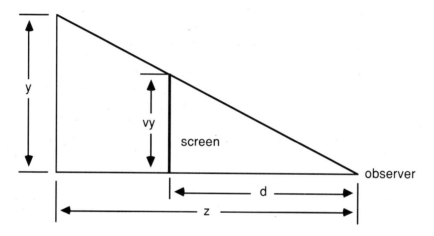

The distance d is that from the observer to the screen, and z is the distance from the observer to the projection of the observed point on the z axis. The triangle formed by the observer, the observed point, and the projection on the z axis is similar to the one formed by the observer, the projection of the observed point on the screen, and the z coordinate of that projected point, so the ratio of two sides is the same for each triangle. Thus:

```
y/z = vy/d        (Eq. 18-9)
```

The projection of y on the screen (resulting from correction for z) is therefore:

```
vy = dy/z         (Eq. 18-10)
```

Exactly the same geometry applies to scaling x, giving

```
vx = dx/z         (Eq. 18-11)
```

Most of the time, the result of looking at a three-dimensional figure with this orientation is very uninteresting. To obtain an interesting display, we need to rotate the three-dimensional figure in some manner. Traditionally, we do this in terms of three angles: *roll* around the z axis, *pitch* around the x axis, and *yaw* around the y axis, all in a clockwise direction. The original derivation of these angles can be understood if you imagine yourself in an airplane flying in the -z direction. Roll will spin you clockwise or counterclockwise. Pitch will spin you forward or backward, a bit like a bucking horse, and yaw will spin you to the left or right. Assuming that the roll, pitch, and yaw angles have been specified, we need to make three rotations in order to reorient the coordinate system to the new position. We shall call the original coordinates $(x_0 y_0 z_0)$ and the rotated coordinates (x,y,z). The first rotation is about the y axis through the yaw angle. Calling the angles R (roll), P (pitch) and Y (yaw) for short, the matrix expression for this rotation is:

$$
\begin{bmatrix} x_1 \\ y_0 \\ z_1 \end{bmatrix} = \begin{bmatrix} -\cos Y & 0 & -\sin Y \\ 0 & 1 & 0 \\ -\sin Y & 0 & \cos Y \end{bmatrix} \begin{bmatrix} x_0 \\ y_0 \\ z_0 \end{bmatrix} \qquad \text{(Eq. 18-12)}
$$

The next rotation is around the new z axis (z1) through the roll angle. The matrix expression is:.

$$
\begin{bmatrix} x \\ y_1 \\ y_1 \end{bmatrix} = \begin{bmatrix} \cos R & \sin R & 0 \\ -\sin R & \cos R & 0 \\ 0 & 0 & 1 \end{bmatrix} \begin{bmatrix} x_1 \\ y_0 \\ z_1 \end{bmatrix} \qquad \text{(Eq. 18-13)}
$$

The final rotation is around the x axis (the final x axis, which was determined in the previous step) through the pitch angle. The matrix expression is:

$$
\begin{bmatrix} x \\ y \\ z \end{bmatrix} = \begin{bmatrix} 1 & 0 & 0 \\ 0 & \cos P & \sin P \\ 0 & -\sin P & \cos P \end{bmatrix} \begin{bmatrix} x \\ y_1 \\ z_1 \end{bmatrix} \qquad \text{(Eq. 18-14)}
$$

These three rotations can easily be combined into a single transformation matrix, but for computer calculations it is actually more efficient to perform the operations separately. Figure 18-4 lists a function which rotates and translates three-dimensional points and then converts them to their projection on a two-dimensional surface. The first parameter passed by the function *number_of_points* is the number of points that are to be converted in this manner. The next parameter, *rot_pts*, is an array that stores the rotated and translated points. The next parameter, *pt*, is the array of original points that are to be processed. The final two parameters, *vx* and *vy*, are arrays of the x and y coordinates, respectively, which are the two-dimensional representation of the rotated and translated points.

Figure 18-4: Function to Rotate and Translate a Solid

```
void perspective(int no_of_points,float rot_pts[][3],
    float pt[][3],int vx[], int vy[])
{
    int i,j;

    float x,y,z,x1,y1,z1;

    for (i=0; i<no_of_points; i++)
    {
        x1 = -cos(yaw)*pt[i][0] - sin(yaw)*pt[i][2];
        z1 = -sin(yaw)*pt[i][0] + cos(yaw)*pt[i][2];
        x = cos(roll)*x1 + sin(roll)*pt[i][1];
        y1 = cos(roll)*pt[i][1] - sin(roll)*x1;
        z = cos(pitch)*z1 - sin(pitch)*y1;
        y = sin(pitch)*z1 + cos(pitch)*y1;
        x += mx;
        y += my;
        z += mz;
        rot_pts[i][0] = x;
        rot_pts[i][1] = y;
        rot_pts[i][2] = z;
        vx[i] = -d*x/z+off_x;
        vy[i] = -d*y/z+off_y;
    )

}
```

The beginning of this function represents the rotations of the solid around the three axes as described above. We are going to describe below the technique for removing hidden surfaces of the solid so that the resulting figure is a realistic representation of what we would see if we look at the solid object it and does not contain any representations of surfaces that cannot be seen from the observer's position. For this hidden surface removal technique to work, the coordinates of the points that define the solid (vertices or corners of polygons that make up its surface) must surround the coordinate (0,0,0). However, this may not result in a figure that is positioned where we want it on the screen. During the second part of the function, mx, my, and mz are added to the coordinates x, y, and z, respectively, to translate the figure to a new position.

These coordinate translations, however, behave as if the solid were moved to a different position with respect to the observer, so that the resulting figure will appear differently. If you want to keep precisely the same perspective, but reposition the figure on the screen, the translation needs to occur after each point is projected onto the two-dimensional surface. The next part of the function preserves the rotated and translated points in an array *rot_pts*. Equations 18-10 and 18-11 are then used to project the points onto the two-dimensional surface.

Any translation which is required without change in the relation of the point to the observer is achieved by adding *off_x* and *off_y* to the two-dimensional x and y coordinates respectively. Calling this function rotates, translates, and projects the specified number of points onto the two-dimensional surface. The three-dimensional representations of the rotated and translated points are stored in the array *rot_pts*, where they are available for processing to determine whether the surface is hidden. The resulting two-dimensional projections of the points (translated as necessary) are stored in the *vx* and *vy* arrays, respectively. All of the collections of points are stored in arrays, which means that what is actually passed to the function is the starting address of each array. Thus the function places data in the proper array addresses, where it is available to the calling routine. Note that C does not require that the first dimension of a multiple array be passed to the function; it can be specified by the array definition in the calling program. However, the second dimension must be passed and must be identical to that in the array definition in the calling program.

Removing Hidden Surfaces

The technique to be used to remove hidden surfaces from the drawing is known as the "plane equation method," and is applied to each side after any desired rotation of the cube takes place. The equation of a plane is:

$$Ax + By + Cz + D \qquad \text{(Eq. 18-16)}$$

If the parameters A, B, and C remain constant, then varying the value of D results in a whole family of parallel planes, one of which (when D is zero) contains the origin of the coordinate system. If D is less than zero, the plane is in front of the origin (toward the observer) and if D is positive, the plane is behind the origin (away from the observer). If we cleverly defined our cube to have its center at the origin, then all those surfaces that are viewable will have negative D's and the unviewable surfaces will have positive D's. Our hidden surface removal routine, then, simply defines the plane corresponding to one of the cube's surfaces, from the coordinates of three points on it, and then computes D. If D is positive, the surface is not drawn; if D is negative, the surface is drawn. For this to work, the cube must first be in the proper orientation and location and each plane must be defined in a consistent manner, with the coordinates listed in counter-clockwise rotation from the starting point. Figure 18-5 is the function which determines whether a surface should be drawn or should be hidden.

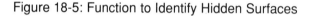

Figure 18-5: Function to Identify Hidden Surfaces

```
surface_test() = Function to Identify Hidden Surfaces.
                 Returns a positive number if surface
                 is hidden and a negative number if it
                 is not
```

```
float surface_test(float x1, float y1, float z1, float x2,
    float y2, float z2, float x3, float y3, float z3)
{
    float stest;

    stest = x1*(y3*z2-y2*z3) - x2*(y3*z1-y1*z3)
        x3*(y1*z2 - y2*z1);
    return (stest);
}
```

Drawing a Cube

The principal information that we need in order to draw a cube is the position of the eight vertices that define the eight corners of the cube. First, we must perform the rotations and translations using the function of Figure 18-4 to orient and position the cube where we want it. Next, the function shown in Figure 18-6 is used to draw the cube. It calls the function *draw_side* to draw each of the six surfaces of the cube. First, the function of Figure 18-5 is used to determine whether the surface is hidden or visible. If the surface is visible, the *drawPoly* function is used to draw the outlines of the polygon which forms that side of the cube.

Normally, we would think of the sides of the cube as being squares, be we must remember that the projection of these squares on the screen display plane are distorted by the cube having been rotated so that they may appear as rectangles, parallelograms, or trapezoids. The only certainty is that they are all four-sided polygons. The three-dimensional demonstration program, which is described in Chapter 20, uses a random number routine to choose the roll, pitch, and yaw angles for each of six cubes, and then draws the six cubes on a single display. Each time the display is repeated, different random orientations are selected. Figure 18-7 shows a typical display of cubes (see color section).

Figure 18-6: Function to Draw a Cube

```
draw_cube()  =  Function  to  draw  a  three-dimensional
                cube
```

```c
void draw_cube(float rot_pts[8][3],int vx[],int vy[])
{

    draw_side(7,0,3,6,rot_pts,vx,vy);
    draw_side(6,5,4,7,rot_pts,vx,vy);
    draw_side(3,2,5,6,rot_pts,vx,vy);
    draw_side(0,1,2,3,rot_pts,vx,vy);
    draw_side(7,4,1,0,rot_pts,vx,vy);
    draw_side(1,4,5,2,rot_pts,vx,vy);
}

void draw_side(int i1, int i2, int i3, int i4,
    float rot_pts[8][3],int vx[],int vy[])
{
    float sp;

    sp = surface_test(rot_pts[i1][0],rot_pts[i1][1],
        rot_pts[i1][2],rot_pts[i2][0],rot_pts[i2][1],
        rot_pts[i2][2],rot_pts[i3][0],rot_pts[i3][1],
        rot_pts[i3][2]);
    if (sp<=0)
        drawPoly(color,vx[i1],+vy[i1],vx[i2],+vy[i2],
            vx[i3],+vy[i3],vx[i4],+vy[i4],-999);
}
```

Drawing a Sphere

Figure 18-8 lists a function for drawing a sphere. The sphere consists of a network of longitude and latitude lines. Without these lines to give the illusion of depth, the sphere would be a featureless oval. The drawing of the sphere begins by determining the points for a band of triangles. The apex of each triangle is at one pole of the sphere and the other two points for each triangle are 10 degrees down from the pole in longitude and at 10 degrees latitude increments in a belt around the sphere. After these points are computed and stored in an array, the *perspective* function is used to rotate each triangle and displace it to the sphere's proposed orientation. The *surface_test* function is then used to determine whether the triangle is hidden or visible; if visible, the *drawPoly* function is used to draw the triangle. In a similar fashion, bands of four-sided polygons around the sphere are computed and drawn if visible. For each polygon, the two points nearest the starting pole have already been computed in the previous step, so that only the two remaining points need to be calculated.

Figure 18-8: Function to Draw a Sphere

```
draw_sphere() = Function to draw a three-dimensional
                sphere
```

```c
void draw_sphere()
{
    float sp;
    int i,j,k,radius;
    float latitude,longitude;

    radius = 30;
    pt1[0][0] = 0;
    pt1[0][1] = radius;
    pt1[0][2] = 0;
    perspective(1,rot_pts1,pt1,vx1,vy1);
    longitude = .17453;
    for (latitude=0,i=0; i<36; i++,latitude +=.17453)
    {
        pt2[i][0] = cos(latitude)*sin(longitude)*radius;
        pt2[i][1] = cos(longitude)*radius;
        pt2[i][2] = sin(latitude)*sin(longitude)*radius;
    }
    pt2[36][0] = pt2[0][0];
    pt2[36][1] = pt2[0][1];
```

```
pt2[36][2] = pt2[0][2];
perspective(37,rot_pts2,pt2,vx2,vy2);
for (i=0; i<36; i++)
{
    sp = surface_test(rot_pts2[i+1][0],
        rot_pts2[i+1][1],rot_pts2[i+1][2],
        rot_pts2[i][0],rot_pts2[i][1],rot_pts2[i][2],
        rot_pts1[0][0],rot_pts1[0][1],rot_pts1[0][2]);
    if (sp<=0)
        drawPoly(color,vx2[i+1],vy2[i+1],vx2[i],
            vy2[i],vx1[0],vy1[0],-999);
}
for (j=0; j<16; j++)
{
    longitude += .17453;
    for (latitude=0,i=0; i<36; i++,latitude+=.17453)
    {
        pt2[i][0] = cos(latitude)*sin(longitude)*
            radius;
        pt2[i][1] = cos(longitude)*radius;
        pt2[i][2] = sin(latitude)*sin(longitude)*
            radius;
    }
    pt2[36][0] = pt2[0][0];
    pt2[36][1] = pt2[0][1];
    pt2[36][2] = pt2[0][2];
    for (i=0; i<37; i++)
    {
        for (k=0; k<3; k++)
            rot_pts1[i][k] = rot_pts2[i][k];
        vx1[i] = vx2[i];
        vy1[i] = vy2[i];
    }
    perspective(37,rot_pts2,pt2,vx2,vy2);
    for (i=0; i<36; i++)
    {
        sp = surface_test(rot_pts1[i][0],
            rot_pts1[i][1],rot_pts1[i][2],
            rot_pts1[i+1][0],rot_pts1[i+1][1],
            rot_pts1[i+1][2],rot_pts2[i+1][0],
            rot_pts2[i+1][1],rot_pts2[i+1][2]);
        if (sp<=0)
```

291

```
                    drawPoly(color,vx1[i],vy1[i],vx1[i+1],
                        vy1[i+1],vx2[i+1],vy2[i+1],
                        vx2[i],vy2[i],-999);
            }
    }
    pt1[0][0] = 0;
    pt1[0][1] = -x;
    pt1[0][2] = 0;
    perspective(1,rot_pts1,pt1,vx1,vy1);
    for (i=0; i<36; i++)
    {
        sp = surface_test(rot_pts2[i][0],rot_pts2[i][1],
            rot_pts2[i][2],rot_pts2[i+1][0],
            rot_pts2[i+1][1],rot_pts2[i+1][2],
            rot_pts1[0][0],rot_pts1[0][1],rot_pts1[0][2]);
        if (sp<=0)
            drawPoly(color,vx2[i+1],vy2[i+1],vx2[i],
                vy2[i],vx1[0],vy1[0],-999);
    }

}
```

When within 10 degrees of longitude from the opposite pole, another group of triangles is computed using the two points of each of the last band of four-sided polygons and the opposite pole as the coordinates. In the demonstration program described in Chapter 21, a new random orientation is determined for the sphere on each repetition of the display. Figure 18-9 shows a typical sphere (see color section).

Other Geometric Figures

The examples of the cube and the sphere are typical of the kinds of figures that can be drawn using the techniques described in this chapter. The same techniques can be used to draw any type of solid which can be decomposed into a number of connected polygons. The same *perspective, surface_test,* and *drawPoly* functions can then be used to create the drawing of the desired solid.

19

Shading
Three-Dimensional Figures

In Chapter 18, we learned how to make line drawings of three-dimensional figures. A much more realistic representation of these figures can be produced by making the sides of the figures appear solid and filling them with a color that varies with the distance from a light source projected onto the solid. Ideally, every point on a surface would be represented by a slightly different shade of the base figure to represent the light reflected from that particular point on the surface. Practically speaking, however, we don't have enough different color shades on the IBM PC to create all of these colors, nor do we have enough time for the computer to calculate the exact shade needed at every point on a surface. Clearly, some compromises are in order.

Selecting Palette Colors

The IBM PC, using the VGA high resolution mode, can display 16 out of a possible 256K shades of color. We shall use this for our optimum shaded display. The EGA can also display 16 different colors, but since it must select them from a range of only 64 colors, we have to do some adaptation to obtain a satisfactorily shaded display. If we wanted to sacrifice resolution, there is a VGA mode (mode 13H) that has the same resolution as the CGA, but displays 256 colors on the same display. We will leave it to the reader to design a shaded display using that mode. The techniques are much the same as we will show in the rest of this chapter, although the sides of the cubes might have to be broken up into smaller areas, or the polygons that make up the sphere might need to be smaller.

We will start with a description of how we solve the shading problem for the EGA. After that, the changes required for the VGA will be noted. The techniques for the CGA, which are similar but less effective to those used for the EGA, will not be discussed, but the three-dimensional demonstration program for the CGA is listed in Appendix F.

For the EGA, we can select somewhere around five shades of a particular color to use for our shading. The easiest way to decide which colors to use is to have a palette of colors on the screen, and change one of them at a time, scanning through the 64 possible colors until you come upon one that you want to include in your final palette. This can then be entered into the proper position, and another color searched for. Figure 19-1 is a program which you can use to perform this operation. The program displays on the screen the selected 16 colors, with their palette numbers above them. You are instructed to enter first a palette number and then a color number. The selected palette on the display then changes to that color and the selected color number appears below it. Note that palette 0 should probably be black (color 0) if you want a black background to be available. Once you have selected the color numbers for your 16 palettes, you need to jot them down so that you can create the proper statements in your program to recreate this set of colors. Then you can terminate the *palette* program by typing in a color number greater than 150.

Figure 19-1: Program to Select Colors for Palette

```
  palette = Program to select the colors for a palette
```

```
#include <stdio.h>
#include <math.h>
#include <dos.h>
#include "gtools.h"
#include "gdraws.h"

int LINEWIDTH=1, OPERATOR=0, ANGLE, XCENTER, YCENTER;
unsigned long int PATTERN=0xFFFFFFFF;

main ()
{
    int i,j,k=0;
    setMode(16);
    gotoxy(4,6,0);
    printf("0    1    2    3    4    5    6    7    8    9   10"
        "   11   12   13   14   15");
```

```
for (i=0; i<16; i++)
    fillRect((32*i-303),100,(32*(i+1)-303),0,i);
while (k<150)
{
    gotoxy(20,22,0);
    printf("                          ");
    gotoxy(20,23,0);
    printf("                          ");
    gotoxy(20,22,0);
    printf("Enter palette number: ");
    scanf("%d",&j);
    gotoxy(20,23,0);
    printf("Enter color number: ");
    scanf("%d",&k);
    if (k > 150)
        break;
    setEGApalette(j,k);
    gotoxy(3+4*j,13,0);
    printf("%2d",k);
}
}
```

Creating Shades by Halftoning

The term *halftoning* comes from the printing industry, where all black and white reproductions of photographs that appear to have innumerable shades of gray actually are printed with a single-color (usually black) ink. This is achieved by making a *halftone* plate for photo reproduction by photographing the original photo through a fine screen so that the image is broken into a series of very small dots. The dots are of differing sizes depending upon the original shade of gray in the particular area of the photograph, and the result is the appearance of a number of different shades of gray. Of course we can't do exactly this with the computer, since the screen pixels are of a fixed size. We can, however, produce shaded areas consisting of two colors mixed in some pattern so as to give the appearance of a shade intermediate between the two colors that are mixed. The use of the term *halftoning* has carried over from the printing industry to describe this process. Figure 19-2 lists a function that provides this shading process for plotting points and gives you a lot of flexibility in mixing colors.

Figure 19-2: Function to Provide Shaded Surfaces

```
pattern_plot() = plots points alternating between
                 two colors according to a specified
                 pattern
```

```c
void pattern_plot(int x, int y, int color)
{
    unsigned int mask;
    int pattern[4][8]={{0xFFFF,0xFFFF,0xFFFF,0xFFFF,
        0xFFFF,0xFFFF,0xFFFF,0xFFFF},{0x2020,0x0202,
        0x8080,0x0808,0x2020,0x0202,0x8080,0x0808},
        {0x4444,0x1111,0x4444,0x1111,0x4444,0x1111,
        0x4444,0x1111},{0xAAAA,0x5555,0xAAAA,0x5555,
        0xAAAA,0x5555,0xAAAA,0x5555}},foreground,
        background,fill;

    foreground = color & 0x0F;
    background = (color & 0xF0) >> 4;
    fill = (color & 0xF00) >> 8;
    mask = 0x8000 >> (x % 16);
    if (pattern[fill][y%8] & mask)
        plot(x,y,foreground);
    else
        plot(x,y,background);
}
```

The principal difference between this and a simple plotting routine is in the parameter *color*. This parameter is a composite of three different parameters, one of which selects the fill pattern, one the background color, and one the foreground color. If the contents of *color* are established with a hexidecimal input, like *0xABC*, then *A* will be the fill number, which must be between 0 and 3, *B* is the background color, and *C* is the foreground color. The parameter *color* is split up into these three separate parameters at the beginning of the function. Note that the function is set up so that if the fill and background parameters are not present (so that *color* contains an ordinary color of the type we would pass to the *plot* function), then the function behaves exactly as if it were the ordinary *plot* function. If the other parameters are present, then *fill* is used to select one of four sets of patterns. The function then performs a modulo eight operation on the line number to determine which of eight pattern words is to be used. It then performs a modulo 16 operation on the column number to determine which of the 16 bits in the pattern is to be used for a test. If the selected pattern bit is a one, the point to be plotted is plotted in the foreground color; if it is a zero, the point is plotted in the background color. The patterns are set up so that if *fill* is zero, all of the points are plotted in the foreground color. If *fill* is one, 12.5% of the points are in the foreground color and the rest in the background color. If *fill* is two, 25% of the points are in the foreground color and the rest in the background color. If *fill* is three, the foreground and background colors are split, 50% to each. The use of eight different words for each set of patterns allows a different positioning of the bits for eight different lines to prevent objectionable repetitions from occurring. If you don't like the patterns that are produced, you can change the words in the *pattern* array to create any kind of patterns that you like.

Determining Which Colors and Patterns to Display

You will remember that in Chapter 18 we set up a function called *surface_test* which determined whether a surface should be displayed or not. That function simply returned a floating point number which was positive if the surface was hidden and negative if the surface should be displayed. To provide shading of surfaces, we create a new function called *shaded_surface_test*. This function returns an integer that is the color that should be used in the *pattern_plot* function. The function begins by performing the same test done by *surface_test* to decide whether a surface should be hidden or displayed. If the surface is hidden, the color is returned as 9999, which is a signal to the calling program not to display the surface. Otherwise, the function determines the plane defined by the surface coordinates and sets up a unit vector perpendicular to this plane. It then takes the cross product of this unit vector and the unit vector representing the direction of the source of illumination for the surface. The resulting cross product is a number between -1 and +1. If it is less than zero, the surface is not illuminated, so we return the darkest shade of color (to distinguish it from the black background). A *switch* statement is used to set the foreground, background, and fill pattern parameters (combined into a single parameter *color*) for whichever of the 16 possible values occurs. The function assumes that you have set up the colors that you want it to modulate between as colors 1 through 5 of the palette. The function is listed in Figure 19-3.

Figure 19-3: Function to Determine Shades for a Surface

```
shaded_surface_test() = function to determine whether a
                        surface should be hidden or
                        visible and if visible what color
                        it should be displayed in
```

```
int shaded_surface_test(float x1, float y1, float z1,
    float x2, float y2,float z2, float x3, float y3,
    float z3)

{
    float v_mag,vert_x1,vert_x2,vert_y1,vert_y2,
        vert_z1,vert_z2,stest,vxn,vyn,vzn;
    int test;

    stest = x1*(y3*z2-y2*z3) - x2*(y3*z1 - y1*z3) -
        x3*(y1*z2-y2*z1);
    color = 9999;
    if (stest < 0)
    {
        vert_x1 = x2 - x1;
        vert_y1 = y2 - y1;
        vert_z1 = z2 - z1;
        vert_x2 = x3 - x1;
        vert_y2 = y3 - y1;
        vert_z2 = z3 - z1;
        vxn = (vert_y1*vert_z2) - (vert_z1*vert_y2);
        vyn = (vert_x1*vert_z2) - (vert_z1*vert_x2);
        vzn = (vert_y1*vert_x2) - (vert_x1*vert_y2);
        v_mag = 1.0/sqrt(vxn*vxn + vyn*vyn + vzn*vzn);
        v_mag = v_mag*(vxn*xls + vyn*yls + vzn*zls);
        test = 9*v_mag;
        if (test < 0)
            color = 0x101;
        else
        {
            switch(test)
            {
                case 0:
                    color = 0x201;
                    break;
```

```
case 1:
    color = 0x01;
    break;
case 2:
    color = 0x112;
    break;
case 3:
    color = 0x212;
    break;
case 4:
    color = 0x312;
    break;
case 5:
    color = 0x221;
    break;
case 6:
    color = 0x02;
    break;
case 7:
    color = 0x223;
    break;
case 8:
    color = 0x323;
    break;
case 9:
    color = 0x232;
    break;
case 10:
    color = 0x03;
    break;
case 11:
    color = 0x134;
    break;
case 12:
    color = 0x234;
    break;
case 13:
    color = 0x334;
    break;
case 14:
    color = 0x243;
    break;
```

```
            case 15:
                color = 0x143;
            break;
            case 16:
                color = 0x04;
        }
    }
    return (color);
}
```

Displaying a Shaded Cube

Figure 19-4 lists a function for displaying a shaded cube. Note how similar this function is to that used to draw a three-dimensional cube. The only differences are that the *shaded_surface_test* function is used to not only test whether a surface should be drawn, but also to determine what color and fill should be used if the surface is to be displayed; and that the *fillPoly* function is used to fill in the surfaces instead of simply outlining them with the *drawPoly* function.

Figure 19-4: Function to Draw a Shaded Cube

```
 fill_cube() = Function to draw a three-dimensional
               cube with shaded surfaces

void fill_cube(float rot_pts[8][3],int vx[],int vy[])
{

    fill_side(7,0,3,6,rot_pts,vx,vy);
    fill_side(6,5,4,7,rot_pts,vx,vy);
    fill_side(3,2,5,6,rot_pts,vx,vy);
    fill_side(0,1,2,3,rot_pts,vx,vy);
    fill_side(7,4,1,0,rot_pts,vx,vy);
    fill_side(1,4,5,2,rot_pts,vx,vy);
}

void fill_side(int i1, int i2, int i3, int i4,
    float rot_pts[8][3],int vx[],int vy[])
{

    color = shaded_surface_test(rot_pts[i1][0],
        rot_pts[i1][1], rot_pts[i1][2],rot_pts[i2][0],
```

```
            rot_pts[i2][1], rot_pts[i2][2],rot_pts[i3][0],
            rot_pts[i3][1], rot_pts[i3][2]);
    if (color < 999)
        fillPoly(color,vx[i1],+vy[i1],vx[i2],+vy[i2],
            vx[i3],+vy[i3],vx[i4],+vy[i4],-999);
}
```

Displaying a Shaded Sphere

Figure 19-5 lists a function for displaying a shaded sphere. Again, the function is very similar to the corresponding function for drawing a sphere. The only differences are that the *shaded_surface_test* function is used to not only test whether a surface should be drawn, but also to determine what color and fill should be used if the surface is to be displayed; and that the *fillPoly* function is used to fill in the surfaces instead of simply outlining them with the *drawPoly* function.

Figure 19-5: Setting Palette and Color Registers

```
fragment of program to set the palette registers to
point to the first 16 color registers and set the color
registers to black and 15 shades of green
```

```
for (i=0; i<16; i++)
{
    setEGApalette(i,i);
    writeColorReg(i,0,4*i,0);
}
```

Shading with the VGA

With the high resolution mode of the VGA, we can do our shading with 15 different shades of green, plus a black background. Of course, this uses up all the colors, as far as that particular display is concerned. We use the *writeColorReg* function, which is a part of the *gtools* library for the VGA. This function permits setting each of the 256 color registers to a six bit value for red, blue, and green. The shades of color that you want to use are limited only by your imagination.

One approach, which has been used here, is to use only the green color and simply increase its intensity for each of 16 registers which we are going to use. Figure 19-5 shows a small section of code which is used to set the color registers and the palette registers instead of the settings that were used for the EGA. You need to remember that the VGA high resolution mode has 16 palette registers, which set the 16 colors that we can display. Each palette register directs the VGA to one of the 256 color registers. To assure compatibility with the EGA, these palette registers are set by default to point to 16 color registers that contain the same 16 shades of color that the EGA normally displays. These are not color registers 0 through 15. If you want to, you can write a program to use the *readColorReg* function to read the 16 palette registers and determine which color registers need to be set to bring the 16 shades of green to the display. It's probably easier to do what was done here; namely to first assign the 16 palette registers to the first 16 color registers and then assign the first 16 color registers to the 16 shades of green.

Another approach is to not only increase green intensity, but add in some blue and red so that the brightest shades of green become whiter. If you want to experiment with assigning colors, the program listed in Figure 19-6 will let you display the 16 colors and change them any way you want.

Figure 19-6: Function to Set Up VGA Color Palette

```
color setting = sets color registers to desired values
```

```c
#include <stdio.h>
#include <math.h>
#include <dos.h>
#include "gtools.h"
#include "gdraws.h"

int color,register_no;
int LINEWIDTH=1, OPERATOR=0, ANGLE, XCENTER, YCENTER;
unsigned long int PATTERN=0xFFFFFFFF;
unsigned long int style[8] = { 0xFFFFFFFF,0xC0C0C0C0,
    0xFF00FF00,0xFFF0FFF0,0xF000F000,
    0xFFFF0000,0xFFFFF0F0,0xFFF0F0F0};
char ch;

main ()

{
```

```
int i,j,angle,palette, red,green,blue;

setMode(0x12);
cls(0);
for (i=0; i<16; i++)
setEGApalette(i,i);
for (i=-310,j=0; i<=170; i+=30,j++)
{
    fillRect(i,100,i+30,40,j);
}
for (;;)
{
    gotoxy(20,20);
    printf("Enter palette no: ");
    scanf("%d",&palette);
    if (palette > 16)
        break;
    gotoxy(20,21);
    printf("Enter red value: ");
    scanf("%d",&red);
    gotoxy(20,22);
    printf("Enter green value: ");
    scanf("%d",&green);
    gotoxy(20,23);
    printf("Enter blue value no: ");
    scanf("%d",&blue);
    writeColorReg(palette,red,green,blue);
    gotoxy(20,20);
    printf("                          ");
    gotoxy(20,21);
    printf("                          ");
    gotoxy(20,22);
    printf("                          ");
    gotoxy(20,23);
    printf("                          ");
}
}
```

Figure 19-7 lists a section of the *shaded_surface_test* function to show the changes that are made for the VGA. For this adapter, this part of the function is almost trivial. You should note for both this and the corresponding EGA function that negative values of *test* represent parts of the figure that are not illuminated by the light source. We could color them black, but if we do, they would not be differentiated from the black background. Therefore, we set the unillumi-nated color to the darkest shade of green. Figure 19-8 (color section) shows the shaded VGA cubes.

Figure 19-7: Portion of Shaded Surface Test for VGA

```
shaded_surface_test() = portion of function showing
                        changes for use with VGA
```

```
test = 13*v_mag;
if (test <0)   color = 1;
switch(test)
{
    case 0:
        color = 0x02;
        break;
    case 1:
        color = 0x03;
        break;
    case 2:
        color = 0x04;
        break;
    case 3:
        color = 0x05;
        break;
    case 4:
        color = 0x06;
        break;
    case 5:
        color = 0x07;
        break;
    case 6:
        color = 0x08;
        break;
    case 7:
        color = 0x09;
        break;
    case 8:
        color = 0x0A;
        break;
```

```
case 9:
    color = 0x0B;
    break;
case 10:
    color = 0x0C;
    break;
case 11:
    color = 0x0D;
    break;
case 12:
    color = 0x0E;
    break;
case 13:
    color = 0x0F;
```

20

Creating
a Graphics Library

At this point, you should have a good understanding of a number of useful graphics functions. The time has come to put them together in a useful and efficient manner for transportation between C programs. Of course, you could take every function that you need for a particular program and include it as part of the program. This is apt to be inefficient. Even more inefficient is making one big package of graphics functions to include in every program that requires graphics. This inflicts the overhead of all the graphics code on every program, even if it only requires a single graphics function.

Fortunately, you can create one or more libraries to store your graphics functions. There are three main advantages to having all of your graphics functions in libraries:

1. Functions are stored in the library in object code. Therefore C does not have to recompile them every time it compiles your C program. If you're making frequent changes and debugging new software, this decrease in compilation time can result in substantial time savings.

2. The C linker is set up so that when it links your program, it searches whatever library files you have specified each time it encounters an unrecognizable function name. If it finds the function, it extracts it from the library and adds it to the final code. Thus only those functions that are actually called by your software are included in the final package; other functions in the library are ignored. This minimizes the size of your final program and does not occupy a lot of memory with functions that you aren't using. Furthermore, if you make a change in the program that requires a previously unused library function, it will be incor-

porated automatically the next time you compile and link the program. Microsoft C does this using the following command line:

```
cl cprogrm.c /lgraphic.lib
```

where *cl* activates the Microsoft C compiler and linker, *cprogrm.c* is the file name of your C program, */l* indicates that the name of a library follows, and *graphic.lib* is the name of the library. Turbo C, using the integrated environment, requires that, before you compile and link, you have a project file that includes all of the names of the library files and the name of your C language file. When you compile and link, the linker will abstract those functions that are needed from the libraries you have specified.

3. If you are using in-line assembly language in any of your functions (the *plot* routine is one that is a good candidate) you cannot compile the function within the Turbo C integrated environment. You can, however, compile the module with the command line compiler and then store the object code in a library, which can be used by a program which is being edited, compiled, and linked within the total integrated environment.

It's possible for the generation of libraries to get a little cumbersome and complex, but with a little care, a procedure can be worked out that makes the whole process relatively simple. First, it is best to have more than one library. For example, those useful tools that are derived from ROM BIOS video services (as described in Chapter 6) can be grouped together in one library. A second library can contain drawing routines for drawing lines; drawing and filling rectangles; drawing and filling ovals, circles, and polygons; and generating horizontal, vertical, big, and video characters. The fundamental point-plotting function can be included in this library. The character table that is used with the custom text writing functions is quite large, so it's best not to have it included in your program if you can get along with the ROM BIOS video service-based character writing routines. It can be in a separate header file that is included only when you are using the character writing functions.

Preparing to Create a Library

I recommend that you first group together the functions that you want to put into a library in a separate program. Call it BIOSVID.C, for example. To make this work together with your main C program, the main program must have at its beginning an include statement of one of the two following forms:

```
#include "BIOSVID.c"

#include <BIOSVID.c>
```

In Turbo C, these two forms are not interchangeable. The first, where the file name is included in quotation marks, indicates that the file is to be found in the same directory as the Turbo C editor/compiler/linker. The second form indicates that there is a header file for the program in the subdirectory of the main Turbo C directory called INCLUDE and a library file in the subdirectory LIB. At this point, you should have the file of graphics functions in the same directory as your Turbo C compiler and program, so the first form is the one to use. You now should get your program (or a demonstration program that makes use of all of the functions that are to be in the library) debugged and working with the proposed library functions. This is the time to correct any errors in the functions and to freeze their coding in its final form.

Setting Up a Header File

Once the demonstration program is running well, its time to begin the process of getting all of the functions into a library. First, you need a header file that contains the description of each function that is to be in the library. This is the same as the description that will be at the head of the function, except that it is immediately followed by a semicolon. For example:

```
void SetCursor (int start, int end);
```

The header file may also contain definitions of any global variables that are needed by the library functions, or at least reference them as *extern* variables. The listings in this book have adopted the convention that such variables are in all capital letters. Thus, when you see such a variable, you know where to find it; it is a global variable. By convention, each header file ends in a *.h*; for example:

```
gtools.h
```

It is also a good idea to give the header file and its associated library the same name, so that the library associated with *gtools.h* will be *gtools.lib*.

309

Making Object Code Modules

Next, you need to make an object code file for each function separately. In order to be able to compile each module to object code, you must first separate that module from the total function file (BIOSVID.C, for example). Unless the module contains in-line assembly code, you can do this from the Turbo C integrated environment. Hit F10 and select the *LOAD* option. Select a unique file name for the particular function you are working on. The screen will come up blank to indicate that the file is currently empty. Type a control-K followed by an R to load the contents of another file into the new one you have opened. Turbo C will ask you for a file name, and you can specify the name of the total function file (BIOSVID.C). The entire file will be loaded. (Note that after you have gone through this procedure once, each time you repeat it Turbo C will offer up the name of the file that you specified after the control-K R commmand. If you are keeping the same total function file, which will normally be the case, you only need to hit the RET key at this point to have it loaded into each newly created file.)

You now need to delete all material that is extraneous to the one function that you are going to compile. At the start of the file, hit control-K followed by B to set the beginning mark. Then scroll the cursor down to the point just before the desired function begins and hit control-K followed by K to set the end marker and then control-K followed by Y to erase all of the material between the markers. Then you can move the cursor to the end of the function you have currently selected, mark it with control-K followed by B, hit control-Q followed by C to go to the end of the file, and then again hit control-K, K, control-K and Y to mark and erase all of the material. At this point, all that should be left in your file is the listing of the desired function.

In order to be able to compile this function successfully, there is some material that must be at the the beginning of your function listing. First is an include statement for the header file. At this point you need to decide where you want the header file and library files to be kept. If you don't mind having them in the same directory with your program and the Turbo C compiler, your include statement can read:

```
#include "gtools.h"
```

If you would prefer to keep the header file with other header files in the INCLUDE directory and the library file with other library files in the LIB directory, you can use the form:

```
#include <gtools.h>
```

If your function makes use of any of the functions that are a part of one of the standard libraries, you need to put an include statement for each of those libraries at the beginning of your listing. Also, if you function makes use of any global variables that are not defined in the function, you need to define them with an *extern* statement, as for example:

```
extern int LINEWIDTH, OPERATOR;
```

The function should now be ready to compile. Type F10, select the Compile option, and then hit a return to choose the first sub-option, Compile to Object Code. The compilation should now take place. If Turbo C reports success, you are done with this function; if it reports errors, the most common causes are lack of an include statement for a library that is being used by the function and failure to define an external variable with an *extern* statement. If compilation was successful, you can type F10 and select the Load option again and repeat the process to create the object module for the next function.

The same basic procedure is used to edit the function files using whatever editor you normally use with Microsoft C. You then return to DOS and enter the command line:

```
cl filename.c /c
```

to compile the file without linking it.

Using the LIB Program

When all of the desired functions have been reduced to object code, you need to make use of the Turbo C *tlib* or the MicroSoft LIB program to combine them into a library. For easiest operation, copy this program to the same directory where your object modules are located. You remain in this directory, but leave Turbo C and return to DOS. The LIB program can perform the functions shown in Figure 20-1.

Figure 20-1: LIB Program Functions

1. Create a new library

2. Check the consistency of an existing library

3. Create a library-reference listing file

4. Maintain an existing library

Figure 20-2: LIB Program Tasks

Symbol	Action to be Taken
+	Add Module
-	Delete Module
-+	Replace Module
*	Copy Module to an external file
-*	Copy Module to an external file and then delete module from library

LIB tasks are assigned by symbols placed before the name of the object code module which is to be operated upon. The tasks are defined in Figure 20-2. You can run LIB in either of two ways. If you just type *LIB* and a return, LIB will prompt you through the necessary inputs. Alternately, you can enter the necessary information on the command line so that the program proceeds to run immediately. Upon typing just *LIB*, the program will ask:

```
Library name:
```

At this point you type in the name that you have selected for your library file. You do not have to include the extension *LIB*; LIB will add that to the file name automatically. If there already is a library file having that name, LIB will proceed to execute tasks on that file; if no file exists with the selected name, LIB will ask:

```
Library file does not exist.   Create?
```

If your reply is *y*, the new library file will be created. When the library is ready for work, the program prompts:

```
Operations:
```

You can now type in as many tasks as you want to perform, following each one with the name of an object module. If the name you type does not include an extension, LIB will assume that the extension is *.obj.*. If you want to perform more tasks than will fit on a single line, type an *&* following the last command that will fit on the line and then when you hit *RET*, LIB will prompt you for additional tasks. After you have completed entering tasks and hit the return button, LIB will prompt:

```
List file:
```

If you want to make a library-reference listing file, type in the name to be assigned to it at this point; if you don't want to, hit *RET*. The file, if created, will contain the latest information on your library file after the tasks you have assigned have been performed. You can print or view it with standard DOS commands.

When you have hit *RET*, LIB will prompt:

```
Output library:
```

If you hit the *RET* key at this point, the new library will replace the one (if it exists) whose name you assigned at the beginning of the LIB program. If you enter a file name at this point, the new file will be stored to the new name, and the old file name will contain the unchanged old file contents.

Running LIB from the Command Line

You can run the library program by typing something like the following:

```
LIB GTOOLS + FSTFILE + SCNDFILE + THRDFILE;
```

where GTOOLS is the name you are going to give to your library, and FST-FILE, SCNDFILE, and THRDFILE are names that you have assigned to the individual function modules. The LIB program assumes that your modules are all present and have the extension *.OBJ*. If this is not true, you will get an error message. If everything is correct, the modules will be added to a library called *GTOOLS.LIB*. You can add as many modules to the library in one pass as you want. In fact, one statement can be used for a single operation to add all of the functions you want in the library, but it is probably simpler to run the program several times, adding a few more files each time. The semicolon at the end of this command tells LIB to use the default responses for any LIB prompts that you have not responded to. The default responses are simply carriage returns, so that with the semicolon, you will not create a library-reference list file, nor will you change the name of the new library to be created.

The Turbo C *tlib* program works in essentially the same way as the Microsoft library program. It may be somewhat faster.

This is all you really need to know to create your library, but the other tasks may come in handy if you need to update it. If you want to delete a module, you can do it with the - task and if you want to replace a module with an updated version, you can use the -+ task.

Some Concerns with Header Files

In order to compile correctly, some of your functions may need generic header files such as *dos.h*. The normal inclination is to put the include statement at the beginning of each function, before the function definition. If you do this, the Microsoft library program is very forgiving; when you add several such functions to the library, it simply reports that you are attempting to repeat some definitions and then ignores the duplicate definitions. The Turbo C library program is not so forgiving and won't let you add functions to the library that redefine.

Next, you might think about putting the include statement inside each function. This works fine if you are going to compile a single function at a time; if not, you will get multiple definition errors during compilation. What seems to work with Turbo C is that if you are compiling a single function, the *include* statements must be within the function, but if you are compiling several functions at the same time, the include statement can be before the beginning of the functions.

The Library-Reference Listing File

The library-reference listing file provides a useful summary of the contents of your library. You can create it with the command line:

```
LIB GTOOLS,GTOOLS
```

where GTOOLS.LIB is the name of your library, and GTOOLS is the name you wish to assign to the library-reference listing file. These do not have to be the same except for the extension; you can assign any name to the library-reference listing file that you desire. If it does have the same name as the library file, however, you won't forget what to look for. Figure 20-3 shows the beginning of the library-reference listing file, which cross-references each Turbo C function to the name of the object file that contains it. Figure 20-4 shows the remainder of the library-reference listing file, which includes the offset from the library beginning and the size of each module.

Figure 20-3: Library-Reference Listing File - Summary Part

```
_cls ........................cls              _getAdapter ......getadap
_getMode...............getmode
_getPage ...............getpage
_getxy....................getxy              _gotoxy............gotoxy
_readChar...............readchar
_readPixel ..............readpix
_reg .......................setmode
_scrollWindowDn. ....scrolldn
_scrollWindowUp .....scrollup
_setBackground ......setback
_setCGAPalette.......setcga
_setMode...............setmode
_setPage................setpage
_setWindow............setwndo
_writChar ................writchar
_writString ..............writstng
```

Finally, it is not necessary to have a separate module for each C function. However, it makes it a lot easier to revise library functions if you don't have too many of them within a single compiled object file.

Using the Library

When your library is complete, you can now include it in whatever program you are working on. At the beginning of your program, you need the same include statement for the header file that was used in your function modules. You also need to remove include statements for any default libraries that have already been referenced in the functions you included in your new library. If you don't remove them, Turbo C will report a redefinition error, and it is much less forgiving of these than was the LIB program.

You can no longer use the F9 MAKE option to directly compile and link your program. You must have a project file. You can create this with the Turbo C editor. It has the file name:

```
nnnnnnnn.PRJ
```

where *nnnnnnnn* is any eight character name acceptable to DOS. In its simplest form, the project file has only two lines; the first is the filename of your library file and the second is the name of your current Turbo C program, of which the library file is to be a part.

Now each time you start up Turbo C to work on this program within the integrated environment, you must first go to the PROJECT option and insert the project file name that you have assigned. You can then go back to editing your program with the assurance that it will be properly compiled and linked whenever you hit the F9 key. If you are using Microsoft C, you can include the library names after your program name, preceeded with a */l*.

Figure 20-4: Balance of Library-Reference Listing File

```
setmode       Offset: 00000010H  Code and data size: 31H
  _reg                _setMode

getmode       Offset: 00000110H  Code and data size: 3aH
  _getMode

gotoxy        Offset: 00000220H  Code and data size: 3dH
  _gotoxy

getxy         Offset: 00000330H  Code and data size: 45H
  _getxy

setpage       Offset: 00000450H  Code and data size: 31H
  _setPage

getpage       Offset: 00000550H  Code and data size: 2dH
  _getPage

cls           Offset: 00000650H  Code and data size: 4dH
  _cls

setwndo       Offset: 00000790H  Code and data size: 53H
  _setWindow

scrollup      Offset: 000008d0H  Code and data size: 4eH
  _scrollWindowUp

scrolldn      Offset: 00000a10H  Code and data size: 4eH
  _scrollWindowDn

readchar      Offset: 00000b50H  Code and data size: 3eH
  _readChar

writchar      Offset: 00000c70H  Code and data size: 43H
  _writChar
writstng      Offset: 00000d90H  Code and data size: 7bH
  _writString

setcga        Offset: 00000ef0H  Code and data size: 36H
  _setCGAPalette
```

```
setback      Offset: 00001000H  Code and data size: 75H
  _setBackground


readpix      Offset: 00001180H  Code and data size: 37H
  _readPixel
getadap      Offset: 00001290H  Code and data size: 98H
  _getAdapter
```

Color
Graphics

Figure 11-4: Filled-in Ovals

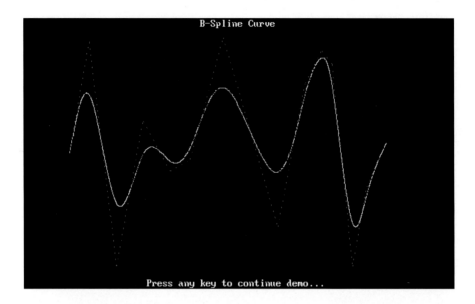

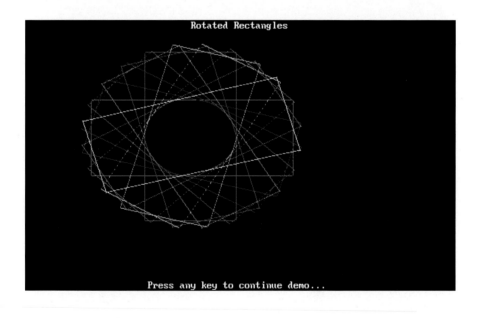

Top
Figure 13-5: B-Spline Curve

Bottom
Figure 14-3: Rotated Rectangles

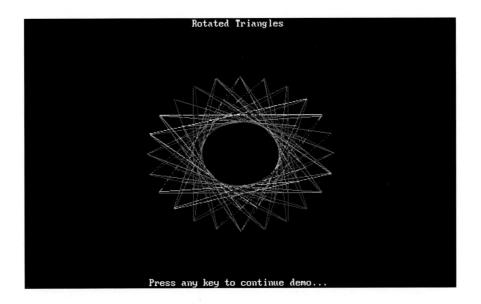

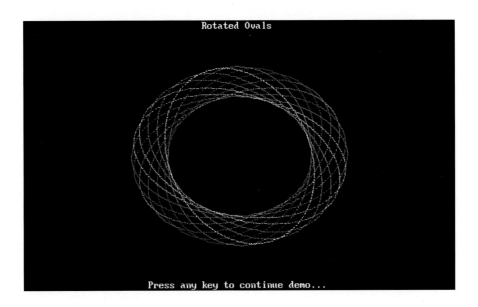

Top
Figure 14-5: Rotated Triangles

Bottom
Figure 14-7: Rotated Ovals

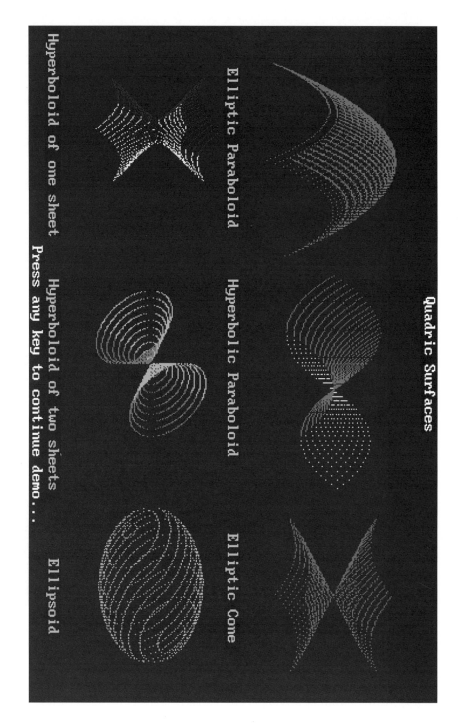

Figure 18-2: Quadric Surfaces

Figure 18-9: Three-Dimensional Sphere

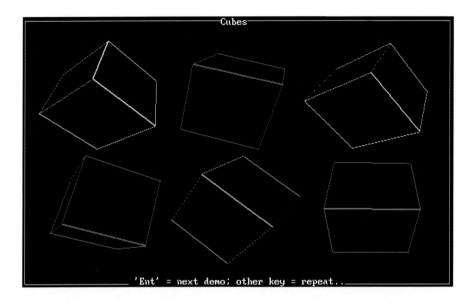

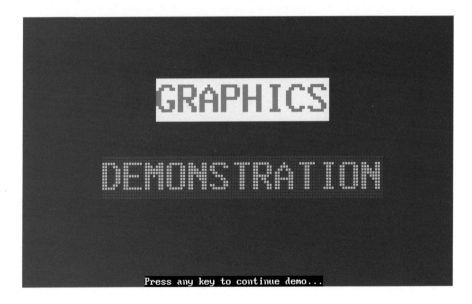

Top
Figure 18-7: Three-Dimensional Cubes

Bottom
Figure 21-2: Three-Dimensional Demonstration

Figure 21-7: City Skyline at Night

Figure 21-8: Stars

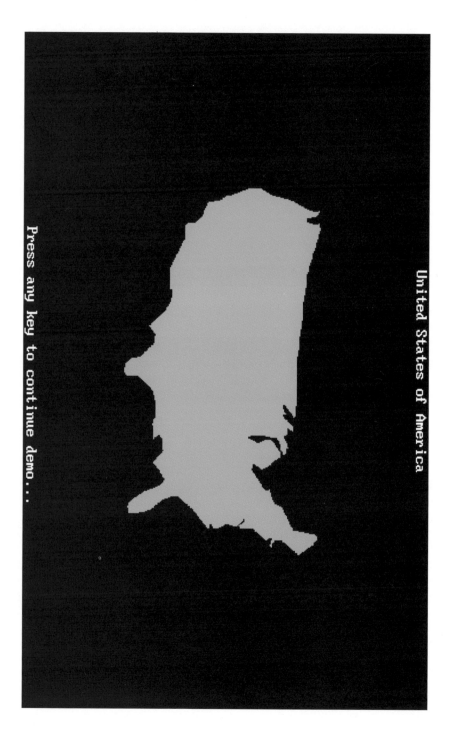

Figure 21-10: United States of America

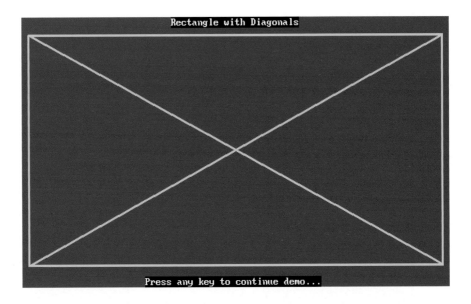

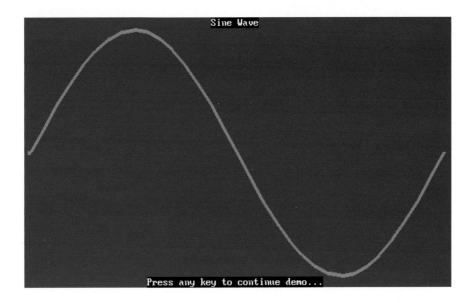

Top
Figure 21-3: Rectangle with Diagonals

Bottom
Figure 21-4: Sine Wave

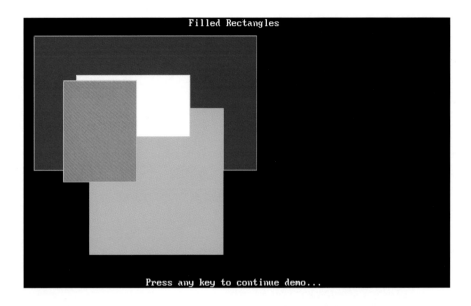

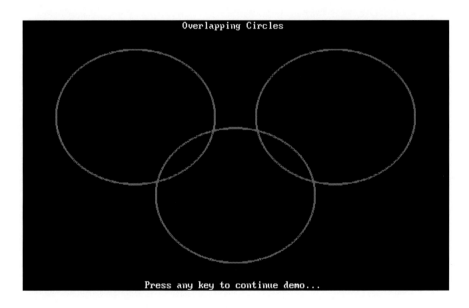

Top
Figure 21-5: Filled Rectangles

Bottom
Figure 21-11: Overlapping Circles

Figure 21-9: Irregular Polygons

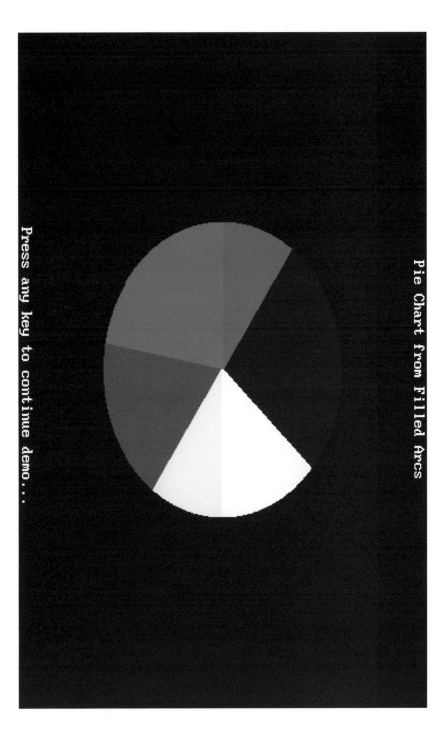

Figure 21-6: Pie Chart from Filled Arcs

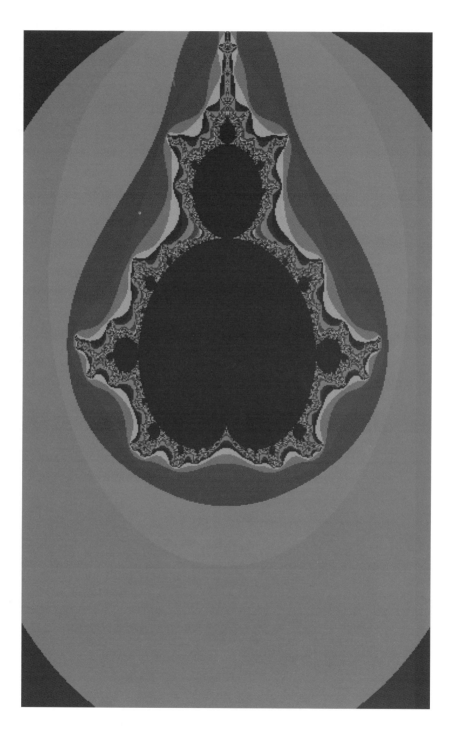

Figure 23-2: Mandelbrot Set

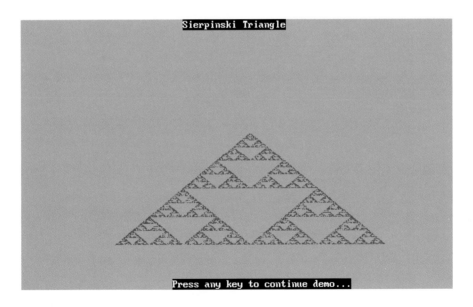

Top
Figure 23-4: Fern Leaf

Bottom
Figure 23-5: Sierpinski Triangle

Figure 19-8: VGA Shaded Cubes

21

Demonstration Programs

The ultimate test of the quality and usefulness of a set of graphics functions is how well and how easily they work when you use them in your programs. But it is not always easy to get started. There are always a few questions about how the functions should be used that don't seem to be answered by any book or instruction manual. Furthermore, if you are typing in the functions from this book, there may well be a few errors inserted that make the functions behave differently from what you expected. In order to help alleviate these difficulties, listings for two demonstration programs are provided.

The first demonstration program presents a number of displays, each of which features several of the functions described in previous chapters. It demonstrates the operation of all of the the functions in the *gtools* and *gdraws* libraries. You first need to create these libraries, as described in Chapter 20. You should then be able to run the first demonstration program. By observing this program in action, you should be able to resolve any questions about the functions that are still unanswered. Furthermore, this demonstration program is designed so that you can use it to debug your software and create an error-free set of graphics functions in the libraries.

The second demonstration program provides displays of all of the three-dimensional functions that are given in chapters 18 and 19. Since these functions are much more dependent on your exact requirements than are the more generic functions, these functions were not included in the libraries. The program does, however, make use of a number of functions from both the *gtools* and *gdraws* libraries. Each of the displays in this demonstration program randomly selects the three rotation angles for each of the six cubes or for the sphere. You may rerun each of the displays by typing any key except *Enter* to display the same basic display again with a new set of random orientations. When you finally hit *Enter*, the demonstration program moves on to the next display. This program can also be used in debugging your functions.

Using the Graphics Disk

If you bought the disk of graphics programs along with this book, you will find that it contains six archived files. One of these contains all of the files for the Hercules graphics card. If you have this card, you need to copy *arce.exe* and *herc.arc* to a fresh disk and then type:

```
arce herc.arc
```

to dearchive all of the Hercules programs. If you have a CGA, EGA, or VGA, you need to copy the *.arc* file for your particular card to a fresh disk, together with *demos.arc*, *source.arc*, and *arce.exe* and then type;

```
arce *.arc
```

to dearchive all of the programs for your adapter card. You will find that there are files for the gtools and gdraws libraries for use with Turbo C, and an *mcgraph* library for use with Microsoft C. In addition are source code listings for all of the library functions, in case you want to change them. There are also several demonstration programs. These include the two described in this chapter, the *cursor* program from Chapter 15, the *quadrics* program from Chapter 18, and the *image* program from Chapter 23. These programs can all be run using the CGA, EGA, or VGA. The Hercules file does not contain part of the three-dimensional demonstration program, since the shaded figures were not implemented for that card.

First Demonstration Program

Figure 21-1 is a listing of the first demonstration program for systems utilizing the CGA, EGA, or VGA. You can emulate one of the lower order cards with the more advanced card by changing the program to force the desired graphics mode and using the correct library; otherwise the demo selects the highest resolution mode for the card installed. The *gtools* library is set up to work with the VGA, EGA, or CGA, and is listed in Appendix D. The CGA, EGA, and VGA use the same source code for their *gdraws* libraries, but compile it with a different *#define* statement (*#define CGA*, *#define EGA* or *#define VGA*). The library contents is listed in Appendix E. The demonstration programs are listed in Appendix F for the CGA, EGA, or VGA and Appendix I for the Hercules Card. The appropriate *gtools* library for the Hercules card is listed in Appendix G and the *gdraws* library in Appendix H. The displays which make up the first demonstration program are described below.

Figure 21-1: Demonstration Program

```
/*    demo() = PROGRAM TO DEMONSTRATE THE USE OF THE
               TURBO C GRAPHICS FUNCTIONS            */


/*                    INCLUDES                       */

   #include <stdio.h>
   #include <math.h>
   #include <dos.h>
   #include <conio.h>

/*              USER WRITTEN INCLUDES                */

   #include "gtools.h"
   #include "gdraws.h"


/*    GLOBAL VARIABLES USED BY GRAPHICS FUNCTIONS    */



   char adapt;
   int color = 2;
   int LINEWIDTH=1, OPERATOR=0, ANGLE, XCENTER, YCENTER;
   int pt[12][2]={{-20,0},{0,0},{0,-120},{-200,-120},
       {-200,200},{90,150},{60,0},{200,0},{0,0}},x,y,z;
   unsigned long int PATTERN=0xFFFFFFFF;

   unsigned long int style[8] = { 0xFFFFFFFF,0xC0C0C0C0,
       0xFF00FF00,0xFFF0FFF0,0xF000F000,0xFFFF0000,
       0xFFFFF0F0,0xFFF0F0F0};

   int usa[600] = {-151,111,-146,107,-144, 96,-140, 96,-138,
       103,-139,111,-135,112,-111,
```

```
        103,-91, 96,-65, 92,-39, 89,-13, 85, 13, 85, 44, 82, 32,
        71, 30, 68, 35, 68, 41, 72, 41, 68, 44, 68, 54, 81, 57,
        81, 53, 74, 61, 72, 62, 70, 73, 75, 73, 72, 79, 71, 79,
        70, 75, 67, 69, 66, 63, 61, 61, 48, 61, 34, 63, 27, 65,
        27, 69, 38, 66, 48, 67, 55, 71, 60, 78, 66, 82, 66, 84,
        66, 84, 66, 87, 66, 86, 66, 89, 55, 93, 45, 87, 34, 93,
        31,114, 48,113, 53,127, 59,130, 68,152, 82,156,107,158,
        110,162,107,162,105,165,105,174, 89,160, 68,160, 61,165,
        55,167, 56,147, 59,158, 59,158, 55,160, 50,149, 34,149,
        20,147, 17,143, 24,140, 24,147, 15,144,  1,147, -2,149,
        -8,149,-13,145,-15,145,-19,149,-19,130,-39,119,-55,119,
        -61,123,-75,123,-75,130,-85,132,-89,134,-96,135,-103,134,
        -114,130,-115,123,-110,115,-96,110,-79,106,-72,104,-71,
        96, -77, 87,-85, 75,-71, 74,-74, 65,-74, 61,-78,65,-85,
        52,-86, 45,-82, 28,-83, 19, -85, 13,-92,  5,-103,  5,
        -116,  2,-119, -1,-119, -7,-116, -9,-114,-11,-111,-12,
        -104,-13,-100,-21,-90,-26,-83,-33,-82,-42,-90,-57,-70,
        -65,-64,-77,-61,-78,-66,-98,-64,-124,-48,-137,-48,-139,
        -45,-139,-37,-146,-27,-159,-20,-161, -6,-165,  0,-165,
        4,-170, 20,-172, 27,-172, 41,-165, 55,-160, 78,-152, 96,
        -150,103,-151,111,-999};


/*                   FUNCTION DEFINITIONS                    */

    void building();
    void wait(char title[]);
    void print_scr();

/*                      MAIN PROGRAM                         */

    main()
    {
        int i, j, k, x, y, oldx, oldy, midpoint;
        double xd,yd,ampl,aspect;
        char ch;

        cls (1);
        adapt = getAdapter();
        if ((adapt != 'E') && (adapt != 'C') && (adapt != 'V'))
        printf("Cannot Run Demo -- No CGA, EGA or VGA"
            " Installed!");
```

```
else
{
    if (adapt == 'V')
    {
        setMode(0x12);
        cls(1);
        write_big_str(-119,131,"GRAPHICS",226);
        write_vid_str(-200,-6,"DEMONSTRATION",91);
    }
    if (adapt == 'E')
    {
        setMode(16);
        cls(1);
        write_big_str(-119,131,"GRAPHICS",226);
        write_vid_str(-200,-6,"DEMONSTRATION",91);
    }
    if (adapt == 'C')
    {
        setMode(4);
        setCGAPalette(0);
        cls(1);
        write_big_str(-319,131,"GRAPHICS",226);
        write_vid_str(-319,-6,"DEMONSTRATION",91);
    }
    wait("");

    LINEWIDTH = 3;
    cls(4);
    drawRect(-309,210,310,-200,11);
    drawLine(-309,210,310,-200,11);
    drawLine(-309,-200,310,210,11);

    wait("Rectangle with Diagonals");

    LINEWIDTH = 5;
    ampl = 220;
    oldx = -315;
    oldy = 0;
    cls(1);
    for (i=0; i<=32; i++)
    {
        y = ampl * sin(6.283 * ((double)i)/32);
```

```
        x = 620 * (double)i/32 - 310;
        drawLine (oldx, oldy, x, y, 12);
        oldx = x;
        oldy = y;
    }
    wait("Sine Wave");

    cls(0);
    PATTERN = style[0];
    drawRect(-310,230,-280,200,1);
    PATTERN = style[1];
    drawRect(-300,160,-240,75,2);
    PATTERN = style[2];
    drawRect(-280,35,-220,-100,3);
    PATTERN = style[3];
    LINEWIDTH = 1;
    drawRect(-200,230,20,100,5);
    PATTERN = style[4];
    drawRect(-180,90,-70,-200,6);
    PATTERN = style[5];
    drawRect(40,75,60,200,7);
    PATTERN = style[6];
    drawRect(100,230,230,-175,9);
    PATTERN = style[7];
    drawRect(250,180,300,-90,10);
    PATTERN = style[0];
    wait("Examples of Dashed Lines");

    LINEWIDTH = 1;
    fillRect(-304,210,30,-30,1);
    drawRect(-304,210,30,-30,11);
    fillRect(-220,80,-20,-180,10);
    drawRect(-220,80,-20,-180,11);
    fillRect(-240,140,-70,30,15);
    drawRect(-240,140,-70,30,11);
    fillRect(-260,130,-150,-50,13);
    drawRect(-260,130,-150,-50,11);
    wait("Filled Rectangles");

    LINEWIDTH = 1;
    drawOval(-175,0,90,13,0.7);
    LINEWIDTH = 3;
```

```
drawOval(65,0,90,15,1.0);
LINEWIDTH = 5;
drawOval(240,0,90,10,1.3);
wait("Ovals and Circle");

LINEWIDTH = 3;
drawOval(-150,70,120,9,1.);
drawOval(0,-70,120,9,1.);
drawOval(150,70,120,9,1.);
wait("Overlapping Circles");

fillOval(-120,0,110,9,0.8);
fillOval(180,0,110,14,1.);
fillOval(220,50,20,0,1.);
fillOval(140,50,20,0,1.);
LINEWIDTH= 5;
drawLine(150,-60,210,-60,0);
drawLine(130,-53,150,-60,0);
drawLine(230,-53,210,-60,0);
drawLine(120,-40,130,-53,0);
drawLine(240,-40,230,-53,0);
wait("Filled Ovals");

aspect = .50;
for (i=0; i<3; i++)
{
    LINEWIDTH = 3;
    drawArc(0,0,120,0,450,5,aspect);
    drawArc(0,0,120,450,900,15,aspect);
    drawArc(0,0,120,900,1350,2,aspect);
    drawArc(0,0,120,1350,1800,15,aspect);
    drawArc(0,0,120,1800,2250,9,aspect);
    drawArc(0,0,120,2250,2700,15,aspect);
    drawArc(0,0,120,2700,3150,10,aspect);
    drawArc(0,0,120,3150,3590,15,aspect);
    wait("Oval Drawn By Combining Arcs");
    aspect +=.5;
}

fillArc(0,0,140,480,1380,1,1.);
fillArc(0,0,140,1380,1800,2,1.);
fillArc(0,0,140,1800,2600,3,1.);
```

```
fillArc(0,0,140,2600,3150,9,1.);
fillArc(0,0,140,3150,3600,14,1.);
fillArc(0,0,140,0,480,15,1.);
wait("Pie Chart from Filled Arcs");

LINEWIDTH = 1;
PATTERN = style[1];
for (i=0; i<7; i++)
drawLine(pt[i][0],pt[i][1],pt[i+1][0],pt[i+1][1],3);
PATTERN = style[0];

drawBezier(160,14,-20,0,0,0,0,-120,-200,-120,-200,
   200,90,150,60,0,200,0,-999);
wait("Bezier Curve");

PATTERN = style[1];
drawLine(-250,-25,-300,240,3);
drawLine(-300,240,-80,210,3);
drawLine(-80,210,-40,-25,3);
drawLine(-40,-25,160,-25,3);
drawLine(160,-25,300,-25,5);
drawLine(300,-25,300,220,5);
drawLine(300,220,40,240,5);
drawLine(40,240,-80,-239,5);
PATTERN = style[0];
drawBezier(160,13,-250,-25,-300,240,-80,210,-40,-25,
    160,-25,-999);
drawBezier(160,14,160,-25,300,-25,300,220,40,240,
    -80,-239,-999);
wait("Two Bezier Curves");

PATTERN = style[1];
drawLine(-250,0,-220,200,3);
drawLine(-220,200,-180,-200,3);
drawLine(-180,-200,-140,60,3);
drawLine(-140,60,-100,-30,3);
drawLine(-100,-30,-70,-10,3);
drawLine(-70,-10,-20,208,3);
drawLine(-20,208,+60,-130,3);
drawLine(+60,-130,100,125,3);
drawLine(100,125,125,185,3);
drawLine(125,185,140,160,3);
```

```
drawLine(140,160,170,-200,3);
drawLine(170,-200,190,-60,3);
drawLine(190,-60,220,20,3);
PATTERN = style[0];
drawBspline(160,14,-250,0,-220,200,-180,-200,
    -140,60,-100,-30,-70,-10,-20,208,60,-130,
    100,125,125,185,140,160,170,-200,190,-60,
    220,20,-999);
wait("B-Spline Curve");

x= -275;
y= 200;
for (k=0; k<37; k++)
{
    write_horz_char(x, y, k+33, 31);
    x += 16;
}
x = -275;
y = 180;
for (k=37; k<74; k++)
{
    write_horz_char(x, y, k+33, 31);
    x += 16;
}
x = -275;
y = 160;
for (k=74; k<93; k++)
{
    write_horz_char(x, y, k+33, 31);
    x += 16;
}
x= -319;
y= -210;
for (k=0; k<17; k++)
{
    write_vert_char(x, y, k+33, 47);
    y += 20;
}
x = -303;
y = -210;
for (k=17; k<34; k++)
{
```

```
        write_vert_char(x, y, k+33, 47);
        y += 20;
    }
    x = -287;
    y = -210;
    for (k=34; k<51; k++)
    {
        write_vert_char(x, y, k+33, 47);
        y += 20;
    }
    x = -271;
    y = -210;
    for (k=51; k<68; k++)
    {
        write_vert_char(x, y, k+33, 47);
        y += 20;
    }
    x = -255;
    y = -210;
    for (k=68; k<85; k++)
    {
        write_vert_char(x, y, k+33, 47);
        y += 20;
    }
    x = -239;
    y = -210;
    for (k=85; k<93; k++)
    {
        write_vert_char(x, y, k+33, 47);
        y += 20;
    }
    write_horz_str(-150,35, "HELLO WORLD!",62);
    write_vert_str(80,-200, "HOW ARE YOU TODAY?",109);
    wait("Alphanumerics");

    LINEWIDTH = 3;
    drawRoundRect(-300,210,300,-210,60,11);
    wait("Rounded Rectangle");

    fillRoundRect(-300,210,300,-210,60,13);
    wait("Filled Rounded Rectangle");
```

```
building();
wait("City Skyline at Night");

drawPoly(11,-259, 90,-59, 90,-159,-90,-999);
drawPoly(11,-259,-20,-159,160,-59,-20,-999);
fillOval(161,34,107,9,1.0);
fillPoly(14,60,66,262,66,104,-55,161,140,218,-55,
    -999);
wait("Stars");

fillPoly(13,-129,103,-69,172,-59,158,-64,144,-39,
    130,-34,151,-24,158,-19,116,1, 75,-9, 48, -49,
    61,-19, -6,-59,-34,-79,-6,-109,-48,-149,-6,
    -129,48,-149,61,-159,20,-179,61,-209,-34,-229,
    -6,-299,89,-249,103,-299,103,-299,130,-249,130,
    -269,172,-259,185,-999);

PATTERN = style[1];
LINEWIDTH = 1;
drawPoly(11,-129,103,-69,172,-59,158,-64,144,-39,
    130,-34,151,-24,158,-19,116,1, 75,-9, 48, -49,
    61,-19, -6,-59,-34,-79,-6,-109,-48,-149,-6,-129,
    48,-149,61,-159,20,-179,61,-209,-34,-229,-6,
    -299,89,-249,103,-299,103,-299,130,-249,130,
    -269,172,-259,185,-999);

fillPoly(14,120,0,168,-96,232,-96,232,-144,168,
    -144,72,-192,24,-160,24,-128,56,-128,40,-144,
    88,-128,88,-96,24,-64,120,32,-999);
drawPoly(15,120,0,168,-96,232,-96,232,-144,168,-144,
    72,-192,24,-160,24,-128,56,-128,40,-144,88,-128,
    88,-96,24,-64,120,32,-999);
wait ("Irregular Polygons");

PATTERN = style[0];
fill2Poly(10,usa);
wait("United States of America");

LINEWIDTH = 1;
cls(0);
color=3;
XCENTER = -70;
```

```
        YCENTER = 35;
        for (ANGLE=0; ANGLE<180; ANGLE+=15)
        {
            rotateRect(-220,100,80,-35,color);
            color++;
            if ((color % 4 == 0) && (adapt == 'C'))
                color++;
        }
        wait("Rotated Rectangles");

        cls(0);
        color=3;
        XCENTER = 0;
        YCENTER = 0;
        for (ANGLE=0; ANGLE<360; ANGLE+=15)
        {
            rotatePoly(color,-120,-70,0,100,120,-70,-999);
            color++;
            if ((color % 4 == 0) && (adapt == 'C'))
                color++;
            if (color == 0) color++;
        }
        wait("Rotated Triangles");

        cls(0);
        color=3;
        for (ANGLE=0; ANGLE<180; ANGLE+=15)
        {
            rotateOval(0,0,160,color,1.5);
            color++;
            if ((color % 4 == 0) && (adapt == 'C'))
                color++;
        }
        wait("Rotated Ovals");

    }
}

void wait(char title[])
{
    int tab,width,line,mode;
```

```
    mode = getMode(&width);
    if ((mode == 0x11) || (mode == 0x12))
    line = 29;
    else
    line = 24;
    tab = (width - strlen(title))/2;
    gotoxy(tab,0);
    writString(title,15,0);
    tab = (width - 33)/2;
    gotoxy(tab,line);
    writString("Press any key to continue demo...", WHITE,0);
    getch();
    cls(0);
}


void building()
{
    int i,j,hue;

    cls(0);
    fillRect(-280,130,-220,-200,9);
    for(i=-275; i<=-235; i+=20)
    {
        for(j=125; j>=-170; j-=40)
        {
            hue = ((rand()%2)*14);
            fillRect(i,j,i+10,j-25,hue);
        }
    }
    fillRect(-140,160,-60,-230,10);
    for(i=-130; i<=-80; i+=20)
    {
        for(j=155; j>=-190; j-=42)
        {
            hue = ((rand()%2)*14);
            fillRect(i,j,i+10,j-25,hue);
        }
    }
    fillRect(-80,-7,60,-200,11);
    fillRect(-40,50,30,-7,11);
    for(i=-75; i<=45; i+=20)
```

```
{
    for(j=-12; j>=-185; j-=30)
    {
        hue = ((rand()%2)*14);
        fillRect(i,j,i+10,j-10,hue);
    }
}
fillRect(40,80,100,-230,5);
for(i=45; i<=85; i+=20)
{
    for(j=75; j>=-215; j-=30)
    {
        hue = ((rand()%2)*14);
        fillRect(i,j,i+10,j-10,hue);
    }
}
fillRect(-220,50,-120,-175,3);
for(i=-215; i<=-135; i+=20)
{
    for(j=45; j>=-160; j-=30)
    {
        hue = ((rand()%2)*14);
        fillRect(i,j,i+10,j-10,hue);
    }
}
fillRect(200,100,280,-175,3);
for(i=205; i<=265; i+=20)
{
    for(j=95; j>=-160; j-=35)
    {
        hue = ((rand()%2)*14);
        fillRect(i,j,i+10,j-15,hue);
    }
}
fillRect(180,190,240,-200,13);
fillRect(200,75,220,190,13);
for(i=185; i<=225; i+=20)
{
    for(j=185; j>=-185; j-=30)
    {
        hue = ((rand()%2)*14);
        fillRect(i,j,i+10,j-10,hue);
```

```
        }
    }
    fillRect(90,75,190,-230,9);
    fillRect(110,105,170,75,9);
    fillRect(130,130,150,105,9);
    for(i=95; i<=175; i+=20)
    {
        for(j=67; j>=-215; j-=30)
        {
            hue = ((rand()%2)*14);
            fillRect(i,j,i+10,j-10,hue);
        }
    }
    for(i=115; i<=155; i+=20)
    {
        for(j=100; j>=90; j-=30)
        {
            hue = ((rand()%2)*14);
            fillRect(i,j,i+10,j-10,hue);
        }
    }
    fillRect(-220,105,-180,50,13);
    fillRect(-215,70,-205,55,0);
    fillRect(-195,70,-185,55,0);
    fillRect(-215,90,-205,75,14);
    fillRect(-195,90,-185,75,0);
    fillOval(-20,195,20,14,1.);
    fillOval(-30,195,20,0,1.);
}
```

Title Display

The demonstration program begins with the title display (Figure 21-2; see color section). The word "GRAPHICS" appears in large letters followed by the large word "DEMONSTRATION". The first word is a demonstration of the use of the *write_big_str* function and the second word uses the *write_vid_str* function. These two functions make use of the same dot matrix fonts used for other text material, but produce them at four times normal size. The *write_big_str* function fills in a 4x4 matrix for each original character pixel; the *write_vid_str* function only fills in a 3x3 section of the 4x4 matrix. This gives an effect as if the characters were generated on a light bulb display. If these characters appear properly on the display, you can be assured that the text character table and the described functions are working properly.

Rectangle with Diagonals

The next display, Figure 21-3 (see color section), is a rectangle that nearly fills the screen, with two diagonal lines drawn across it. The line width for these lines is three pixels. If the lines appear to be correct, it means that the *plot*, *drawLine* and *drawRect* functions are working correctly.

Sine Wave

Figure 21-4 (see color section) display draws a sine wave across the screen. It is created with a series of small line segments having line widths of 5 pixels. This again demonstrates the satisfactory working of the line drawing function.

Examples of Dashed Lines

This display shows a number of rectangles drawn with the different styles of lines that are available. The line styles are defined at the beginning of the program in the variable *style*. Eight line styles are available. You can experiment with different line styles by initializing the eight values of *style* in different patterns.

Filled Rectangles

Figure 21-5 (see color section) shows a set of overlapping rectangles, all outlined in a different color. From it, you can verify that the *fillRect* function is working satisfactorily. You can also note whether the *drawRect* function, which draws a line around the filled rectangles, is correctly coordinated with the *fillRect* function so that they both have the same boundaries.

Ovals and Circle

This display shows an oval whose width is greater than its height, a circle, and an oval whose height is greater than its width. The line width in pixels of the first oval is 1, of the second is 3, and of the third is 5. The linewidths are supposed to be set so that the center of the line is at the specified coordinates for the oval, but the successive ovals or circles are drawn so fast that you probably cannot see this. If you need to verify it, you can add more statements to the part of the program that generates this display and cause an oval of the same coordinates but with a different color and a one pixel linewidth to be superimposed on one of the ovals which uses the wider lines. The new line should be right in the middle of the wider one. The display demonstrates the proper functioning of the *drawOval* function. If the circle does not appear quite circular to you, you may need to adjust the vertical height of the display on your monitor. (The system coordinates are defined so that if you draw an oval with an aspect ratio of 1.0, it should appear on the screen as a circle.) If you feel that the circle is not circular enough, don't begin modifying the aspect ratio at this time, since looking at circles is not an adequate way to judge whether the monitor is properly adjusted. Later in this chapter, while describing the "Rotated Rectangles" display, we shall explain how to adjust your display for the best circularity.

Filled Ovals

This display shows a filled oval and a filled circle having a smiling face. It is created with the *fillOval* and *drawLine* functions. Its purpose is to verify the proper functioning of the *fillOval* function.

Oval Drawn By Combining Arcs

This set of three displays shows first an oval with its width greater than its height, then a circle, and finally an oval with its height greater than its width. Each oval or circle is generated by using the *drawArc* function to draw a series of arcs, each of which covers an adjacent 45 degree sector and each of which is drawn in a different color. You can determine from this display whether the *drawArc* function is working correctly. If the function's tests for the beginning and end point of each arc are working properly, there should be no overlapping and no gaps between arc segments. One thing to note is that the statement:

```
#include <math.h>
```

must be at the beginning of your program for this function to work correctly, since it makes use of sines and cosines that are in the math library. If you leave out the statement, C does not give you any kind of warning, but when you program runs, calls to sine or cosine functions return zeroes or garbage values which can be very confusing. It is particularly important when you begin breaking up your graphics functions into modules and compiling them to create a library that the above *include* statement be at the beginning of each module that uses math functions. Otherwise, you are apt to find that the function works perfectly while it is part of your program, but mysteriously quits as soon as it is transferred to the library of graphics functions. Another thing to observe on this display is that arcs covering 45 degrees only have equal length when the resulting figure is a circle. When an oval is being produced, different portions of the curve will have different lengths of arc subtending a 45-degree angle.

Pie Chart from Filled Arcs

Figure 21-6 (see color section) shows a pie chart, with each segment a different color. It is drawn with a series of *fillArc* statements. It is pretty slow, since filling an arc is one of our less efficient functions. This display determines whether the *fillArc* function is doing its job correctly.

Bezier Curves

These two displays show the drawing of Bezier curves. The first is a single Bezier curve, together with the convex hull that generates it. The second shows two joined Bezier curves and their convex hulls. Comparing the curves with the generating convex hulls will give an indication of whether the functions are working correctly. Funny curve responses usually indicate the use of integer variables where floating point ones are needed.

B-Spline Curve

This display shows a B-Spline curve and its generating convex hull. It should show pretty quickly whether this function is working correctly.

Alphanumerics

Figure 21-2 provided information on whether the *big* and *vid* functions were producing large characters and also gave some indication of whether the character font was properly programmed. The alphanumerics display shows the entire normal sized horizontal and vertical character fonts together with a sample message written in each direction. If the characters are correct, the text routines and character font are satisfactory.

Rounded Rectangle

This display draws a rounded rectangle that nearly fills the screen and has a linewidth of three pixels and a rounding radius of 50. If you are not satisfied with the fit of the straight line segments with the rounded corners, this is the diplay to use when you are tinkering with the *drawRoundRect* function.

Filled Rounded Rectangle

This display fills a rounded rectangle of the same size as the one in the previous display. This is the display to use to check the functioning of the *fillRoundRect* function and to verify the results of any modifications that you may wish to make to it.

City Skyline at Night

This fanciful display is shown in Figure 21-7 (see color section). It is designed to test the working of the *fillRect* function, which is called upon many times to create this display. If it does indeed look like a city at night, the *fillRect* function is working properly. The black or yellow color of the windows in the buildings is controlled by a random number function, so each time the display is produced, different windows are lighted.

Stars

This display appears in Figure 21-8 (see color section). The six-pointed star is produced by generating two equilateral triangles with the *drawPoly* function. The blue circle is generated by the *fillOval* function. The five-pointed star is generated using the *fillPoly* function. This is an example of the fact that the *fillPoly* function only guarantees to fill a polygon which is specified as a set of lines that bound a surface and do not intersect within it. The five-pointed star does not meet this criteria and as a consequence a polygon within it does not get filled. In addition to testing the functioning of the *drawPoly*, *fillPoly*, and *fillOval* functions, this display makes the point that the *drawPoly* and *fillPoly* functions can be used with any set of coordinates, though the result of using them with sets of lines that do not truly bound a surface may need to be determined by experimentation. Sometimes, as in the case of the five-pointed star, the result is quite pleasing. Also, if you do have a figure like this, you may use another *fillPoly* call to trace out the internal unfilled part of the figure and fill it in a separate step.

Irregular Polygons

Figure 21-9 (see color section) shows an irregular polygon in light magenta with a dashed white border and a yellow irregular polygon with a dashed white border. Its first purpose is to verify that the *fillPoly* function is working properly. As discussed in Chapter 12, the joints between the line segments composing the polygon offer critical points at which a fill function may create an error. When such errors occur, there will be black lines across the polygon or colored lines between points that are really outside the polygon. These will readily show up on this display. If any do, you need to go back and check the function carefully against the listing in Chapter 12. A single dropped value can make a big difference in performance, even if it does not appear to contribute much in the listing. The second purpose of this display is to verify that the 'drawPoly' function and the 'fillPoly' function place the same boundaries on the polygon. If the line drawn around the polygon is offset from the colored internal fill, there is a mistake in one or both functions which must be corrected.

United States of America

This display, shown in Figure 21-10 (see color section), verifies the functioning of the *fill2Poly* function. This function draws a polygon using the sets of coordinates from a coordinate array. It is almost certain to bomb out the complier if the *fillPoly* function is used instead. If the *fill2Poly* function is working correctly, the display should produce a reasonable representation of the United States.

Overlapping Circles

Figure 21-11 is a display of three overlapping circles. It verifies the proper operation of the *fillOval* function.

Rotated Rectangles

This display shows a rectangle at its original position and then rotated in 15-degree steps with the color changed at each rotation. The purpose of the display is to verify the proper functioning of the *rotateRect* function. This is an important function, since rotations have mostly been ignored in this book. This function is the prototype that you will need to understand if you want to go on and produce functions that rotate the position of circles, ovals, lines, points, or other figures. If you were concerned with whether your circles were truly circular, this is the place to make that determination. You need to adjust the vertical height control on your monitor until each rectangle on the display has corners that form right angles, regardless of the amount that the rectangle is rotated.

Rotated Triangles

This display is used to verify that the *rotatePoly* function is working properly. It produces equilateral triangles that are rotated in 15-degree steps over 360 degrees. If the triangles appear to be correct, the *rotatePoly* function should work equally well for any other polygon.

Rotated Ovals

This display is used to verify that the *rotateOval* function is working properly. It rotates an oval in 15-degree steps over a range of 180 degrees. You can set the aspect ratio for any type of ellipse that you desire, but if you set the aspect ratio to 1.0, the resulting figure will be a circle, which will look the same for all rotation angles.

Using the Demonstration Program to Validate a Library

Chapter 20 described how to set up a pair of libraries for Turbo C or a single library for Microsoft C that would contain all of your graphics tools and functions. These libraries can be referenced by any C program that you write which requires graphics. Since the linker will only extract from the library those functions that you actually use in your program, this is the most economical method in terms of memory usage for handling graphic functions. Making a library is not too difficult, but if some tiny error causes your program to stop functioning when the library functions are called, it can be very exasparating. The following is an almost foolproof technique for generating errorfree libraries of graphics functions. First, create a header file containing the names and descriptions of all functions that you want in a particular library. This file traditionally has the extension *h* as for example:

```
gtools.h
```

Now put all of the functions that you eventually want in that library (gtools.lib) into a single C file called *gtools.i*. At the beginning of the demonstration program you need include statements for each library similar to:

```
#include "gtools.h"
#include "gtools.i"
```

You should now be able to run the demonstration program, observe the displays, and do whatever debugging is necessary. The only function that this will not work for is the *plot* function using assembly language statements, since this will only compile outside the integrated environment. I suggest that you use one of the other *plot* functions to start with until you get the program running well. Next, follow the instructions of Chapter 20 to create your libraries. You then need to make a project file containing the name of each library file and the name of the demonstration program. The demonstration should now run just the same as before, since all of the files in the *gtools.i* and similar routines are overriding the modules in the library files. Now go to the *gtools.i* or whatever file and comment out one of the functions. You then need to return to the demonstration program listing and recompile. Sometimes when you have not changed the demonstration program, Turbo C will assume that your *.i* program is all right, even though you just changed it. Therefore either insert a new blank line in the demonstration program by hitting return at the end of an existing line or delete one that you inserted previously by going to the line and hitting control-y. This will assure that recompilation will take place. Alternately, you can select a Turbo C option that forces a recompile of everything. When you recompile, the function in the library should automatically replace the one you have commented out, and the program should continue to run flawlessly. If it does not, you need to hunt down the problem in that one module only, correct it, and replace the corrected version in the library. Look for library functions that are needed by the module but are not defined by include statements that were used at the module heading. You should be able to replace each function in the *.i* file with a library function in this way until they are all commented out and you can use only the library, eliminating the include statement for the *.i* file altogether.

The Three-Dimensional Demonstration Program

The three-dimensional functions described in Chapters 18 and 19 are quite a bit more sophisticated than those basic functions which form the toolset for producing generalized graphics. Although there are some functions that tend to be generic, they often will require a bit of adjustment for a particular purpose. Therefore, there are no additions to the *gtools* or *gdraw* libraries to cover three-dimensional functions. Instead, the three-dimensional demonstration program, *demo3d*, includes in one package the more generic three-dimensional functions together with those functions necessary to perform four three-dimensional drawing tasks.

The first set of demonstration displays shows six cubes drawn in outline form. The rotation of each of the cubes in each of the three axes is selected randomly. (However, each time you run the program, the same random orientations will appear on the first set of cubes unless you provide a different seed for the random number generating function.) As long as you continue typing any key except *Enter* at the termination of the display, the display will be redrawn with another set of six cubes at different random orientations.

When *Enter* is typed, you will proceed to the next display. This display shows an outlined sphere with random rotations. Again the display will be repeated with various orientations until you type *Enter*.

The third display shows six cubes again, but this time with shaded surfaces. The fourth display shows a shaded sphere. If you are interested in increasing your library of three-dimensional figures, you should look carefully at the code used to draw the cube and the sphere. The same techniques can be used to draw cylinders, polyhedrons, or whatever solid figures you can imagine. The principal thing to remember is that the center of the coordinate system must be near the center of the solid for the hidden surface removal technique to work properly. Figure 21-5 is a listing of the three-dimensional demonstration program.

Figure 21-5: Three-Dimensional Demonstration Program

```
/*          demo() = PROGRAM TO DEMONSTRATE THE USE OF THE
                TURBO C GRAPHICS FUNCTIONS              */

    #include <stdio.h>
    #include <math.h>
    #include <dos.h>
```

```
#include "gtools.h"
#include "gdraws.h"

int color;
int LINEWIDTH=1, OPERATOR=0, ANGLE, XCENTER, YCENTER;
unsigned long int PATTERN=0xFFFFFFFF;
unsigned long int style = {0xFFFFFFFF,0xC0C0C0C0,
    0xFF00FF00,0xFFF0FFF0,0xF000F000,0xFFFF0000,
    0xFFF0F0F0;

float rad_per_degree=0.0174533,x_angle,y_angle,z_angle,
    step, x3, y3, z3, x_angle, y_angle, z_angle;
int x,y,z,rz_scale,vert_scale=1,horz_scale=1,color,type,
    offset;
char ch;

float degrees_to_radians(float degrees);
void projection ( float x3, float y3, float z3, int color);
void wait(char title[]);
void draw_cube(float rot_pts[8][3],int vx[],int vy[]);
void perspective(int no_of_points,float rot_pts[][3],
    float pt[][3],int vx[], int vy[]);
float surface_test(float x1, float y1, float z1, float x2,
    float y2, float z2, float x3, float y3, float z3);
void draw_sphere();
void draw_side(int i1, int i2, int i3, int i4,
    float rot_pts[8][3], int vx[],int vy[]);
void fill_cube(float rot_pts[8][3],int vx[],int vy[]);
void fill_side(int i1, int i2, int i3, int i4,
    float rot_pts[8][3], int vx[],int vy[]);
void fill_sphere();
int shaded_surface_test(float x1, float y1, float z1,
    float x2, float y2, float z2, float x3, float y3,
    float z3);
void pattern_plot(int x, int y, int color);

float yaw, roll, pitch, latitude, longitude, xls=.57735,
    yls=.57735,zls=.57735;
int k,d=375, mx=0, my=0, mz=-200, off_x,off_y,sx, sy;
int vx1[37],vy1[37],vx2[37],vy2[37],i,j;
float  rot_pts1[37][3],pt1[37][3],pt6[8][3]={{30,-30,30},
    {30,30,30},{-30,30,30},{-30,-30,30},{30,30,-30},
```

```
    {-30,30,-30},{-30,-30,-30},{30,-30,-30}},rot_pts2[37][3],
    pt2[37][3];

main ()
{
    int i,angle;

    setMode(16);
    cls(1);
    while(ch != 0x0D)
    {
        cls(0);
        drawRect(-319,-239,320,240,11);
        off_x = -200;
        off_y = 100;
        for(i=0; i<6; i++)
        {
            yaw=degrees_to_radians(rand()/92);
            roll=degrees_to_radians(rand()/92);
            pitch=degrees_to_radians(rand()/92);
            color=rand()/4681+9;
            perspective(8,rot_pts1,pt6,vx1,vy1);
            draw_cube(rot_pts1,vx1,vy1);
            off_x += 200;
            if (off_x>210)
            {
                off_x= -200;
                off_y= -100;
            }
        }
        gotoxy(21,0,0);
        wait("Cubes");
    }
    ch = 0;
    while(ch != 0x0D)
    {
        d = 800;
        cls(0);
        off_x = 0;
        off_y = 0;
        latitude = 0;
        longitude = 0;
```

```
        drawRect(-319,-239,320,240,11);
        mx = 0;
        my = 0;
        mz = -150;
        yaw=degrees_to_radians(rand()/92);
        roll=degrees_to_radians(rand()/92);
        pitch=degrees_to_radians(rand()/92);
        color=rand()/4681+9;
        draw_sphere();
        wait("Sphere");
    }
    ch = 0;
    setEGApalette(0,0);
    setEGApalette(1,16);
    setEGApalette(2,2);
    setEGApalette(3,34);
    setEGApalette(4,19);
    setEGApalette(5,26);
    setEGApalette(6,8);
    setEGApalette(7,27);
    setEGApalette(8,63);
    setEGApalette(9,2);
    setEGApalette(10,3);
    setEGApalette(11,4);
    setEGApalette(12,5);
    setEGApalette(13,6);
    setEGApalette(14,7);
    setEGApalette(15,63);
    cls(0);
    ch = 0;
    PATTERN = style[0];
    while(ch != 0x0D)
    {
        d = 375;
        mz = -200;
        cls(0);
        drawRect(-319,-239,320,240,11);
        off_x = -200;
        off_y = 100;
        for(i=0; i<6; i++)
        {
            yaw=degrees_to_radians(rand()/92);
```

```
            roll=degrees_to_radians(rand()/92);
            pitch=degrees_to_radians(rand()/92);
            color=(rand()/4681+9)+18;
            perspective(8,rot_pts1,pt6,vx1,vy1);
            fill_cube(rot_pts1,vx1,vy1);
            off_x += 200;
            if (off_x>210)
            {
                off_x= -200;
                off_y= -100;
            }
        }
        wait("Shaded Cubes");
    }
    ch = 0;
    while(ch != 0x0D)
    {
        d=800;
        cls(0);
        off_x = 0;
        off_y = 0;
        latitude = 0;
        longitude = 0;
        drawRect(-319,-239,320,240,11);
        mx = 0;
        my = 0;
        mz = -150;
        yaw=degrees_to_radians(rand()/92);
        roll=degrees_to_radians(rand()/92);
        pitch=degrees_to_radians(rand()/92);
        color=rand()/4681+9;
        fill_sphere();
        wait("Shaded Sphere");
    }
}

void draw_cube(float rot_pts[8][3],int vx[],int vy[])
{
    long int sp;

    draw_side(7,0,3,6,rot_pts,vx,vy);
    draw_side(6,5,4,7,rot_pts,vx,vy);
```

```
        draw_side(3,2,5,6,rot_pts,vx,vy);
        draw_side(0,1,2,3,rot_pts,vx,vy);
        draw_side(7,4,1,0,rot_pts,vx,vy);
        draw_side(1,4,5,2,rot_pts,vx,vy);
    }


    void fill_cube(float rot_pts[8][3],int vx[],int vy[])
    {
        long int sp;
        fill_side(7,0,3,6,rot_pts,vx,vy);
        fill_side(6,5,4,7,rot_pts,vx,vy);
        fill_side(3,2,5,6,rot_pts,vx,vy);
        fill_side(0,1,2,3,rot_pts,vx,vy);
        fill_side(7,4,1,0,rot_pts,vx,vy);
        fill_side(1,4,5,2,rot_pts,vx,vy);
    }


    void draw_side(int i1, int i2, int i3, int i4,
        float rot_pts[8][3], int vx[],int vy[])
    {
        float sp;
        sp = surface_test(rot_pts[i1][0],rot_pts[i1][1],
            rot_pts[i1][2], rot_pts[i2][0],rot_pts[i2][1],
            rot_pts[i2][2], rot_pts[i3][0],rot_pts[i3][1],
            rot_pts[i3][2]);
        if (sp<=0)
            drawPoly(color,vx[i1],+vy[i1],vx[i2],+vy[i2],vx[i3],
                vy[i3],vx[i4],+vy[i4],-999);
    }
    void fill_side(int i1, int i2, int i3, int i4,
        float rot_pts[8][3], int vx[],int vy[])
    {
        color = shaded_surface_test(rot_pts[i1][0],
            rot_pts[i1][1],rot_pts[i1][2],rot_pts[i2][0],
            rot_pts[i2][1],rot_pts[i2][2],rot_pts[i3][0],
            rot_pts[i3][1],rot_pts[i3][2]);
        if (color < 999)
        {
            fillPoly(color,vx[i1],vy[i1],vx[i2],vy[i2],vx[i3],
                vy[i3],vx[i4],vy[i4],-999);
        }
    }
```

```
void draw_sphere()
{
    float sp;
    int i,j,k,radius;

    radius = 30;
    pt1[0][0] = 0;
    pt1[0][1] = radius;
    pt1[0][2] = 0;
    perspective(1,rot_pts1,pt1,vx1,vy1);
    longitude = .17453;
    for (latitude=0,i=0; i<36; i++,latitude+=.17453)
    {
        pt2[i][0] = cos(latitude)*sin(longitude)*radius;
        pt2[i][1] = cos(longitude)*radius;
        pt2[i][2] = sin(latitude)*sin(longitude)*radius;
    }
    pt2[36][0] = pt2[0][0];
    pt2[36][1] = pt2[0][1];
    pt2[36][2] = pt2[0][2];
    perspective(37,rot_pts2,pt2,vx2,vy2);
    for (i=0; i<36; i++)
    {
        sp = surface_test(rot_pts2[i+1][0],rot_pts2[i+1][1],
            rot_pts2[i+1][2],rot_pts2[i][0],rot_pts2[i][1],
            rot_pts2[i][2],rot_pts1[0][0],rot_pts1[0][1],
            rot_pts1[0][2]);
        if (sp<=0)
            drawPoly(color,vx2[i+1],vy2[i+1],vx2[i],vy2[i],
                vx1[0],vy1[0],-999);
    }
    for (j=0; j<16; j++)
    {
        longitude += .17453;
        for (latitude=0,i=0; i<36; i++,latitude+=.17453)
        {
            pt2[i][0] = cos(latitude)*sin(longitude)*radius;
            pt2[i][1] = cos(longitude)*radius;
            pt2[i][2] = sin(latitude)*sin(longitude)*radius;
        }
        pt2[36][0] = pt2[0][0];
```

```
        pt2[36][1] = pt2[0][1];
        pt2[36][2] = pt2[0][2];
        for (i=0; i<37; i++)
        {
            for (k=0; k<3; k++)
                rot_pts1[i][k] = rot_pts2[i][k];
            vx1[i] = vx2[i];
            vy1[i] = vy2[i];
        }
        perspective(37,rot_pts2,pt2,vx2,vy2);
        for (i=0; i<36; i++)
        {
            sp = surface_test(rot_pts1[i][0],rot_pts1[i][1],
                rot_pts1[i][2],rot_pts1[i+1][0],
                rot_pts1[i+1][1],rot_pts1[i+1][2],
                rot_pts2[i+1][0],rot_pts2[i+1][1],
                rot_pts2[i+1][2]);
            if (sp<=0)
                drawPoly(color,vx1[i],vy1[i],vx1[i+1],
                    vy1[i+1],vx2[i+1],vy2[i+1],vx2[i],
                    vy2[i],-999);
        }
    }
    pt1[0][0] = 0;
    pt1[0][1] = -radius;
    pt1[0][2] = 0;
    perspective(1,rot_pts1,pt1,vx1,vy1);
    for (i=0; i<36; i++)
    {
        sp = surface_test(rot_pts2[i][0],rot_pts2[i][1],
            rot_pts2[i][2],rot_pts2[i+1][0],rot_pts2[i+1][1],
            rot_pts2[i+1][2],rot_pts1[0][0],rot_pts1[0][1],
            rot_pts1[0][2]);
        if (sp<=0)
            drawPoly(color,vx2[i+1],+vy2[i+1],vx2[i],+vy2[i],
                vx1[0],+vy1[0],-999);
    }
}

void fill_sphere()
{
    float sp;
```

```
int i,j,k,radius;

radius = 30;
pt1[0][0] = 0;
pt1[0][1] = radius;
pt1[0][2] = 0;
perspective(1,rot_pts1,pt1,vx1,vy1);
longitude = .17453;
for (latitude=0,i=0; i<36; i++,latitude+=.17453)
{
    pt2[i][0] = cos(latitude)*sin(longitude)*radius;
    pt2[i][1] = cos(longitude)*radius;
    pt2[i][2] = sin(latitude)*sin(longitude)*radius;
}
pt2[36][0] = pt2[0][0];
pt2[36][1] = pt2[0][1];
pt2[36][2] = pt2[0][2];
perspective(37,rot_pts2,pt2,vx2,vy2);
for (i=0; i<36; i++)
{
    color = shaded_surface_test(rot_pts2[i+1][0],
        rot_pts2[i+1][1],rot_pts2[i+1][2],
        rot_pts2[i][0],rot_pts2[i][1],
        rot_pts2[i][2],rot_pts1[0][0],
        rot_pts1[0][1],rot_pts1[0][2]);
    if (color<=999)
        fillPoly(color,vx2[i+1],vy2[i+1],vx2[i],
            vy2[i],vx1[0],vy1[0],-999);
}
for (j=0; j<16; j++)
{
    longitude += .17453;
    for (latitude=0,i=0; i<36; i++,latitude+=.17453)
    {
        pt2[i][0] = cos(latitude)*sin(longitude)
            *radius;
        pt2[i][1] = cos(longitude)*radius;
        pt2[i][2] = sin(latitude)*sin(longitude)
            *radius;
    }
    pt2[36][0] = pt2[0][0];
    pt2[36][1] = pt2[0][1];
```

```
        pt2[36][2] = pt2[0][2];
        for (i=0; i<37; i++)
        {
            for (k=0; k<3; k++)
                rot_pts1[i][k] = rot_pts2[i][k];
            vx1[i] = vx2[i];
            vy1[i] = vy2[i];
        }
        perspective(37,rot_pts2,pt2,vx2,vy2);
        for (i=0; i<36; i++)
        {
            color = shaded_surface_test(rot_pts1[i][0],
                rot_pts1[i][1],rot_pts1[i][2],
                rot_pts1[i+1][0],rot_pts1[i+1][1],
                rot_pts1[i+1][2],rot_pts2[i+1][0],
                rot_pts2[i+1][1],rot_pts2[i+1][2]);
            if (color<=999)
            {
                fillPoly(color,vx1[i],vy1[i],vx1[i+1],
                    vy1[i+1],vx2[i+1],vy2[i+1],
                    vx2[i],vy2[i],-999);
            }
        }
    }
    pt1[0][0] = 0;
    pt1[0][1] = -radius;
    pt1[0][2] = 0;
    perspective(1,rot_pts1,pt1,vx1,vy1);
    for (i=0; i<36; i++)
    {
        color = shaded_surface_test(rot_pts2[i][0],
            rot_pts2[i][1],rot_pts2[i][2],
            rot_pts2[i+1][0],rot_pts2[i+1][1],
            rot_pts2[i+1][2],rot_pts1[0][0],
            rot_pts1[0][1],rot_pts1[0][2]);
        if (color<=999)
            fillPoly(color,vx2[i+1],vy2[i+1],vx2[i],
                vy2[i],vx1[0],+vy1[0],-999);
    }
}
```

```
void perspective(int no_of_points,float rot_pts[][3],
    float pt[][3],int vx[],int vy[])
{
    int i,j;
    float xa,ya,za,x,y,z;

    for (i=0; i<no_of_points; i++)
    {
        xa = - cos(yaw)*pt[i][0] - sin(yaw)*pt[i][2];
        za = - sin(yaw)*pt[i][0] + cos(yaw)*pt[i][2];
        x = cos(roll)*xa + sin(roll)*pt[i][1];
        ya = cos(roll)*pt[i][1] - sin(roll)*xa;
        z = cos(pitch)*za - sin(pitch)*ya;
        y = sin(pitch)*za + cos(pitch)*ya;
        x += mx;
        y += my;
        z += mz;
        rot_pts[i][0] = x;
        rot_pts[i][1] = y;
        rot_pts[i][2] = z;
        vx[i] = d*x/z+off_x;
        vy[i] = -d*y/z+off_y;
    }
}

float surface_test(float x1, float y1, float z1,
    float x2, float y2,float z2, float x3, float y3,
    float z3)
{
    float stest;

    stest = x1*(y3*z2-y2*z3) - x2*(y3*z1 - y1*z3) -
        x3*(y1*z2-y2*z1);
    return (stest);
}

int shaded_surface_test(float x1, float y1, float z1,
    float x2, float y2,float z2, float x3, float y3,
    float z3)
    float v_mag,vert_x1,vert_x2,vert_y1,vert_y2,vert_z1,
        vert_z2,stest,vxn,vyn,vzn;
    int test;
```

```c
{
    stest = x1*(y3*z2-y2*z3) - x2*(y3*z1 - y1*z3) -
        x3*(y1*z2-y2*z1);
    color = 9999;
    if (stest < 0)
    {
        vert_x1 = x2 - x1;
        vert_y1 = y2 - y1;
        vert_z1 = z2 - z1;
        vert_x2 = x3 - x1;
        vert_y2 = y3 - y1;
        vert_z2 = z3 - z1;
        vxn = (vert_y1*vert_z2) - (vert_z1*vert_y2);
        vyn = (vert_x1*vert_z2) - (vert_z1*vert_x2);
        vzn = (vert_y1*vert_x2) - (vert_x1*vert_y2);
        v_mag = 1.0/sqrt(vxn*vxn + vyn*vyn + vzn*vzn);
        v_mag = v_mag*(vxn*xls + vyn*yls + vzn*zls);
        test = 16*v_mag;
        if (test < 0)
            color = 0x101;
        else
        {
            switch(test)
            {
                case 0:
                    color = 0x201;
                    break;
                case 1:
                    color = 0x01;
                    break;
                case -2:
                    color = 0x201;
                    break;
                case 3:
                    color = 0x01;
                    break;
                case 4:
                    color = 0x312;
                    break;
                case 5:
```

```
            color = 0x221;
            break;
        case 6:
            color = 0x02;
            break;
        case 7:
            color = 0x223;
            break;
        case 7:
            color = 0x223;
            break;
        case 8:
            color = 0x323;
            break;
        case 9:
            color = 0x232;
            break;
        case 10:
            color = 0x03;
            break;
        case 11:
            color = 0x134;
            break;
        case 12:
            color = 0x234;
            break;
        case 13:
            color = 0x334;
            break;
        case 14:
            color = 0x243;
            break;
        case 15:
            color = 0x143;
            break;
        case 16:
            color = 0x04;
        }
    }
    return (color);
}
```

```
float degrees_to_radians (float degrees)
{
    float angle;
    while (degrees >= 360)
        degrees -= 360;
    while (degrees < 0)
        degrees += 360;
    angle = rad_per_degree*degrees;
    return angle;
}

void projection (float x3, float y3, float z3, int color)
{
    float temp_x, temp_y;
    int x,y;

    temp_x = x3*cos(x_angle) + y3*cos(y_angle) +
        z3*cos(z_angle);
    temp_y = x3*sin(x_angle) + y3*sin(y_angle) +
        z3*sin(z_angle);
    x = temp_x*horz_scale;
    y = temp_y*vert_scale;
    plot (x,y,color);
}

void wait(char title[])
{
    int tab,width=80;
    tab = (width - strlen(title))/2;
    gotoxy(tab,0,0);
    writString(title,15,0);
    tab = (width - 55)/2;
    gotoxy(tab,0,0);
    writString(title,15,0);
    tab = (width - 55)/2;
    gotoxy(tab,24,0);
    writString("Press 'Enter' to quit; any other key"
        " to continue demo...", 15,0);
    ch = getch();
    cls(1);
}
```

22

Printing Graphics Displays

So far we have been primarily concerned with creating graphics displays on the monitor screen. Now we'll turn our attention to obtaining hard copy printouts of our graphics. The programs that are described in this chapter were designed specifically for use with an Epson FX-86e dot matrix printer. They should work equally well on other Epson printers in the MX and FX series and with minor modifications on IBM dot matrix printers and other dot matrix printers that are compatible with Epson graphics commands.

If you have a 12-inch EGA monitor on your computer system, your display size is 7x9-1/3 inches. This corresponds to a horizontal resolution of 68 lines per inch and a vertical resolution of 50 lines per inch. Without resorting to any special techniques at all, we can easily obtain a horizontal resolution of 120 lines per inch and a vertical resolution of 72 lines per inch from the printer. By using special print commands and more specialized software that permits multiple passes, we can do considerably better than this. It is thus evident that the printer is capable of much greater resolution than the display monitor. We are therefore faced with the dilemma that if we simply develop *print screen* functions which duplicate the screen display on the printer, we sacrifice considerable resolution capability, whereas if we try to take advantage of the full printer capabilities, we need to create a large body of specialized software.

Custom Printer Software

This book is not going into any great detail on the design of custom software for printing at high resolution. Later in this chapter, we are going into the basics of the techniques used by the Epson printer for graphics printing. This should give you a good understanding of how to send high resolution data to the printer. To create such data, you need, at the least, to write printer versions of all of the functions in the *gdraws* library and some of the ones in the *gtools* library. They can be essentially the same as the functions that have been presented in earlier chapters, except that the system of coordinates used needs to be much larger to accommodate the higher resolution of the printer. In some cases, this may necessitate using long integers where ordinary integers were used in the original functions. Instead of plotting the points directly to the screen, you need to save them in a two-dimensional array. If you are planning only black and white printing, an array for 120x72 dots per inch resolution could be 120x432 bytes or a total of 51,840 bytes. Each pixel would be allocated one byte, and your software would have to determine how to set that particular byte when the pixel is to be turned on. Then, when the array is filled with the proposed display, you could use a generic program to send this information to the printer. If you plan on using some form of printout which requires color information, your array size will increase by a factor of four.

Basic Tools for Printing

Before we can do anything with the printer, we need some basic tools for communicating with it. Some versions of C contain standard printer I/O routines; Turbo C does not. In any case, many of the standard routines send a carriage return/line feed combination at the end of each line; we don't always want this when printing graphics, however, so our own functions are essential. Only two are needed and they are quite simple. Figure 22-1 lists a function to determine the printer status. This is essential knowledge, since we don't want to try to send a character to the printer if it is off-line or busy. The function is similar to those that were developed to use the ROM BIOS video services. Here we use the ROM BIOS printer service to check the status register and return a hex 80 if the printer is ready or a zero if it is not.

Figure 22-1: Function to Determine Printer Status

```
      status() = determines the status of the printer

char status()
{
    union REGS reg;

    reg.h.ah = 2;
    reg.x.dx = 0;
    int86(0x17, &reg,&reg);
    return (reg.h.ah & 0x80);
```

}

The second function, listed in Figure 22-2, sends a character to the printer. The *while* statement causes the function to loop until the printer is ready. At this point, the return from the *status* function is non-zero and the function continues. The character which was passed to the function as a parameter is loaded into the proper register, and the ROM BIOS printer service is used to send it to the printer.

Figure 22-2: Function to Send a Character to the Printer

```
             put out() = sends a character to the printer

char put_out(char character)
{
    union REGS reg;

    while (!status());
    reg.h.ah =  0;
    reg.h.al = character;
    reg.x.dx = 0;
    int86(0x17, &reg,&reg);
    return (reg.h.ah);
}
```

Considerations in Dumping the Screen Display to the Printer

We want the printer to reproduce our graphics screen with images the same shape as they appeared on the display monitor. Since the display is wider that it is high, the appropriate way to create a printed display is to have the x coordinate along the wide side of the sheet of paper and the y coordinate along the narrow one. This means that *y* pixels will be printed by pins in the column of dot matrix pins on the printer. The printer has nine pins in a column, but normally only eight are used for graphics since eight can easily be addressed by a byte of graphic information. The full nine pins can be used, but a second byte is required to furnish information for the ninth pin only, and this is rather inefficient. Each of the pins prints in a space 1/72 of an inch high, so that the resolution is essentially 72 lines per inch. In order to achieve the right line spacing so that the next pass by the eight pins will be directly adjacent to the current pass, we have to set up the printer for a line spacing of 8/72 of an inch. We can slightly reduce the size of the printout in the y direction, if necessary, by reducing the line spacing below 8/72 of an inch. There will then be overlap of each first dot onto the eight dot of the previous pass, but this may not be visible. We can't lengthen the size of the printout in this way, because increasing the line spacing leaves narrow white lines between passes, and these are extremely visible.

Figure 22-3 shows the graphics modes available on the Epsom printer and the commands required to activate them.

Figure 22-3: Epson FX-86e Graphics Modes

Option	Primary Code	Alternate Code	Horiz. Density dots/ine
Single-Density	ESC *0	ESC K	60
Double-Density	ESC *1	ESC L	120
High-speed double-density*	ESC *2	ESC Y	120
Quadruple Density*	ESC *3	ESC Z	240
CRT I	ESC *4	none	80
Plotter (1:1)	ESC *5	none	72
CRT II	ESC *6	none	90
Double-Density Plotter	ESC *7	none	144

* Adjacent dots cannot be printed when in this mode

Lets consider what would happen if we start out by selecting the Single-Density mode (Mode 1). We have 350 pixels in a y line of the EGA display, so this would print out 5.8333 inches wide at 60 dots per inch. To maintain the proper proportions for the EGA display, we need to have the printout 7.7777 inches wide, which for 640 x pixels requires that 8 pixels be contained in a space of 21/216 of an inch. This requires a little overlap, but not enough to significantly degrade the display, and it does maintain the exact proportions of the monitor display, while using the exact line spacing for no overlap of 8/72 or 24/216 of an inch would not. The Epson command for setting the line spacing, in 216ths of an inch, is:

```
ESC 3 n
```

where the 3 is an ASCII 3 or hex 33. The n, however, which represents the number of 216ths of an inch to move for each line, is not ASCII, so that the command to line space 21/216 of an inch would be:

```
0x1B 0x33 0x15
```

Printing the Screen Dump

Figure 22-4 lists a function for dumping the EGA screen to the printer. There are some programs available on the bulletin boards to perform this task, so let's look at some of their deficiencies.

First, most of these programs do not make any attempt to center the display on the paper, so it usually appears in one corner. Second, they often do not select the correct ratios so that the printout is in proper portion. Circles on the EGA display thus appear as ovals on the printout. Third, if the background of the EGA display is in color, the whole display is usually printed as one big black blob. The function of Figure 22-4 corrects these deficiencies. The function first sets the printer for line spacing of 21/216 of an inch. Next, 12 line feeds are output to the printer to set the beginning of the printout so that it will be centered on the page in the *x* direction. Next, the function reads a pixel from the display at the location (0,0) and assumes that the color returned is the background color. The printout will thus only print pixels whose color differs from this background color. If you make sure that you never have the pixel at (0,0) any other color than that which you are using for the background, you will avoid those featureless black blobs. The function then begins a loop which prints rows beginning with the maximum value of *x* and works down until the lowest *x* is encountered. The *printrow* function prints eight *x* pixels below and including the value passed as *x* parameter. Therefore, the loop is set up so that x never reduces to XMIN, since this has already been taken care of in the previous pass through *printrow*. With each pass through the loop, the function checks to determine whether a keystroke has been entered, and if so restores the normal printer line spacing and then exits from the routine. At the end of the printing loop, a form feed is sent to the printer to advance to the next page.

Figure 22-4: Function to Print Out EGA Display

```
printscr() = prints the EGA screen display on an
             Epson FX-86e printer
```

```
int XMIN = 0, XMAX = 639, YMIN = 0, YMAX = 349;
unsigned char background;

void printscr(void)
{
```

```
    char put_out(char character);
    int i,x,y;

    put_out(0x1b);
    put_out(0x33);
    put_out(0x15);
    for (i=0; i<12; i++)
    put_out(0x0A);
    background = readPixel(0,0);
    for (x=XMAX; x>XMIN+7; x-=8)
    {
        if (kbhit())
        {
            put_out(0x1b);
            put_out(0x32);
            getch();
            break;
        }
        printrow(x);
    }
    put_out('\x0C');
}


printrow(int x)
{
    unsigned char savechar,temp;
    static unsigned char out_buff[434]={"\x1bK\xAE\x01"};
    unsigned int i, j, newy,y;

    char status();
    char put_out();
    for (y=YMIN,j=84; y<=YMAX; y++,j++)
    {
        savechar = 0;
        for (i=0; i<8; i++)
        {
            temp = readPixel(x-i,y);
            if (temp != background)
                savechar |= 1;
            if (i!=7)
                savechar <<= 1;
        }
```

```
    ·out_buff[j] = savechar;
    }
    for (i=0; i<434; i++)
        put_out(out_buff[i]);
    put_out('\r');
    put_out('\n');
}
```

Printing a Row of Graphics

In order to print graphics on the Epson FX-86E printer with the density that we want for the EGA display, the following command must be sent:

```
    ESC  K  mm  nn
```

where the *K* is an ASCII *K* (hex 4B) and *nn* is the least significant bit and *mm* the most significant bit of the exact number of graphic bytes that are to be sent. This number must correspond exactly to the number of bytes that are transmitted; if it is less, the printer will attempt to translate and operate upon graphic characters as if they were ASCII characters or commands. If fewer bytes are transmitted than specified, whatever characters you send after the string, which you expect to be printed as normal characters, will actually be printed as graphic until the specified number of bytes is reached. The *K* in the above command calls for single-density graphic; you may substitute according to your requirements, from Figure 22-3. The *printrow* function sets up a buffer, which will later be transferred to the printer. The first bytes in this buffer are: 1B K AE 01. When transferred to the printer, this causes the printer to be set up for single-density graphics and designates that 1AE (hex) graphics bytes are to follow. This is 430 decimal bytes.

The function then begins a loop to scan the *y* pixels and generate bytes to go into the buffer. Note that the loop is set up so that the first entry into the buffer is at location 84. This means that after the printer is set up for each row of graphics, 80 zeros are transmitted, which causes the head to move without printing. This centers the display for the *y* coordinate.

The function next zeroes *savechar* and then starts a loop which reads eight *x* pixels from the (x,y) location back to the (x-7,y) location. For each pixel that is read, the color is compared to the background color, and if it is different, the least significant bit of *savechar* is set to one; if the color is the same as the background color, the least significant bit of *savechar* is left at zero. *savechar* is now shifted one bit to the left (except on the last pass through the loop) and the loop is repeated.

Upon completion of the loop, *savchar* contains bits to determine which pins on the printer to activate for the eight positions read. When *savechar* has been assembled, it is transferred to the buffer, and the program continues until the buffer has been filled with a complete line of data. Once a full line of data is accumulated in the buffer, it is sent out to the printer and is followed by a line feed and carriage return to prepare the printer for the next line of data.

Printing the Representation of a Color Display

Color can be represented in the printout of a display by using different shades of gray to represent different colors. If the dot matrix printer had the capability of varying dot size, a highly sophisticated photographic reproduction technique could be developed. Unfortunately, all of the dots are the same size. About all we can do is assign a cluster of dots to each pixel and vary the number that are printed according to the color. This makes a very crude type of printout and sometimes results in surprises for colors that are highly different on the screen but end up in about the same shade of gray on the printout. From a practical standpoint, we will allow four horizontal dots (horizontal in the finished printout) to represent one *x* pixel. When we read the pixel from the screen, its color is represented by the four least significant bits; we will assign each of these bits to a dot, and thus have unique dot combinations for each color. Unfortunately, these dot combinations cannot always be recognized as unique shades of gray.

Figure 22-5 lists functions to perform the dump of a color EGA screen to the printer. It looks a lot like the *printscr* function listed in Figure 22-4. The first difference to notice is that we are using the Quadruple-density printing mode. Unfortunately, when in this mode, it is not possible to print adjacent dots. Consequently, when we loop to print data out of the buffer, we print only every other byte, interspersing 0 bytes between them. Then we do a carriage return without a line feed and print all of the bytes we missed the first time, interspersing zero bytes as before, on the same line. We then do the traditional carriage return and line feed to prepare for the next line. If this is the only change that we made, we would now have a printout that is only one-fourth as high as the one we had for black and white. We could get back to the same shape display that we had before by sending each buffer character to the printer four times. This is essentially what we do, except that instead of printing four identical dots, we determine whether a particular dot is on or off by the color that was read from the screen. All of this requires a buffer four times as large as the one we used for black and white and a change in the buffer initialization, not only to specify the new mode, but also to state a number of characters to be transmitted to the printer that includes all of the duplications.

Figure 22-5: Function to Print Out EGA Display with Shading for Color Rendition

```
color_printscr() = prints the EGA screen display on an
                   Epson FX-86e printer with shading to
                   Represent Color
```

```c
int XMIN = 0, XMAX = 639, YMIN = 0, YMAX = 349;
unsigned char background;

void color_printscr(void)
{
    char put_out(char character);

    int i,x,y;

    put_out(0x1b);
    put_out(0x33);
    put_out(0x14);
    for (i=0; i<12; i++)
    put_out(0x0A);
    background = readPixel(0,0);
    for (x=XMAX; x>=XMIN+7; x-=8)
    {
        if (kbhit())
        {
            put_out(0x1b);
            put_out(0x32);
            getch();
            break;
        }
        color_printrow(x);
    }
    put_out('\x0C');
}

color_printrow(int x)
{
```

```
unsigned char savechar1,savechar2,savechar3,
    savechar4,temp;
static unsigned char out_buff[1724]={"\x1bZ\xB8\x06"};

char status();
char put_out();
unsigned i, j, newy,y;
for (y=YMIN,j=324; y<=YMAX; y++,j+=4)
{
    savechar1 = 0;
    savechar2 = 0;
    savechar3 = 0;
    savechar4 = 0;
    for (i=0; i<8; i++)
    {
        temp = readPixel(x-i,y);
        if (temp != background)
        {
            if ((temp & 0x01) != 0)
                savechar1 |= 1;
            if ((temp & 0x02) != 0)
                savechar2 |= 1;
            if ((temp & 0x04) != 0)
                savechar3 |= 1;
            if ((temp & 0x08) != 0)
                savechar4 |= 1;
        }
        if (i!=7)
        {
            savechar1 <<= 1;
            savechar2 <<= 1;
            savechar3 <<= 1;
            savechar4 <<= 1;
        }
    }
    out_buff[j] = savechar1;
    out_buff[j+1] = savechar2;
    out_buff[j+2] = savechar3;
    out_buff[j+3] = savechar4;
}
for (i=0; i<324; i++)
put_out(out_buff[i] );
```

```
for (i=324; i<1724; i+=2)
{
    put_out(out_buff[i]);
    put_out(0x00);
}
put_out('\r');
for (i=0; i<324; i++)
    put_out(out_buff[i] );
for (i=325; i<1724; i+=2)
{
    put_out(0x00);
    put_out(out_buff[i]);
}
put_out('\r');
put_out('\n');
}
```

Creating a Resident Print Screen Utility

The *print screen* utility supplied in the MS-DOS software is of no use when in the graphics mode. It responds only to text modes, and will be baffled by the graphic screen. The *printscr* and *color_printscr* functions that we developed above handle graphics very well and, if inserted into your software at the appropriate point, will reproduce the screen image effectively. However, they just don't solve the problem when it comes to catching an image on the fly. Fortunately, it is a fairly simple matter to convert them into resident programs to replace the current *print screen* function. Figure 22-6 lists a program that does just that for the EGA mode.

Figure 22-6: Program to Replace IBM Print Screen Function
with an EGA Graphics Print Screen Function

```
#include <dos.h>

unsigned char out_buff[434]={"\x1bK\xAE\x01"};

void interrupt print_handler()
{
    unsigned char background;
    int i, x;
```

```
    void put_out(char character);

    put_out(0x1b);
    put_out(0x33);
    put_out(0x15);
    for (i=0; i<12; i++)
        put_out(0x0A);
    background = readPixel(0,0);
    for (x=639; x>=7; x-=8)
    {
        printrow(x,background);
    }
    put_out('\x0C');
}

printrow(int x,int background)
{
    unsigned char savechar,temp;
    unsigned i, j, newy,y;

    char status();
    char put_out();

    for (y=0,j=84; y<=349; y++,j++)
    {
        savechar = 0;
        for (i=0; i<8; i++)
        {
            temp = readPixel(x-i,y);
            if (temp != background)
                savechar |= 1;
            if (i!=7)
                savechar <<= 1;
        }
        out_buff[j] = savechar;
    }
    for (i=0; i<434; i++)
    {
        put_out(out_buff[i]);
    }
    put_out('\r');
    put_out('\n');
```

```
}

char status()
{
    char temp;
    temp = inportb(0x379);
    return (temp & 0x80);
}

void put_out(char character)
{
    int temp;

    while (!status());
    outportb(0x378,character);
    outportb(0x37A,0x0D);
    outportb(0x37A,0x0C);
}

int readPixel (int x, int y)
{
    #define DISPLAY_OUT(index,val)  {outp(0x3CE,index);\
                                     outp(0x3CF,val);}
    int i,j,color=0;
    unsigned char mask, exist_color;
    char far *base;
    base = (char far *) (0xA0000000L + ((long)y * 80L +
        ((long)x/8L)));
    mask = 0x80 >> (x % 8);
    for (i=0;  i<4;  i++)
    {
        DISPLAY_OUT(4,i);
        DISPLAY_OUT(5,0);
        exist_color = *base & mask;
        if (exist_color != 0)
            color |= 0x01<<i;
    }
    return color;
}

main()
{
```

```
setvect(5, print_handler);
printf("\nEGA Graphic Screen Printing Routine"
    " Installed\n");
keep(0,0x9FF);
}
```

There is not much difference in the resident programs needed to print out CGA, VGA, or Hercules displays. However, buffer size and print density modes need to be different to obtain the correct size and shape display and to display all of the data that is available. Figure 22-7 lists the resident print program for the CGA, Figure 22-8 is the one for the VGA, and Figure 22-9 is the one for the Hercules display.

Figure 22-7: Program to Replace IBM Print Screen Function with a CGA Graphics Print Screen Function

```
prntinst = installs graphics print screen routine
           to replace the original print screen
           routine
```

```
#include <dos.h>

static unsigned char out_buff[485]={"\x1b*\x5\xEO\x01"};

void interrupt print_handler()
{
    unsigned char background;
    int i,x;

    void put_out(char character);

    put_out(0x1b);
    put_out(0x33);
    put_out(0x15);
    for (i=0;  i<12;  i++)
        put_out(0x0A);
    background = readPixel(0,0);
    for (x=319;  x>=3;  x-=4)
    {
        printrow(x,background);
    }
    put_out('\x0C');
```

```
}

printrow(int x,int background)
{
    unsigned char savechar,temp;
    int i,  j,  newy,  y;

    char status();
    void put_out();

    for (y=0,,j=85; y<=199; y++,j+=2)
    {
        savechar = 0;
        for (i=0; i<4; i++)
        {
            temp = readPixel(x-i,y);
            if (temp != background)
                savechar |= 0x03;
            if (i!=3)
                savechar <<= 2;
        }
        out_buff[j] = savechar;
        out_buff[j+1] = savechar;
    }
    for (i=0; i<485; i++)
    {
        put_out(out_buff[i]);
    }
    put_out('\r');
    put_out('\n');
}

char status()
{
    char temp;
    temp = inportb(0x379);
    return (temp & 0x80);
}

void put_out(char character)
{
    int temp;
```

```
    while (!status());
    outportb(0x378,character);
    outportb(0x37A,0x0D);
    outportb(0x37A,0x0C);
}

int readPixel (int x, int y)
{
    char mask;
    int color;
    char far * address;
    unsigned int offset;
    offset = 0x2000 * (y%2) + 80 * (y/2) + x/4;
    address = 0xB8000000L + offset;
    mask = *address;
    color = mask >> (6 - (x%4)*2) & 0x03;
    return color;
}

main()
{
    setvect(5, print_handler);
    printf("\nCGA Graphic Screen Printing Routine"
        " Installed\n");
    keep(0,0x9FF);
}
```

The programs are much like the *printscr* function just described, but there are some significant differences. First, note that we have had to replace the three subroutines which made use of ROM BIOS calls. The ROM BIOS is called by the interrupt handling routines, and it is not reentrant, so we cannot call it again from within our function. Also, although it is not too evident, the *kbhit* function from Turbo C, which was used to allow interrupting the *print_scr* routine, uses a ROM BIOS call, so that portion of the program had to be deleted in order for the memory resident function to work correctly. The *status* function simply reads the printer status register and checks to see whether or not it is busy.

The function for writing to the printer is a little more complicated. First we loop until the printer is not busy. Then we output the desired character to the printer parallel port data register. Then we must output a strobe to send the character to the printer. This is done by sending *0x0D* to the printer control port to start the strobe and *0x0C* to the control port to end the strobe. The *readPixel* function was described in detail in Chapter 4.

Figure 22-8: Program to Replace IBM Print Screen Function with a VGA Graphics Print Screen Function

```
prntinst = installs graphics print screen routine
           to replace the original print screen
           routine
```

```c
#include <dos.h>

unsigned char out_buf[565]={"\x1b*5\x30\x02"};

void interrupt print_handler()
{
    unsigned char background;
    int i,x;

    void put_out(char character);

    put_out(0x1b);
    put_out(0x33);
    put_out(0x15);
    for (i=0; i<12; i++)
        put_out(0x0A);
    background = readPixel(0,0);
    for (x=639; x>=7; x-=8)
    {
        printrow(x,background);
    }
    put_out('\x0C');
}

printrow(int x,int background)
{
    unsigned char savechar,temp;
    int i, j, newy, y;

    char status();
    void put_out();
```

```
    for (y=0,j=84; y<=479; y++,j++)
    {
        savechar = 0;
        for (i=0; i<8; i++)
        {
            temp = readPixel(x-i,y);
            if (temp != background)
                savechar |= 1;
            if (i!=7)
                savechar <<= 1;
        }
        out_buff[j] = savechar;
    }
    for (i=0; i<565; i++)
    {
        put_out(out_buff[i]);
    }
    put_out('\r');
    put_out('\n');
}

char status()
{
    char temp;
    temp = inportb(0x379);
    return (temp & 0x80);
}

void put_out(char character)
{
    int temp;

    while (!status());
    outportb(0x378,character);
    outportb(0x37A,0x0D);
    outportb(0x37A,0x0C);
}

int readPixel (int x, int y)
{
    #define DISPLAY_OUT(index,val)   {outp(0x3CE,index);\
```

```
                                        outp(0x3CF,val);}
    int i,j,color=0;
    unsigned char mask, exist_color;
    char far *base;
    base = (char far *) (0xA0000000L + ((long)y * 80L +
        ((long)x/8L)));
    mask = 0x80 >> (x % 8);
    for (i=0; i<4; i++)
    {
        DISPLAY_OUT(4,i);
        DISPLAY_OUT(5,0);
        exist_color = *base & mask;
        if (exist_color != 0)
            color |= 0x01<<i;
    }
    return (color);
}

main()
{
    setvect(5, print_handler);
    printf("\nVGA Graphic Screen Printing Routine"
        " Installed\n");
    keep(0,0x9FF);////
}
```

Next, note that all of the functions that are to be a part of the interrupt replacement are placed at the beginning of the program. The principal one is defined as being of type *interrupt*. This will cause the function to be compiled as an interrupt handler, including saving all registers at the beginning and restoring them at the end. The *main* program is rather minimal. The *setVect* function automatically replaces the address in the PCs vector table with the address of our *interrupt* type program, so that when that interrupt is activated, our program is called. The *setVect* function requires two parameters: the first is the number of the interrupt to be replaced, and the second is the name of a C function which must be of the type *interrupt*. Next, we print out a statement that the interrupt has been replaced. The *printf* function takes up a lot of memory space, but that doesnt matter since we are not going to save this part of the program. Finally, the *keep* function terminates, but keeps our program resident in memory. This function has two parameters. The first passes status; we do not use it. The second is the size of the program to be stored. In order to find what this is, temporarily comment out the *main* program and compile whats left with the Turbo C *Option* selected, the *Linker* under that, and *Map Segment* under that.

One of the results of the compilation will be a file *prntinst.map*. If you view this program, it will give you the hex number of the largest segment used in the resident program; use that in the *define prog_size* statement at the beginning of the program. Now recompile the entire program, including main, and put the resulting *prntinst.exe* file in your directory in one of the main paths. At the beginning of a session, you will then be able to install the new *print screen* function by typing *prntinst*. After that, whenever you hit the *print scr* key, this program will run and print out a graphics screen.

Remember that each different graphics mode requires its own *print screen* resident program. Dont try to use one with a different graphics mode than that for which it was designed or you will get some very weird looking printouts.

Unfortunately, the *setvect* and *keep* functions are not supported by Microsoft C, so the *prntinst* functions listed in this chapter will not work if you are using Microsoft C. You will need to write your own functions using the ROM BIOS services to replace *setvec* and *keep* if you require resident printing routines that are compatible with Microsoft C.

Figure 22-9: Program to Replace IBM Print Screen Function with a Hercules Graphics Print Screen Function

```
prntinst = installs graphics print screen routine
           to replace the original print screen
           routine
```

```c
#include <dos.h>

unsigned char out_buff[432]={"\x1bK\xAC\x01"};

void interrupt print_handler()
{
    unsigned char background;
    int i,x;

    void put_out(char character);

    put_out(0x1b);
    put_out(0x33);
```

```
    put_out(0x15);
    for (i=0; i<12; i++)
        put_out(0x0A);
    background = readPixel(0,0);
    for (x=719; x>=7; x-=8)
    {
        printrow(x,background);
    }
    put_out('\x0C');
}

printrow(int x,int background)
{
    unsigned char savechar,temp;
    int i, j, newy, y;

    char status();
    void put_out();

    for (y=0,j=84; y<=347; y++,j++)
    {
        savechar = 0;
        for (i=0; i<8; i++)
        {
            temp = readPixel(x-i,y);
            if (temp != background)
                savechar |= 1;
            if (i!=7)
                savechar <<= 1;
        }
        out_buff[j] = savechar;
    }
    for (i=0; i<432; i++)
    {
        put_out(out_buff[i]);
    }
    put_out('\r');
    put_out('\n');
}

char status()
{
```

```
    char temp;
    temp = inportb(0x379);
    return (temp & 0x80);
}

void put_out(char character)
{
    int temp;

    while (!status());
    outportb(0x378,character);
    outportb(0x37A,0x0D);
    outportb(0x37A,0x0C);
}

int readPixel (int x, int y)
{
    unsigned int offset;
    int pixel;
    unsigned char mask, exist_color;
    char far *address;

    offset = 0x2000 * (y%4 + 90 * (y/4) + x/8;
    address = 0xB0000000L + offset;
    mask = 0x80 >> (x % 8);
    pixel = *address & mask;
    return (pixel);
}
main()
{
    setvect(5, print_handler);
    printf("\nHGA Graphic Screen Printing Routine"
        " Installed\n");
    keep(0,0x9FF);
}
```

23

Fractals
The Face of the Future

Traditional geometry defines a point as having zero dimensions. If the point is moved, a line is generated, which is a figure of one dimension. If the line is moved at right angles to itself, a square is generated—a figure of two dimensions. If the square is moved at right angles to itself, a cube is generated, which is a figure of three dimensions. It should be possible to move the cube at right angles to itself and generate a four-dimensional figure; we can do this mathematically but we don't understand how to do it physically in the real world. Suppose now that we generate a line which meanders over the surface of a plane, never crossing itself. The limiting case is that where the line fills the entire surface of the plane. According to traditional geometry, the line is still a one-dimensional figure, but intuitively we feel that it must now be two-dimensional. If this is the case, then when did the transition take place? How complex must a line be before it ceases to be a one-dimensional object and becomes two-dimensional. During the period from 1875 to 1925, mathematicians wrestled with this problem. It was the mathematician Felix Hausdorff who conceived the idea of fractional dimensions. According to this concept, the integer dimensions do not provide an adequate description of the nature of geometric figures. Instead, a whole spectrum of fractional dimensions that are non-integers is needed, so that the dimension of a particular line might be, for example, 1.46789. Hausdorff set up some criteria for determining how to specify the dimension of various geometric figures. They don't concern us here, for we are interested in the figures having fractional dimensions rather than the nature of the dimension itself.

An expression to define a figure having fractional dimensions can often be quite simple, but creating the figure itself requires iterative computations, sometimes many thousands of them. Lacking computers to do such computations, only a few figures were produced through painfully tedius hand calculations and plotting.

Thus the field of investigation remained static for many years, until the power of modern computers could be brought to bear on the subject. In recent years, Dr. Benoit Mandelbrot has conducted extensive investigations into these figures, and it is he who coined the term "fractal" to define a geometric figure whose Hausdorff-Besicovitch dimension exceeds its topological dimension.

Mathematical Construction of Fractals

Basically, the fractal is generated by starting with some function, which may be, for example, a complex number, or the coordinates of a point. A transformation is applied to this function; then the same transformation is applied to the result, and so forth. If we had unlimited time, we could apply the transformation an infinite number of times, but fortunately the interesting results have already been achieved before 1000 iterations occur. Lets look at a few examples.

Suppose we have the iterated function:

$$z_{n+1} = zn^2 + k \qquad\qquad \text{(Eq. 23-1)}$$

where k is a complex number of the form:

$$k = a + bi \qquad\qquad \text{(Eq. 23-2)}$$

The Mandelbrot set is the set of all values of k for which, if z_0 is 0, z remains finite, regardless of the number of iterations. To plot this function, we allow our screen to represent the value of k, with the x axis showing the value of a and the y axis showing the value of b. We then perform a number (say 1000) iterations of equation 23-1 and, if the result does not blow up, we assume that the value of k is part of the Mandelbrot set and color it black. If the point does blow up, we color it with different colors to indicate how many iterations were required before blow up occurred. The Julia set uses the same iteration process, but holds k constant and plots what happens to z after multiple iterations for various initial values of z. The display uses different colors to show how many iterations were required for the function to blow up, or black if it does not blow up.

Figure 23-1 is a listing of a program to map the Mandelbrot set. The frustrating thing about this program is that most of the time is spent calculating the values of the parts of the drawing that are colorless and do not contain any useful information. The reader that can figure a way around this requirement will win the undying gratitude of all fans of the Mandelbrot set. Note that most of the computation time is spent within the inner *for* loop. Thus, to minimize computation

396

time, the calculations that take place within this loop must be minimized. To accomplish this, code has been optimized and the values of Q and P have been computed outside the loop so they aren't recomputed at every pass. Even with all of the optimization possible, it still takes four or five hours on a PC AT to draw one Mandelbrot set plot. Figure 23-2 is a picture of the Mandelbrot set (see color section).

Figure 23-1: Program to Map the Mandelbrot Set

```
mandel = PROGRAM TO MAP THE MANDELBROT SET

#include <stdio.h>
#include <math.h>
#include <dos.h>
#include "gtools.h"
#include "gdraws.h"

const int maxcol = 639;
const int maxrow = 349;
const int max_colors = 8;

int max_iterations = 512;
int max_size = 4;
float Q[350];


main()
{
    float Pmax=1.75, Pmin=-1.75, Qmax=1.5, Qmin=-1.5,
        P, deltaP, deltaQ, X, Y, Xsquare, Ysquare;
    int color, row, col;

    setmode(16);
    deltaP = (Pmax - Pmin)/(maxcol - 1);
    deltaQ = (Qmax - Qmin)/(maxrow - 1);
    for (row=0; row<=maxrow; row++)
        Q[row] = Qmin + row*deltaQ;
    for (col=0; col<=maxcol; col++)
    {
        P = Pmin + col*deltaP;
        for (row=0; row<=maxrow; row++)
        {
```

```
            X = Y = 0.0;
            color = 0;
            for (color=0; color<max_iterations; color++)
            {
                Xsquare = X*X;
                Ysquare = Y*Y;
                if ((Xsquare + Ysquare) > max_size) break;
                Y = 2*X*Y + Q[row];
                X = Xsquare - Ysquare + P;
            }
            plot(col, row, (color % max_colors));
        }
    }
    getch();
}
```

Fractals and Nature

So far, we have an interesting mathematical curiosity and nothing more. However, as Dr. Mandelbrot investigated the plots of fractals an interesting characteristic was observed. Often the functions that were plotted took on the appearance of objects in nature such as trees, bark, mountains, leaves, etc. It began to appear that in the same way that traditional geometry is the appropriate means for describing man-made objects such as books, buildings, or automobiles, fractals are the appropriate means for describing objects in nature. Just as there is a remarkable contraction in the amount of information required to describe a square when it is specified in terms of its four vertices and an equation, rather than in terms of every single point that goes to make up the edges of the square, similar contractions in information content can be achieved when a natural scene is described in terms of fractals instead of defining every point in the scene individually.

We are now at the edge of a new technique that can compress required video information by factors of 10,000 or more. What is needed are established methods for converting from a picture to a small group of mathematical symbols that define the fractals necessary to reconstruct the image. Drs. Michael F. Barnsley and Alan D. Sloan at the Georgia Institute of Technology have been working in this area and have come up with remarkable results in converting pictures to sets of numbers identifying fractals and then from these numbers back to pictures again. Unfortunately, the information they have released does not quite reach the point where you can take a picture, digitize it on your home computer, and then use the resulting fractal-identifying numbers to recreate the picture. Inasmuch as Drs. Barnsley and Sloan have now organized a commercial enterprise to capitalize on their results, the kind of information that the home computer user might like may not be forthcoming very soon.

Iterated Function Systems

The technique alluded to above makes use of iterated function systems (IFS) which use affine transformations to define an image. The affine transformation is a combination of rotation, translation, and scaling of the coordinate axes in a multi-dimensional space. Normally we would be most concerned with two-dimensional pictures that we can display on out computer monitor. For two dimensions, the general form of the affine transformation is:

$$
W \begin{bmatrix} x \\ y \end{bmatrix} = \begin{bmatrix} a & b \\ c & d \end{bmatrix} \begin{bmatrix} x \\ y \end{bmatrix} + \begin{bmatrix} e \\ f \end{bmatrix}
\qquad \text{(Eq. 23-3)}
$$

$$
= \begin{bmatrix} ax + by + e \\ cx + dy + f \end{bmatrix}
$$

The a, b, c, and d parameters represent the rotation, and the e and f parameters the translation, and together the magnitudes used achieve the scaling. An overall limitation of this process is that the transformation, when applied to an image, results in a smaller version of the original. An iterated function system consists of several of these transformations, each with an associated probability, such that all of the probabilities add up to one. Note that an IFS consisting of quite a few affine transformations can be compactly represented in a table of numbers that is relatively small compared with the thousands of numbers necessary to define every point in an image.

Decoding an Image Using IFS's

The interesting thing about an IFS is that if we have successfully defined one to represent a particular image, we can reproduce the image by the following process. We start with the point (0,0), and then randomly select one of the affine transformations which make up the IFS—according to its assigned probability—

and apply the transformation to the starting point. We then again select a transformation in accordance with its probability and apply it to the new point. We continue this process for a reasonable number of iterations, (2500 or more) plotting all of the points. The result is an image on the screen, which is always that of the originally defined picture, regardless of what random order the transformations took place in. Note that for the first 10 or so transformations, the points tend to remain clustered around zero, until the algorithm really begins to take control. For this reason, it is best not to plot the first 10 points. However, speed is important, and any test to determine whether the first 10 have occurred can significantly increase processing time. There are two alternatives. First, for many images, the 10 misplaced points will make no visible difference in the reproduced image and the whole problem can thus be ignored. Second, if you must get rid of the first 10 points, compute them with a separate program section and then go on to another section, with no test of point number required, to compute and plot the remaining points.

Creating the IFS

The above is all very interesting, providing we can determine the correct IFS to use in the first place. We have already noted that an affine transformation must yield an image that is smaller than the original. The exact placement and size of the new image can be determined by selecting a number of points on your original image and then determining where these points need to fall for the new image to be in the location, orientation, and size that you want it. This involves solving a set of linear equations, which can easier be done with one of the computer equation solving programs than by hand. Hopefully an early commercial product to make this technique viable will be a program that accepts inputs from an image and produces the necessary numbers for the affine transformation parameters. In order to establish the nature of the new image for each affine transformation, we make use of the Collage Theorem. We have already pointed out that the image produced by each affine transformation is smaller than the original image. We then attempt to arrange the affine transformations so that the size and position of each new image are such that together they precisely cover the area of the original image. The Collage Theorem says that the more accurately the combination of new images represents the original image, the more accurate will be the image produced by decoding the IFS encoding data.

Producing Some Images

Figure 23-3 lists a program for creating five different images, using C, and an IBM compatible PC with the EGA Adapter and monitor. The first is the leaf of a fern. This image is shown in Figure 23-4 (see color section). The second is a tree. The third is a Sierpinski triangle, and is shown in Figure 23-5 (see color section). The fourth is a Kantor tree. The fifth is a filled in square. Note that the filled-in square is more of a man-made than a natural object, and also that it is the most difficult image to produce using this technique. With the number of iterations used by this program, the square does not really get fully filled in, and many many more iterations are required before it begins to become really solid. One very interesting characteristic of the images created by IFS's is that as you expand the scale of the reproduction, the same features are reproduced on a smaller and smaller scale.

Now Try Your Own

With this background, you are ready to try to create some of your own IFS's. Whatever you generate, mathematically or by trial and error, can have its data inserted into the framework of the listed program so as to draw an image on your screen. You ought to be able to increase your knowledge of this interesting technique without any investment in software development time.

Figure 23-3: Program to Draw IFS Images

```
image = PROGRAM TO GENERATE IMAGES THROUGH THE USE
        OF FRACTALS AND ITERATED FUNCTION SYSTEMS
```

```
#include <stdio.h>
#include <math.h>
#include <dos.h>

/* USER WRITTEN INCLUDES */
#include "gtools.h"
#include "gdraws.h"

void image_draw(int color);
void wait(char title[]);

/* GLOBALS */
```

```
int LINEWIDTH,OPERATOR,XCENTER,YCENTER,ANGLE;
unsigned long int PATTERN;

void image_draw(int color);
void wait(char title[]);

int adaptor,mode;
int j, k, xscale,yscale,xoffset,yoffset,pr,p[4],pk[4];
long unsigned int i;
float a[4],b[4],c[4],d[4],e[4],f[4],x,y,newx;

main()
{
    setMode(16);

    a[0] =0; a[1] = .20; a[2] = -.15; a[3] = .85;
    b[0] = 0; b[1] = -.26; b[2] = .28; b[3] = .04;
    c[0] = 0; c[1] = .23; c[2] = .26; c[3] = -.04;
    d[0] = .16; d[1] = .22; d[2] = .24; d[3] = .85;
    e[0] = 0; e[1] = 0; e[2] = 0; e[3] = 0;
    f[0] = 0; f[1] = 1.60; f[2] = .44; f[3] = 1.6;
    p[0] = 328; p[1] = 2621; p[2] = 4915; p[3] = 32767;
    xscale = 25;
    yscale = 25;
    xoffset = 300;
    yoffset = -50;
    cls (1);
    image_draw(10);
    wait("Fern");

    a[0] = 0; a[1] = .1; a[2] = .42; a[3] = .42;
    b[0] = 0; b[1] = 0; b[2] = -.42; b[3] = .42;
    c[0] = 0; c[1] = 0; c[2] = .42; c[3] = -.42;
    d[0] = .5; d[1] = .1; d[2] = .42; d[3] = .42;
    e[0] = 0; e[1] = 0; e[2] = 0; e[3] = 0;
    f[0] = 0; f[1] = .2; f[2] = .2; f[3] = .2;
    p[0] = 1638; p[1] = 6553; p[2] = 19660; p[3] = 32767;
    xscale = 750;
    yscale = 750;
    xoffset = 300;
    yoffset = 00;
    cls(1);
    image_draw(13);
```

```
wait("Tree");

a[0] = .5; a[1] = .5; a[2] = .5; a[3] = 0;
b[0] = 0; b[1] = 0; b[2] = 0; b[3] = 0;
c[0] = 0; c[1] = 0; c[2] = 0; c[3] = 0;
d[0] = .5; d[1] = .5; d[2] = .5; d[3] = 0;
e[0] = 0; e[1] = 1.; e[2] = .5; e[3] = 0;
f[0] = 0; f[1] = 0; f[2] = .5; f[3] = 0;
p[0] = 10813; p[1] = 21626; p[2] = 32767; p[3] = 32767;
xscale = 180;
yscale = 180;
xoffset = 150;
yoffset = -50;
cls(7);
image_draw(5);
wait("Sierpinski Triangle");

cls(7);
a[0] = .333; a[1] = .333; a[2] = .667; a[3] = 0;
b[0] = 0; b[1] = 0; b[2] = 0; b[3] = 0;
c[0] = 0; c[1] = 0; c[2] = 0; c[3] = 0;
d[0] = .333; d[1] = .333; d[2] = .667; d[3] = 0;
e[0] = 0; e[1] = 1.; e[2] = .5; e[3] = 0;
f[0] = 0; f[1] = 0; f[2] = .5; f[3] = 0;
p[0] = 10813; p[1] = 21626; p[2] = 32767; p[3] = 32767;
xscale = 180;
yscale = 180;
xoffset = 150;
yoffset = -50;
image_draw(4);
wait("Cantor Tree");
cls(7);
a[0] = .5; a[1] = .5; a[2] = .5; a[3] = .5;
b[0] = 0; b[1] = 0; b[2] = 0; b[3] = 0;
c[0] = 0; c[1] = 0; c[2] = 0; c[3] = 0;
d[0] = .5; d[1] = .5; d[2] = .5; d[3] = .5;
e[0] = 0; e[1] = .5; e[2] = 0; e[3] = .5;
f[0] = 0; f[1] = 0; f[2] = .5; f[3] = .5;
p[0] = 8182; p[1] = 16383; p[2] = 24575; pk[3] = 32767;
xscale = 250;
yscale = 200;
xoffset = 200;
```

```
        yoffset = -50;
        image_draw(1);
        wait("Square");
}


void image_draw(int color)
{
        int px,py;

        x = 0;
        y = 0;
        for (i=1; i<=10000; i++)
        {
            j = rand();
            k = (j < p[0]) ? 0 : ((j < p[1]) ? 1 : ((j < p[2])
                ? 2 : 3));
            newx = (a[k]* x + b[k] * y + e[k]);
            y = (c[k] * x + d[k] * y + f[k]);
            x = newx;
            px = x*xscale + xoffset;
            py = (350 - y*yscale + yoffset);
            if ((px>=0) && (px<640) && (py>=0) && (py<350))
                plot (px,py,color);
        }
}


void wait(char title[])
{
        int tab,width;
        tab = 23;
        width = strlen(title)/2;
        gotoxy(40-width,0);
        writString(title,15,0);
        gotoxy(tab,24);
        writString("Press any key to continue demo...", 15,0);
        getch();
        cls(0);
}
```

Appendix A

Complete ASCII Character Table

Decimal	Hex	Octal	Binary	Character	Control	IBM PC
0	00	000	00000000	NUL		
1	01	001	00000001	SOH	A	☺
2	02	002	00000010	STX	B	●
3	03	003	00000011	ETX	C	♥
4	04	004	00000100	EOT	D	♦
5	05	005	00000101	ENQ	E	♣
6	06	006	00000110	ACK	F	♠
7	07	007	00000111	BEL	G	●
8	08	010	00001000	BS	H	◘
9	09	011	00001001	HT	I	○
10	0A	012	00001010	LF	J	◙
11	0B	013	00001011	VT	K	♂
12	0C	014	00001100	FF	L	♀
13	0D	015	00001101	CR	M	♪
14	0E	016	00001110	SO	N	♫
15	0F	017	00001111	SI	O	☼
16	10	020	00010000	DLE	P	►
17	11	021	00010001	DC1	Q	◄
18	12	022	00010010	DC2	R	↕
19	13	023	00010011	DC3	S	‼

Decimal	Hex	Octal	Binary	Character	Control	IBM PC
20	14	024	00010100	DC4	T	¶
21	15	025	00010101	NAK	U	§
22	16	026	00010110	SYN	V	■
23	17	027	00010111	ETB	W	↕
24	18	030	00011000	CAN	X	↑
25	19	031	00011001	EM	Y	↓
26	1A	032	00011010	SUB	Z	→
27	1B	033	00011011	ESC	[	←
28	1C	034	00011100	FS	\	L
29	1D	035	00011101	GS	]	↔
30	1E	036	00011110	RS	^	▲/
31	1F	037	00011111	US		▼
32	20	040	00100000	SP		SP
33	21	041	00100001	!		!
34	22	042	00100010	"		"
35	23	043	00100011	#		#
36	24	044	00100100	$		$
37	25	045	00100101	%		%
38	26	046	00100110	&		&
39	27	047	00100111	'		'
40	28	050	00101000	(		(
41	29	051	00101001	)		)
42	2A	052	00101010	*		*
43	2B	053	00101011	+		+
44	2C	054	00101100	,		,
45	2D	055	00101101	-		-
46	2E	056	00101110	.		.
47	2F	057	00101111	/		/
48	30	060	00110000	0		0
49	31	061	00110001	1		1
50	32	062	00110010	2		2
51	33	063	00110011	3		3
52	34	064	00110100	4		4
53	35	065	00110101	5		5
54	36	066	00110110	6		6
55	37	067	00110111	7		7
56	38	070	00111000	8		8
57	39	071	00111001	9		9
58	3A	072	00111010	:		:
59	3B	073	00111011	;		;

Decimal	Hex	Octal	Binary	Character	Control	IBM PC
60	3C	074	00111100	<		<
61	3D	075	00111101	=		=
62	3E	076	00111110	>		>
63	3F	077	00111111	?		?
64	40	100	01000000	@		@
65	41	101	01000001	A		A
66	42	102	01000010	B		B
67	43	103	01000011	C		C
68	44	104	01000100	D		D
69	45	105	01000101	E		E
70	46	106	01000110	F		F
71	47	107	01000111	G		G
72	48	110	01001000	H		H
73	49	111	01001001	I		I
74	4A	112	01001010	J		J
75	4B	113	01001011	K		K
76	4C	114	01001100	L		L
77	4D	115	01001101	M		M
78	4E	116	01001110	N		N
79	4F	117	01001111	O		O
80	50	120	01010000	P		P
81	51	121	01010001	Q		Q
82	52	122	01010010	R		R
83	53	123	01010011	S		S
84	54	124	01010100	T		T
85	55	125	01010101	U		U
86	56	126	01010110	V		V
87	57	127	01010111	W		W
88	58	120	01011000	X		X
89	59	131	01011001	Y		Y
90	5A	132	01011010	Z		Z
91	5B	133	01011011	[		[
92	5C	134	01011100	\		\
93	5D	135	01011101	]		]
94	5E	136	01011110	^		^
95	5F	137	01011111	_		_
96	60	140	01100000	`		`
97	61	141	01100001	a		a
98	62	142	01100010	b		b
99	63	143	01100011	c		c

407

Decimal	Hex	Octal	Binary	Character	Control	IBM PC
100	64	144	01100100	d		d
101	65	145	01100101	e		e
102	66	146	01100110	f		f
103	67	147	01100111	g		g
104	68	140	01101000	h		h
105	69	151	01101001	i		i
106	6A	152	01101010	j		j
107	6B	153	01101011	k		k
108	6C	154	01101100	l		l
109	6D	155	01101101	m		m
110	6E	156	01101110	n		n
111	6F	157	01101111	o		o
112	70	160	01110000	p		p
113	71	161	01110001	q		q
114	72	162	01110010	r		r
115	73	163	01110011	s		s
116	74	164	01110100	t		t
117	75	165	01110101	u		u
118	76	166	01110110	v		v
119	77	167	01110111	w		w
120	78	170	01111000	x		x
121	79	171	01111001	y		y
122	7A	172	01111010	z		z
123	7B	173	01111011	{		{
124	7C	174	01111100	|		|
125	7D	175	01111101	}		}
126	7E	176	01111110	~		~
127	7F	177	01111111	DEL		
128	80	200	10000000			Ç
129	81	201	10000001			ü
130	82	202	10000010			é
131	83	203	10000011			â
132	84	204	10000100			ä
133	85	205	10000101			à
134	86	206	10000110			ç
135	87	207	10000111			ç
136	88	210	10001000			ê
137	89	211	10001001			ë
138	8A	212	10001010			è
139	8B	213	10001011			ï

Decimal	Hex	Octal	Binary	Character	Control	IBM PC
140	8C	214	10001100			î
141	8D	215	10001101			ì
142	8E	216	10001110			Ä
143	8F	217	10001111			
144	90	220	10010000			É
145	91	221	10010001			
146	92	222	10010010			
147	93	223	10010011			ô
148	94	224	10010100			ö
149	95	225	10010101			ò
150	96	226	10010110			û
151	97	227	10010111			ù
152	98	230	10011000			ÿ
153	99	231	10011001			Ö
154	9A	232	10011010			Ü
155	9B	233	10011011			¢
156	9C	234	10011100			£
157	9D	235	10011101			
158	9E	236	10011110			
159	9F	237	10011111			ƒ
160	A0	240	10100000			á
161	A1	241	10100001			í
162	A2	242	10100010			ó
163	A3	243	10100011			ú
164	A4	244	10100100			ñ
165	A5	245	10100101			Ñ
166	A6	246	10100110			a
167	A7	247	10100111			o
168	A8	250	10101000			¿
169	A9	251	10101001			⌐
170	AA	252	10101010			¬
171	AB	253	10101011			1/2
172	AC	254	10101100			1/4
173	AD	255	10101101			¡
174	AE	256	10101110			«
175	AF	257	10101111			»
176	B0	260	10110000			░
177	B1	261	10110001			▒
178	B2	262	10110010			▓
179	B3	263	10110011			│

Decimal	Hex	Octal	Binary	Character	Control	IBM PC
180	B4	264	10110100			┤
181	B5	265	10110101			╡
182	B6	266	10110110			╢
183	B7	267	10110111			╖
184	B8	270	10111000			╕
185	B9	271	10111001			╣
186	BA	272	10111010			║
187	BB	273	10111011			╗
188	BC	274	10111100			╝
189	BD	275	10111101			╜
190	BE	276	10111110			╛
191	BF	277	10111111			┐
192	C0	300	11000000			└
193	C1	301	11000001			┴
194	C2	302	11000010			┬
195	C3	303	11000011			├
196	C4	304	11000100			─
197	C5	305	11000101			┼
198	C6	306	11000110			╞
199	C7	307	11000111			╟
200	C8	310	11001000			╚
201	C9	311	11001001			╔
202	CA	312	11001010			╩
203	CB	313	11001011			╦
204	CC	314	11001100			╠
205	CD	315	11001101			═
206	CE	316	11001110			╬
207	CF	317	11001111			╧
208	D0	320	11010000			╨
209	D1	321	11010001			╤
210	D2	322	11010010			╥
211	D3	323	11010011			╙
212	D4	324	11010100			╘
213	D5	325	11010101			╒
214	D6	326	11010110			╓
215	D7	327	11010111			╫
216	D8	330	11011000			╪
217	D9	331	11011001			┘
218	DA	332	11011010			┌
219	DB	333	11011011			█

Decimal	Hex	Octal	Binary	Character	Control	IBM PC
220	DC	334	11011100			▄
221	DD	335	11011101			▌
222	DE	336	11011110			▐
223	DF	337	11011111			▀
224	E0	340	11100000			α
225	E1	341	11100001			β
226	E2	342	11100010			Γ
227	E3	343	11100011			π
228	E4	344	11100100			Σ
229	E5	345	11100101			σ
230	E6	346	11100110			μ
231	E7	347	11100111			τ
232	E8	350	11101000			Φ
233	E9	351	11101001			θ
234	EA	352	11101010			Ω
235	EB	353	11101011			δ
236	EC	354	11101100			∞
237	ED	355	11101101			φ
238	EE	356	11101110			ε
239	EF	357	11101111			∩
240	F0	360	11110000			≡
241	F1	361	11110001			±
242	F2	362	11110010			≥
243	F3	363	11110011			≤
244	F4	364	11110100			⌠
245	F5	365	11110101			⌡
246	F6	366	11110110			÷
247	F7	367	11110111			≈
248	F8	370	11111000			°
249	F9	371	11111001			●
250	FA	372	11111010			•
251	FB	373	11111011			√
252	FC	374	11111100			n
253	FD	375	11111101			²
254	FE	376	11111110			■
255	FF	377	11111111			

411

Appendix B

Keyboard Code Assignments

Keyboard entries return either one or two bytes. If the key produces a two-byte sequence, the first byte is 00. The following table shows the return codes from the keyboard when accessed through the Turbo C functions, such as *getch()*. You will notice that some of the keys do not produce any return sequence. This does not mean that the keys are inactive, but rather they cannot be accessed directly through Turbo C or the ROM BIOS services. Instead, direct reads of the keyboard port are necessary.

KEY	FIRST BYTE DECIMAL	HEX	SECOND BYTE DECIMAL	HEX
F1	0	00	59	3B
F2	0	00	60	3C
F3	0	00	61	3D
F4	0	00	62	3E
F5	0	00	63	3F
F6	0	00	64	40
F7	0	00	65	41
F8	0	00	66	42
F9	0	00	67	43
F10	0	00	68	44
Shift F1	0	00	84	54
Shift F2	0	00	85	55
Shift F3	0	00	86	56
Shift F4	0	00	87	57
Shift F5	0	00	88	58
Shift F6	0	00	89	59
Shift F7	0	00	90	5A
Shift F8	0	00	91	5B
Shift F9	0	00	92	5C
Shift F10	0	00	93	5D

KEY	FIRST BYTE		SECOND BYTE	
	DECIMAL	HEX	DECIMAL	HEX
Alternate F1	0	00	104	68
Alternate F2	0	00	105	69
Alternate F3	0	00	106	6A
Alternate F4	0	00	107	6B
Alternate F5	0	00	108	6C
Alternate F6	0	00	109	6D
Alternate F7	0	00	110	6E
Alternate F8	0	00	111	6F
Alternate F9	0	00	112	70
Alternate F10	0	00	113	71
Control F1	0	00	94	5E
Control F2	0	00	95	5F
Control F3	0	00	96	60
Control F4	0	00	97	61
Control F5	0	00	98	62
Control F6	0	00	99	63
Control F7	0	00	90	64
Control F8	0	00	101	65
Control F9	0	00	102	66
Control F10	0	00	103	67
SPACE	32	20	—	—
!	33	21	—	—
"	34	22	—	—
#	35	23	—	—
$	36	24	—	—
%	37	25	—	—
&	38	26	—	—
'	39	27	—	—
(	40	28	—	—
)	41	29	—	—
*	42	2A	—	—
+	43	2B	—	—
,	44	2C	—	—
-	45	2D	—	—
.	46	2E	—	—
/	47	2F	—	—
0	48	30	—	—
1	49	31	—	—
2	50	32	—	—
3	51	33	—	—

KEY	FIRST BYTE		SECOND BYTE	
	DECIMAL	HEX	DECIMAL	HEX
4	52	34	—	—
5	53	35	—	—
6	54	36	—	—
7	55	37	—	—
8	56	38	—	—
9	57	39	—	—
:	58	3A	—	—
;	59	3B	—	—
<	60	3C	—	—
=	61	3D	—	—
>	62	3E	—	—
?	63	3F	—	—
@	64	40	—	—
SHIFT A	65	41	—	—
SHIFT B	66	42	—	—
SHIFT C	67	43	—	—
SHIFT D	68	44	—	—
SHIFT E	69	45	—	—
SHIFT F	70	46	—	—
SHIFT G	71	47	—	—
SHIFT H	72	48	—	—
SHIFT I	73	49	—	—
SHIFT J	74	4A	—	—
SHIFT K	75	4B	—	—
SHIFT L	76	4C	—	—
SHIFT M	77	4D	—	—
SHIFT N	78	4E	—	—
SHIFT O	79	4F	—	—
SHIFT P	80	50	—	—
SHIFT Q	81	51	—	—
SHIFT R	82	52	—	—
SHIFT S	83	53	—	—
SHIFT T	84	54	—	—
SHIFT U	85	55	—	—
SHIFT V	86	56	—	—
SHIFT W	87	57	—	—
SHIFT X	88	58	—	—
SHIFT Y	89	59	—	—
SHIFT Z	90	5A	—	—

KEY	FIRST BYTE DECIMAL	FIRST BYTE HEX	SECOND BYTE DECIMAL	SECOND BYTE HEX
[	91	5B	—	—
\	92	5C	—	—
]	93	5D	—	—
^	94	5E	—	—
_	95	5F	—	—
`	96	60	—	—
a	97	61	—	—
b	98	62	—	—
c	99	63	—	—
d	100	64	—	—
e	101	65	—	—
f	102	66	—	—
g	103	67	—	—
h	104	68	—	—
i	105	69	—	—
j	106	6A	—	—
k	107	6B	—	—
l	108	6C	—	—
m	109	6D	—	—
n	110	6E	—	—
o	111	6F	—	—
p	112	70	—	—
q	113	71	—	—
r	114	72	—	—
s	115	73	—	—
t	116	74	—	—
u	117	75	—	—
v	118	76	—	—
w	119	77	—	—
x	120	78	—	—
y	121	79	—	—
z	122	7A	—	—
{	123	7B	—	—
		124	7C	—	—
}	125	7D	—	—
~	126	7E	—	—
Alternate A	0	00	30	18
Alternate B	0	00	48	30
Alternate C	0	00	46	2E
Alternate D	0	00	32	20

KEY	FIRST BYTE		SECOND BYTE	
	DECIMAL	HEX	DECIMAL	HEX
Alternate E	0	00	18	12
Alternate F	0	00	33	21
Alternate G	0	00	34	22
Alternate H	0	00	35	23
Alternate I	0	00	23	17
Alternate J	0	00	36	24
Alternate K	0	00	37	25
Alternate L	0	00	38	26
Alternate M	0	00	50	32
Alternate N	0	00	49	31
Alternate O	0	00	24	18
Alternate P	0	00	25	19
Alternate Q	0	00	16	10
Alternate R	0	00	19	13
Alternate S	0	00	31	1F
Alternate T	0	00	20	14
Alternate U	0	00	22	16
Alternate P	0	00	25	19
Alternate Q	0	00	16	10
Alternate R	0	00	19	13
Alternate S	0	00	31	1F
Alternate T	0	00	20	14
Alternate U	0	00	22	16
Alternate V	0	00	47	2F
Alternate W	0	00	17	11
Alternate X	0	00	45	2D
Alternate Y	0	00	21	15
Alternate Z	0	00	44	2C
Alternate 1	0	00	120	78
Alternate 2	0	00	121	79
Alternate 3	0	00	122	7A
Alternate 4	0	00	123	7B
Alternate 5	0	00	124	7C
Alternate 6	0	00	125	7D
Alternate 7	0	00	126	7E
Alternate 8	0	00	127	7F
Alternate 9	0	00	128	80
Alternate 0	0	00	129	81

KEY	FIRST BYTE DECIMAL	HEX	SECOND BYTE DECIMAL	HEX
Home	0	00	71	47
End	0	00	79	4F
PgUp	0	00	73	49
PgDn	0	00	81	51
Up arrow	0	00	72	48
Down arrow	0	00	80	50
Right arrow	0	00	77	4D
Left arrow	0	00	75	4B
Ins	0	00	82	52
Del	0	00	83	53
Control Home	0	00	119	77
Control End	0	00	117	75
Control PgUp	0	00	132	83
Control PgDn	0	00	118	76
Control Right	0	00	116	74
Control Left	0	00	115	73
Control PrtSc	0	00	114	72

Appendix C

Character Tables

The following is the character table used for generating the 8x14 characters for the VGA, EGA, and Hercules cards.

```
char char_table[1316] = {

    0x00, 0x00, 0x00, 0x00, 0x00, 0x00, 0x00, 0x00,
    0x00, 0x00, 0x00, 0x00, 0x00, 0x00,
    0x00, 0x00, 0x18, 0x18, 0x18, 0x18, 0x18, 0x18,
    0x00, 0x00, 0x18, 0x00, 0x00, 0x00, 0x00, 0x66,
    0x66, 0x66, 0x00, 0x00, 0x00, 0x00, 0x00, 0x00,
    0x00, 0x00, 0x00, 0x00, 0x00, 0x00, 0x6C, 0x6C,
    0xFE, 0x6C, 0x6C, 0x6C, 0xFE, 0x6C, 0x6C, 0x00,
    0x00, 0x00, 0x00, 0x10, 0x7C, 0xD6, 0xD0, 0xD0,
    0x7C, 0x16, 0x16, 0xD6, 0x7C, 0x10, 0x00, 0x00,
    0x00, 0x00, 0x00, 0x00, 0xC2, 0xC4, 0x08, 0x10,
    0x20, 0x46, 0x86, 0x00, 0x00, 0x00, 0x00, 0x00,
    0x38, 0x6C, 0x6C, 0x38, 0x76, 0xDC, 0xCC, 0xCC,
    0x76, 0x00, 0x00, 0x00, 0x00, 0x30, 0x30, 0x30,
    0x00, 0x00, 0x00, 0x00, 0x00, 0x00, 0x00, 0x00,
    0x00, 0x00, 0x00, 0x00, 0x0C, 0x18, 0x30, 0x30,
    0x30, 0x30, 0x30, 0x18, 0x0C, 0x00, 0x00, 0x00,

    0x00, 0x00, 0x30, 0x18, 0x0C, 0x0C, 0x0C, 0x0C,
    0x0C, 0x18, 0x30, 0x00, 0x00, 0x00, 0x00, 0x00,
    0x00, 0x00, 0x66, 0x3C, 0xFF, 0x3C, 0x66, 0x00,
    0x00, 0x00, 0x00, 0x00, 0x00, 0x00, 0x00, 0x00,
    0x18, 0x18, 0x7E, 0x18, 0x18, 0x00, 0x00, 0x00,
    0x00, 0x00, 0x00, 0x00, 0x00, 0x00, 0x00, 0x00,
    0x00, 0x00, 0x00, 0x1C, 0x18, 0x30, 0x00, 0x00,
    0x00, 0x00, 0x00, 0x00, 0x00, 0x00, 0xFC, 0x00,
    0x00, 0x00, 0x00, 0x00, 0x00, 0x00, 0x00, 0x00,
    0x00, 0x00, 0x00, 0x00, 0x00, 0x00, 0x00, 0x18,
```

```
0x18, 0x00, 0x00, 0x00, 0x00, 0x00, 0x02, 0x06,
0x0C, 0x18, 0x30, 0x60, 0xC0, 0x80, 0x00, 0x00,
0x00, 0x00, 0x00, 0x00, 0x7C, 0xC6, 0xC6, 0xC6,
0xD6, 0xC6, 0xC6, 0xC6, 0x7C, 0x00, 0x00, 0x00,
0x00, 0x00, 0x18, 0x38, 0x18, 0x18, 0x18, 0x18,

0x18, 0x18, 0x7E, 0x00, 0x00, 0x00, 0x00, 0x00,
0x7C, 0xC6, 0x06, 0x0C, 0x18, 0x30, 0x60, 0xC0,
0xFE, 0x00, 0x00, 0x00, 0x00, 0x00, 0x7C, 0xC6,
0x06, 0x06, 0x3C, 0x06, 0x06, 0xC6, 0x7C, 0x00,
0x00, 0x00, 0x00, 0x00, 0x0C, 0x1C, 0x3C, 0x6C,
0xCC, 0xFE, 0x0C, 0x0C, 0x0C, 0x00, 0x00, 0x00,
0x00, 0x00, 0xFE, 0xC0, 0xC0, 0xC0, 0xFC, 0x06,
0x06, 0xC6, 0x7C, 0x00, 0x00, 0x00, 0x00, 0x00,
0x3C, 0x60, 0xC0, 0xC0, 0xFC, 0xC6, 0xC6, 0xC6,
0x7E, 0x00, 0x00, 0x00, 0x00, 0x00, 0xFE, 0x06,
0x06, 0x0C, 0x18, 0x30, 0x30, 0x30, 0x30, 0x00,
0x00, 0x00, 0x00, 0x00, 0x7C, 0xC6, 0xC6, 0xC6,
0x7C, 0xC6, 0xC6, 0xC6, 0x7C, 0x00, 0x00, 0x00,
0x00, 0x00, 0x7C, 0xC6, 0xC6, 0xC6, 0x7E, 0x06,
0x06, 0x0C, 0x78, 0x00, 0x00, 0x00, 0x00, 0x00,

0x00, 0x18, 0x18, 0x00, 0x00, 0x00, 0x18, 0x18,
0x00, 0x00, 0x00, 0x00, 0x00, 0x00, 0x00, 0x18,
0x18, 0x00, 0x00, 0x00, 0x18, 0x18, 0x30, 0x00,
0x00, 0x00, 0x00, 0x00, 0x06, 0x0C, 0x18, 0x30,
0x60, 0x30, 0x18, 0x0C, 0x06, 0x00, 0x00, 0x00,
0x00, 0x00, 0x00, 0x00, 0x00, 0x7E, 0x00, 0x00,
0x7E, 0x00, 0x00, 0x00, 0x00, 0x00, 0x00, 0x00,
0x60, 0x30, 0x18, 0x0C, 0x06, 0x0C, 0x18, 0x30,
0x60, 0x00, 0x00, 0x00, 0x00, 0x00, 0x7C, 0xC6,
0x06, 0x0C, 0x18, 0x18, 0x00, 0x00, 0x18, 0x00,
0x00, 0x00, 0x00, 0x00, 0x7C, 0xC6, 0xC6, 0xDE,
0xDE, 0xDE, 0xDC, 0xC0, 0x7C, 0x00, 0x00, 0x00,
0x00, 0x00, 0x10, 0x38, 0x6C, 0xC6, 0xC6, 0xFE,
0xC6, 0xC6, 0xC6, 0x00, 0x00, 0x00, 0x00, 0x00,
0xFC, 0xC6, 0xC6, 0xC6, 0xFC, 0xC6, 0xC6, 0xC6,
0xFC, 0x00, 0x00, 0x00, 0x00, 0x00, 0x3C, 0x66,

0xC0, 0xC0, 0xC0, 0xC0, 0xC0, 0x66, 0x3C, 0x00,
0x00, 0x00, 0x00, 0x00, 0xF8, 0xCC, 0xC6, 0xC6,
0xC6, 0xC6, 0xC6, 0xCC, 0xF8, 0x00, 0x00, 0x00,
```

```
0x00, 0x00, 0xFE, 0xC0, 0xC0, 0xC0, 0xFC, 0xC0,
0xC0, 0xC0, 0xFE, 0x00, 0x00, 0x00, 0x00, 0x00,
0xFE, 0xC0, 0xC0, 0xC0, 0xFC, 0xC0, 0xC0, 0xC0,
0xC0, 0x00, 0x00, 0x00, 0x00, 0x00, 0x3C, 0x66,
0xC0, 0xC0, 0xC0, 0xCE, 0xC6, 0x66, 0x3C, 0x00,
0x00, 0x00, 0x00, 0x00, 0xC6, 0xC6, 0xC6, 0xC6,
0xFE, 0xC6, 0xC6, 0xC6, 0xC6, 0x00, 0x00, 0x00,
0x00, 0x00, 0x3C, 0x18, 0x18, 0x18, 0x18, 0x18,
0x18, 0x18, 0x3C, 0x00, 0x00, 0x00, 0x00, 0x00,
0x1E, 0x0C, 0x0C, 0x0C, 0x0C, 0x0C, 0x0C, 0xCC,
0x78, 0x00, 0x00, 0x00, 0x00, 0x00, 0xC6, 0xCC,
0xD8, 0xF0, 0xE0, 0xF0, 0xD8, 0xCC, 0xC6, 0x00,
0x00, 0x00, 0x00, 0x00, 0xC0, 0xC0, 0xC0, 0xC0,

0xC0, 0xC0, 0xC0, 0xC0, 0xFE, 0x00, 0x00, 0x00,
0x00, 0x00, 0xC6, 0xEE, 0xFE, 0xFE, 0xD6, 0xC6,
0xC6, 0xC6, 0xC6, 0x00, 0x00, 0x00, 0x00, 0x00,
0xC6, 0xE6, 0xF6, 0xFE, 0xDE, 0xCE, 0xC6, 0xC6,
0xC6, 0x00, 0x00, 0x00, 0x00, 0x00, 0x7C, 0xC6,
0xC6, 0xC6, 0xC6, 0xC6, 0xC6, 0xC6, 0x7C, 0x00,
0x00, 0x00, 0x00, 0x00, 0xFC, 0xC6, 0xC6, 0xC6,
0xFC, 0xC0, 0xC0, 0xC0, 0xC0, 0x00, 0x00, 0x00,
0x00, 0x00, 0x7C, 0xC6, 0xC6, 0xC6, 0xC6, 0xC6,
0xD6, 0xCC, 0x7A, 0x00, 0x00, 0x00, 0x00, 0x00,
0xFC, 0xC6, 0xC6, 0xC6, 0xFC, 0xD8, 0xCC, 0xC6,
0xC6, 0x00, 0x00, 0x00, 0x00, 0x00, 0x7C, 0xC6,
0xC0, 0x60, 0x38, 0x0C, 0x06, 0xC6, 0x7C, 0x00,
0x00, 0x00, 0x00, 0x00, 0x7E, 0x18, 0x18, 0x18,
0x18, 0x18, 0x18, 0x18, 0x18, 0x00, 0x00, 0x00,
0x00, 0x00, 0xC6, 0xC6, 0xC6, 0xC6, 0xC6, 0xC6,

0xC6, 0xC6, 0x7C, 0x00, 0x00, 0x00, 0x00, 0x00,
0xC6, 0xC6, 0xC6, 0xC6, 0xC6, 0xC6, 0x6C, 0x38,
0x10, 0x00, 0x00, 0x00, 0x00, 0x00, 0xC6, 0xC6,
0xC6, 0xC6, 0xD6, 0xD6, 0xFE, 0xEE, 0xC6, 0x00,
0x00, 0x00, 0x00, 0x00, 0xC6, 0xC6, 0x6C, 0x38,
0x10, 0x38, 0x6C, 0xC6, 0xC6, 0x00, 0x00, 0x00,
0x00, 0x00, 0x66, 0x66, 0x66, 0x66, 0x3C, 0x18,
0x18, 0x18, 0x18, 0x00, 0x00, 0x00, 0x00, 0x00,
0xFE, 0x06, 0x0C, 0x18, 0x30, 0x60, 0xC0, 0xC0,
0xFE, 0x00, 0x00, 0x00, 0x00, 0x00, 0x3C, 0x30,
0x30, 0x30, 0x30, 0x30, 0x30, 0x30, 0x3C, 0x00,
```

```
0x00, 0x00, 0x00, 0x00, 0x00, 0x80, 0xC0, 0x60,
0x30, 0x18, 0x0C, 0x06, 0x02, 0x00, 0x00, 0x00,
0x00, 0x00, 0x3C, 0x0C, 0x0C, 0x0C, 0x0C, 0x0C,
0x0C, 0x0C, 0x3C, 0x00, 0x00, 0x00, 0x10, 0x38,
0x6C, 0xC6, 0x00, 0x00, 0x00, 0x00, 0x00, 0x00,

0x00, 0x00, 0x00, 0x00, 0x00, 0x00, 0x00, 0x00,
0x00, 0x00, 0x00, 0x00, 0x00, 0x00, 0x00, 0x00,
0xFE, 0x00, 0x30, 0x30, 0x18, 0x00, 0x00, 0x00,
0x00, 0x00, 0x00, 0x00, 0x00, 0x00, 0x00, 0x00,
0x00, 0x00, 0x00, 0x00, 0x00, 0x7C, 0x06, 0x7E,
0xC6, 0xC6, 0x7E, 0x00, 0x00, 0x00, 0x00, 0x00,
0xC0, 0xC0, 0xC0, 0xFC, 0xC6, 0xC6, 0xC6, 0xC6,
0xFC, 0x00, 0x00, 0x00, 0x00, 0x00, 0x00, 0x00,
0x00, 0x7C, 0xC6, 0xC0, 0xC0, 0xC6, 0x7C, 0x00,
0x00, 0x00, 0x00, 0x00, 0x06, 0x06, 0x06, 0x7E,
0xC6, 0xC6, 0xC6, 0xC6, 0x7E, 0x00, 0x00, 0x00,
0x00, 0x00, 0x00, 0x00, 0x00, 0x7C, 0xC6, 0xFE,
0xC0, 0xC6, 0x7C, 0x00, 0x00, 0x00, 0x00, 0x00,
0x3C, 0x66, 0x60, 0x60, 0xF0, 0x60, 0x60, 0x60,
0x60, 0x00, 0x00, 0x00, 0x00, 0x00, 0x00, 0x00,
0x00, 0x7E, 0xC6, 0xC6, 0xC6, 0x7E, 0x06, 0x06,

0x7C, 0x00, 0x00, 0x00, 0xC0, 0xC0, 0xC0, 0xFC,
0xC6, 0xC6, 0xC6, 0xC6, 0xC6, 0x00, 0x00, 0x00,
0x00, 0x00, 0x18, 0x18, 0x00, 0x00, 0x18, 0x18,
0x18, 0x18, 0x18, 0x00, 0x00, 0x00, 0x00, 0x00,
0x06, 0x06, 0x00, 0x00, 0x06, 0x06, 0x06, 0x06,
0x06, 0xC6, 0x7C, 0x00, 0x00, 0x00, 0xC0, 0xC0,
0xC0, 0xCC, 0xD8, 0xF0, 0xD8, 0xCC, 0xC6, 0x00,
0x00, 0x00, 0x00, 0x00, 0x38, 0x18, 0x18, 0x18,
0x18, 0x18, 0x18, 0x18, 0x3C, 0x00, 0x00, 0x00,
0x00, 0x00, 0x00, 0x00, 0x00, 0xEC, 0xD6, 0xD6,
0xD6, 0xD6, 0xC6, 0x00, 0x00, 0x00, 0x00, 0x00,
0x00, 0x00, 0x00, 0xFC, 0xC6, 0xC6, 0xC6, 0xC6,
0xC6, 0x00, 0x00, 0x00, 0x00, 0x00, 0x00, 0x00,
0x00, 0x7C, 0xC6, 0xC6, 0xC6, 0xC6, 0x7C, 0x00,
0x00, 0x00, 0x00, 0x00, 0x00, 0x00, 0x00, 0xFC,
0xC6, 0xC6, 0xC6, 0xC6, 0xFC, 0xC0, 0xC0, 0x00,

0x00, 0x00, 0x00, 0x00, 0x00, 0x7E, 0xC6, 0xC6,
0xC6, 0xC6, 0x7E, 0x06, 0x06, 0x00, 0x00, 0x00,
```

```
0x00, 0x00, 0x00, 0xFC, 0xC6, 0xC0, 0xC0, 0xC0,
0xC0, 0x00, 0x00, 0x00, 0x00, 0x00, 0x00, 0x00,
0x00, 0x7C, 0xC0, 0x70, 0x1C, 0x06, 0x7C, 0x00,
0x00, 0x00, 0x00, 0x00, 0x00, 0x30, 0x30, 0xFC,
0x30, 0x30, 0x30, 0x30, 0x1C, 0x00, 0x00, 0x00,
0x00, 0x00, 0x00, 0x00, 0x00, 0xC6, 0xC6, 0xC6,
0xC6, 0xC6, 0x7C, 0x00, 0x00, 0x00, 0x00, 0x00,
0x00, 0x00, 0x00, 0xC6, 0xC6, 0xC6, 0x6C, 0x38,
0x10, 0x00, 0x00, 0x00, 0x00, 0x00, 0x00, 0x00,
0x00, 0xC6, 0xC6, 0xD6, 0xD6, 0xFE, 0xC6, 0x00,
0x00, 0x00, 0x00, 0x00, 0x00, 0x00, 0x00, 0xC6,
0x6C, 0x38, 0x38, 0x6C, 0xC6, 0x00, 0x00, 0x00,
0x00, 0x00, 0x00, 0x00, 0x00, 0xC6, 0xC6, 0xC6,
0xC6, 0x7E, 0x06, 0x06, 0x7C, 0x00, 0x00, 0x00,

0x00, 0x00, 0x00, 0xFE, 0x0C, 0x18, 0x30, 0x60,
0xFE, 0x00, 0x00, 0x00, 0x00, 0x00, 0x0E, 0x18,
0x18, 0x18, 0x60, 0x18, 0x18, 0x18, 0x0E, 0x00,
0x00, 0x00, 0x00, 0x00, 0x18, 0x18, 0x18, 0x18,
0x00, 0x18, 0x18, 0x18, 0x18, 0x00, 0x00, 0x00,
0x00, 0x00, 0x70, 0x18, 0x18, 0x18, 0x06, 0x18,
0x18, 0x18, 0x70, 0x00, 0x00, 0x00};
```

The following is the character table used for generating the 8x8 characters for the CGA card.

```
char char_table[1316] = {

0x00, 0x00, 0x00, 0x00, 0x00, 0x00, 0x00, 0x00,
0x30, 0x78, 0x78, 0x30, 0x30, 0x00, 0x30, 0x00,
0x6C, 0x6C, 0x6C, 0x00, 0x00, 0x00, 0x00, 0x00,
0x6C, 0x6C, 0xFE, 0x6C, 0xFE, 0x6C, 0x6C, 0x00,
0x30, 0x7C, 0xC0, 0x78, 0x0C, 0xF8, 0x30, 0x00,
0x00, 0xC6, 0xCC, 0x18, 0x30, 0x66, 0xC6, 0x00,
0x38, 0x6C, 0x38, 0x76, 0xDC, 0xCC, 0x76, 0x00,
0x60, 0x60, 0xC0, 0x00, 0x00, 0x00, 0x00, 0x00,
0x18, 0x30, 0x60, 0x60, 0x60, 0x30, 0x18, 0x00,
0x60, 0x30, 0x18, 0x18, 0x18, 0x30, 0x60, 0x00,
0x00, 0x66, 0x3C, 0xFF, 0x3C, 0x66, 0x00, 0x00,
0x00, 0x30, 0x30, 0xFC, 0x30, 0x30, 0x00, 0x00,
0x00, 0x00, 0x00, 0x00, 0x00, 0x30, 0x30, 0x60,
0x00, 0x00, 0x00, 0xFC, 0x00, 0x00, 0x00, 0x00,
```

```
0x00, 0x00, 0x00, 0x00, 0x00, 0x30, 0x30, 0x00,
0x06, 0x0C, 0x18, 0x30, 0x60, 0xC0, 0x80, 0x00,

0x7C, 0xC6, 0xCE, 0xDE, 0xF6, 0xE6, 0x7C, 0x00,
0x30, 0x70, 0x30, 0x30, 0x30, 0x30, 0xFC, 0x00,
0x78, 0xCC, 0x0C, 0x38, 0x60, 0xCC, 0xFC, 0x00,
0x78, 0xCC, 0x0C, 0x38, 0x0C, 0xCC, 0x78, 0x00,
0x1C, 0x3C, 0x6C, 0xCC, 0xFE, 0x0C, 0x1E, 0x00,
0xFC, 0xC0, 0xF8, 0x0C, 0x0C, 0xCC, 0x78, 0x00,
0x38, 0x60, 0xC0, 0xF8, 0xCC, 0xCC, 0x78, 0x00,
0xFC, 0xCC, 0x0C, 0x18, 0x30, 0x30, 0x30, 0x00,
0x78, 0xCC, 0xCC, 0x78, 0xCC, 0xCC, 0x78, 0x00,
0x78, 0xCC, 0xCC, 0x7C, 0x0C, 0x18, 0x70, 0x00,
0x30, 0x30, 0x30, 0x00, 0x00, 0x30, 0x30, 0x00,
0x00, 0x30, 0x30, 0x00, 0x00, 0x30, 0x30, 0x60,
0x18, 0x30, 0x60, 0xC0, 0x60, 0x30, 0x18, 0x00,
0x00, 0x00, 0xFC, 0x00, 0x00, 0xFC, 0x00, 0x00,
0x60, 0x30, 0x18, 0x0C, 0x18, 0x30, 0x60, 0x00,
0x78, 0xCC, 0x0C, 0x18, 0x30, 0x00, 0x30, 0x00,

0x7C, 0xC6, 0xDE, 0xDE, 0xDE, 0xC0, 0x78, 0x00,
0x30, 0x78, 0xCC, 0xCC, 0xFC, 0xCC, 0xCC, 0x00,
0xFC, 0x66, 0x66, 0x7C, 0x66, 0x66, 0xFC, 0x00,
0x3C, 0x66, 0xC0, 0xC0, 0xC0, 0x66, 0x3C, 0x00,
0xF8, 0x6C, 0x66, 0x66, 0x66, 0x6C, 0xF8, 0x00,
0xFE, 0x62, 0x68, 0x78, 0x68, 0x62, 0xFE, 0x00,
0xFE, 0x62, 0x68, 0x78, 0x68, 0x60, 0xF0, 0x00,
0x3C, 0x66, 0xC0, 0xC0, 0xCE, 0x66, 0x3E, 0x00,
0xCC, 0xCC, 0xCC, 0xFC, 0xCC, 0xCC, 0xCC, 0x00,
0x78, 0x30, 0x30, 0x30, 0x30, 0x30, 0x78, 0x00,
0x1E, 0x0C, 0x0C, 0x0C, 0xCC, 0xCC, 0x78, 0x00,
0xE6, 0x66, 0x6C, 0x78, 0x6C, 0x66, 0xE6, 0x00,
0xF0, 0x60, 0x60, 0x60, 0x62, 0x66, 0xFE, 0x00,
0xC6, 0xEE, 0xFE, 0xFE, 0xD6, 0xC6, 0xC6, 0x00,
0xC6, 0xE6, 0xF6, 0xDE, 0xCE, 0xC6, 0xC6, 0x00,
0x38, 0x6C, 0xC6, 0xC6, 0xC6, 0x6C, 0x38, 0x00,

0xFC, 0x66, 0x66, 0x7C, 0x60, 0x60, 0xF0, 0x00,
0x78, 0xCC, 0xCC, 0xCC, 0xDC, 0x78, 0x1C, 0x00,
0xFC, 0x66, 0x66, 0x7C, 0x6C, 0x66, 0xE6, 0x00,
0x78, 0xCC, 0xE0, 0x70, 0x1C, 0xCC, 0x78, 0x00,
0xFC, 0xB4, 0x30, 0x30, 0x30, 0x30, 0x78, 0x00,
```

```
0xCC, 0xCC, 0xCC, 0xCC, 0xCC, 0xCC, 0xFC, 0x00,
0xCC, 0xCC, 0xCC, 0xCC, 0xCC, 0x78, 0x30, 0x00,
0xC6, 0xC6, 0xC6, 0xD6, 0xFE, 0xEE, 0xC6, 0x00,
0xC6, 0xC6, 0x6C, 0x38, 0x38, 0x6C, 0xC6, 0x00,
0xCC, 0xCC, 0xCC, 0x78, 0x30, 0x30, 0x78, 0x00,
0xFE, 0xC6, 0x8C, 0x18, 0x32, 0x66, 0xFE, 0x00,
0x78, 0x60, 0x60, 0x60, 0x60, 0x60, 0x78, 0x00,
0xC0, 0x60, 0x30, 0x18, 0x0C, 0x06, 0x02, 0x00,
0x78, 0x18, 0x18, 0x18, 0x18, 0x18, 0x78, 0x00,
0x10, 0x38, 0x6C, 0xC6, 0x00, 0x00, 0x00, 0x00,
0x00, 0x00, 0x00, 0x00, 0x00, 0x00, 0x00, 0xFF,

0x30, 0x30, 0x18, 0x00, 0x00, 0x00, 0x00, 0x00,
0x00, 0x00, 0x78, 0x0C, 0x7C, 0xCC, 0x76, 0x00,
0xE0, 0x60, 0x60, 0x7C, 0x66, 0x66, 0xDC, 0x00,
0x00, 0x00, 0x78, 0xCC, 0xC0, 0xCC, 0x78, 0x00,
0x1C, 0x0C, 0x0C, 0x7C, 0xCC, 0xCC, 0x76, 0x00,
0x00, 0x00, 0x78, 0xCC, 0xFC, 0xC0, 0x78, 0x00,
0x38, 0x6C, 0x60, 0xF0, 0x60, 0x60, 0xF0, 0x00,
0x00, 0x00, 0x76, 0xCC, 0xCC, 0x7C, 0x0C, 0xF8,
0xE0, 0x60, 0x6C, 0x76, 0x66, 0x66, 0xE6, 0x00,
0x30, 0x00, 0x70, 0x30, 0x30, 0x30, 0x78, 0x00,
0x0C, 0x00, 0x0C, 0x0C, 0x0C, 0xCC, 0xCC, 0x78,
0xE0, 0x60, 0x66, 0x6C, 0x78, 0x6C, 0xE6, 0x00,
0x70, 0x30, 0x30, 0x30, 0x30, 0x30, 0x78, 0x00,
0x00, 0x00, 0xCC, 0xFE, 0xFE, 0xD6, 0xC6, 0x00,
0x00, 0x00, 0xF8, 0xCC, 0xCC, 0xCC, 0xCC, 0x00,
0x00, 0x00, 0x78, 0xCC, 0xCC, 0xCC, 0x78, 0x00,

0x00, 0x00, 0xDC, 0x66, 0x66, 0x7C, 0x60, 0xF0,
0x00, 0x00, 0x76, 0xCC, 0xCC, 0x7C, 0x0C, 0x1E,
0x00, 0x00, 0xDC, 0x76, 0x66, 0x60, 0xF0, 0x00,
0x00, 0x00, 0x7C, 0xC0, 0x78, 0x0C, 0xF8, 0x00,
0x10, 0x30, 0x7C, 0x30, 0x30, 0x34, 0x18, 0x00,
0x00, 0x00, 0xCC, 0xCC, 0xCC, 0xCC, 0x76, 0x00,
0x00, 0x00, 0xCC, 0xCC, 0xCC, 0x78, 0x30, 0x00,
0x00, 0x00, 0xC6, 0xD6, 0xFE, 0xFE, 0x6C, 0x00,
0x00, 0x00, 0xC6, 0x6C, 0x38, 0x6C, 0xC6, 0x00,
0x00, 0x00, 0xCC, 0xCC, 0xCC, 0x7C, 0x0C, 0xF8,
0x00, 0x00, 0xFC, 0x98, 0x30, 0x64, 0xFC, 0x00,
0x1C, 0x30, 0x30, 0xE0, 0x30, 0x30, 0x1C, 0x00,
0x18, 0x18, 0x18, 0x00, 0x18, 0x18, 0x18, 0x00,
```

```
0xE0, 0x30, 0x30, 0x1C, 0x30, 0x30, 0xE0, 0x00,
0x76, 0xDC, 0x00, 0x00, 0x00, 0x00, 0x00, 0x00,
0x00, 0x10, 0x38, 0x6C, 0xC6, 0xC6, 0xFE, 0x00,
 };
```

Appendix D

GTools Library for CGA, EGA, and VGA

```
/*  HEADER FILE FOR CGA and EGA GRAPHICS TOOLS  */


void cls(char colors);
char getAdaptor();
int getMode(int *ncols);
int getPage(void);
void getxy(int *column, int *row, int page);
void gotoxy(int column, int row, int page);
int readChar(int page, char *attr);
void readColorReg(int color_reg, int *red, int *green, int *blue);
int readPixel(int x, int y);
void scrollWindowDn(int x1, int y1, int x2, int y2, int color);
void scrollWindowUp(int x1, int y1, int x2, int y2, int color);
void setBackground(int color);
void setCGAPalette(int paletteNo);
void setColorPage(int page_no);
void setColorPageMode(int mode);
void setEGApalette(int palette, int color);
void setMode(int mode);
void setPage(int page);
void setWindow(int x1, int y1, int x2, int y2, int color);
void writChar(char ch, int color, int page);
void writeColorReg(int color_reg, int red, int green, int blue);
void writString(char *str, int color, int page);
```

'gtools' library directory

Publics by module

CLS   size = 150
        _cls

GETADAP   size = 222
        _getAdapter

GETMODE   size = 47
        _getMode

GETPAGE   size = 37
        _getPage

GETXY   size = 58
        _getxy

GOTOXY   size = 48
        _gotoxy

READCHAR   size = 51
        _readChar

READPIX   size = 49
        _readPixel

SCROLLDN   size = 66
        _scrollWindowDn

SCROLLUP   size = 66
        _scrollWindowUp

SETBACK   size = 97
        _setBackground

SETCGA   size = 42
        _setCGAPalette

SETCOLPG   size = 212
        _readColorReg   _setColorPage

```
        _setColorPageMode                    _writeColorReg

SETEGA      size = 48
        _setEGApalette

SETMODE     size = 38
        _setMode

SETPAGE     size = 38
        _setPage

SETWNDO     size = 66
        _setWindow

WRITCHAR    size = 55
        _writChar

WRITSTNG    size = 107
        _writString
```

```c
/*                cls() = Clears the Screen              */

#include "gtools.h"

void cls(char colors)
{

    #include <dos.h>

    union REGS reg;

    char ch;
    int columns,mode;

    mode = getMode(&columns);
    if (columns == 80)
    {
        if ((mode == 0x11) || (mode == 0x12))
            reg.x.dx = 0x1D4F;
        else
            reg.x.dx = 0x184F;
```

```c
        reg.h.bh = colors;
    }
    else
    {
        reg.x.dx = 0x1828;
        switch (colors)
        {
            case 1:  reg.h.bh = 0x55;
                     break;
            case 2:  reg.h.bh = 0xAA;
                     break;
            case 3:  reg.h.bh = 0xFF;
                     break;
            default:
                     reg.h.bh = 0;
                     break;
        }
    }
    reg.x.ax = 0x0600;
    reg.x.cx = 0;
    int86(0x10,&reg,&reg);
    gotoxy(0,0);
}


/*              getAdapter = Returns Adapter Type        */

#include "gtools.h"


char getAdapter()
{
    #include <dos.h>

    union REGS reg;
    struct SREGS inreg;

    int EGA, adapter, mode, herc, i, n;
    char type,buffer[64];
    char far *address;
    segread(&inreg);
    inreg.es = inreg.ds;
```

```
reg.x.di = (int) buffer;
reg.x.ax = 0x1B00;
reg.x.bx = 0;
int86x(0x10,&reg,&reg,&inreg);
if (reg.h.al == 0x1B)
    type = 'V';
else
{
    int86(0x11,&reg,&reg);
    adapter = (reg.h.al & 0x30) >> 4;
    mode = getMode(&n);
    address = (char far *)0x00000487;
    EGA = *address;
    type = 'O';
    if (EGA)
        type = 'E';
    else
    {
        if(adapter == 3)
        {
            for (i=0; i<=0x1000; i++)
            {
                if (inp(0x3BA) & 0x80)
                {
                    type = 'H';
                    break;
                }
            }
            if (type == 'O')
                type = 'M';
        }
        else
        {
            if ((adapter == 2) || (adapter == 0))
            {
                if (mode == 2)
                    type = 'Q';
                else
                    type = 'C';
            }
        }
    }
}
```

```
    }
    return (type);
}

/*          getMode() = Returns Current  Video Mode       */

#include "gtools.h"


int getMode(int *ncols)
{
    #include <dos.h>
    union REGS reg;

    reg.h.ah = 0x0F;
    int86 (0x10,&reg,&reg);
    *ncols = reg.h.ah;
    return reg.h.al;
}



/*          getPage() = Returns Active Page Number       */

#include "gtools.h"


int getPage(void)
{
    #include <dos.h>

    union REGS reg;

    reg.h.ah =0x0F;
    int86(0x10,&reg,&reg);
    return (reg.h.bh);
}
```

```
/*      getxy() = Gets the Current Cursor Position    */

#include "gtools.h"


void getxy(int *column, int *row, int page)
{
    #include <dos.h>

    union REGS reg;

    reg.h.ah = 3;
    reg.h.bh = page;
    int86 (0x10,&reg,&reg);
    *row = reg.h.dh;
    *column = reg.h.dl;
}



/*   gotoxy() = Moves Cursor to Specified x,y Position  */
                and Page

#include "gtools.h"


void gotoxy(int column, int row, int page)
{
    #include <dos.h>

    union REGS reg;

    reg.h.ah = 2;
    reg.h.bh = page;
    reg.h.dh = row;
    reg.h.dl = column;
    int86 (0x10,&reg,&reg);
}

/*     readChar = Reads a Character from the Screen    */

#include "gtools.h"
```

```
int readChar(int page, char *attr)
{
    #include <dos.h>

    union REGS reg;

    reg.h.ah = 8;
    reg.h.bh = page;
    int86 (0x10,&reg,&reg);
    *attr = reg.h.ah;
    return (reg.h.al);
}


/*      readPixel = Read a Pixel from the Screen      */

#include "gtools.h"


int readPixel(int x, int y)
{
    #include <dos.h>

    union REGS reg;

    reg.h.ah = 0x0D;
    reg.x.cx = x;
    reg.x.dx = y;
    int86 (0x10,&reg,&reg);
    return (reg.h.al);
}


/*      scrollWindowDn = Scrolls Window One Line Down    */

#include "gtools.h"


void scrollWindowDn(int x1, int y1, int x2, int y2, int color)
{
    #include <dos.h>
```

```
    union REGS reg;

    reg.h.ah = 7;
    reg.h.al = 1;
    reg.h.bh = color;
    reg.h.cl = x1;
    reg.h.ch = y1;
    reg.h.dl = x2;
    reg.h.dh = y2;
    int86 (0x10,&reg,&reg);
}


/*   scrollWindowUp() = Scrolls Window One Line Upward  */

#include "gtools.h"


void scrollWindowUp(int x1, int y1, int x2, int y2, int color)
{
    #include <dos.h>

    union REGS reg;

    reg.h.ah = 6;
    reg.h.al = 1;
    reg.h.bh = color;
    reg.h.cl = x1;
    reg.h.ch = y1;
    reg.h.dl = x2;
    reg.h.dh = y2;
    int86 (0x10,&reg,&reg);
}



/*        setBackground = Sets Background Color       */

#include "gtools.h"

void setBackground(int color)
{
    #include <dos.h>
```

```
    union REGS reg;

    int mode,n;
    mode = getMode(&n);
    if (mode >= 10)
    {
        reg.h.ah = 0x10;
        reg.h.al = 0;
        reg.h.bl = 0;
        reg.h.bh = color;
        int86 (0x10,&reg,&reg);
    }
    else
    {
        reg.h.ah = 0x0B;
        reg.h.bl = color;
        reg.h.bh = 0;
        int86 (0x10,&reg,&reg);
    }
}



/*       setPage() = Sets the Active Display Page      */

#include "gtools.h"


void setPage(int page)
{
    #include <dos.h>

    union REGS reg;

    reg.h.ah = 5;
    reg.h.al = page;
    int86 (0x10,&reg,&reg);
}
```

```c
/*      setCGAPalette = Sets Palette for CGA Modes      */

#include "gtools.h"


void setCGAPalette(int paletteNo)
{
    #include <dos.h>

    union REGS reg;

    reg.h.ah = 0x0B;
    reg.h.bl = paletteNo;
    reg.h.bh = 1;
    int86 (0x10,&reg,&reg);
}

/*   setEGApalette() = sets the color for an EGA palette  */

#include "gtools.h"

void setEGApalette(int palette, int color)
{
    #include <dos.h>

    union REGS reg;

    reg.h.ah = 0x10;
    reg.h.al = 0;
    reg.h.bh = color;
    reg.h.bl = palette;
    int86(0x10,&reg,&reg);
}

/*              setMode() = Sets Video Mode              */

#include "gtools.h"


void setMode(int mode)
{
    #include <dos.h>
```

```
    union REGS reg;

    reg.h.ah = 0;
    reg.h.al = mode;
    int86 (0x10,&reg,&reg);
}

/*        setWindow() = Creates an Empty Window        */

#include "gtools.h"


void setWindow(int x1, int y1, int x2, int y2, int color)
{
    #include <dos.h>

    union REGS reg;

    reg.h.ah = 6;
    reg.h.al = 0;
    reg.h.bh = color;
    reg.h.cl = x1;
    reg.h.ch = y1;
    reg.h.dl = x2;
    reg.h.dh = y2;
    int86 (0x10,&reg,&reg);
}

/*      writChar = Writes a Character to the Screen      */
                with Specified Attribute

#include "gtools.h"

void writChar(char ch, int color, int page)
{
    #include <dos.h>

    union REGS reg;

    reg.h.ah = 9;
    reg.h.al = ch;
```

```
    reg.h.bl = color;
    reg.h.bh = page;
    reg.x.cx = 1;
    int86 (0x10,&reg,&reg);
}


/*      writString = Writes a String to the Screen      */

#include "gtools.h"

void writString(char *str, int color, int page)
{
    int col, row, width, i = 0;
    getMode (&width);
    getxy(&col,&row,page);
    while (str[i])
    {
        writChar(str[i++], color, page);

        if (col++ > (width - 1))
        {
            col = 0;
            row++;
        }
        gotoxy(col, row, page);
    }
}
```

The remaining 'gtools' functions are used with the VGA board only.


```
#include <dos.h>

/*   setColorPageMode() = sets the color paging mode     */
                        number.

#include "gtools.h"

void setColorPageMode(int mode)
{

    union REGS reg;
```

```
    reg.x.ax = 0x1013;
    reg.h.bh = mode;
    reg.h.bl = 0;
    int86(0x10,&reg,&reg);
}

/*  setColorPage() = sets page of color registers      */

void setColorPage(int page_no)
{

    union REGS reg;

    reg.x.ax = 0x1013;
    reg.h.bh = page_no;
    reg.h.bl = 1;
    int86(0x10,&reg,&reg);
}

/*   readColorReg() = Reads Individual Color Register  */
                     Settings


void readColorReg(int color_reg, int *red, int *green, int *blue)
{

    union REGS reg;

    reg.x.ax = 0x1015;
    reg.x.bx = color_reg;
    int86(0x10,&reg,&reg);
    *green = reg.h.ch;
    *blue = reg.h.cl;
    *red = reg.h.dh;
}

/*   writeColorReg() = Writes Color Data to Individual */
                     Color Register

void writeColorReg(int color_reg, int red, int green, int blue)
{
```

```
    union REGS reg;

    reg.x.ax = 0x1010;
    reg.x.bx = color_reg;
    reg.h.ch = green;
    reg.h.cl = blue;
    reg.h.dh = red;
    int86(0x10,&reg,&reg);
}
```

Appendix E

GDraws Library
for CGA, EGA, and VGA

GDRAWS LIBRARY FOR CGA, EGA, and VGA

```
/*        gdraws.h = Header file for gdraws library     */

float bs_blend(int i, int n, float u);
void drawArc (int xc, int yc, int b, int start_angle,
    int end_angle, int color, float aspect);
void drawBezier(int segments,int color,...);
void drawBspline(int segments, int color,...);
void drawLine(int x1, int y1, int x2, int y2, int color);
void drawOval(int x, int y, int b, int color, float aspect);
void drawPoly(int color, ...);
void drawRect(int x1, int y1, int x2, int y2, int color);
void drawRoundRect(int x1, int y1, int x2, int y2, int b,
    int color);
void fillArc (int xc, int yc, int b, int start_angle,int
    end_angle, int color, float aspect);
void fillArc1 (int xc, int yc,int x, int y, int sector,
    int arcTest[], int x_start_test, int x_end_test, int color);
void fillOval(int x, int y, int r, int color, float aspect);
void fillPoly(int color, ...);
void fill2Poly(int color,int point[600]);
void fillRect(int x1, int y1, int x2, int y2, int color);
void fillRoundRect(int x1, int y1, int x2, int y2, int r,
    int color);
void plot(int x, int y, int color);
void plots(int x, int y, int color);
void plotArc1 (int x, int y, int sector, int color,
```

```
    int arcTest[], int x_start_test, int x_end_test);
void plotArc2 (int x, int y, int sector, int color,
    int arcTest[], int x_start_test, int x_end_test);
void plot_char(int x, int y, int char_offset,int color,
    int type);
void sort(int index, int x_coord[], int y_coord[]);
void write_horz_char(int x, int y, int ch, int color);
void write_vert_char(int x, int y, int ch, int color);
void write_horz_str(int x, int y, char *string, int color);
void write_vert_str(int x, int y, char *string, int color);
void write_big_char(int x, int y, int ch, int color);
void write_vid_char(int x, int y, int ch, int color);
void write_big_str(int x, int y, char *string, int color);
void write_vid_str(int x, int y, char *string, int color);

extern int OPERATOR, LINEWIDTH, ANGLE, XCENTER, YCENTER;
extern unsigned long PATTERN, style[8];

#define VGA

#ifdef VGA
#define convert(x,y)   {x = (x + 319);   y = (240 - y);}
#endif

#ifdef EGA
#define convert(x,y)   {x = (x + 319);   y = (175 - ((93*y) >> 7));}
#endif

#ifdef CGA
#define convert(x,y)   {x = ((x >> 1) + 159);   y = (100 - ((53*y)\
                >> 7));}
#endif
```

                gdraws library listing file

Publics by module

```
CHARS       size = 2355
_char_table                    _plot_char
_write_big_char                _write_big_str
_write_horz_char               _write_horz_str
```

```
_write_vert_char                    _write_vert_str
_write_vid_char                     _write_vid_str


DRAWARC      size = 1537
_drawArc                            _plotArc1
_plotArc2


DRAWBEZ      size = 533
_blend                              _drawBezier


DRAWBSPL     size = 821
_drawBspline


DRAWLINE     size = 492
_drawLine


DRAWOVAL     size = 743
_drawOval


DRAWPOLY     size = 210
_drawPoly


DRAWRECT     size = 171
_drawRect


DRAWRNDR     size = 955
_drawRoundRect


FIL2POLY     size = 696
_fill2Poly


FILLARC      size = 2283
_fillArc                            _fillArc1


FILLOVAL     size = 1244
_fillOval


FILLPOLY     size = 888
_fillPoly


FILLRECT     size = 676
_fillRect
```

```
FILLRNDR     size = 901
_fillRoundRect

PATPLOT      size = 264
_pattern_plot

PLOT         size = 285
_plot

PLOTS        size = 274
_plots

ROTOVAL      size = 1918
_rotateOval

ROTPOLY      size = 996
_rotatePoly

ROTRECT      size = 1490
_rotateRect

SORT         size = 249
_sort


    /*   drawArc() = draws an arc centered at (xc,yc) with
                 radius 'b' in y direction from starting
                 angle 'start_angle' in tenths of a
                 degree to ending angle 'end_angle' in
                 tenths of a degree with aspect ratio
                 'aspect' and in color 'color'.  */


#include <math.h>
#include "gdraws.h"

void drawArc (int xc, int yc, int b, int start_angle,
    int end_angle, int color, float aspect)

{
    #include <dos.h>
```

```
int col, i, row,start_sector,end_sector,x_start_test,
    x_end_test;
int arcTest[9],j;
float aspect_square;
long a_square, b_square, two_a_square, two_b_square,
    four_a_square, four_b_square,d;

void plotArc1 (int x, int y, int sector, int color,
    int arcTest[], int x_start_test, int x_end_test);
void plotArc2 (int x, int y, int sector, int color,
    int arcTest[], int x_start_test, int x_end_test);

aspect_square = aspect*aspect;
b -= LINEWIDTH/2;
for (j=0; j<8; j++)
    arcTest[j] = 0;
for (j=1; j<=LINEWIDTH; j++)
{
    b_square = b*b;
    a_square = b*b/aspect_square;
    row = b;
    col = 0;
    two_a_square = a_square << 1;
    four_a_square = a_square << 2;
    four_b_square = b_square << 2;
    two_b_square = b_square << 1;
    d = two_a_square * ((row  -1)*(row )) + a_square +
        two_b_square*(1-a_square);
    start_sector = start_angle/450;
    end_sector = end_angle/450;
    x_start_test = xc+sqrt(a_square)*cos(start_angle*
        .0017453);
    x_end_test = xc+sqrt(a_square)*cos(end_angle*
        .0017453);
    if (start_sector == end_sector)
        arcTest[start_sector] = 4;
    else
    {
        arcTest[start_sector] = 1;
        arcTest[end_sector] = 3;
        for (i=start_sector+1; i!=end_sector; i++)
```

```
        {
            arcTest[i] = 2;
            if (i==8)
                i=-1;
        }
    }
    while (a_square*(row ) > b_square * (col))
    {
        plotArc1 (xc+col, yc-row, 6, color, arcTest,
            x_start_test, x_end_test);
        plotArc2 (xc+col, yc+row, 1, color, arcTest,
            x_start_test, x_end_test);
        plotArc1 (xc-col, yc-row, 5, color, arcTest,
            x_start_test, x_end_test);
        plotArc2 (xc-col, yc+row, 2, color, arcTest,
            x_start_test, x_end_test);
        if (d>= 0)
        {
            row--;
            d -= four_a_square*(row);
        }
        d += two_b_square*(3 + (col << 1));
        col++;
    }

    d = two_b_square * (col + 1)*col + two_a_square*(row *
        (row  -2) +1) + (1-two_a_square)*b_square;
    while ((row) + 1)
    {
        plotArc1 (xc+col, yc-row, 7, color, arcTest,
            x_start_test, x_end_test);
        plotArc2 (xc+col, yc+row, 0, color, arcTest,
            x_start_test, x_end_test);
        plotArc1 (xc-col, yc-row, 4, color, arcTest,
            x_start_test, x_end_test);
        plotArc2 (xc-col, yc+row, 3, color, arcTest,
            x_start_test, x_end_test);
        if (d<= 0)
        {
            col++;
            d += four_b_square*col;
        }
```

```
            row--;
            d += two_a_square * (3 - (row <<1));
        }
        b++;
    }
}


void plotArc1 (int x, int y, int sector, int color,
    int arcTest[], int x_start_test, int x_end_test)
{
    if (arcTest[sector] == 0)
        return;
    if (arcTest[sector] == 2)
        plots(x,y,color);
    if ((arcTest[sector] == 1) && (x>=x_start_test))
        plots(x,y,color);
    if ((arcTest[sector] == 3) && (x<=x_end_test))
        plots(x,y,color);
    if ((arcTest[sector] == 4) && (x>=x_start_test) &&
        (x<=x_end_test))
        plots(x,y,color);
}


void plotArc2 (int x, int y, int sector, int color,
    int arcTest[], int x_start_test, int x_end_test)
{
    if (arcTest[sector] == 0)
        return;
    if (arcTest[sector] == 2)
        plots(x,y,color);
    if ((arcTest[sector] == 1) && (x<=x_start_test))
        plots(x,y,color);
    if ((arcTest[sector] == 3) && (x>=x_end_test))
        plots(x,y,color);
    if ((arcTest[sector] == 4) && (x>=x_end_test) &&
        (x<=x_start_test))
        plots(x,y,color);
}


    /*  drawBezier() = draws a Bezier curve      */
```

```
#include "gdraws.h"


void drawBezier(int segments, int color,...)
{
    #include <dos.h>
    #include <stdarg.h>
    #include <stdio.h>

    union REGS reg;

    float blend(int i, int n, float u);

    va_list coord;
    int xpoint[20],ypoint[20],i=0,j,oldx,oldy,px,py,last;
    float b,u,x,y;

    va_start(coord,color);
    while (((xpoint[i]=va_arg(coord,int)) >= -320 &&
        ((ypoint[i]=va_arg(coord,int)) >= -320) && (i<=20))
        i++;
    va_end(coord);
    last = (i-1);
    for (i=0; i<=segments; i++)
    {
        u = (float)i/segments;
        x = 0;
        y = 0;
        for (j=0; j<=last; j++)
        {
            b = blend (j,last,u);
            x += xpoint[j]*b;
            y += ypoint[j]*b;
        }
        px = x;
        py = y;
        if (i>0)
            drawLine(oldx,oldy,x,y,color);
        oldx = x;
        oldy = y;
    }
}
```

```
float blend(int i, int n, float u)
{
    int c,j,k=1,g=1;
    float f;

    for (c=n; c>i; c--)
        k *= c;
    for (c=n-i; c>1; c--)
        g *= c;
    f = (float)k/g;
    for (j=1; j<=i; j++)
        f *= u;
    for (j=1; j<=n-i; j++)
        f *= (1-u);
    return (f);
}


    /* drawBspline() = draws a B-Spline Curve    */

#include "gdraws.h"


void drawBspline(int segments, int color,...)
{
    #include <dos.h>
    #include <stdarg.h>
    #include <stdio.h>

    union REGS reg;

    va_list coord;
    int xpoint[20],ypoint[20],i=1,j,x,y,oldx,oldy,last;
    float u,nc1,nc2,nc3,nc4;

    va_start(coord,color);
    while (((xpoint[i]=va_arg(coord,int)) >= -320) &&
        ((ypoint[i]=va_arg(coord,int)) >= -320) && (i<=20))
        i++;
    va_end(coord);
    xpoint[0]=xpoint[1];
```

```
    ypoint[0]=ypoint[1];
    oldx=xpoint[0];
    oldy=ypoint[0];
    for (j=i;j<=i+1;j++)
    {
        xpoint[j]=xpoint[j-1];
        ypoint[j]=ypoint[j-1];
    }
    last = j;
    for(i=1; i<=last-3; i++)
    {
        for (u=0; u<=1; u+=1.0/segments)
        {
            nc1=-(u*u*u/6)+u*u/2-u/2+1.0/6;
            nc2=u*u*u/2-u*u+2.0/3;
            nc3=(-u*u*u+u*u+u)/2+1.0/6;
            nc4=u*u*u/6;
            x = (nc1*xpoint[i-1]+nc2*xpoint[i]+nc3*xpoint[i+1]
                +nc4*xpoint[i+2]);
            y = (nc1*ypoint[i-1]+nc2*ypoint[i]+nc3*ypoint[i+1]
                +nc4*ypoint[i+2]);
            drawLine(oldx,oldy,x,y,color);
            oldx=x;
            oldy=y;
        }
    }
}


        /*  drawLine() = draws a line from one set of coordinates
                       to another in a designated color  */

#include "gdraws.h"


extern unsigned long int PATTERN;
extern int LINEWIDTH;

void drawLine(int x1, int y1, int x2, int y2, int color)
{
    #include <dos.h>

    union REGS reg;
```

```c
#define sign(x)  ((x) > 0 ? 1:  ((x) == 0 ? 0:  (-1)))

int dx, dy, dxabs, dyabs, i, j, px, py, sdx, sdy, x, y;
unsigned long int mask=0x80000000;

convert(x1,y1);
convert(x2,y2);
dx = x2 - x1;
dy = y2 - y1;
sdx = sign(dx);
sdy = sign(dy);
dxabs = abs(dx);
dyabs = abs(dy);
x = 0;
y = 0;
px = x1;
py = y1;
if (dxabs >= dyabs)
{
    for (i=0; i<dxabs; i++)
    {
        mask = mask ? mask : 0x80000000;
        y += dyabs;
        if (y>=dxabs)
        {
            y -= dxabs;
            py += sdy;
        }
        px += sdx;
        if (PATTERN & mask)
        {
            for (j=-LINEWIDTH/2; j<=LINEWIDTH/2; j++)
                plot(px,py+j,color);
        }
        mask >>= 1;
    }
}
else
{
    for (i=0; i<dyabs; i++)
    {
```

```
                mask = mask ? mask : 0x80000000;
                x += dxabs;
                if (x>=dyabs)
                {
                    x -= dyabs;
                    px += sdx;
                }
                py += sdy;
                if (PATTERN & mask)
                {
                    for (j=-LINEWIDTH/2; j<=LINEWIDTH/2; j++)
                        plot(px+j,py,color);
                }
                mask >>= 1;
            }
        }
}


    /* drawOval() = draws an oval with specified center,
                    radius, color and aspect ratio.      */

#include "gdraws.h"



void drawOval(int x, int y, int b, int color, float aspect)
{
    #include <dos.h>

    union REGS reg;

    int col, i, row, bnew;
    float aspect_square;
    long a_square, b_square, two_a_square, two_b_square,
        four_a_square, four_b_square,d;

    aspect_square = aspect*aspect;
    b -= LINEWIDTH/2;
    for (i=1; i<=LINEWIDTH; i++)
    {
        b_square = b*b;
        a_square = (b*b)/aspect_square;
```

```
        row = b;
        col = 0;
        two_a_square = a_square << 1;
        four_a_square = a_square << 2;
        four_b_square = b_square << 2;
        two_b_square = b_square << 1;
        d = two_a_square * ((row  -1)*(row )) + a_square +
            two_b_square*(1-a_square);
        while (a_square*(row ) > b_square * (col))
        {
            plots(col+x,row+y,color);
            plots(col+x,y-row, color);
            plots(x-col,row+y,color);
            plots(x-col,y-row,color);
            if (d>= 0)
            {
                row--;
                d -= four_a_square*(row);
            }
            d += two_b_square*(3 + (col << 1));
            col++;
        }

        d = two_b_square * (col + 1)*col + two_a_square*(row *
            (row  -2) +1) + (1-two_a_square)*b_square;
        while ((row) + 1)
        {
            plots(col+x,row+y,color);
            plots(col+x,y-row, color);
            plots(x-col,row+y,color);
            plots(x-col,y-row,color);
            if (d<= 0)
            {
                col++;
                d += four_b_square*col;
            }
            row--;
            d += two_a_square * (3 - (row <<1));
        }
        b++;
    }
}
```

```
    /*  drawPoly() = draws a polygon in specified color by
                     connecting specified sets of points in
                     order given and then connecting last
                     point to first.                             */

#include "gdraws.h"

void drawPoly(int color,...)
{
    #include <stdarg.h>
    #include <stdio.h>

    va_list coord;
    int xpoint[150],ypoint[150],i=0,j;
    va_start(coord,color);
    while (((xpoint[i]=va_arg(coord,int)) >= -320) &&
        ((ypoint[i]=va_arg(coord,int)) >= -320) && (i<=150))
        i++;
    if (i<3) return;
    for (j=0; j<i-1; j++)
    drawLine(xpoint[j],ypoint[j],xpoint[j+1],ypoint[j+1],color);
    drawLine(xpoint[0],ypoint[0],xpoint[i-1],ypoint[i-1],color);
    va_end(coord);

    /*  drawRect() = draws a rectangle with top left and
                     bottom right corners specified in
                     specified color               */

#include "gdraws.h"

extern int LINEWIDTH;


void drawRect(int x1, int y1, int x2, int y2, int color)
{
    #include <dos.h>

    union REGS reg;

    int i,j;
```

```
        drawLine(x1-LINEWIDTH/2,y1,x2+LINEWIDTH/2,y1,color);
        drawLine(x1-LINEWIDTH/2,y2,x2+LINEWIDTH/2,y2,color);
        drawLine(x1,y1+LINEWIDTH/2,x1,y2-LINEWIDTH/2,color);
        drawLine(x2,y1+LINEWIDTH/2,x2,y2-LINEWIDTH/2,color);


}



    /*    drawRoundRect() = draws a rectangle with rounded
            corners of radius 'b' with upper right
            corner 'x1,y1', lower left corner 'x2,y2',
            in specified color 'color'.            */

#include "gdraws.h"

void drawRoundRect(int x1, int y1, int x2, int y2, int b,
    int color)
{
    int a, xr, yr, col,i,j,row,xend,yend;
    long a_square, b_square, two_a_square, two_b_square,
        four_a_square, four_b_square,d;
    yr = b;
    xr = b;
    xend = x2-xr;
    yend = y2+yr;
    for (j=-LINEWIDTH/2; j<=LINEWIDTH/2; j++)
    {
        for (i=x1+xr; i<=xend; i++)
        {
            plots(i,y1-j,color);
            plots(i,y2-j,color);
        }
    }
    for (j=-LINEWIDTH/2; j<=LINEWIDTH/2; j++)
    {
        for (i=y1-yr; i>=yend; i--)
        {
            plots(x1+j,i,color);
            plots(x2+j,i,color);
        }
    }
    b -= LINEWIDTH/2;
```

```
a = b;
for (i=0; i<LINEWIDTH; i++)
{
    b_square = b*b;
    a_square = a*a;
    row = b;
    col = 0;
    two_a_square = a_square << 1;
    four_a_square = a_square << 2;
    four_b_square = b_square << 2;
    two_b_square = b_square << 1;
    d = two_a_square * ((row  -1)*(row )) + a_square +
        two_b_square*(1-a_square);
    while (a_square*(row ) > b_square * (col))
    {
        plots(col+xend,yend-row,color);
        plots(col+xend,y1-yr+row, color);
        plots(x1+xr-col,yend-row,color);
        plots(x1+xr-col,y1-yr+row,color);
        if (d>= 0)
        {
            row--;
            d -= four_a_square*(row);
        }
        d += two_b_square*(3 + (col << 1));
        col++;
    }

    d = two_b_square * (col + 1)*col + two_a_square*(row *
        (row  -2) +1) + (1-two_a_square)*b_square;
    while (row)
    {
        plots(col+xend,yend-row,color);
        plots(col+xend,y1-yr+row, color);
        plots(x1+xr-col,yend-row,color);
        plots(x1+xr-col,y1-yr+row,color);
        if (d<= 0)
        {
            col++;
            d += four_b_square*col;
        }
        row--;
```

```
        d += two_a_square * (3 - (row <<1));
    }
    b++;
    a++;
}
}


/*  fil2Poly() = fills a polygon in specified color by
               filling in boundaries resulting from
               connecting specified points in the
               order given and then connecting last
               point to first.  Uses an array to
               store coordinates.

#include <math.h>
#include "gdraws.h"

void fill2Poly(int color,int point[600])
{
    #include <dos.h>

    #define sign(x) ((x) > 0 ? 1:  ((x) == 0 ? 0:  (-1)))

    int dx, dy, dxabs, dyabs, i, index=0, j, k, px, py, sdx,
        sdy, x, y, toggle, old_sdy, sy0;
    int *x_coord, *y_coord;

    x_coord = (int *) malloc(4000 * sizeof(int));
    y_coord = (int *) malloc(4000 * sizeof(int));
    for (i=0; i<=600; i++)
        if (point[i] < -320)
            break;
    point[i] = point[0];
    point[i+1] = point[1];
    if (i<=5) return;
    px = point[0];
    py = point[1];
    if (point[1] == point[3])
    {
        x_coord[index] = px;
        y_coord[index++] = py;
```

```
        }
    for (j=0; j<i-2; j+=2)
    {
        dx = point[j+2] - point[j];
        dy = point[j+3] - point[j+1];
        sdx = sign(dx);
        sdy = sign(dy);
        if (j==0)
        {
            old_sdy = sdy;
            sy0 = sdy;
        }
        dxabs = abs(dx);
        dyabs = abs(dy);
        x = 0;
        y = 0;
        if (dxabs >= dyabs)
        {
            for (k=0; k<dxabs; k++)
            {
                y += dyabs;
                if (y>=dxabs)
                {
                    y -= dxabs;
                    py += sdy;
                    if (old_sdy != sdy)
                    {
                        old_sdy = sdy;
                        index--;
                    }
                    x_coord[index] = px+sdx;
                    y_coord[index++] = py;
                }
                px += sdx;
                plots(px,py,color);
            }
        }
        else
        {
            for (k=0; k<dyabs; k++)
            {
                x += dxabs;
```

```
            if (x>=dyabs)
            {
                x -= dyabs;
                px += sdx;
            }

            py += sdy;
            if (old_sdy != sdy)
            {
                old_sdy = sdy;
                if (sdy != 0)
                    index--;
            }
            plots(px,py,color);
            x_coord[index] = px;
            y_coord[index] = py;
            index++;
        }
    }
}
index--;
if (sy0 + sdy == 0)
    index--;
sort(index,x_coord,y_coord);
toggle = 0;
for (i=0; i<index; i++)
{
    if ((y_coord[i] == y_coord[i+1]) &&
        (toggle == 0))
    {
        for (j=x_coord[i]; j<=x_coord[i+1]; j++)
            plots(j,y_coord[i],color);
        toggle = 1;
    }
    else
        toggle = 0;
}
}


/*      fillArc() = fills an arc centered at (xc,yc) having
                radius 'b' in y direction from starting
```

```
                      angle  'start_angle' in tenths of a
                      degree to ending angle 'end_angle' in
                      tenths of a degree and aspect ratio
                      'aspect' with   color 'color'.       */

#include <math.h>
#include "gdraws.h"
#include <dos.h>


void fillArc (int xc, int yc, int b, int start_angle,
    int end_angle, int color, float aspect)

{

    int col, i, row,start_sector,end_sector,x_start_test,
        x_end_test;
    int arcTest[9];
    float aspect_square;
    long a_square, b_square, two_a_square, two_b_square,
        four_a_square, four_b_square,d;

    for (i=0; i<8; i++)
        arcTest[i] = 0;
    aspect_square = aspect*aspect;
    a_square = b*b/aspect_square;
    b_square = b*b;
    row = b;
    col = 0;
    convert(xc,yc);
    two_a_square = a_square << 1;
    four_a_square = a_square << 2;
    four_b_square = b_square << 2;
    two_b_square = b_square << 1;
    d = two_a_square * ((row  -1)*(row )) + a_square +
        two_b_square*(1-a_square);
    start_sector = start_angle/450;
    end_sector = end_angle/450;
    x_start_test = xc+sqrt(a_square)*cos(start_angle*.0017453);
    x_end_test = xc+sqrt(a_square)*cos(end_angle*.0017453);
    if (start_sector == end_sector)
        arcTest[start_sector] = 4;
    else
```

```
{
    arcTest[start_sector] = 1;
    arcTest[end_sector] = 3;
    for (i=start_sector+1; i!=end_sector; i++)
    {
        arcTest[i] = 2;
        if (i==8)
            i=-1;
    }
}
while (a_square*(row ) > b_square * (col))
{
    fillArc1 (xc,yc,xc+col, yc+row, 6, arcTest,
        x_start_test, x_end_test,color);
    fillArc1 (xc,yc,xc+col, yc-row, 1, arcTest,
        x_start_test, x_end_test,color);
    fillArc1 (xc,yc,xc-col, yc+row, 5, arcTest,
        x_start_test, x_end_test,color);
    fillArc1 (xc,yc,xc-col, yc-row, 2, arcTest,
        x_start_test, x_end_test,color);
    if (d>= 0)
    {
        row--;
        d -= four_a_square*(row);
    }
    d += two_b_square*(3 + (col << 1));
    col++;
}

d = two_b_square * (col + 1)*col + two_a_square*(row *
    (row  -2) +1) + (1-two_a_square)*b_square;
while ((row) + 1)
{
    fillArc1 (xc,yc,xc+col, yc+row, 7, arcTest,
        x_start_test, x_end_test,color);
    fillArc1 (xc,yc,xc+col, yc-row, 0, arcTest,
        x_start_test, x_end_test,color);
    fillArc1 (xc,yc,xc-col, yc+row, 4, arcTest,
        x_start_test, x_end_test,color);
    fillArc1 (xc,yc,xc-col, yc-row, 3, arcTest,
        x_start_test, x_end_test,color);
    if (d<= 0)
```

```
        {
            col++;
            d += four_b_square*col;
        }
        row--;
        d += two_a_square * (3 - (row <<1));
    }
}


    /*   fillArc1() = subroutine for fillArc       */



void fillArc1 (int xc, int yc,int x, int y, int sector,
    int arcTest[], int x_start_test, int x_end_test, int color)
{
    union REGS reg;
    #define seq_out(index,val)     {outp(0x3C4,index);\
                                    outp(0x3C5,val);}
    #define graph_out(index,val)   {outp(0x3CE,index);\
                                    outp(0x3CF,val);}

    unsigned int offset;
    int dummy, mask,dx,dy,i,tx=0,ty=0,sdx,sdy,dxabs,dyabs;
    char far * mem_address;

    switch (sector)
    {
        case 4:
        case 5:
        case 6:
        case 7:
            if (arcTest[sector] == 2)
                break;
            if ((arcTest[sector] == 1) && (x>=x_start_test))
                break;
            if ((arcTest[sector] == 3) && (x<=x_end_test))
                break;
            if ((arcTest[sector] == 4) && (x>=x_start_test)
                && (x<=x_end_test))
                break;
            return;
```

```
    case 0:
    case 1:
    case 2:
    case 3:
        if (arcTest[sector] == 2)
            break;
        if ((arcTest[sector] == 1) && (x<=x_start_test))
            break;
        if ((arcTest[sector] == 3) && (x>=x_end_test))
            break;
        if ((arcTest[sector] == 4) && (x>=x_end_test)
            && (x<=x_start_test))
            break;
        return;
}
if ((sector <= 1) || (sector >= 6))
    sdx = 1;
else
    sdx = -1;
if (sector > 3)
    sdy = 1;
else
    sdy = -1;
dxabs = (x-xc)*sdx;
dyabs = (y-yc)*sdy;
if (dxabs >= dyabs)
{
    for (i=0; i<= dxabs; i++)
    {
        ty+= dyabs;
        if (ty>dxabs)
        {
            ty -= dxabs;
            yc +=sdy;
        }
        #ifdef CGA
        plot(xc,yc,color);
        plot(xc,yc+1,color);
        #endif

        #ifndef CGA
        offset = (long)yc * 80L + ((long)xc / 8L);
```

```
                        mem_address = (char far *) 0xA0000000L + offset;
                        mask = 0x80 >> (xc % 8);
                        graph_out(8,mask);
                        seq_out(2,0x0F);
                        dummy = *mem_address;
                        *mem_address = 0;
                        seq_out(2,color);
                        *mem_address = 0xFF;
                        offset = (long)(yc + 1) * 80L + ((long)xc / 8L);
                        mem_address = (char far *) 0xA0000000L + offset;
                        graph_out(8,mask);
                        seq_out(2,0x0F);
                        dummy = *mem_address;
                        *mem_address = 0;
                        seq_out(2,color);
                        *mem_address = 0xFF;
                        seq_out(2,0x0F);
                        graph_out(3,0);
                        graph_out(8,0xFF);
                        #endif

                        xc+= sdx;
                }
        }
        else
        {
                for (i=0; i<= dyabs; i++)
                {
                        tx+= dxabs;
                        if (tx>dyabs)
                        {
                                tx -= dyabs;
                                xc +=sdx;
                        }

                        #ifdef CGA
                        plot(xc,yc,color);
                        plot(xc+1,yc,color);
                        #endif

                        #ifndef CGA
                        offset = (long)yc * 80L + ((long)xc / 8L);
```

```
            mem_address = (char far *) 0xA0000000L + offset;
            mask = 0x80 >> (xc % 8);
            graph_out(8,mask);
            seq_out(2,0x0F);
            dummy = *mem_address;
            *mem_address = 0;
            seq_out(2,color);
            *mem_address = 0xFF;
            offset = (long)yc * 80L + ((long)(xc + 1) / 8L);
            mem_address = (char far *) 0xA0000000L + offset;
            mask = 0x80 >> ((xc + 1) % 8);
            graph_out(8,mask);
            seq_out(2,0x0F);
            dummy = *mem_address;
            *mem_address = 0;
            seq_out(2,color);
            *mem_address = 0xFF;
            seq_out(2,0x0F);
            graph_out(3,0);
            graph_out(8,0xFF);
            #endif

            yc+= sdy;
        }
    }
}


/*  fillOval() = draws an oval centered at (x,y) with
                 radius in y direction of 'b' with
                 aspect ratio 'aspect' and fills it
                 with color 'color'.                   */


#include "gdraws.h"


void fillOval(int x, int y, int b, int color, float aspect)
{
    #include <dos.h>

    union REGS reg;
```

```
#define seq_out(index,val)      {outp(0x3C4,index);\
                                 outp(0x3C5,val);}
#define graph_out(index,val)    {outp(0x3CE,index);\
                                 outp(0x3CF,val);}

unsigned int offset;
char far * mem_address;
int col, col1, row, row1, dummy, i, mask;
float aspect_square;
long a_square, b_square, two_a_square, two_b_square,
    four_a_square, four_b_square,d;


char far *base;

aspect_square = aspect*aspect;
a_square = b*b/aspect_square;

#ifdef CGA
a_square >>= 2;
b = (53*b) >> 7;
#endif

#ifdef EGA
b = (93*b) >> 7;
#endif

b_square = b*b;
row = b;
col = 0;
convert(x,y);
two_a_square = a_square << 1;
four_a_square = a_square << 2;
four_b_square = b_square << 2;
two_b_square = b_square << 1;
d = two_a_square * ((row  -1)*(row )) + a_square +
    two_b_square*(1-a_square);
while (a_square*(row ) > b_square * (col))
{
    for (i=y-row; i<=y+row; i++)
    {
        #ifdef CGA
```

```
        plot(x+col,i,color);
        plot(x-col,i,color);
        #endif

        #ifndef CGA
        offset = (long)i * 80L + ((long)(x + col) / 8L);
        mem_address = (char far *) 0xA0000000L + offset;
        mask = 0x80 >> ((x + col) % 8);
        graph_out(8,mask);
        seq_out(2,0x0F);
        dummy = *mem_address;
        *mem_address = 0;
        seq_out(2,color);
        *mem_address = 0xFF;
        offset = (long)i * 80L + ((long)(x - col) / 8L);
        mem_address = (char far *) 0xA0000000L + offset;
        mask = 0x80 >> ((x - col) % 8);
        graph_out(8,mask);
        seq_out(2,0x0F);
        dummy = *mem_address;
        *mem_address = 0;
        seq_out(2,color);
        *mem_address = 0xFF;
        seq_out(2,0x0F);
        graph_out(3,0);
        graph_out(8,0xFF);
        #endif

    }
    if (d>= 0)
    {
        row--;
        d -= four_a_square*(row);
    }
    d += two_b_square*(3 + (col << 1));
    col++;
}

d = two_b_square * (col + 1)*col + two_a_square*(row *
    (row  -2) +1) + (1-two_a_square)*b_square;
while ((row) + 1)
{
```

```
for (i=y-row; i<=y+row; i++)
{
    #ifdef CGA
    plot(x+col,i,color);
    plot(x-col,i,color);
    #endif

    #ifndef CGA
    offset = (long)i * 80L + ((long)(x + col) / 8L);
    mem_address = (char far *) 0xA0000000L + offset;
    mask = 0x80 >> ((x + col) % 8);
    graph_out(8,mask);
    seq_out(2,0x0F);
    dummy = *mem_address;
    *mem_address = 0;
    seq_out(2,color);
    *mem_address = 0xFF;
    offset = (long)i * 80L + ((long)(x - col) / 8L);
    mem_address = (char far *) 0xA0000000L + offset;
    mask = 0x80 >> ((x - col) % 8);
    graph_out(8,mask);
    seq_out(2,0x0F);
    dummy = *mem_address;
    *mem_address = 0;
    seq_out(2,color);
    *mem_address = 0xFF;
    seq_out(2,0x0F);
    graph_out(3,0);
    graph_out(8,0xFF);

    #endif

}
if (d<= 0)
{
    col++;
    d += four_b_square*col;
}
row--;
d += two_a_square * (3 - (row <<1));
}
}
```

```
/*      fillPoly() = fills a polygon in specified color by
                     filling in boundaries resulting from
                     connecting specified points in the
                     order given and then connecting last
                     point to first.               */

#include "gdraws.h"
void fillPoly(int color,...)
{
    #include <dos.h>
    #include <stdarg.h>
    #include <stdio.h>

    #define sign(x)  ((x) > 0 ? 1:  ((x) == 0 ? 0:  (-1)))

    int dx, dy, dxabs, dyabs, i, index=0, j, k, px, py, sdx,
        sdy, x, y, xpoint[150], ypoint[150], toggle, old_sdy,sy0;
    long int check;
    int *x_coord, *y_coord;

    va_list coord;

    x_coord = (int *) malloc(4000 * sizeof(int));
    y_coord = (int *) malloc(4000 * sizeof(int));
    va_start(coord,color);
    for (i=0; i<150; i++)
    {
        xpoint[i] = va_arg(coord,int);
        ypoint[i] = va_arg(coord,int);
        convert(xpoint[i], ypoint[i]);
        if ((xpoint[i] < 0) || (ypoint[i] > 480))
            break;
    }
    va_end(coord);
    xpoint[i] = xpoint[0];
    ypoint[i] = ypoint[0];
    if (i<3) return;
    px = xpoint[0];
    py = ypoint[0];
    if (ypoint[1] == ypoint[0])
    {
```

```
    x_coord[index] = px;
    y_coord[index++] = py;
}
for (j=0; j<i; j++)
{
    dx = xpoint[j+1] - xpoint[j];
    dy = ypoint[j+1] - ypoint[j];
    sdx = sign(dx);
    sdy = sign(dy);
    if (j==0)
    {
        old_sdy = sdy;
        sy0 = sdy;
    }
    dxabs = abs(dx);
    dyabs = abs(dy);
    x = 0;
    y = 0;
    if (dxabs >= dyabs)
    {
        for (k=0; k<dxabs; k++)
        {
            y += dyabs;
            if (y>=dxabs)
            {
                y -= dxabs;
                py += sdy;
                if (old_sdy != sdy)
                {
                    old_sdy = sdy;
                    index--;
                }
                x_coord[index] = px+sdx;
                y_coord[index++] = py;
            }
            px += sdx;
            pattern_plot(px,py,color);
        }
    }
    else
    {
        for (k=0; k<dyabs; k++)
```

```
        {
            x += dxabs;
            if (x>=dyabs)
            {
                x -= dyabs;
                px += sdx;
            }
            py += sdy;
            if (old_sdy != sdy)
            {
                old_sdy = sdy;
                if (sdy != 0)
                    index--;
            }

            pattern_plot(px,py,color);
            x_coord[index] = px;
            y_coord[index++] = py;
        }
    }
}
index--;
if (sy0 + sdy== 0)
index--;
sort(index,x_coord,y_coord);
toggle = 0;
for (i=0; i<index; i++)
{
    if ((y_coord[i] == y_coord[i+1]) &&
        (toggle == 0))
    {
        for (j=x_coord[i]; j<=x_coord[i+1]; j++)
            pattern_plot(j,y_coord[i],color);
        toggle = 1;
    }
    else
        toggle = 0;
}

free(x_coord);
free(y_coord);
}
```

```
/*         fillRect() = fills a rectangle whose top left and
                        bottom right corners are specified
                        with a specified color      */

#include "gdraws.h"

void fillRect(int x1, int y1, int x2, int y2, int color)
{
    #include <dos.h>

    int i,first,last,begin,end,start_mask,end_mask,mask,
        dumm  y,page,xs,xe;
    long int y1L, y2L,j;
    #define seq_out(index,val)      {outp(0x3C4,index);\
                                     outp(0x3C5,val);}
    #define graph_out(index,val)    {outp(0x3CE,index);\
                                     outp(0x3CF,val);}
    unsigned int offset;
    char far * mem_address;

    convert(x1,y1);
    convert(x2,y2);

    #ifdef CGA

    page = getPage();
    xs = x1 - (x1%4) +4;
    xe = x2 - (x1%4);

    for (i=y1; i<=y2; i++)
    {
        for (j=x1; j<xs; j++)
        {
            offset = 0x2000 * (i%2) + 4000 * page + 80 * (i/2)
                + j/4;
            mask = 0xC0 >> ((j%4)*2);
            mem_address = 0xB8000000L +offset;
            *mem_address &= ~mask);
            mask = (color & 0x03) << (6 - (j%4) * 2);
            *mem_address |= mask;
        }
```

```
    for (j=xs; j<xe; j+=4)
    {
        offset = 0x2000 * (i%2) + 4000 * page + 80 * (i/2)
            + j/4;
        mask = color & 0x03;
        mask += (mask << 2);
        mask += (mask << 4);
        mem_address = 0xB8000000L +offset;
        *mem_address = mask;
    }
    for (j=xe; j<=x2; j++)
    {
        offset = 0x2000 * (i%2) + 4000 * page + 80 * (i/2)
            + j/4;
        mask = 0xC0 >> ((j%4)*2);
        mem_address = 0xB8000000L +offset;
        *mem_address &= ~mask);
        mask = (color & 0x03) << (6 - (j%4) * 2);
        *mem_address |= mask);
    }
}

#endif

#ifndef CGA

y1L = y1*80L;
y2L = y2*80L;
begin = x1/8;
end = x2/8;
first = x1 - begin*8;
last = x2 - end*8 + 1;
start_mask = 0xFF >> first;
end_mask = 0xFF << (8-last);
for (j=y1L; j<=y2L; j+=80)
{
    offset = j + begin;
    mem_address = (char far *) 0xA0000000L + offset;
    graph_out(8,start_mask);
    seq_out(2,0x0F);
    dummy = *mem_address;
    *mem_address = 0;
```

```
            seq_out(2,color);
            *mem_address = start_mask;
            for (i=begin+1; i<end; i++)
            {
                offset = j + i;
                mem_address = (char far *) 0xA0000000L + offset;
                graph_out(8,0xFF);
                seq_out(2,0x0F);
                dummy = *mem_address;
                *mem_address = 0;
                seq_out(2,color);
                *mem_address = 0xFF;
            }
            offset = j + end;
            mem_address = (char far *) 0xA0000000L + offset;
            graph_out(8,end_mask);
            seq_out(2,0x0F);
            dummy = *mem_address;
            *mem_address = 0;
            seq_out(2,color);
            *mem_address = end_mask;
            seq_out(2,0x0F);
            graph_out(3,0);
            graph_out(8,0xFF);
        }
        #endif
}


/*     fillRoundRect() = fills in a rectangle with rounded
                corners of radius 'b' with upper right
                corner 'x1,y1', lower left corner 'x2,y2',
                in specified color 'color'.              */



#include "gdraws.h"

void fillRoundRect(int x1, int y1, int x2, int y2, int b,
    int color)
{
    int a, xr, yr, col,i,j,row,xend,yend,flag;
    long a_square, b_square, two_a_square, two_b_square,
        four_a_square, four_b_square,d;
```

```
yr = b;
xr = b-2;
xend = x2-xr;
yend = y2+yr;
b -= LINEWIDTH/2;
a = b;
b_square = b*b;
a_square = a*a;
fillRect(x1,y1-yr,x2,y2+yr,color);
fillRect(x1+xr,y1,x2-xr,y2,color);
row = b;
col = 0;
two_a_square = a_square << 1;
four_a_square = a_square << 2;
four_b_square = b_square << 2;
two_b_square = b_square << 1;
d = two_a_square * ((row  -1)*(row )) + a_square +
two_b_square*(1-a_square);
while (a_square*(row ) > b_square * (col))
{
    drawLine(xend,yend-row,col+xend,yend-row,color);
    drawLine(xend,y1-yr+row,col+xend,y1-yr+row, color);
    drawLine(x1+xr,yend-row,x1+xr-col,yend-row,color);
    drawLine(x1+xr,y1-yr+row,x1+xr-col,y1-yr+row,color);
    if (d>= 0)
    {
        row--;
        d -= four_a_square*(row);
    }
    d += two_b_square*(3 + (col << 1));
    col++;
}
d = two_b_square * (col + 1)*col + two_a_square*(row *
    (row  -2) +1) + (1-two_a_square)*b_square;
while (row)
{
    drawLine(xend,yend-row,col+xend,yend-row,color);
    drawLine(xend,y1-yr+row,col+xend,y1-yr+row, color);
    drawLine(x1+xr,yend-row,x1+xr-col,yend-row,color);
    drawLine(x1+xr,y1-yr+row,x1+xr-col,y1-yr+row,color);
    if (d<= 0)
```

```
        {
            col++;
            d += four_b_square*col;
        }
        row--;
        d += two_a_square * (3 - (row <<1));
    }
    b++;
    a++;
}



    /* pattern_plot() = plots points alternating between
                        two colors according to a specified
                        pattern.                            */

#include "gdraws.h"

void pattern_plot(int x, int y, int color)
{
    #include <dos.h>

    unsigned int mask, pattern[4][8];
    int i,foreground,background,fill;

    for (i=0; i<8; i++)
    {
        pattern[0][i] = 0xFFFF;
        if (i%2 == 0)
        {
            pattern[2][i] = 0x4444;
            pattern[3][i] = 0xAAAA;
        }
        else
        {
            pattern[2][i] = 0x1111;
            pattern[3][i] = 0x5555;
        }
    }
    pattern[1][0] = 0x2020;
    pattern[1][1] = 0x0202;
    pattern[1][2] = 0x8080;
```

```
    pattern[1][3] = 0x0808;
    pattern[1][4] = 0x2020;
    pattern[1][5] = 0x0202;
    pattern[1][6] = 0x8080;
    pattern[1][7] = 0x0808;
    foreground = color & 0x0F;
    background = (color & 0xF0) >> 4;
    fill = (color & 0xF00) >> 8;
    mask = 0x8000 >> (x % 16);
    if (pattern[fill][y%8] & mask)
    plot(x,y,foreground);
    else
        plot(x,y,background);
}


/*      plot() = plots a point on the screen at designated
                screen coordinates using selected color.  */


#include "gdraws.h"
extern int OPERATOR;

void plot(int x, int y, int color)
{
    #include <dos.h>

    #define seq_out(index,val)      {outp(0x3C4,index);\
                                    outp(0x3C5,val);}
    #define graph_out(index,val)    {outp(0x3CE,index);\
                                    outp(0x3CF,val);}


    unsigned int offset;
    int dummy,mask,page;
    char far * mem_address;

    #ifdef CGA

    page = getPage();
    offset = 0x2000 * (y%2) + 80 * (y/2) + x/4;
    mask = 0xC0   >> ((x%4)*2);
    mem_address = (char far *) 0xB8000000L + offset;
```

479

```c
    *mem_address &= ~mask;
    mask = (color & 0x03) << (6 - (x%4) * 2);
    *mem_address |= mask;

    #endif

    #ifndef  CGA

    offset = (long)y * 80L + ((long)x / 8L);
    mem_address = (char far *) 0xA0000000L + offset;
    mask = 0x80 >> (x % 8);
    graph_out(8,mask);
    seq_out(2,0x0F);
    dummy = *mem_address;
    *mem_address = 0;
    seq_out(2,color);
    *mem_address = 0xFF;
    seq_out(2,0x0F);
    graph_out(3,0);
    graph_out(8,0xFF);

    #endif
}


/* plots() = plots a point on the screen at designated
             system coordinates using selected color. */


#include "gdraws.h"

void plots(int x, int y, int color)      /* plot pixel at x, y */
{

    #include <dos.h>

    #define seq_out(index,val)      {outp(0x3C4,index);\
                                     outp(0x3C5,val);}
    #define graph_out(index,val)    {outp(0x3CE,index);\
                                     outp(0x3CF,val);}

    unsigned int offset;
```

```c
    int dummy,mask,page;
    char far * mem_address;

    convert(x,y);

    #ifdef CGA

    page = getPage();
    offset = 0x2000 * (y%2) + 80 * (y/2) + x/4);
    mask = 0xC0   >> ((x%4)*2);
    mem_address = (char far *) 0xB8000000L + offset;
    *mem_address &= ~mask;
    mask = (color & 0x03) << (6 - (x%4 * 2);
    *mem_address |= mask;

    #endif

    #ifndef CGA

    offset = (long)y * 80L + ((long)x / 8L);
    mem_address = (char far *) 0xA0000000L + offset;
    mask = 0x80 >> (x % 8);
    graph_out(8,mask);
    seq_out(2,0x0F);
    dummy = *mem_address;
    *mem_address = 0;
    seq_out(2,color);
    *mem_address = 0xFF;
    seq_out(2,0x0F);
    graph_out(3,0);
    graph_out(8,0xFF);

    #endif
}

/*      rotateOval() = rotates an oval with center (x,y),
                       radius 'b', and color 'color' through
                       angle 'ANGLE' and draws oval.      */

#include <math.h>
#include "gdraws.h"
```

```c
extern int ANGLE;

int rotateOval(int x, int y, int b, int color, double aspect)
{
    #include <dos.h>

    int col, i, row,px,py;
    double aspect_square;
    long a_square, b_square, two_a_square, two_b_square,
        four_a_square, four_b_square,d;
    float angle,ca,sa;

    angle = .01745329*(360 - ANGLE);
    sa=sin(angle);
    ca=cos(angle);

    aspect_square = aspect*aspect;
    b -= LINEWIDTH/2;
    for (i=1; i<=LINEWIDTH; i++)
    {
        b_square = b*b;
        a_square = b_square/aspect_square;
        row = b;
        col = 0;
        two_a_square = a_square << 1;
        four_a_square = a_square << 2;
        four_b_square = b_square << 2;
        two_b_square = b_square << 1;
        d = two_a_square * ((row  -1)*(row )) + a_square +
            two_b_square*(1-a_square);
        while (a_square*(row ) > b_square * (col))
        {
            px = x + col*ca - (row)*sa;
            py = y + col*sa + row*ca;
            plots(px,py,color);
            px = x + col*ca + row*sa;
            py = y + col*sa - row*ca;
            plots(px,py,color);
            px = x - col*ca - row*sa;
            py = y - col*sa + row*ca;
            plots(px,py,color);
            px = x - col*ca + row*sa;
```

```
            py = y - col*sa - row*ca;
            plots(px,py,color);
            if (d>= 0)
            {
                row--;
                d -= four_a_square*(row);
            }
            d += two_b_square*(3 + (col << 1));
            col++;
        }

    d = two_b_square * (col + 1)*col + two_a_square*(row *
        (row  -2) +1) + (1-two_a_square)*b_square;
    while ((row) + 1)
    {
        px = x+ col*ca - (row)*sa;
        py = y + col*sa + row*ca;
        plots(px,py,color);
        px = x + col*ca + row*sa;
        py = y + col*sa - row*ca;
        plots(px,py,color);
        px = x - col*ca - row*sa;
        py = y - col*sa + row*ca;
        plots(px,py,color);
        px = x - col*ca + row*sa;
        py = y - col*sa - row*ca;
        plots(px,py,color);
        if (d<= 0)
        {
            col++;
            d += four_b_square*col;
        }
        row--;
        d += two_a_square * (3 - (row <<1));
    }
    b++;
    }
}


/*  rotatePoly() = rotates a polygon whose sides and
                color are specified through an
```

```
                              angle 'ANGLE' and draws polygon.    */

#include <math.h>
#include "gdraws.h"
extern int ANGLE,XCENTER,YCENTER;

void rotatePoly(int color,...)
{
    #include <dos.h>
    #include <stdarg.h>
    #include <stdio.h>

    va_list coord;
    int point[600],i=0,j,x1,y1,x2,y2;
    float angle,param;

    va_start(coord,color);
    angle = .01745329*(360 - ANGLE);
    while (((point[i]=va_arg(coord,int)) >= -320) && (i<=600))
        i++;
    va_end(coord);
    point[i++] = point[0];
    point[i] = point[1];
    if (i<=5) return;
    for (j=0; j<i-2; j+=2)
    {
        x1 = (point[j] - XCENTER)*cos(angle) - (point[j+1] -
            YCENTER)*sin(angle) + XCENTER;
        y1 = (point[j] - XCENTER)*sin(angle) + (point[j+1] -
            YCENTER)*cos(angle) + YCENTER;
        x2 = (point[j+2] - XCENTER)*cos(angle) - (point[j+3] -
            YCENTER)*sin(angle) + XCENTER;
        y2 = (point[j+2] - XCENTER)*sin(angle) + (point[j+3] -
            YCENTER)*cos(angle) + YCENTER;
        drawLine(x1,y1,x2,y2,color);
    }
}


    /*    rotateRect() = draws a rectangle with top left and
                    bottom right corners specified in
                    specified color and rotated to a
```

```
                    specified angle.                        */

#include <math.h>
#include "gdraws.h"


void rotateRect(int x1, int y1, int x2, int y2, int color)
{
    #include <dos.h>

    union REGS reg;

    int nx1,nx2,nx3,nx4,ny1,ny2,ny3,ny4;
    float angle,param=.83;

    angle = .01745329*(360 - ANGLE);
    nx1 = (x1 - XCENTER)*cos(angle) - (y1 - YCENTER)*sin(angle)
        + XCENTER;
    ny1 = (x1 - XCENTER)*sin(angle) + (y1 - YCENTER)*cos(angle)
        + YCENTER;
    nx3 = (x2 - XCENTER)*cos(angle) - (y2 - YCENTER)*sin(angle)
        + XCENTER;
    ny3 = (x2 - XCENTER)*sin(angle) + (y2 - YCENTER)*cos(angle)
        + YCENTER;
    nx2 = (x2 - XCENTER)*cos(angle) - (y1 - YCENTER)*sin(angle)
        + XCENTER;
    ny2 = (x2 - XCENTER)*sin(angle) + (y1 - YCENTER)*cos(angle)
        + YCENTER;
    nx4 = (x1 - XCENTER)*cos(angle) - (y2 - YCENTER)*sin(angle)
        + XCENTER;
    ny4 = (x1 - XCENTER)*sin(angle) + (y2 - YCENTER)*cos(angle)
        + YCENTER;

    drawLine(nx1-LINEWIDTH/2,ny1,nx2+LINEWIDTH/2,ny2,color);
    drawLine(nx2-LINEWIDTH/2,ny2,nx3+LINEWIDTH/2,ny3,color);
    drawLine(nx3,ny3+LINEWIDTH/2,nx4,ny4-LINEWIDTH/2,color);
    drawLine(nx4,ny4+LINEWIDTH/2,nx1,ny1-LINEWIDTH/2,color);
}


    /*  sort() = sorts coordinate pairs for drawing and
                filling polygons.                      */
```

```c
#include "gdraws.h"

void sort(int index, int x_coord[], int y_coord[])
{
    int d=4,i,j,k,temp;

    while (d<=index)
    d*=2;
    d-=1;
    while (d>1)
    {
        d/=2;
        for (j=0; j<=(index-d); j++)
        {
            for (i=j; i>=0; i-=d)
            {
                if ((y_coord[i+d] < y_coord[i]) ||
                    ((y_coord[i+d] == y_coord[i]) &&
                    (x_coord[i+d] <= x_coord[i])))
                {
                    temp = y_coord[i];
                    y_coord[i] = y_coord[i+d];
                    y_coord[i+d] = temp;
                    temp = x_coord[i];
                    x_coord[i] = x_coord[i+d];
                    x_coord[i+d] = temp;
                }
            }
        }
    }
}


/*      chars = functions to write characters with specified
                foreground and background colors.       */

#include <stdio.h>
#include <dos.h>
#include "chars.h"
#include "gdraws.h"
```

```
void write_horz_char(int x, int y, int ch, int color)
{
    #define seq_out(index,val)      {outp(0x3C4,index);\
                                     outp(0x3C5,val);}
    #define graph_out(index,val)    {outp(0x3CE,index);\
                                     outp(0x3CF,val);}

    unsigned int offset;
    char far * mem_address;
    int char_offset,dummy,i,j,mask;
    unsigned char char_test, exist_color;

    convert(x,y);

    #ifdef CGA

    char_offset = (ch - 32) * 8;

    #endif

    #ifndef CGA

    char_offset = (ch - 32) * 14;

    #endif

    plot_char(x,y,char_offset,color,0);
}

void write_vert_char(int x, int y, int ch, int color)
{
    #define seq_out(index,val)      {outp(0x3C4,index);\
                                     outp(0x3C5,val);}
    #define graph_out(index,val)    {outp(0x3CE,index);\
                                     outp(0x3CF,val);}

    unsigned int offset;
    char far * mem_address;
    int char_offset,dummy,i,j,mask;
    unsigned char char_test, exist_color;
```

```
    convert(x,y);

    #ifdef CGA

    char_offset = (ch - 32) * 8;

    #endif

    #ifndef CGA

    char_offset = (ch - 32) * 14;

    #endif

    plot_char(x,y,char_offset,color,1);
}


void write_horz_str(int x, int y, char *string, int color)
{
    #define seq_out(index,val)      {outp(0x3C4,index);\
                                     outp(0x3C5,val);}
    #define graph_out(index,val)    {outp(0x3CE,index);\
                                     outp(0x3CF,val);}

    unsigned int offset;
    char far * mem_address;
    int char_offset,dummy,i,j,mask,p=0;
    unsigned char char_test, exist_color;

    convert(x,y);
    while (string[p])
    {

        #ifdef CGA

        char_offset = (string[p] - 32) * 8;

        #endif

        #ifndef CGA
```

```c
        char_offset = (string[p] - 32) * 14;

        #endif

        plot_char(x,y,char_offset,color,0);
        x += 8;

        #ifdef CGA

        if (x>312)
        {
            x=0;
            y -= 8;
        }
        #endif

        #ifndef CGA
        if (x>632)
        {
            x=0;
            y -= 14;
        }
        #endif
        p++;
    }
}

void write_vert_str(int x, int y, char *string, int color)
{
    #define seq_out(index,val)      {outp(0x3C4,index);\
                                     outp(0x3C5,val);}
    #define graph_out(index,val)    {outp(0x3CE,index);\
                                     outp(0x3CF,val);}

    unsigned int offset;
    char far * mem_address;
    int char_offset,point_color,dummy,i,j,mask,p=0;
    unsigned char char_test, exist_color;

    convert(x,y);
    while (string[p])
    {
```

```
        #ifdef CGA

        char_offset = (string[p] - 32) * 8;

        #endif

        #ifndef CGA

        char_offset = (string[p] - 32) * 14;

        #endif

        plot_char(x,y,char_offset,color,1);
        y -= 8;
        if (y<8)
        {
            #ifdef VGA
            y=472;
            x += 14;
            #endif

            #ifdef EGA
            y=342;
            x += 14;
            #endif

            #ifdef VGA
            y=192;
            x += 8;
            #endif
        }
        p++;
    }
}

void write_big_char(int x, int y, int ch, int color)
{
    #define seq_out(index,val)      {outp(0x3C4,index);\
                                     outp(0x3C5,val);}
    #define graph_out(index,val)    {outp(0x3CE,index);\
                                     outp(0x3CF,val);}
```

```
    unsigned int offset;
    char far * mem_address;
    int char_offset,dummy,i,j,k,m,mask;
    unsigned char char_test, exist_color;

    convert(x,y);

    #ifdef CGA
    char_offset = (ch - 32) * 8;
    #endif

    #ifndef CGA
    char_offset = (ch - 32) * 14;
    #endif

    plot_char(x,y,char_offset,color,2);
}

void write_vid_char(int x, int y, int ch, int color)
{
    #define seq_out(index,val)      {outp(0x3C4,index);\
                                     outp(0x3C5,val);}
    #define graph_out(index,val)    {outp(0x3CE,index);\
                                     outp(0x3CF,val);}

    unsigned int offset;
    char far * mem_address;
    int char_offset,dummy,i,j,k,m,mask;
    unsigned char char_test, exist_color;

    convert(x,y);

    #ifdef CGA
    char_offset = (ch - 32) * 8;
    #endif

    #ifndef CGA
    char_offset = (ch - 32) * 14;
    #endif

    plot_char(x,y,char_offset,color,3);
}
```

```c
void write_big_str(int x, int y, char *string, int color)
{
    int p=0,char_offset;

    convert(x,y);

    while (string[p])
    {
        #ifdef CGA
        char_offset = (string[p] - 32) * 8;
        #endif

        #ifndef CGA
        char_offset = (string[p] - 32) * 14;
        #endif

        plot_char(x,y,char_offset,color,2);
        x += 32;

        #ifdef CGA
        if (x>287)
        {
            x=0;
            y += 32;
        }
        #endif

        #ifndef CGA

        if (x>607)
        {
            x=0;
            y += 56;
        }
        #endif
        p++;
    }
}

void write_vid_str(int x, int y, char *string, int color)
{
```

```c
    int p=0,char_offset;

convert(x,y);
while (string[p])
{
    #ifdef CGA
    char_offset = (string[p] - 32) * 8;
    #endif

    #ifndef CGA
    char_offset = (string[p] - 32) * 14;
    #endif

    plot_char(x,y,char_offset,color,3);
    x += 32;

    #ifdef CGA
    if (x>287)
    {
        x=0;
        y += 32;
    }
    #endif

    #ifndef CGA

    if (x>607)
    {
        x=0;
        y += 56;
    }
    #endif
    p++;
}
}

void plot_char(int x, int y, int char_offset,int color, int type)
{
    #define seq_out(index,val)     {outp(0x3C4,index);\
                                    outp(0x3C5,val);}
    #define graph_out(index,val)   {outp(0x3CE,index);\
                                    outp(0x3CF,val);}
```

```
unsigned int offset;
char far * mem_address;
unsigned char char_test, exist_color;
int i, j, k, m, start, end,height,width,foreground,
    background,
point_color,dummy,mask;

foreground = color & 0x0F;
background = (color & 0xF0) >> 4;
switch(type)
{
    case 0:
    case 1:
        start = 0;
        end = 1;
        break;
    case 2:
        start = 0;
        end = 4;
        break;
    case 3:
        start = 1;
        end = 4;
}
#ifdef CGA
for (i=0; i<8; i++)
#endif
#ifndef CGA
for (i=0; i<14; i++)
#endif
{
    for (j=0; j<8; j++)
    {
        for (m=start; m<end; m++)
        {
            for (k=start; k<end; k++)
            {
                switch(type)
                {
                    case 0:
                        height = y+i;
```

```
                                width = x+j;
                                break;
                        case 1:
                                height = y-j;
                                width = x+i;
                                break;
                        case 2:
                        case 3:
                                height = y+4*i+k;
                                width = x+4*j+m;
                }
                char_test = 0x80 >> j;
                if ((char_table[char_offset+i] &
                    char_test) != 0)
                    point_color = foreground;
                else
                    point_color = background;
                #ifdef CGA
                plot(height,width,point_color);
                #endif

                #ifndef CGA
                offset = (long)(height) * 80L +
                    ((long)(width) / 8L);
                mem_address = (char far *)0xA0000000L
                    + offset;
                mask = 0x80 >> ((width) % 8);
                graph_out(8,mask);
                seq_out(2,0x0F);
                dummy = *mem_address;
                *mem_address = 0;
                seq_out(2,point_color);
                *mem_address = 0xFF;
                #endif
            }
        }
    }
}
#ifndef CGA
seq_out(2,0x0F);
graph_out(3,0);
graph_out(8,0xFF);
```

```
    #endif
}
```

Appendix F

Demonstration Programs for CGA, EGA, and VGA

```c
/*      demo() = PROGRAM TO DEMONSTRATE THE USE OF THE
                 C GRAPHICS FUNCTIONS                        */


                    /*      INCLUDES    */

#include <stdio.h>
#include <math.h>
#include <dos.h>
#include <conio.h>


                /*      USER WRITTEN INCLUDES    */

#include "gtools.h"
#include "gdraws.h"
#include "colors.h"


    /*      GLOBAL VARIABLES USED BY GRAPHICS FUNCTIONS      */



char adapt;
int color = 2;
int LINEWIDTH=1, OPERATOR=0, ANGLE, XCENTER, YCENTER;
int pt[12][2]={{-20,0},{0,0},{0,-120},{-200,-120},
    {-200,200},{90,150},{60,0},{200,0},{0,0}},x,y,z;
unsigned long int PATTERN=0xFFFFFFFF;
```

```
unsigned long int style[8] = { 0xFFFFFFFF,0xC0C0C0C0,0xFF00FF00,
    0xFFF0FFF0,0xF000F000,0xFFFF0000,0xFFFFF0F0,0xFFF0F0F0};

int usa[600] = {-151,111,-146,
    107,-144, 96,-140, 96,-138,103,-139,111,-135,112,-111,
    103,-91, 96,-65, 92,-39, 89,-13, 85, 13, 85, 44, 82, 32,
    71, 30, 68, 35, 68, 41, 72, 41, 68, 44, 68, 54, 81, 57,
    81, 53, 74, 61, 72, 62, 70, 73, 75, 73, 72, 79, 71, 79,
    70, 75, 67, 69, 66, 63, 61, 61, 48, 61, 34, 63, 27, 65,
    27, 69, 38, 66, 48, 67, 55, 71, 60, 78, 66, 82, 66, 84,
    61, 84, 59, 87, 56, 86, 49, 89, 55, 93, 45, 87, 34, 93,
    31,114, 48,113, 53,127, 59,130, 68,152, 82,156,107,158,
    110,162,107,162,105,165,105,174, 89,160, 68,160, 61,165,
    55,167, 56,147, 59,158, 59,158, 55,160, 50,149, 34,149,
    20,147, 17,143, 24,140, 24,147, 15,144,  1,147, -2,149,
    -8,149,-13,145,-15,145,-19,149,-19,130,-39,119,-55,119,
    -61,123,-75,123,-75,130,-85,132,-89,134,-96,135,-103,134,
    -114,130,-115,123,-110,115,-96,110,-79,106,-72,104,-71,
    96, -77, 87,-85, 75,-71, 74,-74, 65,-74, 61,-78, 65,-85,
    52,-86, 45,-82, 28,-83, 19, -85, 13,-92,  5,-103,  5,
    -116,  2,-119, -1,-119, -7,-116, -9,-114,-11,-111,-12,
    -104,-13,-100,-21,-90,-26,-83,-33,-82,-42,-90,-57,-70,
    -65,-64,-77,-61,-78,-66,-98,-64,-124,-48,-137,-48,-139,
    -45,-139,-37,-146,-27,-159,-20,-161, -6,-165,  0,-165,
    4,-170, 20,-172, 27,-172, 41,-165, 55,-160, 78,-152, 96,
    -150,103,-151,111,-999};


                /*        FUNCTION DEFINITIONS    */

void building();
void wait(char title[]);
void print_scr();


        /*                  MAIN PROGRAM            */

main()
{
    int i, j, k, x, y, oldx, oldy, midpoint;
    double xd,yd,ampl,aspect;
```

```
char ch;

cls (1);
adapt = getAdapter();
if ((adapt != 'E') && (adapt != 'C') && (adapt != 'V'))
    printf("Cannot Run Demo--No CGA, EGA or VGA Installed!");
else
{
    if (adapt == 'V')
    {
        setMode(0x12);
        cls(1);
        write_big_str(-119,131,"GRAPHICS",226);
        write_vid_str(-200,-6,"DEMONSTRATION",91);
    }
    if (adapt == 'E')
    {
        setMode(16);
        cls(1);
        write_big_str(-119,131,"GRAPHICS",226);
        write_vid_str(-200,-6,"DEMONSTRATION",91);
    }
    if (adapt == 'C')
    {
        setMode(4);
        setCGAPalette(0);
        cls(1);
        write_big_str(-319,131,"GRAPHICS",0x23);
        write_vid_str(-319,-6,"DEMONSTRATION",91);
    }
    wait("");

    LINEWIDTH = 3;
    cls(4);
    drawRect(-309,210,310,-200,11);
    drawLine(-309,210,310,-200,11);
    drawLine(-309,-200,310,210,11);

    wait("Rectangle with Diagonals");

    LINEWIDTH = 5;
    ampl = 220;
```

```
oldx = -315;
oldy = 0;
cls(1);
for (i=0; i<=32; i++)
{
    y = ampl * sin(6.283 * ((double)i)/32);
    x = 620 * (double)i/32 - 310;
    drawLine (oldx, oldy, x, y, 12);
    oldx = x;
    oldy = y;
}
wait("Sine Wave");

cls(0);
PATTERN = style[0];
drawRect(-310,230,-280,200,1);
PATTERN = style[1];
drawRect(-300,160,-240,75,2);
PATTERN = style[2];
drawRect(-280,35,-220,-100,3);
PATTERN = style[3];
LINEWIDTH = 1;
drawRect(-200,230,20,100,5);
PATTERN = style[4];
drawRect(-180,90,-70,-200,6);
PATTERN = style[5];
drawRect(40,75,60,200,7);
PATTERN = style[6];
drawRect(100,230,230,-175,9);
PATTERN = style[7];
drawRect(250,180,300,-90,10);
PATTERN = style[0];
wait("Examples of Dashed Lines");

LINEWIDTH = 1;
fillRect(-304,210,30,-30,1);
drawRect(-304,210,30,-30,11);
fillRect(-220,80,-20,-180,10);
drawRect(-220,80,-20,-180,11);
fillRect(-240,140,-70,30,15);
drawRect(-240,140,-70,30,11);
fillRect(-260,130,-150,-50,13);
```

```
drawRect(-260,130,-150,-50,11);
wait("Filled Rectangles");

LINEWIDTH = 1;
drawOval(-175,0,90,13,0.7);
LINEWIDTH = 3;
drawOval(65,0,90,15,1.0);
LINEWIDTH = 5;
drawOval(240,0,90,10,1.3);
wait("Ovals and Circle");

LINEWIDTH = 3;
drawOval(-150,70,120,9,1.);
drawOval(0,-70,120,9,1.);
drawOval(150,70,120,9,1.);
wait("Overlapping Circles");

fillOval(-120,0,110,9,0.8);
fillOval(180,0,110,14,1.);
fillOval(220,50,20,0,1.);
fillOval(140,50,20,0,1.);
LINEWIDTH= 5;
drawLine(150,-60,210,-60,0);
drawLine(130,-53,150,-60,0);
drawLine(230,-53,210,-60,0);
drawLine(120,-40,130,-53,0);
drawLine(240,-40,230,-53,0);
wait("Filled Ovals");

aspect = .50;
for (i=0; i<3; i++)
{
    LINEWIDTH = 3;
    drawArc(0,0,120,0,450,5,aspect);
    drawArc(0,0,120,450,900,15,aspect);
    drawArc(0,0,120,900,1350,2,aspect);
    drawArc(0,0,120,1350,1800,15,aspect);
    drawArc(0,0,120,1800,2250,9,aspect);
    drawArc(0,0,120,2250,2700,15,aspect);
    drawArc(0,0,120,2700,3150,10,aspect);
    drawArc(0,0,120,3150,3590,15,aspect);
    wait("Oval Drawn By Combining Arcs");
```

```
        aspect +=.5;
}

fillArc(0,0,140,480,1380,1,1.);
fillArc(0,0,140,1380,1800,2,1.);
fillArc(0,0,140,1800,2600,3,1.);
fillArc(0,0,140,2600,3150,9,1.);
fillArc(0,0,140,3150,3600,14,1.);
fillArc(0,0,140,0,480,15,1.);
wait("Pie Chart from Filled Arcs");

LINEWIDTH = 1;
PATTERN = style[1];
for (i=0;  i<7;  i++)
drawLine(pt[i][0],pt[i][1],pt[i+1][0],pt[i+1][1],3);
PATTERN = style[0];
drawBezier(160,14,-20,0,0,0,0,-120,-200,-120,-200,200,
    90,150,60,0,200,0,-999);
wait("Bezier Curve");

PATTERN = style[1];
drawLine(-250,-25,-300,240,3);
drawLine(-300,240,-80,210,3);
drawLine(-80,210,-40,-25,3);
drawLine(-40,-25,160,-25,3);
drawLine(160,-25,300,-25,5);
drawLine(300,-25,300,220,5);
drawLine(300,220,40,240,5);
drawLine(40,240,-80,-239,5);
PATTERN = style[0];
drawBezier(160,13,-250,-25,-300,240,-80,210,-40,-25,
    160,-25,-999);
drawBezier(160,14,160,-25,300,-25,300,220,40,240,-80,-239,
    -999);
wait("Two Bezier Curves");

PATTERN = style[1];
drawLine(-250,0,-220,200,3);
drawLine(-220,200,-180,-200,3);
drawLine(-180,-200,-140,60,3);
drawLine(-140,60,-100,-30,3);
drawLine(-100,-30,-70,-10,3);
```

```
drawLine(-70,-10,-20,208,3);
drawLine(-20,208,+60,-130,3);
drawLine(+60,-130,100,125,3);
drawLine(100,125,125,185,3);
drawLine(125,185,140,160,3);
drawLine(140,160,170,-200,3);
drawLine(170,-200,190,-60,3);
drawLine(190,-60,220,20,3);
PATTERN = style[0];
drawBspline(160,14,-250,0,-220,200,-180,-200,-140,60,
    -100,-30,-70,-10,-20,208,60,-130,100,125,125,185,
    140,160,170,-200,190,-60,220,20,-999);
wait("B-Spline Curve");

x= -275;
y= 200;
for (k=0; k<37; k++)
{
    write_horz_char(x, y, k+33, 31);
    x += 16;
}
x = -275;
y = 180;
for (k=37; k<74; k++)
{
    write_horz_char(x, y, k+33, 31);
    x += 16;
}
x = -275;
y = 160;
for (k=74; k<93; k++)
{
    write_horz_char(x, y, k+33, 31);
    x += 16;
}
x= -310;
y= -210;
for (k=0; k<17; k++)
{
    write_vert_char(x, y, k+33, 47);
    y += 20;
}
```

```
    x = -294;
    y = -210;
    for (k=17; k<34; k++)
    {
        write_vert_char(x, y, k+33, 47);
        y += 20;
    }
    x = -278;
    y = -210;
    for (k=34; k<51; k++)
    {
        write_vert_char(x, y, k+33, 47);
        y += 20;
    }
    x = -262;
    y = -210;
    for (k=51; k<68; k++)
    {
        write_vert_char(x, y, k+33, 47);
        y += 20;
    }
    x = -246;
    y = -210;
    for (k=68; k<85; k++)
    {
        write_vert_char(x, y, k+33, 47);
        y += 20;
    }
    x = -230;
    y = -210;
    for (k=85; k<93; k++)
    {
        write_vert_char(x, y, k+33, 47);
        y += 20;
    }
    write_horz_str(-150,35, "HELLO WORLD!",62);
    write_vert_str(80,-200, "HOW ARE YOU TODAY?",109);
    wait("Alphanumerics");

    LINEWIDTH = 3;
    drawRoundRect(-300,210,300,-210,60,11);
    wait("Rounded Rectangle");
```

```
fillRoundRect(-300,210,300,-210,60,13);
wait("Filled Rounded Rectangle");

building();
wait("City Skyline at Night");

drawPoly(11,-259, 90,-59, 90,-159,-90,-999);
drawPoly(11,-259,-20,-159,160,-59,-20,-999);
fillOval(161,34,107,9,1.0);
fillPoly(14,60,66,262,66,104,-55,161,140,218,-55,-999);
wait("Stars");

fillPoly(13,-129,103,-69,172,-59,158,-64,144,-39,130,
    -34,151,-24,158,-19,116,1, 75,-9, 48, -49, 61,-19,
    -6,-59,-34,-79,-6,-109,-48,-149,-6,-129,48,-149,61,
    -159,20,-179,61,-209,-34,-229,-6,-299,89,-249,103,
    -299,103,-299,130,-249,130,-269,172,-259,185,-999);

PATTERN = style[1];
LINEWIDTH = 1;
drawPoly(11,-129,103,-69,172,-59,158,-64,144,-39,130,
    -34,151,-24,158,-19,116,1, 75,-9, 48, -49, 61,-19,
    -6,-59,-34,-79,-6,-109,-48,-149,-6,-129,48,-149,61,
    -159,20,-179,61,-209,-34,-229,-6,-299,89,-249,103,
    -299,103,-299,130,-249,130,-269,172,-259,185,-999);

fillPoly(14,120,0,168,-96,232,-96,232,-144,168,-144,72,
    -192,24,-160,24,-128,56,-128,40,-144,88,-128,88,
    -96,24,-64,120,32,-999);
drawPoly(15,120,0,168,-96,232,-96,232,-144,168,-144,72,
    -192,24,-160,24,-128,56,-128,40,-144,88,-128,88,
    -96,24,-64,120,32,-999);
wait ("Irregular Polygons");

PATTERN = style[0];
fill2Poly(10,usa);
wait("United States of America");

LINEWIDTH = 1;
cls(0);
color=3;
```

```
        XCENTER = -70;
        YCENTER = 35;
        for (ANGLE=0; ANGLE<180; ANGLE+=15)
        {
            rotateRect(-220,100,80,-35,color);
            color++;
            if ((color % 4 == 0) && (adapt == 'C'))
                color++;
        }
        wait("Rotated Rectangles");

        cls(0);
        color=3;
        XCENTER = 0;
        YCENTER = 0;
        for (ANGLE=0; ANGLE<360; ANGLE+=15)
        {
            rotatePoly(color,-120,-70,0,100,120,-70,-999);
            color++;
            if ((color % 4 == 0) && (adapt == 'C'))
                color++;
            if (color == 0) color++;
        }

        wait("Rotated Triangles");

        cls(0);
        color=3;
        for (ANGLE=0; ANGLE<180; ANGLE+=15)
        {
            rotateOval(0,0,160,color,1.5);
            color++;
            if ((color % 4 == 0) && (adapt == 'C'))
                color++;
        }
        wait("Rotated Ovals");

    }
}

void wait(char title[])
{
```

```
    int tab,width,line,mode;

    mode = getMode(&width);
    if ((mode == 0x11) || (mode == 0x12))
        line = 29;
    else
        line = 24;
    tab = (width - strlen(title))/2;
    gotoxy(tab,0);
    writString(title,WHITE,0);
    tab = (width - 33)/2;
    gotoxy(tab,line);
    writString("Press any key to continue demo...", 15,0);
    getch();
    cls(0);
}


void building()
{
    int i,j,hue;

    cls(0);

    fillRect(-280,130,-220,-200,9);

    for(i=-275; i<=-235; i+=20)
    {
        for(j=125; j>=-170; j-=40)
        {
            hue = ((rand()%2)*14);
            fillRect(i,j,i+10,j-25,hue);
        }
    }


    fillRect(-140,160,-60,-230,10);

    for(i=-130; i<=-80; i+=20)
    {
        for(j=155; j>=-190; j-=42)
        {
```

```
            hue = ((rand()%2)*14);
            fillRect(i,j,i+10,j-25,hue);
        }
    }


    fillRect(-80,-7,60,-200,11);
    fillRect(-40,50,30,-7,11);

    for(i=-75; i<=45; i+=20)
    {
        for(j=-12; j>=-185; j-=30)
        {
            hue = ((rand()%2)*14);
            fillRect(i,j,i+10,j-10,hue);
        }
    }

    fillRect(40,80,100,-230,5);

    for(i=45; i<=85; i+=20)
    {
        for(j=75; j>=-215; j-=30)
        {
            hue = ((rand()%2)*14);
            fillRect(i,j,i+10,j-10,hue);
        }
    }
    fillRect(-220,50,-120,-175,3);

    for(i=-215; i<=-135; i+=20)
    {
        for(j=45; j>=-160; j-=30)
        {
            hue = ((rand()%2)*14);
            fillRect(i,j,i+10,j-10,hue);
        }
    }
    fillRect(200,100,280,-175,3);

    for(i=205; i<=265; i+=20)
    {
```

```
    for(j=95; j>=-160; j-=35)
    {
        hue = ((rand()%2)*14);
        fillRect(i,j,i+10,j-15,hue);
    }
}

fillRect(180,190,240,-200,13);
fillRect(200,75,220,190,13);

for(i=185; i<=225; i+=20)
{
    for(j=185; j>=-185; j-=30)
    {
        hue = ((rand()%2)*14);
        fillRect(i,j,i+10,j-10,hue);
    }
}
fillRect(90,75,190,-230,9);
fillRect(110,105,170,75,9);
fillRect(130,130,150,105,9);


for(i=95; i<=175; i+=20)
{
    for(j=67; j>=-215; j-=30)
    {
        hue = ((rand()%2)*14);
        fillRect(i,j,i+10,j-10,hue);
    }
}
for(i=115; i<=155; i+=20)
{
    for(j=100; j>=90; j-=30)
    {
        hue = ((rand()%2)*14);
        fillRect(i,j,i+10,j-10,hue);
    }
}

fillRect(-220,105,-180,50,13);
```

```
    fillRect(-215,70,-205,55,0);
    fillRect(-195,70,-185,55,0);
    fillRect(-215,90,-205,75,14);
    fillRect(-195,90,-185,75,0);

    fillOval(-20,195,20,14,1.);
    fillOval(-30,195,20,0,1.);
}




/*      demo3d() = PROGRAM TO DEMONSTRATE THREE DIMENSIONAL
                   GRAPHICS FIGURES IN C               */

#include <stdio.h>
#include <math.h>
#include <dos.h>
#include "gtools.h"
#include "gdraws.h"

int color,register_no;
int LINEWIDTH=1, OPERATOR=0, ANGLE, XCENTER, YCENTER;
unsigned long int PATTERN=0xFFFFFFFF;
unsigned long int style[8] = { 0xFFFFFFFF,0xC0C0C0C0,
    0xFF00FF00,0xFFF0FFF0,0xF000F000,0xFFFF0000,0xFFFFF0F0,
    0xFFF0F0F0};

float rad_per_degree=0.0174533,x_angle,y_angle,z_angle, step,
    x3, y3, z3,x_angle, y_angle, z_angle;
int x,y,z,rz_scale,vert_scale=1,horz_scale=1,color,type,offset;
char ch;

float degrees_to_radians(float degrees);
void projection ( float x3, float y3, float z3, int color);
void wait(char title[]);
void draw_cube(float rot_pts[8][3],int vx[],int vy[]);
void perspective(int no_of_points,float rot_pts[][3],float pt[][3],
    int vx[],int vy[]);
void setColorReg(int reg_no, int blue, int green, int red);
float surface_test(float x1, float y1, float z1, float x2,
    float y2,float z2, float x3, float y3, float z3);
```

```
void draw_sphere();
void draw_side(int i1, int i2, int i3, int i4,
    float rot_pts[8][3],int vx[],int vy[]);
void fill_cube(float rot_pts[8][3],int vx[],int vy[]);
void fill_side(int i1, int i2, int i3, int i4,
    float rot_pts[8][3],int vx[],int vy[]);
void fill_sphere();
int getPalette(int register);
int shaded_surface_test(float x1, float y1, float z1, float x2,
    float y2, float z2, float x3, float y3, float z3);
void pattern_plot(int x, int y, int color);

float yaw, roll, pitch, latitude, longitude, xls=.57735,
    yls=.57735,zls=.57735;
int k,d=375, mx=0, my=0, mz=-200, off_x,off_y,sx, sy;
int vx1[37],vy1[37],vx2[37],vy2[37],i,j;
float  rot_pts1[37][3],pt1[37][3],pt6[8][3]={{30,-30,30},
    {30,30,30},{-30,30,30},{-30,-30,30},{30,30,-30},
    {-30,30,-30},{-30,-30,-30},{30,-30,-30}},rot_pts2[37][3],
    pt2[37][3];

main ()
{
    int i,angle,green;
    char adapt;

    adapt = getAdapter();
    if ((adapt != 'E') && (adapt != 'C') && (adapt != 'V'))
        printf("Cannot Run Demo -- No CGA, EGA or VGA Installed!");
    else
    {
        if (adapt == 'V')
            setMode(0x12);
        if (adapt == 'E')
            setMode(16);
        if (adapt == 'C')
        {
            setMode(4);
            setCGAPalette(1);
        }
        cls(1);
        while(ch != 0x0D)
```

```
    {
        cls(0);
        drawRect(-316,-235,315,235,11);
        off_x = -200;
        off_y = 100;
        for(i=0; i<6; i++)
        {
            yaw=degrees_to_radians(rand()/92);
            roll=degrees_to_radians(rand()/92);
            pitch=degrees_to_radians(rand()/92);
            color=rand()/4681+9;
            perspective(8,rot_pts1,pt6,vx1,vy1);
            draw_cube(rot_pts1,vx1,vy1);
            off_x += 200;
            if (off_x>210)
            {
                off_x= -200;
                off_y= -100;
            }
        }
        gotoxy(21,0);
        wait("Cubes");
    }
    ch = 0;
    while(ch != 0x0D)
    {
        d = 800;
        cls(0);
        off_x = 0;
        off_y = 0;
        latitude = 0;
        longitude = 0;
        drawRect(-316,-235,315,235,11);
        mx = 0;
        my = 0;
        mz = -150;
        yaw=degrees_to_radians(rand()/92);
        roll=degrees_to_radians(rand()/92);
        pitch=degrees_to_radians(rand()/92);
        color=rand()/4681+9;
        draw_sphere();
        wait("Sphere");
```

```
}

#ifdef VGA
for (i=0; i<16; i++)
{
    setEGApalette(i,i);
    writeColorReg(i,0,4*i,0);
}
#endif

#ifdef EGA
setEGApalette(0,0);
setEGApalette(1,16);
setEGApalette(2,2);
setEGApalette(3,34);
setEGApalette(4,19);
setEGApalette(5,26);
setEGApalette(6,8);
setEGApalette(7,27);
setEGApalette(8,63);
setEGApalette(9,2);
setEGApalette(10,3);
setEGApalette(11,4);
setEGApalette(12,5);
setEGApalette(13,6);
setEGApalette(14,7);
setEGApalette(15,63);
#endif

cls(0);
ch = 0;
PATTERN = style[0];
while(ch != 0x0D)
{
    d = 375;
    mz = -200;
    cls(0);
    drawRect(-316,-235,315,235,11);
    off_x = -200;
    off_y = 100;
    for(i=0; i<6; i++)
    {
```

```
            yaw=degrees_to_radians(rand()/92);
            roll=degrees_to_radians(rand()/92);
            pitch=degrees_to_radians(rand()/92);
            color=(rand()/4681+9)+18;
            perspective(8,rot_pts1,pt6,vx1,vy1);
            fill_cube(rot_pts1,vx1,vy1);
            off_x += 200;
            if (off_x>210)
            {
                off_x= -200;
                off_y= -100;
            }
        }
        wait("Shaded Cubes");
    }
    ch = 0;
    while(ch != 0x0D)
    {
        d=800;
        cls(0);
        off_x = 0;
        off_y = 0;
        latitude = 0;
        longitude = 0;
        drawRect(-316,-235,315,235,11);
        mx = 0;
        my = 0;
        mz = -150;
        yaw=degrees_to_radians(rand()/92);
        roll=degrees_to_radians(rand()/92);
        pitch=degrees_to_radians(rand()/92);
        fill_sphere();
        wait("Shaded Sphere");
    }

  }
}


void draw_cube(float rot_pts[8][3],int vx[],int vy[])
{
    long int sp;
```

```
    draw_side(7,0,3,6,rot_pts,vx,vy);
    draw_side(6,5,4,7,rot_pts,vx,vy);
    draw_side(3,2,5,6,rot_pts,vx,vy);
    draw_side(0,1,2,3,rot_pts,vx,vy);
    draw_side(7,4,1,0,rot_pts,vx,vy);
    draw_side(1,4,5,2,rot_pts,vx,vy);
}

void fill_cube(float rot_pts[8][3],int vx[],int vy[])
{
    long int sp;

    fill_side(7,0,3,6,rot_pts,vx,vy);
    fill_side(6,5,4,7,rot_pts,vx,vy);
    fill_side(3,2,5,6,rot_pts,vx,vy);
    fill_side(0,1,2,3,rot_pts,vx,vy);
    fill_side(7,4,1,0,rot_pts,vx,vy);
    fill_side(1,4,5,2,rot_pts,vx,vy);
}

void draw_side(int i1, int i2, int i3, int i4,
    float rot_pts[8][3], int vx[],int vy[])
{
    float sp;

    sp = surface_test(rot_pts[i1][0],rot_pts[i1][1],
        rot_pts[i1][2],rot_pts[i2][0],rot_pts[i2][1],
        rot_pts[i2][2],rot_pts[i3][0],rot_pts[i3][1],
        rot_pts[i3][2]);
    if (sp<=0)
        drawPoly(color,vx[i1],+vy[i1],vx[i2],+vy[i2],vx[i3],
            +vy[i3],vx[i4],+vy[i4],-999);
}

void fill_side(int i1, int i2, int i3, int i4,
    float rot_pts[8][3], int vx[],int vy[])
{

    color = shaded_surface_test(rot_pts[i1][0],rot_pts[i1][1],
        rot_pts[i1][2],rot_pts[i2][0],rot_pts[i2][1],
        rot_pts[i2][2],rot_pts[i3][0],rot_pts[i3][1],
        rot_pts[i3][2]);
```

```
    if (color < 999)
    {
        fillPoly(color,vx[i1],vy[i1],vx[i2],vy[i2]
            ,vx[i3],vy[i3],vx[i4],vy[i4],-999);
    }
}

void draw_sphere()
{
    float sp;
    int i,j,k,radius;

    radius = 30;
    pt1[0][0] = 0;
    pt1[0][1] = radius;
    pt1[0][2] = 0;
    perspective(1,rot_pts1,pt1,vx1,vy1);
    longitude = .17453;
    for (latitude=0,i=0; i<36; i++,latitude+=.17453)
    {
        pt2[i][0] = cos(latitude)*sin(longitude)*radius;
        pt2[i][1] = cos(longitude)*radius;
        pt2[i][2] = sin(latitude)*sin(longitude)*radius;
    }
    pt2[36][0] = pt2[0][0];
    pt2[36][1] = pt2[0][1];
    pt2[36][2] = pt2[0][2];
    perspective(37,rot_pts2,pt2,vx2,vy2);
    for (i=0; i<36; i++)
    {
        sp = surface_test(rot_pts2[i+1][0],rot_pts2[i+1][1],
            rot_pts2[i+1][2],rot_pts2[i][0],rot_pts2[i][1],
            rot_pts2[i][2],rot_pts1[0][0],rot_pts1[0][1],
            rot_pts1[0][2]);
        if (sp<=0)
            drawPoly(color,vx2[i+1],vy2[i+1],vx2[i],vy2[i],
                vx1[0],vy1[0],-999);
    }
    for (j=0; j<16; j++)
    {
        longitude += .17453;
        for (latitude=0,i=0; i<36; i++,latitude+=.17453)
```

```
    {
        pt2[i][0] = cos(latitude)*sin(longitude)*radius;
        pt2[i][1] = cos(longitude)*radius;
        pt2[i][2] = sin(latitude)*sin(longitude)*radius;
    }
    pt2[36][0] = pt2[0][0];
    pt2[36][1] = pt2[0][1];
    pt2[36][2] = pt2[0][2];
    for (i=0; i<37; i++)
    {
        for (k=0; k<3; k++)
            rot_pts1[i][k] = rot_pts2[i][k];
        vx1[i] = vx2[i];
        vy1[i] = vy2[i];
    }
    perspective(37,rot_pts2,pt2,vx2,vy2);
    for (i=0; i<36; i++)
    {
        sp = surface_test(rot_pts1[i][0],rot_pts1[i][1],
            rot_pts1[i][2],rot_pts1[i+1][0],rot_pts1[i+1][1],
            rot_pts1[i+1][2],rot_pts2[i+1][0],
            rot_pts2[i+1][1],rot_pts2[i+1][2]);
        if (sp<=0)
            drawPoly(color,vx1[i],vy1[i],vx1[i+1],
        vy1[i+1],vx2[i+1],vy2[i+1],
        vx2[i],vy2[i],-999);
    }
}
pt1[0][0] = 0;
pt1[0][1] = -radius;
pt1[0][2] = 0;
perspective(1,rot_pts1,pt1,vx1,vy1);
for (i=0; i<36; i++)
{
    sp = surface_test(rot_pts2[i][0],rot_pts2[i][1],
        rot_pts2[i][2],rot_pts2[i+1][0],rot_pts2[i+1][1],
        rot_pts2[i+1][2],rot_pts1[0][0],rot_pts1[0][1],
        rot_pts1[0][2]);
    if (sp<=0)
        drawPoly(color,vx2[i+1],+vy2[i+1],vx2[i],+vy2[i],
    vx1[0],+vy1[0],-999);
}
```

```
}

void fill_sphere()
{
    float sp;
    int i,j,k,radius;

    radius = 30;
    pt1[0][0] = 0;
    pt1[0][1] = radius;
    pt1[0][2] = 0;
    perspective(1,rot_pts1,pt1,vx1,vy1);
    longitude = .17453;
    for (latitude=0,i=0; i<36; i++,latitude+=.17453)
    {
        pt2[i][0] = cos(latitude)*sin(longitude)*radius;
        pt2[i][1] = cos(longitude)*radius;
        pt2[i][2] = sin(latitude)*sin(longitude)*radius;
    }
    pt2[36][0] = pt2[0][0];
    pt2[36][1] = pt2[0][1];
    pt2[36][2] = pt2[0][2];
    perspective(37,rot_pts2,pt2,vx2,vy2);
    for (i=0; i<36; i++)
    {
        color = shaded_surface_test(rot_pts2[i+1][0],
            rot_pts2[i+1][1],rot_pts2[i+1][2],rot_pts2[i][0],
            rot_pts2[i][1],rot_pts2[i][2],rot_pts1[0][0],
            rot_pts1[0][1],rot_pts1[0][2]);
        if (color<=999)
            fillPoly(color,vx2[i+1],vy2[i+1],vx2[i],vy2[i],
        vx1[0],vy1[0],-999);
    }
    for (j=0; j<16; j++)
    {
        longitude += .17453;
        for (latitude=0,i=0; i<36; i++,latitude+=.17453)
        {
            pt2[i][0] = cos(latitude)*sin(longitude)*radius;
            pt2[i][1] = cos(longitude)*radius;
            pt2[i][2] = sin(latitude)*sin(longitude)*radius;
```

```
        }
        pt2[36][0] = pt2[0][0];
        pt2[36][1] = pt2[0][1];
        pt2[36][2] = pt2[0][2];
        for (i=0; i<37; i++)
        {
            for (k=0; k<3; k++)
                rot_pts1[i][k] = rot_pts2[i][k];
            vx1[i] = vx2[i];
            vy1[i] = vy2[i];
        }
        perspective(37,rot_pts2,pt2,vx2,vy2);
        for (i=0; i<36; i++)
        {
            color = shaded_surface_test(rot_pts1[i][0],
                rot_pts1[i][1],rot_pts1[i][2],rot_pts1[i+1][0],
                rot_pts1[i+1][1],rot_pts1[i+1][2],
                rot_pts2[i+1][0],rot_pts2[i+1][1],
                rot_pts2[i+1][2]);
            if (color<=999)
            {
                fillPoly(color,vx1[i],vy1[i],vx1[i+1],
                vy1[i+1],vx2[i+1],vy2[i+1],
                vx2[i],vy2[i],-999);
            }
        }
    }
    pt1[0][0] = 0;
    pt1[0][1] = -radius;
    pt1[0][2] = 0;
    perspective(1,rot_pts1,pt1,vx1,vy1);
    for (i=0; i<36; i++)
    {
        color = shaded_surface_test(rot_pts2[i][0],
            rot_pts2[i][1],rot_pts2[i][2],rot_pts2[i+1][0],
            rot_pts2[i+1][1],rot_pts2[i+1][2],rot_pts1[0][0],
            rot_pts1[0][1],rot_pts1[0][2]);
        if (color<=999)
            fillPoly(color,vx2[i+1],+vy2[i+1],vx2[i],+vy2[i],
        vx1[0],+vy1[0],-999);
    }
}
```

```
void perspective(int no_of_points,float rot_pts[][3],
    float pt[][3],int vx[],int vy[])
{
    int i,j;
    float xa,ya,za,x,y,z;

    for (i=0; i<no_of_points; i++)
    {
        xa = - cos(yaw)*pt[i][0] - sin(yaw)*pt[i][2];
        za = - sin(yaw)*pt[i][0] + cos(yaw)*pt[i][2];
        x = cos(roll)*xa + sin(roll)*pt[i][1];
        ya = cos(roll)*pt[i][1] - sin(roll)*xa;
        z = cos(pitch)*za - sin(pitch)*ya;
        y = sin(pitch)*za + cos(pitch)*ya;
        x += mx;
        y += my;
        z += mz;
        rot_pts[i][0] = x;
        rot_pts[i][1] = y;
        rot_pts[i][2] = z;
        vx[i] = d*x/z+off_x;
        vy[i] = -d*y/z+off_y;
    }
}

float surface_test(float x1, float y1, float z1, float x2,
    float y2, float z2, float x3, float y3, float z3)
{
    float stest;


    stest = x1*(y3*z2-y2*z3) - x2*(y3*z1 - y1*z3) -
        x3*(y1*z2-y2*z1);
    return (stest);
}

int shaded_surface_test(float x1, float y1, float z1, float x2,
    float y2, float z2, float x3, float y3, float z3)

{
    float v_mag,vert_x1,vert_x2,vert_y1,vert_y2,vert_z1,vert_z2,
```

```
    stest,vxn,vyn,vzn;
int test;

stest = x1*(y3*z2-y2*z3) - x2*(y3*z1 - y1*z3) -
    x3*(y1*z2-y2*z1);
color = 9999;
if (stest < 0)
{
    vert_x1 = x2 - x1;
    vert_y1 = y2 - y1;
    vert_z1 = z2 - z1;
    vert_x2 = x3 - x1;
    vert_y2 = y3 - y1;
    vert_z2 = z3 - z1;
    vxn = (vert_y1*vert_z2) - (vert_z1*vert_y2);
    vyn = (vert_x1*vert_z2) - (vert_z1*vert_x2);
    vzn = (vert_y1*vert_x2) - (vert_x1*vert_y2);
    v_mag = 1.0/sqrt(vxn*vxn + vyn*vyn + vzn*vzn);
    v_mag = v_mag*(vxn*xls + vyn*yls + vzn*zls);

    #ifdef VGA
    test = 13*v_mag;
    if (test <0)
        color = 1;
    switch(test)
    {
        case 0:
            color = 0x02;
            break;
        case 1:
            color = 0x03;
            break;
        case 2:
            color = 0x04;
            break;
        case 3:
            color = 0x05;
            break;
        case 4:
            color = 0x06;
            break;
        case 5:
```

```
          color = 0x07;
          break;
     case 6:
          color = 0x08;
          break;
     case 7:
          color = 0x09;
          break;
     case 8:
          color = 0x0A;
          break;
     case 9:
          color = 0x0B;
          break;
     case 10:
          color = 0x0C;
          break;
     case 11:
          color = 0x0D;
          break;
     case 12:
          color = 0x0E;
          break;
     case 13:
          color = 0x0F;
}
#endif

#ifdef EGA
test = 16*v_mag;
if (test <0)
     color = 0x101;
switch(test)
{
     case 0:
          color = 0x201;
          break;
     case 1:
          color = 0x01;
          break;
     case 2:
          color = 0x112;
```

```
          break;
     case 3:
          color = 0x212;
          break;
     case 4:
          color = 0x312;
          break;
     case 5:
          color = 0x221;
          break;
     case 6:
          color = 0x02;
          break;
     case 7:
          color = 0x223;
          break;
     case 8:
          color = 0x323;
          break;
     case 9:
          color = 0x232;
          break;
     case 10:
          color = 0x03;
          break;
     case 11:
          color = 0x134;
          break;
     case 12:
          color = 0x234;
          break;
     case 13:
          color = 0x334;
          break;
     case 14:
          color = 0x243;
          break;
     case 15:
          color = 0x143;
          break;
     case 16:
          color = 0x04;
```

```
                break;
        }
        #endif

        #ifdef CGA
        test = 8*v_mag;
        if (test <0)
            color = 0x101;
        switch(test)
        {
            case 0:
                color = 0x201;
                break;
            case 1:
                color = 0x301;
                break;
            case 2:
                color = 0x01;
                break;
            case 3:
                color = 0x113;
                break;
            case 4:
                color = 0x213;
                break;
            case 5:
                color = 0x313;
                break;
            case 6:
                color = 0x131;
                break;
            case 7:
                color = 0x231;
                break;
            case 8:
                color = 0x03;
                break;
        }
        #endif
    }
    return (color);
}
```

```
float degrees_to_radians (float degrees)
{
    float angle;

    while (degrees >= 360)
        degrees -= 360;
    while (degrees < 0)
        degrees += 360;
    angle = rad_per_degree*degrees;
    return angle;
}

void projection (float x3, float y3, float z3, int color)
{
    float temp_x, temp_y;
    int x,y;

    temp_x = x3*cos(x_angle) + y3*cos(y_angle) + z3*cos(z_angle);
    temp_y = x3*sin(x_angle) + y3*sin(y_angle) + z3*sin(z_angle);
    x = temp_x*horz_scale;
    y = temp_y*vert_scale;
    plot (x,y,color);
}

void wait(char title[])
{
    int tab,width;
    getMode(&width);
    tab = (width - strlen(title))/2;
    gotoxy(tab,0);
    writString(title,15,0);

    #ifdef VGA
    gotoxy((width-40)/2,29);
    #endif

    #ifndef VGA
    gotoxy((width-40)/2,24);
    #endif

    writString(" 'Ent' = next demo; other key = repeat..", 15,0);
```

525

```
    ch = getch();
    cls(1);
}


    /*                    CURSOR DEMONSTRATIONM              */


            /*             INCLUDES              */

#include <stdio.h>
#include <math.h>
#include <dos.h>


    /*               USER WRITTEN INCLUDES              */

#include "colors.h"
#include "gtools.h"
#include "gdraws.h"


    /*     GLOBAL VARIABLES USED BY GRAPHICS FUNCTIONS     */


enum vidTypes {mda, cga, ega, compaq, other};

int color = 2;
int background_color = 0;
int LINEWIDTH=1, OPERATOR=0, ANGLE, XCENTER, YCENTER,CURSOR_X,
    CURSOR_Y;
unsigned long int PATTERN=0xFFFFFFFF;

unsigned long int style[8] = { 0xFFFFFFFF,0xC0C0C0C0,0xFF00FF00,
    0xFFF0FFF0,0xF000F000,0xFFFF0000,0xFFFFF0F0,0xFFF0F0F0};

unsigned int mask, cursor_pattern[2][16] = {0x8000,0xC000,0xE000,
0xF000,0xF800,0xFC00,0xFE00,0xFF00,0xF800,0xD800,0x8C00,
0x0C00,0x0600,0x0600,0x00,0x00,0x0100,0x0100,0x0100,0x0100,
0x0100,0x7FFC,0x0100,0x0100,0x0100,0x0100,0x0100,0x0100};
```

```
    /*                    FUNCTION DEFINITIONS              */

void move_cursor(int type,int color);
void wait(char title[]);




    /*                       MAIN PROGRAM                   */




main()
{
    double xd,yd,ampl,aspect;
    char adapt,ch;

    cls (1);
    adapt = getAdapter();
    if ((adapt != 'E') && (adapt != 'C') && (adapt != 'V'))
        printf("Cannot Run Demo--No CGA, EGA or VGA Installed!");
    else
    {
        if (adapt == 'V')
        {
            setMode(0x12);
            cls(1);
            write_big_str(-119,131,"CURSOR",226);
            write_vid_str(-200,-6,"DEMONSTRATION",91);
        }
        if (adapt == 'E')
        {
            setMode(16);
            cls(1);
            write_big_str(-119,131,"CURSOR",226);
            write_vid_str(-200,-6,"DEMONSTRATION",91);
        }
        if (adapt == 'C')
        {
            setMode(4);
```

```
                setCGAPalette(0);
                cls(1);
                write_big_str(-319,131,"CURSOR",226);
                write_vid_str(-319,-6,"DEMONSTRATION",91);
            }
        }
    wait("Move cursor with arrows");
    LINEWIDTH = 3;
    cls(4);
    drawRect(-309,210,310,-200,11);
    drawLine(-309,210,310,-200,11);
    drawLine(-309,-200,310,210,11);
    wait("Move cursor with arrows");
}

void wait(char title[])
{
    int tab,width,line,mode;
    static int cursor_type,cursor_color;

    cursor_type = cursor_type %2;
    cursor_color = cursor_color %8 + 8;
    mode = getMode(&width);
    if ((mode == 0x11) || (mode == 0x12))
        line = 29;
    else
        line = 24;
    tab = (width - strlen(title))/2;
    gotoxy(tab,0);
    writString(title,WHITE,0);
    tab = (width - 33)/2;
    gotoxy(tab,line);
    writString("Press 'Enter' to continue demo...", WHITE,0);
    move_cursor(cursor_type,cursor_color);
    cursor_color--;
    cursor_type = (++cursor_type)%2;
    cls(0);
}

void move_cursor(int type,int color)
{
    int i,j,k,xoff=0,yoff=0,image_store[3][4][16],ch,
```

```
    fast = 1,temp;
char far *base;

if (type == 1)
{
    xoff = -8;
    yoff = -6;
}
CURSOR_X = -xoff;
CURSOR_Y = -yoff;
temp = OPERATOR;
OPERATOR = 0x18;
do
{
    for (i=0; i<16; i++)
    {
        for (j=0; j<16; j++)
        {
            mask = 0x8000 >> j;
            if ((mask & cursor_pattern[type][i]) != 0)
                plot(CURSOR_X+j+xoff+319,175 -
                    ((CURSOR_Y*93) >> 7)+i+yoff,color);
        }
    }
    ch = getch();
    if (ch == 0)
        ch = getch() + 256;
    for (i=0; i<16; i++)
    {
        for (j=0; j<16; j++)
        {
            mask = 0x8000 >> j;
            if ((mask & cursor_pattern[type][i]) != 0)
                plot(CURSOR_X+j+xoff+319,175 -
                    ((CURSOR_Y*93) >> 7)+i+yoff,color);
        }
    }
    switch(ch)
    {
        case 27:
            fast = (++fast) % 2;
            break;
```

```
                case 333:
                    if ((CURSOR_X < 303) && (fast == 0))
                        CURSOR_X++;
                    if ((CURSOR_X < 294) && (fast == 1))
                        CURSOR_X += 10;
                    break;
                case 331:
                    if ((CURSOR_X > -318)  && (fast == 0))
                        CURSOR_X--;
                    if ((CURSOR_X > -309) && (fast == 1))
                        CURSOR_X -= 10;
                    break;
                case 336:
                    if ((CURSOR_Y > -223) && (fast == 0))
                        CURSOR_Y--;
                    if ((CURSOR_Y > -214) && (fast == 1))
                        CURSOR_Y -= 10;
                    break;
                case 328:
                    if ((CURSOR_Y < 239) && (fast == 0))
                        CURSOR_Y++;
                    if ((CURSOR_Y < 230) && (fast == 1))
                        CURSOR_Y += 10;
                    break;
            }
        }
    while (ch != 0x0D);
    OPERATOR = temp;
}



/*    gmenu() = PROGRAM TO DEMONSTRATE THE USE OF MENUS
                AND WINDOWS IN GRAPHICS MODE            */



                /*        INCLUDES     */

#include <stdio.h>
#include <math.h>
#include <dos.h>
```

```
/*                    USER WRITTEN INCLUDES                   */

#include "gtools.h"
#include "gdraws.h"



/*        GLOBAL VARIABLES USED BY GRAPHICS FUNCTIONS      */

enum vidTypes {mda, cga, ega, compaq, other};

int color = 2;
int background_color = 0;
int LINEWIDTH=1, OPERATOR=0, ANGLE, XCENTER, YCENTER;
unsigned long int PATTERN=0xFFFFFFFF;
char string[5][30]={{"Select choice with arrows -- "},
        {"'Enter' to quit...            "},
        {"Six pointed star              "},
        {"Five pointed star             "},
        {"Rotated rectangles            "}};




/*                    FUNCTION DEFINITIONS                   */

int menu(int x1, int y1, int x2, int y2);
void save_restore (int x1, int y1, int x2, int y2, int type);
void wait(char title[]);
void write_menu_line(int x,int y,char string[], int color);



/*                       MAIN PROGRAM                        */



main()
{
    int i, j, k, x, y, oldx, oldy, midpoint,select;
```

```
double xd,yd,ampl,aspect;
char ch;

cls (1);
ch = getAdapter();
if ((ch != 'V') && (ch != 'E'))
    printf("Cannot Run Demo -- EGA or VGA Not Installed!");
else
{
    setMode(16);
    LINEWIDTH = 3;
    cls(1);
    drawRect(-310,225,310,-220,10);
    drawLine(-310,225,310,-220,10);
    drawLine(310,225,-310,-220,10);
    select = menu(2,2,37,8);

    if (select==1)
    {
        LINEWIDTH = 2;
        drawPoly(11,-259, 90,-59, 90,-159,-90,-999);
        drawPoly(11,-259,-20,-159,160,-59,-20,-999);
    }
    if (select == 2)
    {
        fillOval(161,34,107,9,1.0);
        fillPoly(14,60,66,262,66,104,-55,161,140,218,-55,
            -999);
    }
    if (select == 3)
    {
        LINEWIDTH = 1;
        color=3;
        XCENTER = -70;
        YCENTER = 35;
        for (ANGLE=0; ANGLE<180; ANGLE+=15)
        {
            rotateRect(-220,100,80,-35,color);
            color++;
        }
        wait("Rotated Rectangles");
    }
```

```
    }
}

void wait(char title[])
{
    int tab,width;
    getMode(&width);
    tab = (width - strlen(title))/2;
    gotoxy(tab,0);
    writString(title,WHITE,0);
    tab = (width - 33)/2;    /* starting column for text */
    gotoxy(tab,24);
    writString("Press any key to continue demo...", WHITE,0);
    getch();
    cls(0);
}



int menu(int x1, int y1, int x2, int y2)
{
    int i,j,select=2,temp,ch;

    save_restore(x1,y1,x2,y2,0);
    setWindow(x1,y1,x2,y2,4);
    for (i=0; i<3; i++)
    {
        for (j=y1*14; j<=y2*14+14; j++)
        {
            plot(x1*8+i,j,11);
            plot((x2+1)*8-i,j,11);
        }
        for(j=x1*8+3; j<=x2*8+5; j++)
        {
            plot(j,y1*14+i,11);
            plot(j,(y2+1)*14-i,11);
        }
    }
    write_menu_line(x1*8+10,y1*14+10,string[0],79);
    write_menu_line(x1*8+10,y1*14+24,string[1],79);
    write_menu_line(x1*8+10,y1*14+38,string[2],47);
    write_menu_line(x1*8+10,y1*14+52,string[3],79);
    write_menu_line(x1*8+10,y1*14+66,string[4],79);
```

```
    while ((ch = getch()) != 13)
    {
        if (ch == 0x00)
            ch = getch() +256;
        switch(ch)
        {
            case 336:
                if (select < 4)
                {
                    write_menu_line(x1*8+10,(y1 + select)*14 +
                        10, string[select],79);
                    write_menu_line(x1*8+10,(y1 + select)*14 +
                        10, string[++select],47);
                }
                break;
            case 328:
                if (select > 2)
                {
                    write_menu_line(x1*8+10,(y1 + select)*14 +
                        10, string[select],79);
                    write_menu_line(x1*8+10,(y1 + select)*14 +
                        10, string[--select],47);
                }
        }
    }
    save_restore(x1,y1,x2,y2,1);
    return(select-1);
}

void save_restore (int x1, int y1, int x2, int y2, int type)
{
    #define DISPLAY_OUT(index,val)   {outp(0x3CE,index);\
                                      outp(0x3CF,val);}
    unsigned char exist_color;
    char far *base1;
    char far *base2;
    int x,y;

    DISPLAY_OUT(5,0x01);
    for (y=(y1-1)*14; y<=(y2+2)*14; y++)
    {
        for (x=(x1-1)*8; x<=(x2+1)*8; x+=8)
```

```
    {
        base1 = (char far *) (0xA0000000L + ((long)y *
            80L + ((long)x/8L)));
        base2 = (char far *) (0xA8000000L + ((long)y *
            80L + ((long)x/8L)));
        if (type == 0)
        {
            exist_color = *base1;
            *base2 = 0x00;
        }
        else
        {
            exist_color = *base2;
            *base1 = 0x00;
        }
    }
    }
    DISPLAY_OUT(5,0);
}

void write_menu_line(int x,int y,char string[], int color)
{
    int char_offset,p=0;

    while (string[p])
    {
        char_offset = (string[p] - 32) * 14;
        plot_char(x,y,char_offset,color,0);
        x += 8;
        p++;
    }
}




/*  image() = PROGRAM TO DEMONSTRATE USE OF FRACTALS TO
            CREATE IMAGES                           */

#include <stdio.h>
#include <math.h>
#include <dos.h>
```

```
/* USER WRITTEN INCLUDES */
#include "gdraws.h"
#include "gtools.h"

/* GLOBALS */


int LINEWIDTH,OPERATOR,XCENTER,YCENTER,ANGLE;
unsigned long int PATTERN;

void image_draw(int color);
void wait(char title[]);

int adapt,mode;
int j, k, xscale,yscale,xoffset,yoffset,pr,p[4],pk[4];
long unsigned int i;
float a[4],b[4],c[4],d[4],e[4],f[4],x,y,newx;

main()
{
    adapt = getAdapter();
    if ((adapt != 'E') && (adapt != 'C') && (adapt != 'V'))
        printf("Cannot Run Demo--No CGA, EGA or VGA Installed!");
    else
    {
        if (adapt == 'V')
            setMode(0x12);
        if (adapt == 'E')
            setMode(16);
        if (adapt == 'C')
            setMode(4);
        a[0] =0; a[1] = .20; a[2] = -.15; a[3] = .85;
        b[0] = 0; b[1] = -.26; b[2] = .28; b[3] = .04;
        c[0] = 0; c[1] = .23; c[2] = .26; c[3] = -.04;
        d[0] = .16; d[1] = .22; d[2] = .24; d[3] = .85;
        e[0] = 0; e[1] = 0; e[2] = 0; e[3] = 0;
        f[0] = 0; f[1] = 1.60; f[2] = .44; f[3] = 1.6;
        p[0] = 328; p[1] = 2621; p[2] = 4915; p[3] = 32767;
        xscale = 25;
        yscale = 25;
        xoffset = 0;
```

```
yoffset = -160;
#ifdef CGA
cls (0);
image_draw(1);
#endif

#ifndef CGA
cls (1);
image_draw(10);
#endif

wait("Fern");

a[0] = 0; a[1] = .1; a[2] = .42; a[3] = .42;
b[0] = 0; b[1] = 0; b[2] = -.42; b[3] = .42;
c[0] = 0; c[1] = 0; c[2] = .42; c[3] = -.42;
d[0] = .5; d[1] = .1; d[2] = .42; d[3] = .42;
e[0] = 0; e[1] = 0; e[2] = 0; e[3] = 0;
f[0] = 0; f[1] = .2; f[2] = .2; f[3] = .2;
p[0] = 1638; p[1] = 6553; p[2] = 19660; p[3] = 32767;
xscale = 750;
yscale = 750;
xoffset = 0;
yoffset = -160;

#ifdef CGA
cls (1);
image_draw(2);
#endif

#ifndef CGA
cls (1);
image_draw(13);
#endif
wait("Tree");

a[0] = .5; a[1] = .5; a[2] = .5; a[3] = 0;
b[0] = 0; b[1] = 0; b[2] = 0; b[3] = 0;
c[0] = 0; c[1] = 0; c[2] = 0; c[3] = 0;
d[0] = .5; d[1] = .5; d[2] = .5; d[3] = 0;
e[0] = 0; e[1] = 1.; e[2] = .5; e[3] = 0;
f[0] = 0; f[1] = 0; f[2] = .5; f[3] = 0;
```

```
p[0] = 10813; p[1] = 21626; p[2] = 32767; p[3] = 32767;
xscale = 200;
yscale = 200;
xoffset = -180;
yoffset = -160;

#ifdef CGA
cls (3);
image_draw(0);
#endif

#ifndef CGA
cls (7);
image_draw(5);
#endif
wait("Sierpinski Triangle");

a[0] = .333; a[1] = .333; a[2] = .667; a[3] = 0;
b[0] = 0; b[1] = 0; b[2] = 0; b[3] = 0;
c[0] = 0; c[1] = 0; c[2] = 0; c[3] = 0;
d[0] = .333; d[1] = .333; d[2] = .667; d[3] = 0;
e[0] = 0; e[1] = 1.; e[2] = .5; e[3] = 0;
f[0] = 0; f[1] = 0; f[2] = .5; f[3] = 0;
p[0] = 10813; p[1] = 21626; p[2] = 32767; p[3] = 32767;
xscale = 120;
yscale = 140;
xoffset = -100;
yoffset = -160;

#ifdef CGA
cls (3);
image_draw(2);
#endif

#ifndef CGA
cls (7);
image_draw(4);
#endif
wait("Cantor Tree");

a[0] = .5; a[1] = .5; a[2] = .5; a[3] = .5;
b[0] = 0; b[1] = 0; b[2] = 0; b[3] = 0;
```

```
c[0] = 0; c[1] = 0; c[2] = 0; c[3] = 0;
d[0] = .5; d[1] = .5; d[2] = .5; d[3] = .5;
e[0] = 0; e[1] = .5; e[2] = 0; e[3] = .5;
f[0] = 0; f[1] = 0; f[2] = .5; f[3] = .5;
p[0] = 8182; p[1] = 16383; p[2] = 24575; pk[3] = 32767;
xscale = 250;
yscale = 250;
xoffset = -100;
yoffset = -160;

#ifdef CGA
cls (3);
image_draw(1);
#endif

#ifndef CGA
cls (7);
image_draw(1);
#endif
wait("Square");
    }
}


void image_draw(int color)
{
    int px,py;

    x = 0;
    y = 0;
    for (i=1; i<=10000; i++)
    {
        j = rand();
        k = (j < p[0]) ? 0 : ((j < p[1]) ? 1 :((j<p[2]) ? 2 : 3));
        newx = (a[k]* x + b[k] * y + e[k]);
        y = (c[k] * x + d[k] * y + f[k]);
        x = newx;
        px = x*xscale + xoffset;
        py = (y*yscale + yoffset);
        if ((px>=-320) && (px<320)  && (py>=-240) && (py<240))
            plots (px,py,color);
    }
}
```

```
void wait(char title[])
{
    int tab,width;
    getMode(&width);
    tab = (width - strlen(title))/2;
    gotoxy(tab,0);
    writString(title,WHITE,0);
    tab = (width - 23)/2;

    #ifdef VGA
    gotoxy(tab,29);
    #endif

    #ifndef VGA
    gotoxy(tab,24);
    #endif

    writString("Press any key to continue demo...", WHITE,0);
    getch();
    cls(0);
}


    /*    quadrics = Program to demonstrate the drawing of
                    three dimensional quadric surfaces.      */

#include <dos.h>
#include <stdio.h>
#include <math.h>

#include "gtools.h"
#include "gdraws.h"

float rad_per_degree=0.0174533, x_angle, y_angle,
    z_angle, step, x3, y3, z3;
int x,y,horz_scale,vert_scale,color,type,x_offset,
    y_offset,OPERATOR = 0;
int XCENTER, YCENTER, ANGLE, LINEWIDTH;
unsigned long PATTERN;

float radians_to_degrees(float degrees);
```

```
void projection (float x_angle, float y_angle,
float z_angle, float x3, float y3, float z3, int color);
void wait(char title[]);

main ()
{
    char adapt;

    adapt = getAdapter();
    if ((adapt != 'E') && (adapt != 'C') && (adapt != 'V'))
        printf("Cannot Run Demo -- No CGA,"
            " EGA or VGA Installed!");
    else
    {
        if (adapt == 'V')
            setMode(0x12);
        if (adapt == 'E')
            setMode(16);
        if (adapt == 'C')
            setMode(4);
    }
    cls(0);
    gotoxy(2,10,0);
    printf("Enter x axis angle in degrees: ");
    scanf("%f",&x_angle);
    gotoxy(2,11,0);
    printf("Enter y axis angle in degrees: ");
    scanf("%f",&y_angle);
    gotoxy(2,12,0);
    printf("Enter z axis angle in degrees: ");
    scanf("%f",&z_angle);
    x_angle = radians_to_degrees(x_angle);
    y_angle = radians_to_degrees(y_angle);
    z_angle = radians_to_degrees(z_angle);
    cls(1);
    for (type=1; type<=6; type++)
    {
        switch (type)
        {
            case 1:
                x_offset = 450;
                y_offset = 195;
```

```
    horz_scale = 9;
    vert_scale = 2.2;
    for (y3=-6; y3<=6; y3+=.4)
    {
        color = 3;
        step = .05;
        for (x3=-6; x3<=6; x3+=step)
        {
            z3 = x3*x3 + y3*y3;
            projection(x_angle, y_angle,z_angle,
                x3,y3,z3,color);
            if (x3>=0)
            {
                step = .2;
                color = 12;
            }
        }
    }
    gotoxy(5,12);

    #ifndef CGA
    writString("Elliptic Paraboloid",11,0);
    #endif
    break;
case 2:
    x_offset = 20;
    y_offset = 120;
    horz_scale = 12;
    vert_scale = 2;
    for (y3=-5; y3<=5; y3+=.4)
    {
        step = .1;
        color = 3;
        for (x3=-5; x3<=5; x3+=step)
        {
            z3 = y3*y3 - x3*x3;
            projection(x_angle,y_angle,z_angle,
                x3,y3,z3,color);
            if (x3>=0)
            {
                step = .4;
                color = 14;
```

```
                }
            }
        }
        gotoxy(30,12,0);

        #ifndef CGA
        writString("Hyperbolic Paraboloid ",11,0);
        #endif
        break;
case 3:
        x_offset = 220;
        y_offset = 120;
        horz_scale = 7;
        vert_scale = 3;
        for (y3=-6; y3<=6; y3+=.75)
        {
            step = .2;
            color = 2;
            for (x3=-6; x3<=6; x3+=step)
            {
                z3 = sqrt(y3*y3 + x3*x3)*2;
                projection(x_angle,y_angle,z_angle,
                    x3,y3,z3,color);
                projection(x_angle,y_angle,z_angle,
                    x3,y3,-z3,color);
                if (x3>=0)
                {
                    step = .5;
                    color = 12;
                }
            }
        }
        gotoxy(60,12,0);

        #ifndef CGA
        writString("Elliptic Cone ",11,0);
        #endif
        break;
case 4:
        y_offset = -85;
        x_offset = 420;
        horz_scale = 7;
```

```
        vert_scale = 5;
        for (y3=-4; y3<=4; y3+=.5)
        {
            for (x3=-4; x3<=4; x3+=.2)
            {
                if (x3<0)
                    color = 4;
                else
                    color = 14;
                if (x3*x3+y3*y3>2)
                {
                    z3 = sqrt(y3*y3 + x3*x3-2)*2;
                    projection(x_angle,y_angle,z_angle,
                        x3,y3,z3,color);
                    projection(x_angle,y_angle,z_angle,
                        x3,y3,-z3,color);
                }
            }
        }

        #ifdef VGA
        gotoxy(0,28,0);
        writString(" Hyperboloid of one sheet",11,0);
        #endif

        #ifdef EGA
        gotoxy(0,23,0);
        writString(" Hyperboloid of one sheet",11,0);
        #endif

        break;
    case 5:
        y_offset = -95;
        x_offset = 0;
        horz_scale = 2;
        vert_scale = 2;
        for (y3=-20; y3<=20; y3+=2)
        {
            for (x3=-20; x3<=20; x3+=.3)
            {
                if (x3<0)
                    color = 10;
```

```
            else
                color = 12;
            if (y3*y3>=x3*x3+1)
            {
                z3 = sqrt(y3*y3 - x3*x3 - 1);
                projection(x_angle,y_angle,z_angle,
                    x3,y3,z3,color);
                projection(x_angle,y_angle,z_angle,
                    x3,y3,-z3,color);
            }
        }
    }

    #ifdef VGA
    gotoxy(30,28,0);
    writString("Hyperboloid of two sheets ",11,0);
    #endif

    #ifdef EGA
    gotoxy(30,23,0);
    writString("Hyperboloid of two sheets ",11,0);
    #endif

    break;
case 6:
    y_offset = -95;
    x_offset = 210;
    horz_scale = 60;
    vert_scale = 50;
    for (y3=-.99; y3<=1; y3+=.15)
    {
        step = .015;
        color = 11;
        for (x3=-1; x3<=1; x3+=.03)
        {
            if (x3*x3+y3*y3<1)
            {
                z3 = sqrt(1-x3*x3 - y3*y3);
                projection(x_angle,y_angle,
                    z_angle,x3,y3,z3,color);
                projection(x_angle,y_angle,
                    z_angle,x3,y3,-z3,color);
```

```
                        }
                        if (x3>0)
                        {
                                step = .03;
                                color = 10;
                        }
                    }
                }

                #ifdef VGA
                gotoxy(63,28,0);
                writString("Ellipsoid",11,0);
                #endif

                #ifdef EGA
                gotoxy(63,23,0);
                writString("Ellipsoid",11,0);
                #endif

            }
        }
    wait("Quadric Surfaces");
}

float radians_to_degrees(float degrees)
{
    float angle;

    while (degrees >= 360)
        degrees -= 360;
    while (degrees < 0)
        degrees += 360;
    angle = rad_per_degree*degrees;
    return angle;
}

void projection (float x_angle, float y_angle,
    float z_angle, float x3, float y3, float z3, int color)
{
    float temp_x, temp_y;
    int x,y;
```

```
    temp_x = x3*cos(x_angle) + y3*cos(y_angle) +
        z3*cos(z_angle);
    temp_y = x3*sin(x_angle) + y3*sin(y_angle) +
        z3*sin(z_angle);
    x = x_offset + (temp_x*horz_scale);
    y = y_offset - (temp_y*vert_scale);
    plots (x,y,color);
}

void wait(char title[])
{
    int tab,width;
    getMode(&width);
    tab = (width - strlen(title))/2;
    gotoxy(tab,0,0);
    writString(title,15,0);
    tab = (width - 28)/2;

    #ifdef VGA
    gotoxy(tab,29,0);
    #endif

    #ifndef VGA
    gotoxy(tab,24,0);
    #endif

    #ifdef CGA
    writString("Press any key to end demo...", 2,0);
    #endif

    #ifndef CGA
    writString("Press any key to continue demo...", 15,0);
    #endif

    getch();
    cls(1);
}
```

Appendix G

GTools Library for the Hercules Graphics Card

```
/*            HEADER FILE FOR HERCULES GRAPHICS TOOLS     */

int getMode (int *ncols);
char getAdapter();
void setMode(int mode);
void gotoxy(int column, int row);
void getxy(int *column, int *row);
void setPage(int page);
int getPage(void);
void cls(void);
int readPixel(int x, int y);
```

'gtools' library directory

Publics by module

```
CLS         size = 111
   _cls

GETADAP     size = 232
   _getAdapter

GETMODE     size = 41
   _getMode

GETPAGE     size = 33
   _getPage
```

```
GETXY           size = 66
    _getxy


GOTOXY          size = 57
    _gotoxy


READPIX         size = 129
    _readPixel


SETMODE         size = 245
    _graph_reg_data                    _setMode
    _text_reg_data


SETPAGE         size = 25
    _setPage
```

```
/*                      cls() = Clears the Screen            */



#include "gtools.h"

void cls(void)
{
    #include <dos.h>

    union REGS reg;

    char far *address;
    unsigned char ch;
    unsigned int i;

    outp(0x3B8,2);
    ch = inp(0x3B8);
    if (ch == 0x8A)
        for (i=0; i<0x7FFF; i++)
        {
            address = (char far *) 0xB8000000L + i;
            *address = 0;
            outp(0x3B8,0x8A);
        }
```

```
    else
        for (i=0; i<0x7FFF; i++)
        {
            address = (char far *) 0xB0000000L + i;
            *address = 0;
            outp(0X3B8,0x0A);
        }
}




/*              getAdapter = Returns Adapter Type       */

#include "gtools.h"

char getAdapter()
{
    #include <dos.h>

    union REGS reg;
    struct SREGS inreg;

    int EGA, adapter, mode, herc, i, n;
    char type,buffer[64];
    char far *address;
    segread(&inreg);
    inreg.es = inreg.ds;
    reg.x.di = (int) buffer;
    reg.x.ax = 0x1B00;
    reg.x.bx = 0;
    int86x(0x10,&reg,&reg,&inreg);
    if (reg.h.al == 0x1B)
        type = 'V';
    else
    {
        int86(0x11,&reg,&reg);
        adapter = (reg.h.al & 0x30) >> 4;
        mode = getMode(&n);
        address = (char far *)0x00000487;
        EGA = *address;
        type = 'O';
        if (EGA)
```

```
            type = 'E';
        else
        {
            if(adapter == 3)
            {
                for (i=0; i<=0x1000; i++)
                {
                    if (inp(0x3BA) & 0x80)
                    {
                        type = 'H';
                        break;
                    }
                }
                if (type == 'O')
                    type = 'M';
            }
            else
            {
                if ((adapter == 2) || (adapter == 0))
                {
                    if (mode == 2)
                    type = 'Q';
                else
                    type = 'C';
                }
            }
        }
    }
    return (type);
}



/*          getMode() = Returns Current Video Mode
                    to another in a designated color       */

#include "gtools.h"

int getMode (int *ncols)
{
    char mode;
    char far *address;
```

```
    address = (char far *)0x00000449;
    mode = *address;
    *ncols = 80;
    return mode;
}




/*      getxy() = Gets the Current Cursor Position      */

#include "gtools.h"


void getxy(int *column, int *row, int page)
{
    #include <dos.h>

    union REGS reg;

    outp (0x3B4,14);
    reg.h.ah = inp (0x3B5);
    outp (0x3B4,15);
    reg.h.al = inp (0x3B5);
    *row = reg.x.ax/80;
    *column = reg.x.ax % 80;
}



/*      gotoxy() = Moves Cursor to Specified x,y Position
                   and Page.                            */

#include "gtools.h"


void gotoxy(int column, int row, int page)
{

    #include <dos.h>

    union REGS reg;
```

```
    reg.x.ax = 80*row + column;
    outp (0x3B4,14);
    outp (0x3B5,reg.h.ah);
    outp (0x3B4,15);
    outp (0x3B5,reg.h.al);
    setPage(page);
}




/*          getPage() = Returns Active Page Number       */

#include "gtools.h"

int getPage(void)
{
    #include <dos.h>

    unsigned char ch;

    ch = inp(0x3B8);
    if (ch == 0x8A)
        return 1;
    else
        return(0);
}




/*          readPixel() = Reads a pixel from the screen at
                          point (x,y) for Hercules Graphics
                          Card.                          */

#include "gtools.h"

int readPixel(int x, int y)
{
    unsigned int offset;
    int page,pixel;
    char mask;
    char far *address;
```

```
    page = getPage();
    offset = 0x2000 * (y%4) + 0x8000 * page + 90 * (y/4) + x/8;
    mask = 0x80 >> (x%8);
    address = (char far *) 0xB0000000L + offset;
    pixel = *address & mask;
    if (pixel != 0) pixel = 1;
        return(pixel);
}




/*          setMode() = Sets Video Mode (Text or Graphics    */

#include "gtools.h"

char graph_reg_data[12] = {0x35,0x2D,0x2E,
    0x07,0x5B,0x02,0x57,0x57,0x02,0x03,0x00,
    0x00},text_reg_data[12] = {0x61,0x50,0x52,
    0x0F,0x19,0x06,0x19,0x19,0x02,0x0D,0x0B,0x0C};

void setMode(int mode)
{
    #include <dos.h>

    char far *address;
    unsigned int i;

    if (mode == 0)
    {
        outp (0x3BF,0);
        outp (0x3B8,0);
        for (i=0; i<12; i++)
        {
            outp (0x3B4,i);
            outp (0x3B5,text_reg_data[i]);
        }
        for (i=0; i<=0x7FFF; i+=2)
        {
            address = (char far *)0xB0000000L + i;
            *address = 00;
            *(address + 1) = 0x07;
        }
```

```
        outp (0x3B8,0x28);
    }
    else
    {
        outp (0x3BF,3);
        outp (0x3B8,2);
        for (i=0; i<12; i++)
        {
            outp (0x3B4,i);
            outp (0x3B5,graph_reg_data[i]);
        }
        for (i=0; i<=0x7FFF; i++)
        {
            address = (char far *)0xB0000000L + i;
            *address = 0x00;
            address = (char far *)0xB8000000L + i;
            *address = 0x00;
        }
        outp (0x3B8,0x0A);
    }
    address = (char far *)0x00000449L;
    *address = mode;
}



/*      setPage() = Sets the Active Display Page    */

#include "gtools.h"

void setPage(int page)
{
    #include <dos.h>

    if (page == 1)
        outp (0x3B8, 0x8A);
    else
        outp (0x3B8,0x0A);
}
```

Appendix H

GDraws Library
for the Hercules Card

```
/*    HEADER FOR GDRAWS LIBRARY FOR HERCULES CARD      */


void drawArc (int xc, int yc, int b, int start_angle,
    int end_angle, int color, float aspect);
void drawBezier(int segments, int color, ...);
void drawBspline(int segments, int color, ...);
void drawLine(int x1, int y1, int x2, int y2, int color);
void drawOval(int x, int y, int b, int color, float aspect);
void drawPoly(int color,...);
void drawRect(int x1, int y1, int x2, int y2, int color);
void drawRoundRect(int x1, int y1, int x2, int y2, int b,
    int color);
void fillArc (int xc, int yc, int b, int start_angle,
    int end_angle, int color, float aspect);
void fillArc1 (int xc, int yc,int x, int y, int sector,
    int arcTest[], int x_start_test, int x_end_test, int color);
void fillOval(int x, int y, int b, int color, float aspect);
void fillPoly(int color,...);
void fill2Poly(int color,int point[600]);
void fillRect(int x1, int y1, int x2, int y2, int color);
void fillRoundRect(int x1, int y1, int x2, int y2, int b,
    int color);
void plot(int x, int y, int color);
void plots(int x, int y, int color);
void rotateOval(int x, int y, int b, int color, double aspect);
void rotatePoly(int color,...);
void rotateRect(int x1, int y1, int x2, int y2, int color);
```

```
void sort(int index, int x_coord[], int y_coord[]);
void write_horz_char(int x, int y, int ch, int color);
void write_vert_char(int x, int y, int ch, int color);
void write_horz_str(int x, int y, char *string, int color);
void write_vert_str(int x, int y, char *string, int color);
void write_big_char(int x, int y, int ch, int color);
void write_vid_char(int x, int y, int ch, int color);
void write_big_str(int x, int y, char *string, int color);
void write_vid_str(int x, int y, char *string, int color);
void write_horz_char(int x, int y, int ch, int color);
void write_vert_char(int x, int y, int ch, int color);
void write_horz_str(int x, int y, char *string, int color);
void write_vert_str(int x, int y, char *string, int color);
void write_big_char(int x, int y, int ch, int color);
void write_vid_char(int x, int y, int ch, int color);
void write_big_str(int x, int y, char *string, int color);
void write_vid_str(int x, int y, char *string, int color);
```

gdraws library listing file

Publics by module

```
CHARACT      size = 2715
    _char_table                        _write_big_char
    _write_big_str                     _write_horz_char
    _write_horz_str                    _write_vert_char
    _write_vert_str                    _write_vid_char
    _write_vid_str


DRAWARC      size = 1767
    _drawArc                           _plotArc1
    _plotArc2


DRAWBEZ      size = 533
    _blend                             _drawBezier


DRAWBSPL     size = 821
    _drawBspline


DRAWLINE     size = 550
```

```
    _drawLine

DRAWOVAL     size = 992
   _drawOval

DRAWPOLY     size = 210
   _drawPoly

DRAWRECT     size = 171
   _drawRect

DRAWRNDR     size = 1112
   _drawRoundRect

FIL2POLY     size = 810
   _fill2Poly

FILLARC      size = 1797
   _fillArc                              _fillArc1

FILLOVAL     size = 925
   _fillOval

FILLPOLY     size = 887
   _fillPoly

FILLRECT     size = 144
   _fillRect

FILLRNDR     size = 901
   _fillRoundRect

PLOT         size = 133
   _plot

PLOTS        size = 179
   _plots

ROTOVAL      size = 1912
   _rotateOval

ROTPOLY      size = 996
```

```
    _rotatePoly

ROTRECT      size = 1590
    _rotateRect

SORT         size = 249
    _sort
```

```
/*                CHARACTER WRITING FUNCTIONS

                  write horizontal normal, big,
                  and video characters and strings
                  and vertical characters and strings.   */


#include "gdraws.h"
#include "chars.h"

void write_horz_char(int x, int y, int ch, int color)
{
    int offset,i,j;
    unsigned char char_test;

    x = ((x + 319)*18) >> 4;
    y = 174 - ((93*y) >> 7);
    offset = (ch - 32) * 14;
    for (i=0; i<14; i++)
    {
        for (j=0; j<8; j++)
        {
            char_test = 0x80 >> j;
            if ((char_table[offset+i] & char_test) != 0)
            {
                if (color == 1)
                    plot(x+j,y+i,1);
                else
                    plot(x+j,y+i,0);
            }
            else
            {
```

```
            if (color == 1)
                plot(x+j,y+i,0);
            else
                plot(x+j,y+i,1);
        }
    }
    if (color == 1)
        plot(x+j,y+i,0);
    else
        plot(x+j,y+i,1);
    }
}


void write_vert_char(int x, int y, int ch, int color)
{
    int offset,i,j;
    unsigned char char_test;

    x = ((x + 319)*18) >> 4;
    y = 174 - ((93*y) >> 7);
    offset = (ch - 32) * 14;
    for (i=0; i<14; i++)
    {
        for (j=0; j<8; j++)
        {
            char_test = 0x80 >> j;
            if ((char_table[offset+i] & char_test) != 0)
            {
                if (color == 1)
                    plot(x+i,y-j,1);
                else
                    plot(x+i,y-j,0);
            }
            else
            {
                if (color == 1)
                    plot(x+i,y-j,0);
                else
                    plot(x+i,y-j,1);
            }
        }
    }
}
```

```
}

void write_horz_str(int x, int y, char *string, int color)
{
    int p=0;

    while (string[p])
    {
        write_horz_char(x,y,string[p++],color);
        x += 8;
        if (x>312)
        {
            x=-319;
            y += 20;
        }
    }
}

void write_vert_str(int x, int y, char *string, int color)
{
    int p=0;

    while (string[p])
    {
        write_vert_char(x,y,string[p++],color);
        y += 12;
        if (y>228)
        {
            y=-239;
            x += 14;
        }
    }
}

void write_big_char(int x, int y, int ch, int color)
{
    int offset,i,j,k,m;
    unsigned char char_test;

    x = ((x + 319)*18) >> 4;
    y = 174 - ((93*y) >> 7);
    offset = (ch - 32) * 14;
```

```
for (i=0; i<14; i++)
{
    for (j=0; j<8; j++)
    {
        char_test = 0x80 >> j;
        for(k=0; k<4; k++)
        {
            for(m=0; m<4; m++)
            {
                if ((char_table[offset+i] &
                    char_test) != 0)
                {
                    if (color == 1)
                        plot(x+4*j+m,y+4*i+k,1);
                    else
                        plot(x+4*j+m,y+4*i+k,0);
                }
                else
                {
                    if (color == 1)
                        plot(x+4*j+m,y+4*i+k,0);
                    else
                        plot(x+4*j+m,y+4*i+k,1);
                }
            }
        }
    }
}

void write_vid_char(int x, int y, int ch, int color)
{
    int offset,i,j,k,m;
    unsigned char char_test;

    x = ((x + 319)*18) >> 4;
    y = 174 - ((93*y) >> 7);
    offset = (ch - 32) * 14;
    for (i=0; i<14; i++)
    {
        for (j=0; j<8; j++)
        {
```

```
                char_test = 0x80 >> j;
                for(k=1; k<4; k++)
                {
                    for(m=1; m<4; m++)
                    {
                        if ((char_table[offset+i] &
                            char_test) != 0)
                        {
                            if (color == 1)
                                plot(x+4*j+m,y+4*i+k,1);
                            else
                                plot(x+4*j+m,y+4*i+k,0);
                        }
                        else
                        {
                            if (color == 1)
                                plot(x+4*j+m,y+4*i+k,0);
                            else
                                plot(x+4*j+m,y+4*i+k,1);
                        }
                    }
                }
            }
        }
}

void write_big_str(int x, int y, char *string, int color)
{
    int p=0;

    while (string[p])
    {
        write_big_char(x,y,string[p++],color);
        x += 32;
        if (x>287)
        {
            x=-329;
            y -= 14;
        }
    }
}
```

```c
void write_vid_str(int x, int y, char *string, int color)
{
    int p=0;

    while (string[p])
    {
        write_vid_char(x,y,string[p++],color);
        x += 32;
        if (x>287)
        {
            x=-319;
            y -= 14;
        }
    }
}


/*    drawArc() = draws an arc centered at (xc,yc) with
                radius 'b' in y direction from starting
                angle 'start_angle' in tenths of a
                degree to ending angle 'end_angle' in
                tenths of a degree with aspect ratio
                'aspect' and in color 'color'.          /*

#include <math.h>
#include "gdraws.h"

extern int LINEWIDTH;

void drawArc (int xc, int yc, int b, int start_angle,
    int end_angle, int color, float aspect)

{
    int i, start_sector,end_sector,x_start_test,x_end_test;
    int arcTest[9],j;
    float a_temp;
    long a_square, b_square, two_a_square, two_b_square,
        four_a_square, four_b_square,d,a,row,col;

    void plotArc1 (int x, int y, int sector, int color,
        int arcTest[], int x_start_test, int x_end_test);
    void plotArc2 (int x, int y, int sector, int color,
```

```
        int arcTest[], int x_start_test, int x_end_test);

for (i=0; i<8; i++)
    arcTest[i] = 0;
xc = ((xc + 319)*18) >> 4;
yc = 174 - ((93*yc) >> 7);
a_temp = b/aspect;
a = (((int)(a_temp * 18)) >> 4) - LINEWIDTH/2;
b = ((93*b) >> 7) - LINEWIDTH/2;
for (j=0; j<LINEWIDTH; j++,a++,b++)
{
    b_square = b*b;
    a_square = a*a;
    row = b;
    col = 0;
    two_a_square = a_square << 1;
    four_a_square = a_square << 2;
    four_b_square = b_square << 2;
    two_b_square = b_square << 1;
    d = two_a_square * ((row -1)*(row )) + a_square +
        two_b_square*(1-a_square);
    start_sector = start_angle/450;
    end_sector = end_angle/450;
    x_start_test = xc+sqrt(a_square)*cos(start_angle*
        .0017453);
    x_end_test = xc+sqrt(a_square)*cos(end_angle*
        .0017453);
    if (start_sector == end_sector)
        arcTest[start_sector] = 4;
    else
    {
        arcTest[start_sector] = 1;
        arcTest[end_sector] = 3;
        for (i=start_sector+1; i!=end_sector; i++)
        {
            arcTest[i] = 2;
            if (i==8)
                i=-1;
        }
    }
    while (a_square*(row ) > b_square * (col))
    {
```

```
        plotArc1 (xc+col, yc-row, 6, color, arcTest,
            x_start_test, x_end_test);
        plotArc2 (xc+col, yc+row, 1, color, arcTest,
            x_start_test, x_end_test);
        plotArc1 (xc-col, yc-row, 5, color, arcTest,
            x_start_test, x_end_test);
        plotArc2 (xc-col, yc+row, 2, color, arcTest,
            x_start_test, x_end_test);
        if (d>= 0)
        {
            row--;
            d -= four_a_square*(row);
        }
        d += two_b_square*(3 + (col << 1));
        col++;
    }
    d = two_b_square * (col + 1)*col + two_a_square*(row *
        (row  -2) +1) + (1-two_a_square)*b_square;
    while ((row) + 1)
    {
        plotArc1 (xc+col, yc-row, 7, color, arcTest,
            x_start_test, x_end_test);
        plotArc2 (xc+col, yc+row, 0, color, arcTest,
            x_start_test, x_end_test);
        plotArc1 (xc-col, yc-row, 4, color, arcTest,
            x_start_test, x_end_test);
        plotArc2 (xc-col, yc+row, 3, color, arcTest,
            x_start_test, x_end_test);
        if (d<= 0)
        {
            col++;
            d += four_b_square*col;
        }
        row--;
        d += two_a_square * (3 - (row <<1));
    }
    }
}


void plotArc1 (int x, int y, int sector, int color,
    int arcTest[], int x_start_test, int x_end_test)
```

```
{
    if (arcTest[sector] == 0)
        return;
    if (arcTest[sector] == 2)
        plot(x,y,color);
    if ((arcTest[sector] == 1) && (x>=x_start_test))
        plot(x,y,color);
    if ((arcTest[sector] == 3) && (x<=x_end_test))
        plot(x,y,color);
    if ((arcTest[sector] == 4) && (x>=x_start_test) &&
        (x<=x_end_test))
        plot(x,y,color);
}

void plotArc2 (int x, int y, int sector, int color,
    int arcTest[], int x_start_test, int x_end_test)
{
    if (arcTest[sector] == 0)
        return;
    if (arcTest[sector] == 2)
        plot(x,y,color);
    if ((arcTest[sector] == 1) && (x<=x_start_test))
        plot(x,y,color);
    if ((arcTest[sector] == 3) && (x>=x_end_test))
        plot(x,y,color);
    if ((arcTest[sector] == 4) && (x>=x_end_test) &&
        (x<=x_start_test))
        plot(x,y,color);
}




/*  drawBezier() = draws a Bezier curve            */

#include "gdraws.h"

void drawBezier(int segments, int color,...)
{
    #include <dos.h>
    #include <stdarg.h>
    #include <stdio.h>
```

```
    union REGS reg;

    float blend(int i, int n, float u);

    va_list coord;
    int xpoint[20],ypoint[20],i=0,j,oldx,oldy,px,py,last;
    float b,u,x,y;

    va_start(coord,color);
    while (((xpoint[i]=va_arg(coord,int)) >= -320) &&
        ((ypoint[i]=va_arg(coord,int)) >= -320) && (i<=20))
        i++;
    va_end(coord);
    last = (i-1);
    for (i=0; i<=segments; i++)
    {
        u = (float)i/segments;
        x = 0;
        y = 0;
        for (j=0; j<=last; j++)
        {
            b = blend (j,last,u);
            x += xpoint[j]*b;
            y += ypoint[j]*b;
        }
        px = x;
        py = y;
        if (i>0)
            drawLine(oldx,oldy,px,py,color);
        oldx = x;
        oldy = y;
    }
}

float blend(int i, int n, float u)
{
    int c,j,k=1,g=1;
    float f;

    for (c=n; c>i; c--)
        k *= c;
    for (c=n-i; c>1; c--)
```

```
        g *= c;
    f = (float)k/g;
    for (j-1; j<=i; j++)
        f *= u;
    for (j=1; j<=n-i; j++)
        f *= (1-u);
    return (f);
}




/*  drawBspline() = draws a B-Spline Curve            */

#include "gdraws.h"

void drawBspline(int segments, int color,...)
{
    #include <dos.h>
    #include <stdarg.h>
    #include <stdio.h>

    union REGS reg;

    va_list coord;
    int xpoint[20],ypoint[20],i=1,j,x,y,oldx,oldy,last;
    float u,nc1,nc2,nc3,nc4;

    va_start(coord,color);
    while ((((xpoint[i]=va_arg(coord,int)) >= -320) &&
        ((ypoint[i]=va_arg(coord,int)) >= -320) && (i<=20))
        i++;
    va_end(coord);
    xpoint[0]=xpoint[1];
    ypoint[0]=ypoint[1];
    oldx=xpoint[0];
    oldy=ypoint[0];
    for (j=i;j<=i+1;j++)
    {
        xpoint[j]=xpoint[j-1];
        ypoint[j]=ypoint[j-1];
    }
    last = j;
```

```
    for(i=1; i<=last-3; i++)
    {
        for (u=0; u<=1; u+=1.0/segments)
        {
            nc1=-(u*u*u/6)+u*u/2-u/2+1.0/6;
            nc2=u*u*u/2-u*u+2.0/3;
            nc3=(-u*u*u+u*u+u)/2+1.0/6;
            nc4=u*u*u/6;
            x = (nc1*xpoint[i-1]+nc2*xpoint[i]+nc3*xpoint[i+1]
                +nc4*xpoint[i+2]);
            y = (nc1*ypoint[i-1]+nc2*ypoint[i]+nc3*ypoint[i+1]
                +nc4*ypoint[i+2]);
            drawLine(oldx,oldy,x,y,color);
            oldx=x;
            oldy=y;
        }
    }
}




/* drawLine() = draws a line from one set of coordinates
               to another in a designated color       */

#include "gdraws.h"

extern unsigned long int PATTERN;
extern int LINEWIDTH;

void drawLine(int x1, int y1, int x2, int y2, int color)
{
    #define sign(x) ((x) > 0 ? 1:  ((x) == 0 ? 0:  (-1)))

    int dx, dy, dxabs, dyabs, i, j, px, py, sdx, sdy, x, y;
    unsigned long int mask=0x80000000;

    x1 = ((x1 + 319)*18) >> 4;
    y1 = 174 - ((93*y1) >> 7);
    x2 = ((x2 + 319)*18) >> 4;
    y2 = 174 - ((93*y2) >> 7);

    dx = x2 - x1;
```

```
    dy = y2 - y1;
    sdx = sign(dx);
    sdy = sign(dy);
    dxabs = abs(dx);
    dyabs = abs(dy);
    x = 0;
    y = 0;
    px = x1;
    py = y1;
    if (dxabs >= dyabs)
    {
        for (i=0; i<dxabs; i++)
        {
            mask = mask ? mask : 0x80000000;
            y += dyabs;
            if (y>=dxabs)
            {
                y -= dxabs;
                py += sdy;
            }
            px += sdx;
            if (PATTERN & mask)
            {
                for (j=-LINEWIDTH/2; j<=LINEWIDTH/2; j++)
                    plot(px,py+j,color);
            }
            mask >>= 1;
        }
    }
    else
    {
        for (i-0; i<dyabs; i++)
        {
            mask = mask ? mask : 0x80000000;
            x += dxabs;
            if (x>=dyabs)
            {
                x -= dyabs;
                px += sdx;
            }
            py += sdy;
            if (PATTERN & mask)
```

```
        {
            for (j=-LINEWIDTH/2; j<=LINEWIDTH/2; j++)
                plot(px+j,py,color);
        }
        mask >>= 1;
    }
  }
}




/* drawOval() = draws an oval with specified center,
                radius, color and aspect ratio.        */

#include "gdraws.h"

extern int LINEWIDTH;

void drawOval(int x, int y, int b, int color, float aspect)
{
    int i;
    float a_temp;
    long a_square, b_square, two_a_square, two_b_square,
        four_a_square, four_b_square, d, a, row, col;

    x = ((x + 319)*18) >> 4;
    y = 174 - ((93*y) >> 7);
    a_temp = b/aspect;
    a = (((int)(a_temp * 18)) >> 4) - LINEWIDTH/2;
    b = ((93*b) >> 7) - LINEWIDTH/2;

    for (i=1; i<=LINEWIDTH; i++)
    {
        b_square = b*b;
        a_square = a*a;
        row = b;
        col = 0;
        two_a_square = a_square << 1;
        four_a_square = a_square << 2;
        four_b_square = b_square << 2;
        two_b_square = b_square << 1;
        d = two_a_square * ((row  -1)*(row )) + a_square +
```

```
            two_b_square*(1-a_square);
      while (a_square*(row ) > b_square * (col))
      {
            plot(col+x,row+y,color);
            plot(col+x,y-row, color);
            plot(x-col,row+y,color);
            plot(x-col,y-row,color);
            if (d>= 0)
            {
                  row--;
                  d -= four_a_square*(row);
            }
            d += two_b_square*(3 + (col << 1));
            col++;
      }

      d = two_b_square * (col + 1)*col + two_a_square*(row *
            (row  -2) +1) + (1-two_a_square)*b_square;
      while ((row) + 1)
      {
            plot(col+x,row+y,color);
            plot(col+x,y-row, color);
            plot(x-col,row+y,color);
            plot(x-col,y-row,color);
            if (d<= 0)
            {
                  col++;
                  d += four_b_square*col;
            }
            row--;
            d += two_a_square * (3 - (row <<1));
      }
      b++;
      a++;
   }
}


/* drawPoly() = draws a polygon in specified color by
               connecting specified sets of points in
               order given and then connecting last
```

```
                point to first.                    */

#include "gdraws.h"

void drawPoly(int color,...)
{
    #include <stdarg.h>
    #include <stdio.h>
    va_list coord;
    int xpoint[150],ypoint[150],i=0,j;
    va_start(coord,color);
    while (((xpoint[i]=va_arg(coord,int)) >= -320) &&
        ((ypoint[i]=va_arg(coord,int)) >= -320) && (i<=150))
        i++;
    if (i<3) return;
    for (j=0; j<i-1; j++)
    drawLine(xpoint[j],ypoint[j],xpoint[j+1],ypoint[j+1],color);
    drawLine(xpoint[0],ypoint[0],xpoint[i-1],ypoint[i-1],color);
    va_end(coord);
}



/*   drawRect() = draws a rectangle with top left and
                  bottom right corners specified in
                  specified color

#include "gdraws.h"

extern int LINEWIDTH;

void drawRect(int x1, int y1, int x2, int y2, int color)
{
    int i,j;
    drawLine(x1-LINEWIDTH/2,y1,x2+LINEWIDTH/2,y1,color);
    drawLine(x1-LINEWIDTH/2,y2,x2+LINEWIDTH/2,y2,color);
    drawLine(x1,y1+LINEWIDTH/2,x1,y2-LINEWIDTH/2,color);
    drawLine(x2,y1+LINEWIDTH/2,x2,y2-LINEWIDTH/2,color);
}



  /* drawRoundRect() = draws a rectangle with rounded
```

```
                corners of radius 'b' with upper right
                corner 'x1,y1', lower left corner 'x2,y2',
                in specified color 'color'.              */

#include "gdraws.h"

extern int LINEWIDTH;

void drawRoundRect(int x1, int y1, int x2, int y2, int b,
    int color)
{
    int a, col,i,j,row,xend,yend,xstart,ystart;
    long a_square, b_square, two_a_square, two_b_square,
        four_a_square, four_b_square,d;

    x1 = ((x1 + 319)*18) >> 4;
    y1 = 174 - ((93*y1) >> 7);
    x2 = ((x2 + 319)*18) >> 4;
    y2 = 174 - ((93*y2) >> 7);
    a = (((int)(b * 18)) >> 4) - LINEWIDTH/2;
    b = ((93*b) >> 7) - LINEWIDTH/2;
    b_square = b*b;
    a_square = a*a;
    row = b;
    col = 0;
    xend = x2-a;
    yend = y2-b;
    xstart = x1+a;
    ystart = y1+b;
    for (j=-LINEWIDTH/2; j<=LINEWIDTH/2; j++)
    {
        for (i=x1+a; i<=xend; i++)
        {
            plot(i,y1+j,color);
            plot(i,y2+j,color);
        }
    }
    for (j=-LINEWIDTH/2; j<=LINEWIDTH/2; j++)
    {
        for (i=y1+b; i<=yend; i++)
        {
            plot(x1+j,i,color);
```

```
                plot(x2+j,i,color);
        }
}
a -= LINEWIDTH/2;
b -= LINEWIDTH/2;
for (i=0; i<LINEWIDTH; i++,a++,b++)
{
    b_square = b*b;
    a_square = a*a;
    row = b;
    col = 0;
    two_a_square = a_square << 1;
    four_a_square = a_square << 2;
    four_b_square = b_square << 2;
    two_b_square = b_square << 1;
    d = two_a_square * ((row  -1)*(row )) + a_square +
        two_b_square*(1-a_square);
    while (a_square*(row ) > b_square * (col))
    {
        plot(col+xend,row+yend,color);
        plot(col+xend,ystart-row, color);
        plot(xstart-col,row+yend,color);
        plot(xstart-col,ystart-row,color);
        if (d>= 0)
        {
            row--;
            d -= four_a_square*(row);
        }
        d += two_b_square*(3 + (col << 1));
        col++;
    }

    d = two_b_square * (col + 1)*col + two_a_square*(row *
        (row  -2) +1) + (1-two_a_square)*b_square;
    while (row)
    {
        plot(col+xend,row+yend,color);
        plot(col+xend,ystart-row, color);
        plot(xstart-col,row+yend,color);
        plot(xstart-col,ystart-row,color);
        if (d<= 0)
        {
```

```
                col++;
                d += four_b_square*col;
            }
            row--;
            d += two_a_square * (3 - (row <<1));
        }
    }
}




/*  fil2Poly() = fills a polygon in specified color by
                filling in boundaries resulting from
                connecting specified points in the
                order given and then connecting last
                point to first.  Uses an array to
                store coordinates.                     */

#include "gdraws.h"

void fill2Poly(int color,int point[600])
{
    #define sign(x) ((x) > 0 ? 1:  ((x) == 0 ? 0:  (-1)))

    int dx, dy, dxabs, dyabs, i, index=0, j, k, px, py, sdx,
        sdy, x, y, toggle, old_sdy, sy0;
    int *x_coord, *y_coord, *n_point;

    x_coord = (int *) malloc(4000 * sizeof(int));
    y_coord = (int *) malloc(4000 * sizeof(int));
    n_point = (int *) malloc(600 * sizeof(int));
    for (i=0; i<=600; i+=2)
    {
        if ((point[i] < -320) || (point[i+1] < -320))
            break;
        n_point[i] = (point[i] + 319)*18 >> 4;
        n_point[i+1] = 174 - ((point[i+1]*93) >> 7);
    }
    n_point[i] = n_point[0];
    n_point[i+1] = n_point[1];
    if (i<=5) return;
    px = n_point[0];
```

```
py = n_point[1];
if (n_point[1] == n_point[3])
{
    x_coord[index] = px;
    y_coord[index++] = py;
}
for (j=0; j<i-2; j+=2)
{
    dx = n_point[j+2] - n_point[j];
    dy = n_point[j+3] - n_point[j+1];
    sdx = sign(dx);
    sdy = sign(dy);
    if (j==0)
    {
        old_sdy = sdy;
        sy0 = sdy;
    }
    dxabs = abs(dx);
    dyabs = abs(dy);
    x = 0;
    y = 0;
    if (dxabs >= dyabs)
    {
        for (k=0; k<dxabs; k++)
        {
            y += dyabs;
            if (y>=dxabs)
            {
                y -= dxabs;
                py += sdy;
                if (old_sdy != sdy)
                {
                    old_sdy = sdy;
                    index--;
                }
                x_coord[index] = px+sdx;
                y_coord[index++] = py;
            }
            px += sdx;
            plot(px,py,color);
        }
    }
```

```
    else
    {
        for (k=0; k<dyabs; k++)
        {
            x += dxabs;
            if (x>=dyabs)
            {
                x -= dyabs;
                px += sdx;
            }

            py += sdy;
            if (old_sdy != sdy)
            {
                old_sdy = sdy;
                if (sdy != 0)
                    index--;
            }
            plot(px,py,color);
            x_coord[index] = px;
            y_coord[index] = py;
            index++;
        }
    }
}
index--;
if (sy0 + sdy == 0)
    index--;
sort(index,x_coord,y_coord);
toggle = 0;
for (i=0; i<index; i++)
{
    if ((y_coord[i] == y_coord[i+1]) &&
        (toggle == 0))
    {
        for (j=x_coord[i]; j<=x_coord[i+1]; j++)
            plot(j,y_coord[i],color);
        toggle = 1;
    }
    else
    toggle = 0;
}
```

```
    free(x_coord);
    free(y_coord);
    free(n_point);
}



/*    fillArc() = fills an arc centered at (xc,yc) having
                radius 'b' in y direction from starting
                angle 'start_angle' in tenths of a
                degree to ending angle 'end_angle' in
                tenths of a degree and aspect ratio
                'aspect' with   color 'color'.       */


#include <math.h>
#include "gdraws.h"
#include <dos.h>

extern int LINEWIDTH;

void fillArc (int xc, int yc, int b, int start_angle,
    int end_angle, int color, float aspect)
{
    int a, col, i, row,start_sector,end_sector,x_start_test,
        x_end_test;
    int arcTest[9];
    long a_square, b_square, two_a_square, two_b_square,
        four_a_square, four_b_square,d;

    for (i=0; i<8; i++)
    arcTest[i] = 0;
    xc = ((xc + 319)*18) >> 4;
    yc = 174 - ((93*yc) >> 7);
    a = (((int)(b * 18/aspect)) >> 4) - LINEWIDTH/2;
    b = ((93*b) >> 7) - LINEWIDTH/2;
    b_square = b*b;
      a_square = a*a;
    row = b;
    col = 0;
    two_a_square = a_square << 1;
    four_a_square = a_square << 2;
```

```
        four_b_square = b_square << 2;
        two_b_square = b_square << 1;
        if (end_angle > 3599)
            end_angle = 3599;
        d = two_a_square * ((row  -1)*(row )) + a_square +
            two_b_square*(1-a_square);
        start_sector = start_angle/450;
        end_sector = end_angle/450;
        x_start_test = xc+sqrt(a_square)*cos(start_angle*.0017453);
        x_end_test = xc+sqrt(a_square)*cos(end_angle*.0017453);
        if (start_sector == end_sector)
            arcTest[start_sector] = 4;
        else
        {
            arcTest[start_sector] = 1;
            arcTest[end_sector] = 3;
            for (i=start_sector+1; i!=end_sector; i++)
            {
                arcTest[i] = 2;
                if (i==8)
                    i=-1;
            }
        }
        while (a_square*(row ) > b_square * (col))
        {
            fillArc1 (xc,yc,xc+col, yc+row, 6, arcTest,
                x_start_test, x_end_test,color);
            fillArc1 (xc,yc,xc+col, yc-row, 1, arcTest,
                x_start_test, x_end_test,color);
            fillArc1 (xc,yc,xc-col, yc+row, 5, arcTest,
                x_start_test, x_end_test,color);
            fillArc1 (xc,yc,xc-col, yc-row, 2, arcTest,
                x_start_test, x_end_test,color);
            if (d>= 0)
            {
                row--;
                d -= four_a_square*(row);
            }
            d += two_b_square*(3 + (col << 1));
            col++;
        }
        d = two_b_square * (col + 1)*col + two_a_square*(row *
```

```
               (row  -2) +1) + (1-two_a_square)*b_square;
       while ((row) + 1)
       {
             fillArc1 (xc,yc,xc+col, yc+row, 7, arcTest,
                 x_start_test, x_end_test,color);
             fillArc1 (xc,yc,xc+col, yc-row, 0, arcTest,
                 x_start_test, x_end_test,color);
             fillArc1 (xc,yc,xc-col, yc+row, 4, arcTest,
                 x_start_test, x_end_test,color);
             fillArc1 (xc,yc,xc-col, yc-row, 3, arcTest,
                 x_start_test, x_end_test,color);
             if (d<= 0)
             {
                 col++;
                 d += four_b_square*col;
             }
             row--;
             d += two_a_square * (3 - (row <<1));
       }
   }


/*     fillArc1() = subroutine for fillArc              */

void fillArc1 (int xc, int yc,int x, int y, int sector,
    int arcTest[], int x_start_test, int x_end_test, int color)
{

    union REGS reg;

    int dx,dy,i,tx=0,ty=0,sdx,sdy,dxabs,dyabs;

    switch (sector)
    {
        case 4:
        case 5:
        case 6:
        case 7:
        if (arcTest[sector] == 2)
            break;
        if ((arcTest[sector] == 1) && (x>=x_start_test))
            break;
```

```
        if ((arcTest[sector] == 3) && (x<=x_end_test))
            break;
        if ((arcTest[sector] == 4) && (x>=x_start_test)
            && (x<=x_end_test))
            break;
        return;
    case 0:
    case 1:
    case 2:
    case 3:
        if (arcTest[sector] == 2)
            break;
        if ((arcTest[sector] == 1) && (x<=x_start_test))
            break;
        if ((arcTest[sector] == 3) && (x>=x_end_test))
            break;
        if ((arcTest[sector] == 4) && (x>=x_end_test)
            && (x<=x_start_test))
            break;
        return;
    }
    if ((sector <= 1) || (sector >= 6))
        sdx = 1;
    else
        sdx = -1;
    if (sector > 3)
        sdy = 1;
    else
        sdy = -1;
    dxabs = (x-xc)*sdx;
    dyabs = (y-yc)*sdy;
    if (dxabs >= dyabs)
    {
        for (i=0; i<= dxabs; i++)
        {
            ty+= dyabs;
            if (ty>dxabs)
            {
                ty -= dxabs;
                yc +=sdy;
            }
            plot(xc,yc,color);
```

```
            plot(xc, yc+1,color);
            xc+= sdx;
        }
    }
    else
    {
        for (i=0; i<= dyabs; i++)
        {
            tx+= dxabs;
            if (tx>dyabs)
            {
                tx -= dyabs;
                xc +=sdx;
            }
            plot(xc,yc,color);
            plot(xc+1,yc,color);
            yc+= sdy;
        }

    }
}



/*  fillOval() = draws an oval centered at (x,y) with
                 radius in y direction of 'b' with
                 aspect ratio 'aspect' and fills it
                 with color 'color'.                  */


#include "gdraws.h"

extern int LINEWIDTH;

void fillOval(int x, int y, int b, int color, float aspect)
{
    int i;
    float a_temp;
    long a_square, b_square, two_a_square, two_b_square,
        four_a_square, four_b_square, d, a, row, col;

    x = ((x + 319)*18) >> 4;
```

```
y = 174 - ((93*y) >> 7);
a_temp = b/aspect;
a = (((int)(a_temp * 18)) >> 4) - LINEWIDTH/2;
b = ((93*b) >> 7) - LINEWIDTH/2;
a_square = a*a;
b_square = b*b;
row = b;
col = 0;
two_a_square = a_square << 1;
four_a_square = a_square << 2;
four_b_square = b_square << 2;
two_b_square = b_square << 1;
d = two_a_square * ((row  -1)*(row )) + a_square +
    two_b_square*(1-a_square);
while (a_square*(row ) > b_square * (col))
{
    for (i=y-row; i<=y+row; i++)
    {
        plot(x+col,i,color);
        plot(x-col,i,color);
    }
    if (d>= 0)
    {
        row--;
        d -= four_a_square*(row);
    }
    d += two_b_square*(3 + (col << 1));
    col++;
}
d = two_b_square * (col + 1)*col + two_a_square*(row *
    (row  -2) +1) + (1-two_a_square)*b_square;
while ((row) + 1)
{
    for (i=y-row; i<=y+row; i++)
    {
        plot(x+col,i,color);
        plot(x-col,i,color);
    }
    if (d<= 0)
    {
        col++;
        d += four_b_square*col;
```

```
        }
        row--;
        d += two_a_square * (3 - (row <<1));
    }
}



/* fillPoly() = fills a polygon in specified color by
               filling in boundaries resulting from
               connecting specified points in the
               order given and then connecting last
               point to first.                        */

#include "gdraws.h"

void fillPoly(int color,...)
{
    #include <stdarg.h>
    #include <stdio.h>
    #include <dos.h>

    #define sign(x) ((x) > 0 ? 1:  ((x) == 0 ? 0:  (-1)))

    int dx, dy, dxabs, dyabs, i, index=0, j, k, px, py, sdx,
        sdy, x, y, xpoint[150], ypoint[150], toggle, old_sdy,sy0;
    long int check;
    int *x_coord, *y_coord;

    va_list coord;

    x_coord = (int *) malloc(4000 * sizeof(int));
    y_coord = (int *) malloc(4000 * sizeof(int));
    va_start(coord,color);
    for (i=0; i<150; i++)
    {
        xpoint[i] = (va_arg(coord,int) + 319)*18 >> 4;
        ypoint[i] = 174 - ((va_arg(coord,int)*93) >> 7);
        if ((xpoint[i] < 0) || (ypoint[i] > 350))
            break;
    }
    va_end(coord);
```

```
xpoint[i] = xpoint[0];
ypoint[i] = ypoint[0];
if (i<3) return;
px = xpoint[0];
py = ypoint[0];
if (ypoint[1] == ypoint[0])
{
    x_coord[index] = px;
    y_coord[index++] = py;
}
for (j=0; j<i; j++)
{
    dx = xpoint[j+1] - xpoint[j];
    dy = ypoint[j+1] - ypoint[j];
    sdx = sign(dx);
    sdy = sign(dy);
    if (j==0)
    {
        old_sdy = sdy;
        sy0 = sdy;
    }
    dxabs = abs(dx);
    dyabs = abs(dy);
    x = 0;
    y = 0;
    if (dxabs >= dyabs)
    {
        for (k=0; k<dxabs; k++)
        {
            y += dyabs;
            if (y>=dxabs)
            {
                y -= dxabs;
                py += sdy;
                if (old_sdy != sdy)
                {
                    old_sdy = sdy;
                    index--;
                }
                x_coord[index] = px+sdx;
                y_coord[index++] = py;
            }
```

```
                px += sdx;
                plot(px,py,color);
            }
        }
        else
        {
            for (k=0; k<dyabs; k++)
            {
                x += dxabs;
                if (x>=dyabs)
                {
                    x -= dyabs;
                    px += sdx;
                }
                py += sdy;
                if (old_sdy != sdy)
                {
                    old_sdy = sdy;
                    if (sdy != 0)
                        index--;
                }
                plot(px,py,color);
                x_coord[index] = px;
                y_coord[index++] = py;
            }
        }
    }
    index--;
    if (sy0 + sdy== 0)
        index--;
    sort(index,x_coord,y_coord);
    toggle = 0;
    for (i=0; i<index; i++)
    {
        if ((y_coord[i] == y_coord[i+1]) &&
            (toggle == 0))
        {
            for (j=x_coord[i]; j<=x_coord[i+1]; j++)
                plot(j,y_coord[i],color);
            toggle = 1;
        }
        else
```

```
            toggle = 0;
    }
    free(x_coord);
    free(y_coord);
}
```

```
/*   fillRect() = fills a rectangle whose top left and
                  bottom right corners are specified
                  with a specified color              */
```

```c
#include "gdraws.h"

extern int LINEWIDTH;

void fillRect(int x1, int y1, int x2, int y2, int color)
{
    int i,j,temp;

    temp = LINEWIDTH;
    LINEWIDTH = 1;
    x1 = ((x1 + 319)*18) >> 4;
    y1 = 174 - ((93*y1) >> 7);
    x2 = ((x2 + 319)*18) >> 4;
    y2 = 174 - ((93*y2) >> 7);
    for (i=y1; i<=y2; i++)
    {
        for  (j=x1; j<=x2; j++)
            plot(j,i,color);
    }
    LINEWIDTH = temp;
}
```

```
/*  fillRoundRect() = fills in a rectangle with rounded
            corners of radius 'b' with upper right
            corner 'x1,y1', lower left corner 'x2,y2',
            in specified color 'color'.                */
```

```
#include "gdraws.h"

extern int LINEWIDTH;

void fillRoundRect(int x1, int y1, int x2, int y2, int b,
    int color)
{
    int a, xr, yr, col,i,j,row,xend,yend,flag;
    long a_square, b_square, two_a_square, two_b_square,
        four_a_square, four_b_square,d;

    yr = b;
    xr = b-2;
    xend = x2-xr;
    yend = y2+yr;
    b -= LINEWIDTH/2;
    a = b;
    b_square = b*b;
    a_square = a*a;
    fillRect(x1,y1-yr,x2,y2+yr,color);
    fillRect(x1+xr,y1,x2-xr,y2,color);
    row = b;
    col = 0;
    two_a_square = a_square << 1;
    four_a_square = a_square << 2;
    four_b_square = b_square << 2;
    two_b_square = b_square << 1;
    d = two_a_square * ((row  -1)*(row )) + a_square +
        two_b_square*(1-a_square);
    while (a_square*(row ) > b_square * (col))
    {
        drawLine(xend,yend-row,col+xend,yend-row,color);
        drawLine(xend,y1-yr+row,col+xend,y1-yr+row, color);
        drawLine(x1+xr,yend-row,x1+xr-col,yend-row,color);
        drawLine(x1+xr,y1-yr+row,x1+xr-col,y1-yr+row,color);
        if (d>= 0)
        {
            row--;
            d -= four_a_square*(row);
        }
        d += two_b_square*(3 + (col << 1));
```

```
        col++;
    }
    d = two_b_square * (col + 1)*col + two_a_square*(row *
        (row  -2) +1) + (1-two_a_square)*b_square;
    while (row)
    {
        drawLine(xend,yend-row,col+xend,yend-row,color);
        drawLine(xend,y1-yr+row,col+xend,y1-yr+row, color);
        drawLine(x1+xr,yend-row,x1+xr-col,yend-row,color);
        drawLine(x1+xr,y1-yr+row,x1+xr-col,y1-yr+row,color);
        if (d<= 0)
        {
            col++;
            d += four_b_square*col;
        }
        row--;
        d += two_a_square * (3 - (row <<1));
    }
    b++;
    a++;
}




/*   plot() = plots a point to the screen at designated
             location in screen coordinates in selected
             color.                                    */

#include "gdraws.h"

void plot(int x, int y, int color)
{
    unsigned int offset;
    int page;
    char mask;
    char far *address;

    page = getPage();
    offset = 0x2000 * (y%4) + 0x8000 * page + 90 * (y/4) + x/8;
    mask = 0x80 >> (x%8);
    address = (char far *)0xB0000000L + offset;
    if (color == 1)
```

```
            *address |= mask;
    else
            *address &= ~mask;
}




/*  plots() = plots a point to the screen at designated
              location in system coordinates in selected
              color.                                      */

#include "gdraws.h"

void plots(int x, int y, int color)
{
    unsigned int offset;
    int page;
    char mask;
    char far *address;

    x = ((x + 319)*18) >> 4;
    y = 174 - ((93*y) >> 7);
    page = getPage();
    offset = 0x2000 * (y%4) + 0x8000 * page + 90 * (y/4) + x/8;
    mask = 0x80 >> (x%8);
    address = (char far *)0xB0000000L + offset;
    if (color == 1)
        *address |= mask;
    else
        *address &= ~mask;
}




/* rotateOval() = rotates an oval with center (x,y),
                  radius 'b', and color 'color' through
                  angle 'ANGLE' and draws oval.      */

#include <math.h>
#include "gdraws.h"

extern XCENTER, YCENTER, ANGLE, LINEWIDTH;
```

```
void rotateOval(int x, int y, int b, int color, double aspect)
{
    int col, i, row,px,py;
    double aspect_square;
    long a_square, b_square, two_a_square, two_b_square,
        four_a_square, four_b_square,d;
    float angle,ca,sa;

    angle = .01745329*(360 - ANGLE);
    sa=sin(angle);
    ca=cos(angle);

    aspect_square = aspect*aspect;
    b -= LINEWIDTH/2;
    for (i=1; i<=LINEWIDTH; i++)
    {
        b_square = b*b;
        a_square = b_square/aspect_square;
        row = b;
        col = 0;
        two_a_square = a_square << 1;
        four_a_square = a_square << 2;
        four_b_square = b_square << 2;
        two_b_square = b_square << 1;
        d = two_a_square * ((row  -1)*(row )) + a_square +
            two_b_square*(1-a_square);
        while (a_square*(row ) > b_square * (col))
        {
            px = x + col*ca - (row)*sa;
            py = y + col*sa + row*ca;
            plots(px,py,color);
            px = x + col*ca + row*sa;
            py = y + col*sa - row*ca;
            plots(px,py,color);
            px = x - col*ca - row*sa;
            py = y - col*sa + row*ca;
            plots(px,py,color);
            px = x - col*ca + row*sa;
            py = y - col*sa - row*ca;
            plots(px,py,color);
            if (d>= 0)
```

```
        {
            row--;
            d -= four_a_square*(row);
        }
        d += two_b_square*(3 + (col << 1));
        col++;
    }
    d = two_b_square * (col + 1)*col + two_a_square*(row *
        (row  -2) +1) + (1-two_a_square)*b_square;
    while ((row) + 1)
    {
        px = x+ col*ca - (row)*sa;
        py = y + col*sa + row*ca;
        plots(px,py,color);
        px = x + col*ca + row*sa;
        py = y + col*sa - row*ca;
        plots(px,py,color);
        px = x - col*ca - row*sa;
        py = y - col*sa + row*ca;
        plots(px,py,color);
        px = x - col*ca + row*sa;
        py = y - col*sa - row*ca;
        plots(px,py,color);
        if (d<= 0)
        {
            col++;
            d += four_b_square*col;
        }
        row--;
        d += two_a_square * (3 - (row <<1));
    }
    b++;
    }
}


/* rotatePoly() = rotates a polygon whose sides and
                color are specified through an
                angle 'ANGLE' and draws polygon.    */

#include <math.h>
#include "gdraws.h"
```

```c
extern int XCENTER, YCENTER, ANGLE;

void rotatePoly(int color,...)
{
    #include <stdarg.h>
    #include <stdio.h>

    va_list coord;
    int point[600],i=0,j,x1,y1,x2,y2;
    float angle,param;

    va_start(coord,color);
    angle = .01745329*(360 - ANGLE);
    while (((point[i]=va_arg(coord,int)) >= -320) && (i<=600))
        i++;
    va_end(coord);
    point[i++] = point[0];
    point[i] = point[1];
    if (i<=5) return;
    for (j=0; j<i-2; j+=2)
    {
        x1 = (point[j] - XCENTER)*cos(angle) - (point[j+1] -
            YCENTER)*sin(angle) + XCENTER;
        y1 = (point[j] - XCENTER)*sin(angle) + (point[j+1] -
            YCENTER)*cos(angle) + YCENTER;
        x2 = (point[j+2] - XCENTER)*cos(angle) - (point[j+3] -
            YCENTER)*sin(angle) + XCENTER;
        y2 = (point[j+2] - XCENTER)*sin(angle) + (point[j+3] -
            YCENTER)*cos(angle) + YCENTER;
        drawLine(x1,y1,x2,y2,color);
    }
}



    /*    rotateRect() = draws a rectangle with top left and
                         bottom right corners specified in
                         specified color and rotated to a
                         specified angle.                     */

#include <math.h>
```

```c
#include "gdraws.h"

extern XCENTER, YCENTER, ANGLE, LINEWIDTH;

void rotateRect(int x1, int y1, int x2, int y2, int color)
{
    int nx1,nx2,nx3,nx4,ny1,ny2,ny3,ny4;
    float angle;

    angle = .01745329*(360 - ANGLE);
    nx1 = (x1 - XCENTER)*cos(angle) - (y1 - YCENTER)*sin(angle)
        + XCENTER;
    ny1 = (x1 - XCENTER)*sin(angle) + (y1 - YCENTER)*cos(angle)
        + YCENTER;
      nx3 = (x2 - XCENTER)*cos(angle) - (y2 - YCENTER)*sin(angle)
        + XCENTER;
    ny3 = (x2 - XCENTER)*sin(angle) + (y2 - YCENTER)*cos(angle)
        + YCENTER;
    nx2 = (x2 - XCENTER)*cos(angle) - (y1 - YCENTER)*sin(angle)
        + XCENTER;
    ny2 = (x2 - XCENTER)*sin(angle) + (y1 - YCENTER)*cos(angle)
        + YCENTER;
    nx4 = (x1 - XCENTER)*cos(angle) - (y2 - YCENTER)*sin(angle)
        + XCENTER;
    ny4 = (x1 - XCENTER)*sin(angle) + (y2 - YCENTER)*cos(angle)
        + YCENTER;

    drawLine(nx1-LINEWIDTH/2,ny1,nx2+LINEWIDTH/2,ny2,color);
    drawLine(nx2-LINEWIDTH/2,ny2,nx3+LINEWIDTH/2,ny3,color);
    drawLine(nx3,ny3+LINEWIDTH/2,nx4,ny4-LINEWIDTH/2,color);
    drawLine(nx4,ny4+LINEWIDTH/2,nx1,ny1-LINEWIDTH/2,color);
}


/*          sort() = sorts coordinate pairs for drawing and
            filling polygons.                          */



#include "gdraws.h"

void sort(int index, int x_coord[], int y_coord[])
```

```
{
    int d=4,i,j,k,temp;

    while (d<=index)
        d*=2;
    d-=1;
    while (d>1)
    {
        d/=2;
        for (j=0; j<=(index-d); j++)
        {
            for (i=j; i>=0; i-=d)
            {
                if ((y_coord[i+d] < y_coord[i]) ||
                    ((y_coord[i+d] == y_coord[i]) &&
                    (x_coord[i+d] <= x_coord[i])))
                {
                    temp = y_coord[i];
                      y_coord[i] = y_coord[i+d];
                    y_coord[i+d] = temp;
                    temp = x_coord[i];
                    x_coord[i] = x_coord[i+d];
                    x_coord[i+d] = temp;
                }
            }
        }
    }
}
```

Appendix I

Demonstration Programs for Hercules Graphics Card

```
/*      demo() = PROGRAM TO DEMONSTRATE THE USE OF THE
                 TURBO C GRAPHICS FUNCTIONS WITH HERCULES
                 GRAPHICS CARD.                              */



/*                      INCLUDES                     */

#include <math.h>



/*                 USER WRITTEN INCLUDES             */

#include "gdraws.h"



/*        GLOBAL VARIABLES USED BY GRAPHICS FUNCTIONS      */

char adapt;
int color;
int background_color = 0;
int LINEWIDTH=1, OPERATOR=0, ANGLE, XCENTER, YCENTER;
int pt[12][2]={{-20,0},{0,0},{0,-120},{-200,-120},
   {-200,200},{90,150},{60,0},{200,0},{0,0}},x,y,z;
double xd,yd,ampl,aspect;
```

```
char ch;
int n,k;
int usa[600] = {-151,111,-146,
    107,-144, 96,-140, 96,-138,103,-139,111,-135,112,-111,
    103,-91, 96,-65, 92,-39, 89,-13, 85, 13, 85, 44, 82, 32,
    71, 30, 68, 35, 68, 41, 72, 41, 68, 44, 68, 54, 81, 57,
    81, 53, 74, 61, 72, 62, 70, 73, 75, 73, 72, 79, 71, 79,
    70, 75, 67, 69, 66, 63, 61, 61, 48, 61, 34, 63, 27, 65,
    27, 69, 38, 66, 48, 67, 55, 71, 60, 78, 66, 82, 66, 84,
    61, 84, 59, 87, 56, 86, 49, 89, 55, 93, 45, 87, 34, 93,
    31,114, 48,113, 53,127, 59,130, 68,152, 82,156,107,158,
    110,162,107,162,105,165,105,174, 89,160, 68,160, 61,165,
    55,167, 56,147, 59,158, 59,158, 55,160, 50,149, 34,149,
    20,147, 17,143, 24,140, 24,147, 15,144,  1,147, -2,149,
    -8,149,-13,145,-15,145,-19,149,-19,130,-39,119,-55,119,
    -61,123,-75,123,-75,130,-85,132,-89,134,-96,135,-103,134,
    -114,130,-115,123,-110,115,-96,110,-79,106,-72,104,-71,
    96, -77, 87,-85, 75,-71, 74,-74, 65,-74, 61,-78, 65,-85,
    52,-86, 45,-82, 28,-83, 19, -85, 13,-92,  5,-103,  5,
    -116,  2,-119, -1,-119, -7,-116, -9,-114,-11,-111,-12,
    -104,-13,-100,-21,-90,-26,-83,-33,-82,-42,-90,-57,-70,
    -65,-64,-77,-61,-78,-66,-98,-64,-124,-48,-137,-48,-139,
    -45,-139,-37,-146,-27,-159,-20,-161, -6,-165,  0,-165,
    4,-170, 20,-172, 27,-172, 41,-165, 55,-160, 78,-152, 96,
    -150,103,-151,111,-999};

unsigned long int PATTERN=0xFFFFFFFF;

unsigned long int style[8] = { 0xFFFFFFFF,0xC0C0C0C0,0xFF00FF00,
    0xFFF0FFF0,0xF000F000,0xFFFF0000,0xFFFFF0F0,0xFFF0F0F0};



/*                      FUNCTION DEFINITIONS                */

void building();
void wait(char title[]);
void drawArc (int xc, int yc, int b, int start_angle,
    int end_angle, int color, float aspect);
float blend(int i, int n, float u);
void drawBezier(int segments,int color,...);
```

```c
float bs_blend(int i, int n, float u);
void drawBspline(int segments, int color,...);
void drawBezier2(int segments, int color,...);



/*                         MAIN PROGRAM                    */




main()
{
    int i, j, k, x, y, oldx, oldy, midpoint;
    double xd,yd,ampl;
    float aspect;
    char ch;
    cls();
    setMode(1);
    write_big_str(-119,131,"GRAPHICS",226);
    write_vid_str(-200,-6,"DEMONSTRATION",91);
    wait("");

    LINEWIDTH = 3;
    cls();
    drawRect(-309,210,310,-200,1);
    drawLine(-309,210,310,-200,1);
    drawLine(-309,-200,310,210,1);
    wait("Rectangle with Diagonals");

    LINEWIDTH = 5;
    ampl = 220;
    oldx = -315;
    oldy = 0;
    cls();
    for (i=0; i<=32; i++)
    {
        y = ampl * sin(6.283 * ((double)i)/32);
        x = 620 * (double)i/32 - 310;
        drawLine(oldx, oldy, x, y, 1);
        oldx = x;
        oldy = y;
```

```
    }
wait("Sine Wave");

cls();
PATTERN = style[0];
drawRect(-310,230,-280,200,1);
PATTERN = style[1];
drawRect(-300,160,-240,75,1);
PATTERN = style[2];
drawRect(-280,35,-220,-100,1);
PATTERN = style[3];
LINEWIDTH = 1;
drawRect(-200,230,20,100,1);
PATTERN = style[4];
drawRect(-180,90,-70,-200,1);
PATTERN = style[5];
drawRect(40,75,60,200,1);
PATTERN = style[6];
drawRect(100,230,230,-175,1);
PATTERN = style[7];
drawRect(250,180,300,-90,1);
PATTERN = style[0];
wait("Examples of Dashed Lines");

LINEWIDTH = 1;
fillRect(-304,210,30,-30,1);
fillRect(-220,80,-20,-180,1);
drawRect(-220,80,-20,-180,0);
fillRect(-240,140,-70,30,1);
drawRect(-240,140,-70,30,0);
fillRect(-260,130,-150,-50,1);
drawRect(-260,130,-150,-50,0);
wait("Filled Rectangles");

LINEWIDTH = 1;
drawOval(-175,0,90,1,0.7);
LINEWIDTH = 3;
drawOval(65,0,90,1,1.0);
LINEWIDTH = 5;
drawOval(240,0,90,1,1.3);
wait("Ovals and Circle");
```

```
LINEWIDTH = 3;
drawOval(-150,70,120,1,1.);
drawOval(0,-70,120,1,1.);
drawOval(150,70,120,1,1.);
wait("Overlapping Circles");

fillOval(-120,0,110,1,0.8);
fillOval(180,0,110,1,1.);
fillOval(220,50,20,0,1.);
fillOval(140,50,20,0,1.);
LINEWIDTH= 5;
drawLine(150,-60,210,-60,0);
drawLine(130,-53,150,-60,0);
drawLine(230,-53,210,-60,0);
drawLine(120,-40,130,-53,0);
drawLine(240,-40,230,-53,0);
wait("Filled Ovals");
aspect = .50;
for (i=0; i<3; i++)
{
    LINEWIDTH = 3;
    drawArc(0,0,120,0,450,1,aspect);
    drawArc(0,0,120,450,900,1,aspect);
    drawArc(0,0,120,900,1350,1,aspect);
    drawArc(0,0,120,1350,1800,1,aspect);
    drawArc(0,0,120,1800,2250,1,aspect);
    drawArc(0,0,120,2250,2700,1,aspect);
    drawArc(0,0,120,2700,3150,1,aspect);
    drawArc(0,0,120,3150,3590,1,aspect);
    wait("Oval Drawn By Combining Arcs");
    aspect +=.5;
}

fillArc(0,0,140,480,1380,1,1.);
fillArc(0,0,140,1380,1800,1,1.);
fillArc(0,0,140,1800,2600,1,1.);
fillArc(0,0,140,2600,3150,1,1.);
fillArc(0,0,140,3150,3600,1,1.);
fillArc(0,0,140,0,480,1,1.);
wait("Pie Chart from Filled Arcs");
```

```
LINEWIDTH = 1;
PATTERN = style[1];
for (n=0; n<7; n++)
    drawLine(pt[n][0],pt[n][1],pt[n+1][0],pt[n+1][1],1);
PATTERN = style[0];
drawBezier(160,1,-20,0,0,0,0,-120,-200,-120,-200,200,90,
    150,60,0,200,0,-999);
wait("Bezier Curve");
PATTERN = style[1];
drawLine(-250,-25,-300,240,1);
drawLine(-300,240,-80,210,1);
drawLine(-80,210,-40,-25,1);
drawLine(-40,-25,160,-25,1);
drawLine(160,-25,300,-25,1);
drawLine(300,-25,300,220,1);
drawLine(300,220,40,240,1);
drawLine(40,240,-80,-239,1);
PATTERN = style[0];
drawBezier(160,1,-250,-25,-300,240,-80,210,-40,-25,
    160,-25,-999);
drawBezier(160,1,160,-25,300,-25,300,220,40,240,-80,-239,
    -999);
wait("Two Bezier Curves");

PATTERN = style[1];
drawLine(-250,0,-220,200,1);
drawLine(-220,200,-180,-200,1);
drawLine(-180,-200,-140,60,1);
drawLine(-140,60,-100,-30,1);
drawLine(-100,-30,-70,-10,1);
drawLine(-70,-10,-20,208,1);
drawLine(-20,208,+60,-130,1);
drawLine(+60,-130,100,125,1);
drawLine(100,125,125,185,1);
drawLine(125,185,140,160,1);
drawLine(140,160,170,-200,1);
drawLine(170,-200,190,-60,1);
drawLine(190,-60,220,20,1);
PATTERN = style[0];
drawBspline(160,1,-250,0,-220,200,-180,-200,-140,60,
    -100,-30,-70,-10,-20,208,60,-130,100,125,125,185,
    140,160,170,-200,190,-60,220,20,-999);
```

```
wait("B-Spline Curve");

x= -275;
y= 200;
for (k=0; k<37; k++)
{
    write_horz_char(x, y, k+33, 31);
    x += 16;
}
x = -275;
y = 180;
for (k=37; k<74; k++)
{
    write_horz_char(x, y, k+33, 31);
    x += 16;
}
x = -275;
y = 160;
for (k=74; k<93; k++)
{
    write_horz_char(x, y, k+33, 31);
    x += 16;
}
x= -319;
y= -210;
for (k=0; k<17; k++)
{
    write_vert_char(x, y, k+33, 47);
    y += 20;
}
x = -303;
y = -210;
for (k=17; k<34; k++)
{
    write_vert_char(x, y, k+33, 47);
    y += 20;
}
x = -287;
y = -210;
for (k=34; k<51; k++)
{
    write_vert_char(x, y, k+33, 47);
```

```
        y += 20;
    }
    x = -271;
    y = -210;
    for (k=51; k<68; k++)
    {
        write_vert_char(x, y, k+33, 47);
        y += 20;
    }
    x = -255;
    y = -210;
    for (k=68; k<85; k++)
    {
        write_vert_char(x, y, k+33, 47);
        y += 20;
    }
    x = -239;
    y = -210;
    for (k=85; k<93; k++)
    {
        write_vert_char(x, y, k+33, 47);
        y += 20;
    }
    write_horz_str(-150,35, "HELLO WORLD!",62);
    write_vert_str(80,-200, "HOW ARE YOU TODAY?",109);
    wait("Alphanumerics");

    LINEWIDTH = 3;
    drawRoundRect(-300,210,300,-210,60,1);
    wait("Rounded Rectangle");

    fillRoundRect(-300,210,300,-210,60,1);
    wait("Filled Rounded Rectangle");

    building();
    wait("City Skyline at Night");

    drawPoly(1,-259, 90,-59, 90,-159,-90,-999);
    drawPoly(1,-259,-20,-159,160,-59,-20,-999);
    LINEWIDTH = 1;
    drawOval(161,34,107,1,1.0);
    fillPoly(1,60,66,262,66,104,-55,161,140,218,-55,-999);
```

```
    wait("Stars");

    fillPoly(1,-129,103,-69,172,-59,158,-64,144,-39,130,-34,151,
        -24,158,-19,116,1, 75,-9, 48, -49, 61,-19, -6,
        -59,-34,-79,-6,-109,-48,-149,-6,-129,48,-149,61,
        -159,20,-179,61,-209,-34,-229,-6,-299,89,-249,103,
        -299,103,-299,130,-249,130,-269,172,-259,185,-999);
    fillPoly(1,120,0,168,-96,232,-96,232,-144,168,-144,72,-192,
        24,-160,24,-128,56,-128,40,-144,88,-128,88,-96,24,
        -64,120,32,-999);
    wait ("Irregular Polygons");

    PATTERN = style[0];
    fill2Poly(1,usa);
    wait("United States of America");

    LINEWIDTH = 1;
    cls();
    XCENTER = -70;
    YCENTER = 35;
    for (ANGLE=0; ANGLE<180; ANGLE+=15)
        rotateRect(-220,100,80,-35,1);
    wait("Rotated Rectangles");

    cls();
    XCENTER = 0;
    YCENTER = 0;
    for (ANGLE=0; ANGLE<360; ANGLE+=15)
        rotatePoly(1,-120,-70,0,100,120,-70,-999);

    wait("Rotated Triangles");
    cls();
    for (ANGLE=0; ANGLE<180; ANGLE+=15)
    rotateOval(0,0,160,1,1.5);
    wait("Rotated Ovals");
    setMode(0);
}

void wait(char title[])
{
    int tab;
```

```
    tab = (80 - strlen(title))/2;
    write_horz_str(9*tab-320,240,title,0);
    write_horz_str(-128,-220,"Press any key to continue demo..."
        ,0);
    getch();
    cls();
}


void building()
{
int i,j;


fillRect(-280,130,-220,-200,1);
drawRect(-280,130,-220,-200,0);

for(i=-275; i<=-235; i+=20)
{
    for(j=125; j>=-170; j-=40)
        fillRect(i,j,i+10,j-25,0);
}



fillRect(-140,160,-60,-230,1);
drawRect(-140,160,-60,-230,0);

for(i=-130; i<=-80; i+=20)
{
    for(j=155; j>=-190; j-=42)
        fillRect(i,j,i+10,j-25,0);
}



fillRect(-80,-7,60,-200,1);
fillRect(-40,50,30,-7,1);
drawRect(-80,-7,60,-200,0);
drawRect(-40,50,30,-7,0);

for(i=-75; i<=45; i+=20)
{
    for(j=-12; j>=-185; j-=30)
```

```
            fillRect(i,j,i+10,j-10,0);
}

fillRect(40,80,100,-230,1);
drawRect(40,80,100,-230,0);

for(i=45;  i<=85;  i+=20)
{
    for(j=75;  j>=-215;  j-=30)
        fillRect(i,j,i+10,j-10,0);
}
   fillRect(-220,50,-120,-175,1);
   drawRect(-220,50,-120,-175,0);

for(i=-215;  i<=-135;  i+=20)
{
    for(j=45;  j>=-160;  j-=30)
        fillRect(i,j,i+10,j-10,0);
}
fillRect(200,100,280,-175,1);
drawRect(200,100,280,-175,0);

for(i=205;  i<=265;  i+=20)
{
    for(j=95;  j>=-160;  j-=35)
        fillRect(i,j,i+10,j-15,0);
}

fillRect(180,190,240,-200,1);
fillRect(200,75,220,190,1);
drawRect(180,190,240,-200,0);
drawRect(200,75,220,190,0);

for(i=185;  i<=225;  i+=20)
{
    for(j=185;  j>=-185;  j-=30)
        fillRect(i,j,i+10,j-10,0);
}
fillRect(90,75,190,-230,1);
fillRect(110,105,170,75,1);
fillRect(130,130,150,105,1);
drawRect(90,75,190,-230,0);
```

```
drawRect(110,105,170,75,0);
drawRect(130,130,150,105,0);


for(i=95; i<=175; i+=20)
{
    for(j=67; j>=-215; j-=30)
        fillRect(i,j,i+10,j-10,0);
}
for(i=115; i<=155; i+=20)
{
    for(j=100; j>=90; j-=30)
        fillRect(i,j,i+10,j-10,0);
}

fillRect(-220,105,-180,50,1);
drawRect(-220,105,-180,50,0);

fillRect(-215,70,-205,55,0);
fillRect(-195,70,-185,55,0);
fillRect(-215,90,-205,75,0);
fillRect(-195,90,-185,75,0);



fillOval(-20,195,20,1,1.);
fillOval(-30,195,20,0,1.);
}



/*     demo3d() = PROGRAM TO DISPLAY THREE DIMENSIONAL
                DRAWINGS USING THE HERCULES GRAPHICS CARD.*/


#include <stdio.h>
#include <math.h>
#include <dos.h>
#include "colors.h"
#include "gtools.h"
#include "gdraws.h"
```

```
int color;
int LINEWIDTH=1, OPERATOR=0, ANGLE, XCENTER, YCENTER;
unsigned long int PATTERN=0xFFFFFFFF;

float rad_per_degree=0.0174533,x_angle,y_angle,z_angle, step, x3,
    y3, z3, x_angle, y_angle, z_angle;
int x,y,z,rz_scale,vert_scale=1,horz_scale=1,color,type,offset;
char ch;

float degrees_to_radians(float degrees);
void projection ( float x3, float y3, float z3, int color);
void wait(char title[]);
void draw_cube(float rot_pts[8][3],int vx[],int vy[]);
void perspective(int no_of_points,float rot_pts[][3],float pt[][3],
    int vx[],int vy[]);
float surface_test(float x1, float y1, float z1, float x2,
    float y2, float z2, float x3, float y3, float z3);
void draw_sphere();
void draw_side(int i1, int i2, int i3, int i4,float rot_pts[8][3],
    int vx[],int vy[]);
void fill_cube(float rot_pts[8][3],int vx[],int vy[]);
void fill_side(int i1, int i2, int i3, int i4,float rot_pts[8][3],
    int vx[],int vy[]);
void fill_sphere();
int shaded_surface_test(float x1, float y1, float z1, float x2,
    float y2, float z2, float x3, float y3, float z3);
void pattern_plot(int x, int y, int color);
float yaw, roll, pitch, latitude, longitude, xls=.57735,yls=.57735,
    zls=.57735;
int k,d=375, mx=0, my=0, mz=-200, off_x,off_y,sx, sy;
int vx1[37],vy1[37],vx2[37],vy2[37],i,j;
float  rot_pts1[37][3],pt1[37][3],pt6[8][3]={{30,-30,30},
    {30,30,30},{-30,30,30},{-30,-30,30},{30,30,-30},
    {-30,30,-30},{-30,-30,-30},{30,-30,-30}},rot_pts2[37][3],
    pt2[37][3];

main ()
{
    int i,angle;

    setMode(1);
    while(ch != 0x0D)
```

611

```
    {
        cls();
        drawRect(-319,-239,320,240,11);
        off_x = -200;
        off_y = 100;
        for(i=0; i<6; i++)
        {
            yaw=degrees_to_radians(rand()/92);
            roll=degrees_to_radians(rand()/92);
            pitch=degrees_to_radians(rand()/92);
            color=1;
            perspective(8,rot_pts1,pt6,vx1,vy1);
            draw_cube(rot_pts1,vx1,vy1);
            off_x += 200;
            if (off_x>210)
            {
                off_x= -200;
                off_y= -100;
            }
        }
        wait("Cubes");
    }
    ch = 0;
    while(ch != 0x0D)
    {
        d = 800;
        cls();
        off_x = 0;
        off_y = 0;
        latitude = 0;
        longitude = 0;
        drawRect(-319,-239,320,240,11);
        mx = 0;
        my = 0;
        mz = -150;
        yaw=degrees_to_radians(rand()/92);
        roll=degrees_to_radians(rand()/92);
        pitch=degrees_to_radians(rand()/92);
        color=1;
        draw_sphere();
        wait("Sphere");
    }
```

```
    setMode(0);
}

void draw_cube(float rot_pts[8][3],int vx[],int vy[])
{
    long int sp;

    draw_side(7,0,3,6,rot_pts,vx,vy);
    draw_side(6,5,4,7,rot_pts,vx,vy);
    draw_side(3,2,5,6,rot_pts,vx,vy);
    draw_side(0,1,2,3,rot_pts,vx,vy);
    draw_side(7,4,1,0,rot_pts,vx,vy);
    draw_side(1,4,5,2,rot_pts,vx,vy);
}

void draw_side(int i1, int i2, int i3, int i4,
    float rot_pts[8][3], int vx[],int vy[])
{
    float sp;

    sp = surface_test(rot_pts[i1][0],rot_pts[i1][1],
        rot_pts[i1][2],rot_pts[i2][0],rot_pts[i2][1],
        rot_pts[i2][2],rot_pts[i3][0],rot_pts[i3][1],
        rot_pts[i3][2]);
    if (sp<=0)
        drawPoly(color,vx[i1],vy[i1],vx[i2],+vy[i2],vx[i3],
            vy[i3],vx[i4],vy[i4],-999);
}

void draw_sphere()
{
    float sp;
    int i,j,k,radius;

    radius = 30;
    pt1[0][0] = 0;
    pt1[0][1] = radius;
    pt1[0][2] = 0;
    perspective(1,rot_pts1,pt1,vx1,vy1);
    longitude = .17453;
    for (latitude=0,i=0; i<36; i++,latitude+=.17453)
    {
```

```
        pt2[i][0] = cos(latitude)*sin(longitude)*radius;
        pt2[i][1] = cos(longitude)*radius;
        pt2[i][2] = sin(latitude)*sin(longitude)*radius;
    }
    pt2[36][0] = pt2[0][0];
    pt2[36][1] = pt2[0][1];
    pt2[36][2] = pt2[0][2];
    perspective(37,rot_pts2,pt2,vx2,vy2);
    for (i=0; i<36; i++)
    {
        sp = surface_test(rot_pts2[i+1][0],rot_pts2[i+1][1],
            rot_pts2[i+1][2],rot_pts2[i][0],rot_pts2[i][1],
            rot_pts2[i][2],rot_pts1[0][0],rot_pts1[0][1],
            rot_pts1[0][2]);
        if (sp<=0)
            drawPoly(color,vx2[i+1],vy2[i+1],vx2[i],vy2[i],
                vx1[0],vy1[0],-999);
    }
    for (j=0; j<16; j++)
    {
        longitude += .17453;
        for (latitude=0,i=0; i<36; i++,latitude+=.17453)
        {
            pt2[i][0] = cos(latitude)*sin(longitude)*radius;
            pt2[i][1] = cos(longitude)*radius;
            pt2[i][2] = sin(latitude)*sin(longitude)*radius;
        }
        pt2[36][0] = pt2[0][0];
        pt2[36][1] = pt2[0][1];
        pt2[36][2] = pt2[0][2];
        for (i=0; i<37; i++)
        {
            for (k=0; k<3; k++)
                rot_pts1[i][k] = rot_pts2[i][k];
            vx1[i] = vx2[i];
            vy1[i] = vy2[i];
        }
        perspective(37,rot_pts2,pt2,vx2,vy2);
        for (i=0; i<36; i++)
        {
            sp = surface_test(rot_pts1[i][0],rot_pts1[i][1],
                rot_pts1[i][2],rot_pts1[i+1][0],rot_pts1[i+1][1],
```

```
                rot_pts1[i+1][2],rot_pts2[i+1][0],
                rot_pts2[i+1][1],rot_pts2[i+1][2]);
            if (sp<=0)
                drawPoly(color,vx1[i],vy1[i],vx1[i+1],
            vy1[i+1],vx2[i+1],vy2[i+1],
            vx2[i],vy2[i],-999);
        }
    }
    pt1[0][0] = 0;
    pt1[0][1] = -radius;
    pt1[0][2] = 0;
    perspective(1,rot_pts1,pt1,vx1,vy1);
    for (i=0; i<36; i++)
    {
        sp = surface_test(rot_pts2[i][0],rot_pts2[i][1],
            rot_pts2[i][2],rot_pts2[i+1][0],rot_pts2[i+1][1],
            rot_pts2[i+1][2],rot_pts1[0][0],rot_pts1[0][1],
            rot_pts1[0][2]);
        if (sp<=0)
            drawPoly(color,vx2[i+1],+vy2[i+1],vx2[i],+vy2[i],
        vx1[0],+vy1[0],-999);
    }
}

void perspective(int no_of_points,float rot_pts[][3],
    float pt[][3],int vx[], int vy[])
{
    int i,j;
    float xa,ya,za,x,y,z;

    for (i=0; i<no_of_points; i++)
    {
        xa = - cos(yaw)*pt[i][0] - sin(yaw)*pt[i][2];
        za = - sin(yaw)*pt[i][0] + cos(yaw)*pt[i][2];
        x = cos(roll)*xa + sin(roll)*pt[i][1];
        ya = cos(roll)*pt[i][1] - sin(roll)*xa;
        z = cos(pitch)*za - sin(pitch)*ya;
        y = sin(pitch)*za + cos(pitch)*ya;
        x += mx;
        y += my;
        z += mz;
        rot_pts[i][0] = x;
```

```
        rot_pts[i][1] = y;
        rot_pts[i][2] = z;
        vx[i] = -d*x/z+off_x;
        vy[i] = -d*y/z+off_y;
    }
}

float surface_test(float x1, float y1, float z1, float x2,
    float y2, float z2, float x3, float y3, float z3)
{
    float stest;

    stest = x1*(y3*z2-y2*z3) - x2*(y3*z1 - y1*z3) -
        x3*(y1*z2-y2*z1);
    return(stest);
}

float degrees_to_radians (float degrees)
{
    float angle;

    while (degrees >= 360)
    degrees -= 360;
    while (degrees < 0)
    degrees += 360;
    angle = rad_per_degree*degrees;
    return angle;
}

void projection (float x3, float y3, float z3, int color)
{
    float temp_x, temp_y;
    int x,y;
    temp_x = x3*cos(x_angle) + y3*cos(y_angle) +
        z3*cos(z_angle);
    temp_y = x3*sin(x_angle) + y3*sin(y_angle) +
        z3*sin(z_angle);
    x = temp_x*horz_scale;
    y = temp_y*vert_scale;
    plot (x,y,color);
}
```

```c
void wait(char title[])
{
    int tab,width=80;

    tab = (width - strlen(title))/2;
    write_horz_str(tab*8-320,220,title,1);
    tab = (width - 55)/2;
    write_horz_str(tab*8-320,-220,"Press 'Enter' to quit; any"
    " other key to continue demo...",1);
    ch = getch();
    cls();
}



/*      image() = PROGRAM TO DEMONSTRATE USE OF FRACTILES TO
                  GENERATE IMAGES WITH THE HERCULES GRAPHICS
                  CARD.                                        */

#include <stdio.h>
#include <math.h>
#include <dos.h>

/* USER WRITTEN INCLUDES */
#include "colors.h"
#include "gdraws.h"
#include "gtools.h"

/* GLOBALS */


int LINEWIDTH,OPERATOR,XCENTER,YCENTER,ANGLE;
unsigned long int PATTERN;

void image_draw(int color);
void wait(char title[]);

int adapt,mode;
int j, k, xscale,yscale,xoffset,yoffset,pr,p[4],pk[4];
long unsigned int i;
float a[4],b[4],c[4],d[4],e[4],f[4],x,y,newx;
```

```
main()
{
    setMode(1);
    a[0] =0; a[1] = .20; a[2] = -.15; a[3] = .85;
    b[0] = 0; b[1] = -.26; b[2] = .28; b[3] = .04;
    c[0] = 0; c[1] = .23; c[2] = .26; c[3] = -.04;
    d[0] = .16; d[1] = .22; d[2] = .24; d[3] = .85;
    e[0] = 0; e[1] = 0; e[2] = 0; e[3] = 0;
    f[0] = 0; f[1] = 1.60; f[2] = .44; f[3] = 1.6;
    p[0] = 328; p[1] = 2621; p[2] = 4915; p[3] = 32767;
    xscale = 25;
    yscale = 25;
    xoffset = 0;
    yoffset = -160;
    cls();
    image_draw(1);
    wait("Fern");

    a[0] = 0; a[1] = .1; a[2] = .42; a[3] = .42;
    b[0] = 0; b[1] = 0; b[2] = -.42; b[3] = .42;
    c[0] = 0; c[1] = 0; c[2] = '.42; c[3] = -.42;
    d[0] = .5; d[1] = .1; d[2] = .42; d[3] = .42;
    e[0] = 0; e[1] = 0; e[2] = 0; e[3] = 0;
    f[0] = 0; f[1] = .2; f[2] = .2; f[3] = .2;
    p[0] = 1638; p[1] = 6553; p[2] = 19660; p[3] = 32767;
    xscale = 750;
    yscale = 750;
    xoffset = 0;
    yoffset = -160;
    cls ();
    image_draw(1);
    wait("Tree");

    a[0] = .5; a[1] = .5; a[2] = .5; a[3] = 0;
    b[0] = 0; b[1] = 0; b[2] = 0; b[3] = 0;
    c[0] = 0; c[1] = 0; c[2] = 0; c[3] = 0;
    d[0] = .5; d[1] = .5; d[2] = .5; d[3] = 0;
    e[0] = 0; e[1] = 1.; e[2] = .5; e[3] = 0;
    f[0] = 0; f[1] = 0; f[2] = .5; f[3] = 0;
    p[0] = 10813; p[1] = 21626; p[2] = 32767; p[3] = 32767;
    xscale = 200;
    yscale = 200;
```

618

```
    xoffset = -180;
    yoffset = -160;
    cls ();
    image_draw(1);
    wait("Sierpinski Triangle");

    a[0] = .333; a[1] = .333; a[2] = .667; a[3] = 0;
    b[0] = 0; b[1] = 0; b[2] = 0; b[3] = 0;
    c[0] = 0; c[1] = 0; c[2] = 0; c[3] = 0;
    d[0] = .333; d[1] = .333; d[2] = .667; d[3] = 0;
    e[0] = 0; e[1] = 1.; e[2] = .5; e[3] = 0;
    f[0] = 0; f[1] = 0; f[2] = .5; f[3] = 0;
    p[0] = 10813; p[1] = 21626; p[2] = 32767; p[3] = 32767;
    xscale = 120;
    yscale = 140;
    xoffset = -100;
    yoffset = -160;
    cls ();
    image_draw(1);
    wait("Cantor Tree");

    a[0] = .5; a[1] = .5; a[2] = .5; a[3] = .5;
    b[0] = 0; b[1] = 0; b[2] = 0; b[3] = 0;
    c[0] = 0; c[1] = 0; c[2] = 0; c[3] = 0;
    d[0] = .5; d[1] = .5; d[2] = .5; d[3] = .5;
    e[0] = 0; e[1] = .5; e[2] = 0; e[3] = .5;
    f[0] = 0; f[1] = 0; f[2] = .5; f[3] = .5;
    p[0] = 8182; p[1] = 16383; p[2] = 24575; pk[3] = 32767;
    xscale = 250;
    yscale = 250;
    xoffset = -100;
    yoffset = -160;
    cls ();
    image_draw(1);
    wait("Square");
    setMode(0);
}

void image_draw(int color)
{

    int px,py;
```

```
    x = 0;
    y = 0;

    for (i=1; i<=10000; i++)
    {
        j = rand();
        k = (j < p[0]) ? 0 : ((j<p[1]) ? 1 : ((j<p[2]) ? 2 : 3));
        newx = (a[k]* x + b[k] * y + e[k]);
        y = (c[k] * x + d[k] * y + f[k]);
        x = newx;
        px = x*xscale + xoffset;
        py = (y*yscale + yoffset);
        if ((px>=-320) && (px<320) && (py>=-240) && (py<240))
            plots (px,py,color);
    }
}

void wait(char title[])
{
    int length;

    length = (strlen(title))*4;
    write_horz_str(-length,220,title,1);
    write_horz_str(-136,-220,"Press any key to continue demo..."
        , 1);
    getch();
    cls();
}




/*      quadrics = Program to demonstrate the drawing of
                three dimensional quadric surfaces.        */

#include <dos.h>
#include <stdio.h>
#include <math.h>

#include "gtools.h"
#include "gdraws.h"
```

```
float rad_per_degree=0.0174533, x_angle, y_angle,
    z_angle, step, x3, y3, z3;
int x,y,horz_scale,vert_scale,color,type,x_offset,
    y_offset,OPERATOR = 0;
int XCENTER, YCENTER, ANGLE, LINEWIDTH;
unsigned long PATTERN;

float radians_to_degrees(float degrees);
void projection (float x_angle, float y_angle,
float z_angle, float x3, float y3, float z3, int color);
void wait(char title[]);

main ()
{
    char adapt;

    setMode(1);
    x_angle = 30;
    y_angle = -30;
    z_angle = 90;
    x_angle = radians_to_degrees(x_angle);
    y_angle = radians_to_degrees(y_angle);
    z_angle = radians_to_degrees(z_angle);
    cls();
    color = 1;
    for (type=1; type<=6; type++)
    {
        switch (type)
        {
            case 1:
                x_offset = 450;
                y_offset = 195;
                horz_scale = 9;
                vert_scale = 2.2;
                for (y3=-6; y3<=6; y3+=.4)
                {
                    step = .05;
                    for (x3=-6; x3<=6; x3+=step)
                    {
                        z3 = x3*x3 + y3*y3;
                        projection(x_angle, y_angle,z_angle,
                            x3,y3,z3,color);
```

```
                    if (x3>=0)
                         step = .2;
                }
          }
          write_horz_str(-290,14,"Elliptic Paraboloid",1);
          break;
     case 2:
          x_offset = 20;
          y_offset = 120;
          horz_scale = 12;
          vert_scale = 2;
          for (y3=-5; y3<=5; y3+=.4)
          {
               step = .1;
               for (x3=-5; x3<=5; x3+=step)
               {
                    z3 = y3*y3 - x3*x3;
                    projection(x_angle,y_angle, z_angle,
                         x3,y3,z3,color);
                    if (x3>=0)
                         step = .4;
               }
          }
          write_horz_str(-60,14,"Hyperbolic Paraboloid ",1);
          break;
     case 3:
          x_offset = 220;
          y_offset = 120;
          horz_scale = 7;
          vert_scale = 3;
          for (y3=-6; y3<=6; y3+=.75)
          {
               step = .2;
               for (x3=-6; x3<=6; x3+=step)
               {
                    z3 = sqrt(y3*y3 + x3*x3)*2;
                    projection(x_angle,y_angle, z_angle,
                         x3,y3,z3,color);
                    projection(x_angle,y_angle, z_angle,
                         x3,y3,-z3,color);
                    if (x3>=0)
                         step = .5;
```

```
            }
        }
        write_horz_str(200,14,"Elliptic Cone ",1);
        break;
    case 4:
        y_offset = -85;
        x_offset = 420;
        horz_scale = 7;
        vert_scale = 5;
        for (y3=-4; y3<=4; y3+=.5)
        {
            for (x3=-4; x3<=4; x3+=.2)
            {
                if (x3*x3+y3*y3>2)
                {
                    z3 = sqrt(y3*y3 + x3*x3-2)*2;
                    projection(x_angle, y_angle,z_angle,
                        x3,y3,z3,color);
                    projection(x_angle, y_angle,z_angle,
                        x3,y3,-z3,color);
                }
            }
        }
        write_horz_str(-290,-200," Hyperboloid of one "
            "sheet",1);
        break;
    case 5:
        y_offset = -95;
        x_offset = 0;
        horz_scale = 2;
        vert_scale = 2;
        for (y3=-20; y3<=20; y3+=2)
        {
            for (x3=-20; x3<=20; x3+=.3)
            {
                if (y3*y3>=x3*x3+1)
                {
                    z3 = sqrt(y3*y3 - x3*x3 - 1);
                    projection(x_angle, y_angle,z_angle,
                        x3,y3,z3,color);
                    projection(x_angle, y_angle,z_angle,
                        x3,y3,-z3,color);
```

```
                              }
                        }
                  }
               write_horz_str(-60,-200,"Hyperboloid of two
                     "sheets ",1);
               break;
          case 6:
               y_offset = -95;
               x_offset = 210;
               horz_scale = 60;
               vert_scale = 50;
               for (y3=-.99; y3<=1; y3+=.15)
               {
                    step = .015;
                    for (x3=-1; x3<=1; x3+=.03)
                    {
                         if (x3*x3+y3*y3<1)
                         {
                              z3 = sqrt(1-x3*x3 - y3*y3);
                              projection(x_angle, y_angle,
                                   z_angle,x3,y3,z3, color);
                              projection(x_angle, y_angle,
                                   z_angle,x3,y3,-z3, color);
                         }
                         if (x3>0)
                              step = .03;
                    }
               }
               write_horz_str(200,-200,"Ellipsoid",1);
          }
     }
     wait("Quadric Surfaces");
     setMode(0);
}

float radians_to_degrees(float degrees)
{
     float angle;

     while (degrees >= 360)
          degrees -= 360;
     while (degrees < 0)
```

```
        degrees += 360;
    angle = rad_per_degree*degrees;
    return angle;
}

void projection (float x_angle, float y_angle,
    float z_angle, float x3, float y3, float z3, int color)
{
    float temp_x, temp_y;
    int x,y;

    temp_x = x3*cos(x_angle) + y3*cos(y_angle) + z3*cos(z_angle);
    temp_y = x3*sin(x_angle) + y3*sin(y_angle) + z3*sin(z_angle);
    x = x_offset + (temp_x*horz_scale);
    y = y_offset - (temp_y*vert_scale);
    plots (x,y,color);
}

void wait(char title[])
{
    write_horz_str(-64,224,title,1);
    write_horz_str(-112,-224,"Press any key to end demo...", 1);
    getch();
    cls();
}
```

625

About the Author

Roger T. Stevens graduated from California Western University, in Santa Ana, California, with a PhD in Electrical Engineering, but not before attaining degrees from three other universities, including: a Master of Engineering in Systems Engineering at Virginia Polytechnic Institute in Blacksburg, Virginia; a Master of Arts in Mathematics at Boston University in Boston; and a Bachelor of Arts in English at Union College in Schenectady, New York.

Roger's engineering career spans over 30 years. He is currently a member of the technical staff of the MITRE Corporation, Bedford, Massachusetts, providing system engineering support and software development for the Defense Test and Evaluation Support Agency.

He has written 20 articles for technical magazines and journals, and is the author of *Operational Test and Evaluation: A Systems Engineering Process*. Roger resides with his wife, Barbara, in Albuquerque, New Mexico.

Bibliography

Adams, Lee, *High Performance Interactive Graphics*, Blue Ridge Summit, PA 17214, TAB Books, Inc., 1987.

Artwick, Bruce A., *Microcomputer Displays, Graphics, and Animation*, Englewood Cliffs, NJ 07632, Prentice-Hall, Inc., 1985.

Barkakati, Nabajyoti, "Graphics: Simple Plots with the Enhanced Graphics Adapter," *Dr. Dobb's Journal*, Vol. 11. No. 5, May 1986, pp. 42, 72-77.

Blinn, James F., "How Many Ways Can You Draw a Circle?" *Dr. Dobb's Journal*, Vol. 12, No. 9, September 1987, pp. 18-26.

Cockerham, John T., "Evaluating the EGA: The EGA Standard," *PC Tech Journal*, Vol. 4, No. 10, pp. 48-79.

Davis, Stephen R., *Turbo C: The Art of Advanced Program Design, Optimization, and Debugging*, Redwood City, CA, M&T Publishing, Inc., 1987.

Fogg, Larry, "A Hercules Primer," *Micro Cornucopia*, No. 39, January/February 1988, pp. 24-29.

Fogg, Larry, "Drawing the Mandelbrot and Julia Sets," *Micro Cornucopia*, No. 39, January/February 1988, pp. 6-9.

Harbison, Samuel P. and Steele, Guy L. Jr., *C: A Reference Manual*, Englewood Cliffs, NJ 07632, Prentice-Hall, Inc., 1987.

Hogan, Thom, "Using Decision Variables in Graphics Primitives," *Dr. Dobb's Journal*, No. 103, May 1985, pp. 40-48.

Johnson, Nelson, *Advanced Graphics in C*, Berkeley, CA, Osborne McGraw-Hill, 1987.

Mitchell, Edward, "Searching Techniques," *Creative Computing*, December 1982, pp. 284-294.

Porter, Kent, "A Graphics Toolbox for Turbo C (Part 1)," *Dr. Dobb's Journal*, Vol 12, No. 11, November 1987, pp. 30-36, 82-86.

Porter, Kent, "A Graphics Toolbox for Turbo C (Part 2)," *Dr. Dobb's Journal*, Vol 12, No. 12, December 1987, pp. 54-61, 106-108.

Porter, Kent, "Curves, Bezier-Style," *Turbo Technix*, March/April 1988, pp. 34-39.

Prata, Stephen, *Advanced C Primmer ++*, Indianapolis, IN 46268, Howard W. Sams & Co., 1986.

Robinson, Fred, "Plotting the Mandelbrot Set with the BGI," *Turbo Technix*, May/June 1988, pp. 28-36.

Index

More Programming Tools
from M&T Books

Programming Languages

C

Graphics Programming in C
Roger T. Stevens
Item #019-2 $39.95 (book/disk)
Item #018-4 $24.95 (book)
Details the fundamentals of graphics processes for the IBM PC family and its clones. All the information needed to program graphics in C, including source code, is presented. The provided source code will enable the user to easily modify graphics functions to suit specific needs. Both Turbo C and Microsoft C are supported. Available September 1988.

C Chest and Other C Treasures from *Dr. Dobb's Journal*
Edited by Allen Holub
Item #40-2 $24.95 (book)
Item #49-6 $39.95 (book/disk)
This comprehensive anthology contains the popular "C Chest" columns from *Dr. Dobb's Journal of Software Tools*, along with the lively philosophical and practical discussions they inspired, in addition to other information-packed articles by C experts. The software in the book is also available on disk with full source code. MS-DOS format.

Turbo C: The Art of Advanced Program Design, Optimization, and Debugging

Stephen R. Davis

Item #38-0 $24.95 (book)

Item #45-3 $39.95 (book/disk)

Overflowing with example programs, this book fully describes the techniques necessary to skillfully program, optimize, and debug in Turbo C. All programs are also available on disk with full source code. MS-DOS format.

A Small C Compiler: Language, Usage, Theory, and Design

James E. Hendrix

Item #88-7 $23.95 (book)

Item #97-6 $38.95 (book/disk)

A full presentation of the design and theory of the Small C compiler (including source code) and programming language. The author has implemented many features in this compiler that make it an excellent example for learning basic compiler theory. Some of these features are: recursive descent parsing, one-pass compilation, and the generation of assembly language. Here is a look into a real compiler with the opportunity for hands-on experience in designing one.

Dr. Dobb's Toolbook of C

Editors of *Dr. Dobb's Journal*

Item #89303-615-3 $29.95

From *Dr. Dobb's Journal of Software Tools* and Brady Communications, this book contains a comprehensive library of valuable C code. *Dr. Dobb's Journal of Software Tools'* most popular articles on C are updated and reprinted here, along with new C programming tools. Also included is a complete C compiler, an assembler, text processing programs, and more!

The Small-C Handbook

James E. Hendrix

Item #8359-7012-4 $17.95 (book)

Item #67-4 $37.90 (book and CP/M disk)

Also from *Dr. Dobb's Journal of Software Tools* and Brady Communications, the handbook is a valuable companion to the Small-C compiler, described below. The book explains the language and the compiler, and contains entire source listings of the compiler and its library of arithmetic and logical routines.

Forth

Dr. Dobb's Toolbook of Forth
Edited by Marlin Ouverson
Item #10-0 $22.95 (book)
Item #57-7 $39.95 (book/disk)
This comprehensive collection of useful Forth programs and tutorials contains expanded versions of *Dr. Dobb's Journal of Software Tools'* best Forth articles and other material, including practical code and in-depth discussions of advanced Forth topics. The screens in the book are also available on disk as ASCII files in the following formats: MS/PC-DOS, Apple II, Macintosh, or CP/M: Osborne or 8" SS/SD.

Dr. Dobb's Toolbook of Forth, Volume II
Editors of *Dr. Dobb's Journal*
Item #41-0 $29.95 (book)
Item #51-8 $45.95 (book/disk)
This complete anthology of Forth programming techniques and developments picks up where the Toolbook of Forth, First Edition left off. Included are the best articles on Forth from *Dr. Dobb's Journal of Software Tools,* along with the latest material from other Forth experts. The screens in the book are available on disk as ASCII files in the following formats: MS-DOS, Macintosh, and CP/M: Osborne or 8" SS/SD.

BASIC

The New BASICs: Programming Techniques and Library Development
Namir Clement Shammas
Item #37-2 $24.95 (book)
Item #43-7 $39.95 (book/disk)
This book will orient the advanced programmer to the syntax and programming features of The New BASICs, including Turbo BASIC 1.0, QuickBASIC 3.0, and True BASIC 2.0. You'll learn the details of implementing subroutines, functions, and libraries to permit more structured coding. Programs and subroutines are available on disk with full source code. MS-DOS format.

QuickBASIC: Programming Techniques and Library Development
Namir Clement Shammas
Item #004-4 $34.95 (book/disk)
Item #003-6 $19.95 (book)
This book provides the reader with the opportunity to learn the details of creating subroutines, functions, and libraries to permit more structured coding. The remainder of the book is dedicated to an in-depth discussion of building original libraries and functions to fulfill individual programming needs. Programs and subroutines are available on disk with full source code.

Turbo BASIC: Programming Techniques and Library Development
Namir Clement Shammas
Item #016-8 $34.95 (book/disk)
Item #015-X $19.95 (book)
Advanced programmers will be introduced to the flexible Turbo BASIC environment, programming framework, data types, and the use of libraries, functions and subroutines to permit more structured coding. As with the QuickBASIC book, the techniques discussed in this volume are then put to use building a selection of useful libraries. All programs and subroutines are also available on disk with full source code.

HyperTalk

Dr. Dobb's Essential HyperTalk Handbook
Michael Swaine
Item #99-5 $39.95 (book/disk)
Item #99-0 $24.95 (book)
Well-known columnist Michael Swaine provides a complete analyses of HyperTalk in this new book. Complete coverage of topics such as the move from authoring to scripting, concepts and components of the language, programming style considerations, full language exposition and discussion, and more, are presented. Programs available on disk.

Turbo Pascal

The Turbo Pascal Toolbook
Edited by Namir Clement Shammas
Item #25-9 $25.95 (book)
Item #61-5 $45.95 (book/disk)

This book contains routines and sample programs to make your programming easier and more powerful. You'll find an extensive library of low-level routines; external sorting and searching tools; window management; artificial intelligence techniques; mathematical expression parsers, including two routines that convert mathematical expressions into RPN tokens; and a smart statistical regression model finder. More than 800K of source code is available on disk for MS-DOS systems.

MIDI

C Programming for MIDI
Jim Conger
Item #86-0 $22.95 (book)
Item #90-9 $37.95 (book/disk)
For musicians and programmers alike, here is the source that will help you write programs for music applications. The author begins by outlining the features of MIDI (Musical Instrument Digital Interface) and its support of real-time access to musical devices. An introduction to C programming fundamentals as they relate to MIDI is also provided. The author fully demonstrates these concepts with two MIDI applications: a patch librarian and a simple sequencer.

MIDI Programming for the Macintosh
Steve De Furia and Joe Scacciaferro, Ferro Technologies
Item #022-2 $37.95 (book/disk)
Item #021-4 $22.95 (book)
This book equips the musician and programmer alike with the background necessary to program music applications and to take advantage of all the Macintosh and the MIDI interface have to offer. Specific examples are presented and all source code is available on disk. Available November 1988.

Business

PC Accounting Solutions
Editors of *PC Accounting* (formerly *Business Software*)
Item #008-7 $37.95 (book/disk)
Item #009-5 $22.95 (book)
This anthology serves as a well-rounded source of expert information for managers who want to implement a PC-based accounting system or to gain better control of their existing system. From choosing and maximizing your accounting systems and software to building better spreadsheets and budgets, this book is

an immensely valuable source that will improve your ability to analyze the information that is critical to the success of your business.

Public-Domain Software: Untapped Resources for the Business User
Rusel DeMaria and George R. Fontaine
Item #39-9 $19.95 (book)
Item #47-X $34.95 (book/disk)
Organized into a comprehensive reference, this book introduces the novice and guides the experienced user to a source of often overlooked software—public domain and Shareware. This book will tell you where it is, how to get it, what to look for, and why it's for you. The sample programs and some of the software reviewed is available on disk in MS-DOS format. Includes $15 worth of free access time on CompuServe!

Time and Task Management with dBASE III
Timothy Berry
Item #09-7 $49.95 (manual/MS-DOS disk)
Like an accounting system for time and tasks, this package helps users organize hours, budgets, activities, and resources. Providing both a useful time-management system and a library of dBASE III code and macros, this package has practical as well as educational value. To be used with dBASE III. Source code and documentation is included. MS-DOS disk format.

Sales Management with dBASE III
Timothy Berry
Item #15-1 $49.95 (manual/MS-DOS disk)
Sales management works with dBASE III to provide a powerful information system that will help you to keep track of clients, names, addresses, follow-ups, pending dates, and account data. This system organizes all the day-to-day activities of selling and includes program files, format files, report files, index files, and data bases. Documentation and full source code is included.

Programming Tools and Source Code Libraries

C

Small-Windows: A Library of Windowing Functions for the C Language
James E. Hendrix
Item #35-X $29.95
Small-Windows is a complete windowing library for C. The package includes video functions, menu functions, window functions, and more. The package is available for MS-DOS systems for the following compilers: Microsoft C Version 4.0 and 5.0; Small-C; Turbo C 1.0 and 1.5; and Lattice C 3.1. Documentation and full C source code is included.

Tools

Small Tools: Programs for Text Processing
James E. Hendrix
Item #78-X $29.95 (manual/disk)
This package of text-processing programs written in Small-C is designed to perform specific, modular functions on text files. Source code is included. Small Tools is available in both CP/M and MS/PC-DOS versions and includes complete documentation.

Small Assembler: A Macro Assembler Written in Small C
James E. Hendrix
MS-DOS version: Item #024-9 $29.95 (manual/disk)
CP/M version: Item #77-1 $29.95 (manual/disk)
Here is a full macro assembler which was developed primarily for use with the Small-C compiler. It provides an excellent example for learning the basics of how assembler works. The manual provides an overview of the Small Assembler, documents the command lines that invoke programs, and more. The accompanying disk includes both the executable assembler and full source code.

NR: An Implementation of the UNIX NROFF Word Processor
Allen Holub
Item #33-X $29.95
NR is a text formatter that is written in C and compatible with UNIX's NROFF. *NR* comes configured for any Diablo-compatible printer, as well as Hewlett Packard's ThinkJet and LaserJet. Both the ready-to-use program and full source code are included. For PC compatibles.

Turbo Pascal

Statistical Toolbox for Turbo Pascal
Namir Clement Shammas
Item #22-4 $39.95 (manuals/disks)
Two statistical packages in one! A library disk and reference manual that includes statistical distribution functions, random number generation, basic descriptive statistics, parametric and nonparametric statistical testing, bivariate linear regression, and multiple and polynomial regression. The demonstration disk and manual incorporate these library routines into a fully functioning statistical program. For IBM PCs and compatibles.

Turbo Advantage
Lauer and Wallwitz
Item #26-7 $29.95
A library of more than 200 routines, with source code sample programs and documentation. Routines are organized and documented under the following categories: bit manipulation, file management, MS-DOS support, string operations, arithmetic calculations, data compression, differential equations, Fourier analysis and synthesis, and much more! For MS/PC-DOS systems.

Turbo Advantage: Complex
Lauer and Wallwitz
Item #27-5 $39.95
This library provides the Turbo Pascal code for digital filters, boundary-value solutions, vector and matrix calculations with complex integers and variables, Fourier transforms, and calculations of convolution and correlation functions. Some of the *Turbo Advantage: Complex* routines are most effectively used with Turbo Advantage. Source code and documentation included.

Turbo Advantage: Display
Lauer and Wallwitz
Item #28-3 $39.95
Turbo Advantage: Display includes an easy-to-use form processor and thirty Turbo Pascal procedures and functions to facilitate linking created forms to your program. Full source code and documentation are included. Some of the *Turbo Advantage* routines are necessary to compile *Turbo Advantage: Display*.

Operating Systems

OS/2

The Programmer's Essential OS/2 Handbook
David E. Cortesi
Item #82-8 $24.95   (book)
Item #89-5 $39.95   (book/disk)
Here is a resource no developer can afford to be without! Cortesi succinctly organizes the many features of OS/2 into related topics and illuminates their uses. Detailed indexes and a web of cross referencing provide easy access to all OS/2 topic areas. Equal support for Pascal and C programmers is provided. *The essential reference for programmers developing in the OS/2 environment.*

UNIX

UNIX Programming on the 80286/80386
Alan Deikman
Item #83-6 $24.95   (book)
Item #91-9 $39.95   (book/disk)
A complete professional-level tutorial and reference for programming UNIX and XENIX on 80286/80386-based computers. Succinct coverage of the UNIX program environment, UNIX file system, shells, utilities, and C programming under UNIX are covered. The author also delves into the development of device drivers; some examples of these are video displays, tape cartridges, terminals, and networks.

On Command: Writing a UNIX-Like Shell for MS-DOS
Allen Holub
Item #29-1 $39.95
Learn how to write shells applicable to MS-DOS, as well as to most other programming environments. This book and disk include a full description of a UNIX-like shell, complete C source code, a thorough discussion of low-level DOS interfacing, and significant examples of C programming at the system level. All source code is included on disk.

/util: A UNIX-Like Utility Package for MS-DOS
Allen Holub
Item #12-7 $29.95
This collection of utilities is intended to be accessed through SH but can be used separately. It contains programs and subroutines that, when coupled with SH,

create a fully functional UNIX-like environment. The package includes a disk with full C source code and documentation in a UNIX-style manual.

MS-DOS

Taming MS-DOS, Second Edition
Thom Hogan
Item #87-9 $19.95
Item #92-5 $34.95
Described by reviewers as "small in size, large on content," and "fun." The second edition promises to be just as readable and is updated to cover MS-DOS 3.3. Some of the more perplexing elements of MS-DOS are succinctly described here with time-saving tricks to help customize any MS-DOS system. Each trick is easily implemented into your existing tools and for programmers, Hogan includes many complete source code files that provide very useful utilities. All source code is written in BASIC.

Program Interfacing to MS-DOS
William G. Wong
Item #34-8 $29.95
Program Interfacing to MS-DOS will orient any experienced programmer to the MS-DOS environment. The package includes a ten-part manual with sample program files and a detailed description of how to build device drivers, along with the device driver for a memory disk and a character device driver on disk with macro assembly source code.

Other

Tele Operating System Toolkit
Ken Berry
This task-scheduling algorithm drives the Tele Operating System and is composed of several components. When integrated, they form an independent operating system for any 8086-based machine. Tele has also been designed for compatibility with MS-DOS, UNIX, and the MOSI standard.

SK: THE SYSTEM KERNEL
Item #30-5 $49.95 (manual/disk)
The System Kernel contains an initialization module, general-purpose utility functions, and a real-time task management system. The kernel provides MS-DOS applications with multitasking capabilities. The System Kernel is required by all other components. All source code is included on disk in MS-DOS format.

DS: WINDOW DISPLAY
Item #32-1 $39.95 (manual/disk)
This component contains BIOS level drivers for a memory-mapped display, window management support and communication coordination between the operator and tasks in a multitasking environment. All source code is included on disk in MS-DOS format.

FS: THE FILE SYSTEM
Item #65-8 $39.95 (manual/disk)
The File System supports MS-DOS disk file structures and serial communication channels. All source code is included on disk in MS-DOS format.

XS: THE INDEX SYSTEM
Item #66-6 $39.95 (manual/disk)
The Index System implements a tree-structured free-form database. All source code is included on disk in MS-DOS format.

Chips

Dr. Dobb's Toolbook of 80286/80386 Programming
Edited by Phillip Robinson
Item #42-9 $24.95 (book)
Item #53-4 $39.95 (book/disk)
This toolbook is a comprehensive discussion of the powerful 80X86 family of microprocessors. Editor Phillip Robinson has gathered the best articles from numerous key programming publications to create this valuable resource for all 80X86 programmers. All programs are available on disk with full source code.

Dr. Dobb's Z80 Toolbook
David E. Cortesi
Item #07-0 $25.00 (book)
Item #55-0 $40.00 (book/disk)
This book contains everything users need to write their own Z80 assembly-language programs, including a method of designing programs and coding them in assembly language and a complete, integrated toolkit of subroutines. All the software in the book is available on disk in the following formats: 8" SS/SD, Apple, Osborne, or Kaypro.

Dr. Dobb's Toolbook of 68000 Programming

Editors of *Dr. Dobb's Journal*

Item #13-216649-6 $29.95 (book)

Item #75-5 $49.95 (book/disk)

From *Dr. Dobb's Journal of Software Tools* and Brady Communications, this collection of practical programming tips and tools for the 68000 family contains the best 68000 articles reprinted from *Dr. Dobb's Journal of Software Tools,* along with much new material. The book contains many useful applications and examples. The software in the book is also available on disk in the following formats: MS/PC-DOS, Macintosh, CP/M 8", Osborne, Amiga, and Atari 520ST.

X68000 Cross Assembler

Brian R. Anderson

Item #71-2 $25.00

This manual and disk contain an executable version of the 68000 Cross Assembler discussed in *Dr. Dobb's Toolbook of 68000 Programming,* complete with source code and documentation. The Cross-Assembler requires CP/M 2.2 with 64K or MS-DOS with 128K. The disk is available in the following formats: MS-DOS, 8" SS/SD, and Osborne.

General Interest

Interfacing to S-100/IEEE 696 Microcomputers

Mark Garetz and Sol Libes

Item #85-2 $24.95

This book helps S-100 bus users expand the utility and power of their systems. It describes the S-100 bus with unmatched precision. Various chapters describe its mechanical and functional design, logical and electrical relationships, bus interconnections, and busing techniques.

Building Local Area Networks

Patrick H. Corrigan

Item #025-7 $39.95 (book/disk)

Item #010-9 $24.95 (disk)

The specifics of building and maintaining PC LANs, including hardware configurations, software development, cabling, selection criteria, installation, and on-going management, are described in a detailed, "how-to" manner with numerous illustrations and sample LAN management forms.

Dr. Dobb's Journal Bound Volume Series

Each volume in this series contains a full year's worth of useful code and fascinating history from *Dr. Dobb's Journal of Software Tools*. Each volume contains every issue of *DDJ* for a given year, reprinted and combined into one comprehensive reference.

Volume	1: 1976	*Item #13-5*	*$30.75*
Volume	2: 1977	*Item #16-X*	*$30.75*
Volume	3: 1978	*Item #17-8*	*$30.75*
Volume	4: 1979	*Item #14-3*	*$30.75*
Volume	5: 1980	*Item #18-6*	*$30.75*
Volume	6: 1981	*Item #19-4*	*$30.75*
Volume	7: 1982	*Item #20-8*	*$35.75*
Volume	8: 1983	*Item #00-3*	*$35.75*
Volume	9: 1984	*Item #08-9*	*$35.75*
Volume	10: 1985	*Item #21-6*	*$35.75*
Volume	11: 1986	*Item #72-0*	*$35.75*
Volume	12: 1987	*Item #84-4*	*$39.95*
Volume	13: 1988	*Item #027-3*	*$39.95*

To order any of these products send your payment, along with $2.95 per item for shipping, to M&T Books, 501 Galveston Drive, Redwood City, California 94063. California residents, please include the appropriate sales tax. Or, call toll-free 800-533-4372 (in California 800-356-2002) Monday through Friday between 8 A.M. and 5 P.M. Pacific Standard Time. When ordering disks, please indicate format.